PRACTICING RESEARCH

This book is dedicated to the ones I love:
John C. Beck, Astrid, and Daniella

PRACTICING RESEARCH

Discovering Evidence That Matters

Arlene Fink

University of California at Los Angeles
The Langley Research Institute, Los Angeles

SAGE Publications

Los Angeles • London • New Delhi • Singapore

For information:

Sage Publications, Inc.
2455 Teller Road
Thousand Oaks, California 91320
E-mail: order@sagepub.com

Sage Publications Ltd.
1 Oliver's Yard
55 City Road
London EC1Y 1SP
United Kingdom

Sage Publications India Pvt. Ltd.
B 1/I 1 Mohan Cooperative Industrial Area
Mathura Road, New Delhi 110 044
India

Sage Publications Asia-Pacific Pte. Ltd.
33 Pekin Street #02-01
Far East Square
Singapore 048763

Printed in the United States of America.

Library of Congress Cataloging-in-Publication Data

Fink, Arlene.
Practicing research: discovering evidence that matters / Arlene Fink.
    p. cm.
Includes bibliographical references and index.
ISBN 978-1-4129-3769-6 (cloth)
ISBN 978-1-4129-3770-2 (pbk.)
I. Title.

Q180.A1 .F53 2008
001.4—dc22   2007031740

This book is printed on acid-free paper.

07 08 09 10 11   10 9 8 7 6 5 4 3 2 1

Acquisitions Editors:	Lisa Cuevas Shaw, Vicki Knight
Associate Editor:	Sean Connelly
Editorial Assistant:	Lauren Habib
Production Editor:	Tracy Buyan
Copy Editor:	Karen E. Taylor
Typesetter:	C&M Digitals (P) Ltd.
Proofreader:	Theresa Kay
Indexer:	Judy Hunt
Cover Designer:	Kathleen Kennedy
Marketing Manager:	Stephanie Adams

Contents

List of Figures and Tables

Figures

Preface_____

And when we try to define "evidence" . . . we find it very difficult.

—R. G. Collingwood,
The Idea of History (1956)

"Surely the only possible rule," one may say, "is to believe what is true and disbelieve what is false." And of course that would be the rule if we were in a position to know what was true and what false. But the whole difficulty arises from the fact that we do not and often cannot. What is to guide us then? . . . The ideal is believe no more, but also no less, than what the evidence warrants.

—Brand Blanshard,
Reason and Belief (1974)

This is a book about finding evidence that matters about effective programs, practices, and policies. Collingwood says that we find defining evidence very difficult. Indeed we do. One of my aims in this book was to come up with a definition that is in common use, one that can be a practical guide to you in your search to know, as Blanshard states, "what is true and what is false." But first, let's consider two other questions. Who are "you," and why do you need to search for evidence?

The "you" for whom this book is designed is anyone in the helping professions who prefers to use the scientific method rather than personal testimony or anecdote in making decisions. You—educators, psychologists, social workers, criminal justice advocates, family therapists and researchers, child development specialists, gerontologists, nurses, substance abuse experts, mental health experts—are studying to be or already are research practitioners.

Research practitioners are concerned with the practical applications of research findings. They use research as the basis for making decisions about programs, practices, and policy. These research practitioners, often called research consumers, rely specifically on evaluation researchers for evidence about programs and on evidence-based practitioners for methods to assess the validity of the evidence that researchers produce. The best evaluation research relies on the scientific method to obtain evidence. Research practitioners/consumers also use experience and clinical judgment to match research findings to client needs. That is how they identify evidence that matters. That is why this book takes the perspective of the practitioner or consumer of research who is searching for reliable and valid evidence of effective programs.

The book has eight chapters and a Web site that is designed to reinforce the contents of each chapter. The book and the Web site have one overarching objective: to help research practitioners and consumers, whether they are graduates or undergraduates or "out there" in the world of work, come up with evidence that matters.

The Book

Each chapter follows the same format so that once you become familiar with how the book works, you can easily find your way around. Here's what each chapter has in common.

- Objectives. Each chapter begins with an overview of the contents and a list of objectives. Each objective has a corresponding practice exercise. Often, additional exercises can be found on the Web to reinforce achievement of these objectives. In writing the book, I had many objectives in mind, but I realized that I could not possibly include exercises for all of them. So, you may find that you learn concepts that are not specifically listed in the objectives. (I hope so!)
- A flow diagram that tells you your location on the path to identifying evidence that matters. To get the evidence you need about programs, interventions, and practices, you will need to follow some basic rules and adhere to ordered steps. The flow chart tells you where you are in the process.
- A summary of chapter contents at the conclusion of each chapter.
- A list of words to remember. These words are usually highlighted in the text. They may be entirely new words to you, or they may be words that are used in a new way. You will also find definitions of these words in the stand-alone Glossary.

- A brief description of what you will learn in the next chapters.
- Exercises that are keyed to each objective and, in the Appendix, detailed answers to each exercise.
- References. These may be books, journal articles, or Web sites.

Unique Features of Practicing Research

This book was designed to teach students how to combine methods from both clinical and evaluation research to appraise the reliability and validity of evidence about programs and practices. Although some clinical and evaluation research is similar in process and outcome, these two research perspectives sometimes differ markedly. Consequently, the book provides

- a comparison of clinical and evaluation research, descriptions of the methods and assessment tools used in these forms of research, and strategies for melding them;
- methods for ensuring that the best available evidence is also evidence that matters;
- in-depth information on the systems currently used to evaluate the methodological quality of individual studies, including CONSORT and TREND;
- detailed information on the systems used by international evidence-based practice centers and agencies to create and evaluate syntheses of the literature, e.g., through meta-analysis and meta-synthesis;
- a discussion of the key issues in evaluating the ethics of research and evidence-based practice as well as definitions of concepts such as informed consent, ethics committees (institutional review boards), and research misconduct;
- detailed examples of evidence-based methods, practices, and programs, taken from the actual research literature of numerous disciplines, including psychology, criminal justice, education, social work, substance abuse treatment, nursing, violence-prevention, and many more;
- how-to skills for identifying useful literature and programs online and elsewhere;
- step-by-step instructions on how to identify and use online bibliographic databases such as MEDLINE, PsychINFO, ERIC, and Social Science Abstracts;
- links to online program databases (e.g., Promising Practices Network) containing programs that "work";

- methods of evaluating the evidence that is used to support programs listed in the online databases;
- ways of searching for literature and programs by using special questioning techniques (e.g., PICO) developed by international centers of evidence-based practice;
- information on how to use key words and Boolean terms to search for evidence and programs;
- information on how international evidence-based practice centers evaluate the methodological quality of experimental and observational studies;
- descriptions of the techniques and concepts often specifically associated with the analysis of evidence-based programs and practices, such as effect size, number needed to treat, propensity score analysis, and odds and risks; and
- methods of assessing needs, preferences, and values to ensure that the evidence provided for effective programs matters to individuals and communities, as their preferences are a key variable in the accomplishment of evidence-based practice.

The following is a walk through each chapter.

Chapter 1. The Evaluation Research and Evidence-Based Practice Partnership—This chapter provides the research consumer with an overview of the theoretical and methodological foundations of evaluation research and evidence-based medicine and practice (EBM/EB) and discusses how to use this research to identify evidence that matters. It aims to help the reader define terms such as evaluation research and evidence-based practice and identify the steps in doing evidence-based practice. Evidence-based medicine is described in this book as the foundation for evidence-based practice in the helping professions because it has been around for a while, and its methods have had a chance to be improved over time.

Chapter 2. The Research Consumer as Detective: Investigating Program and Bibliographic Databases—This chapter discusses how to find program databases and establish their quality. It also introduces the research consumer to the research literature review, focusing on the identification of online article databases and other sources of program information. Other objectives of the chapter include helping you develop a plan for identifying evidence-based program databases and for evaluating the quality of these databases. Finally, the chapter aims to assist you in learning all the tasks you need to conduct a research literature review.

Chapter 3. The Practical Research Consumer—This chapter aims to maximize the efficiency with which you identify potentially useful research articles. It begins by discussing the practical screen, which consists of criteria to sift through the huge number of articles that often result from even the most careful searches. Among the criteria are language, research design, program characteristics, outcomes measures, research sponsorship, and the characteristics of the report or article. For consumers who are concerned with the costs of programs, the chapter also provides guidance in screening programs for information on program costs and their relation to the achievement of outcomes.

Chapter 4. The Designing Research Consumer—High quality evaluation research uses the scientific method to investigate the effectiveness of programs and practices. One important index of quality is the rigor of the study's research design. This chapter discusses the most commonly used experimental and observational research designs and discusses criteria for evaluating their quality (including their internal and external validity). This chapter goes into great detail about research design because of how important study design is to the identification of high quality research and practice.

Chapter 5. The Research Consumer Reviews the Measures—Evaluation researchers collect information from their study's participants by relying on measures of process, impact, outcomes, and costs. This chapter discusses measures that are commonly used by evaluators, and it reviews the advantages and limitations of these measures from the perspective of the research consumer. The chapter also compares quantitative and qualitative data collection and the reasons for using multiple measures to study a single concept.

Chapter 6. The Research Consumer Evaluates Measurement Reliability and Validity—Evidence that matters is collected from reliable, valid, responsive, and interpretable measures of program process, outcomes, impact, and costs. This chapter discusses the characteristics of reliable and valid measures and the effects on design and measurement validity of incomplete or missing data.

Chapter 7. Getting Closer: Grading the Literature and Evaluating the Strength of the Evidence—This chapter aims to help you reliably abstract information from the literature and create charts and tables that facilitate analysis and reporting of results. It also provides you with guidance in evaluating the quality of two major types of systematic literature reviews, including meta-analysis, and examines ways of ensuring that the reviews meet the highest quality standards.

Chapter 8. The Ethical Research Consumer Assesses Needs and Evaluates Improvement—This chapter discusses the context in which the process of discovering evidence that matters takes place. It focuses on three topics: identifying clients' needs, determining if programs have met those needs, and applying ethical standards when practicing research.

The Stand-Alone Glossary—The book and Web site include a stand-alone glossary. All important terms that are emphasized in the book ("Words to Remember") are included in the glossary. You can download the glossary and consult it whenever you are involved in defining the terms used to describe evidence-based practices, programs, or policies.

The Web Site—The companion Web site at www.sagepub.com/finkstudy has two separate components. The first is a slide presentation that consists of a detailed summary of each of the book's chapters. The second is a set of additional exercises that are keyed to the printed text's major objectives.

Detailed answers and a set of references are provided for each exercise. All the exercises are interactive in that you must find articles and programs and review their quality, justify your criteria, and propose an answer.

Acknowledgments

Producing a contemporary textbook with all its component parts is a team effort, and I had a great team for this one. Sage is responsible for providing me with Lauren Habib and Tracy Buyan, who were always responsive to my calls for help. Sean Connelly humored me when I needed to be humored and, most important, taught me some secrets about Adobe. I've always loved secrets.

Vicki Knight joined the project later on, but she has been terrific. I am sure we are on to some wonderful future times. Lisa Cuevas Shaw deserves a very special thank you for providing inspiration and real assistance in the conceptualization of this book. Some of its best features are her ideas. I would also like to thank Margo Crouppen for her work in analyzing the reviewers' comments and for adding to the fun of writing the book. Karen E. Taylor, the copy editor, was indispensable to the book's coherence. If you discover errors or inconsistencies in the book, you can be sure they came about because I ignored her comments. Karen is a pleasure to work with, and she is efficient, precise, and almost always correct.

This book may have several flaws, but many of its virtues are due to its reviewers. These wonderful people read earlier versions of the book and were kind enough to offer significant comments. The reviewers are Jean F. Copenhaver-Johnson, Ohio State University at Mansfield; Ellen Tuchman, New York University, School of Social Work; Josephine G. Pryce, University of Alabama, School of Social Work; Marguerite J. Aube, R.N., C.A.S., St. Joseph's College of Maine; Dianne Oakes, J.D., M.S.W., Binghamton University, New York; Diane M. Samdahl, University of Georgia.

1

The Evaluation Research and Evidence-Based Practice Partnership

Evaluation research relies on the scientific method to provide valid evidence on the outcomes, impact, and costs of programs to improve the public's health, education, and welfare. But valid evidence alone may be insufficient to meet the needs and expectations of clients, patients, and other users of the evidence. Evaluators have identified methods for determining those needs and using their expertise to incorporate user values and expectations into their study's purposes and methods.

Evidence-based medicine and its sibling evidence-based practice (EBM/EBP) are concerned with using experience and clinical judgment to integrate best evidence from research with patient values and experience. EBM/EBP practitioners have developed special methods for identifying research studies and grading the quality and strength of the evidence. By design, EBM/EBP combines the best research evidence and brings it together with clinical and professional expertise and patient or client values to make clinical decisions.

This chapter provides the **research consumer** with an overview of the theoretical and methodological foundations of evaluation research and EBM/EBP and discusses how to use them in identifying evidence that matters. Research consumers use research as the basis for making decisions about programs, practices, and policy. Consumers practice research and are concerned with the practical applications of research findings.

Chapter Objectives

After reading this chapter, you will be able to

- Define evaluation research and EBM/EBP
- Distinguish evaluation research from other types of evaluation
- Explain how the research consumer uses evaluation research and EBM
- Distinguish evaluation research from other types of social research
- Find the outcomes and hypotheses in selected evaluation studies
- Identify the five steps of EBM
- Compare the similarities and differences between evaluation research and EBM/EBP

Figure 1.1 shows your location on the way to discovering evidence that matters.

Evaluation Research: What It Is and What It Is Not

Human problems are sometimes solved by enlisting people's participation in programs to improve their health, quality of life, social well-being, and economic prospects. A **program** consists of activities and resources that have been specifically selected to achieve these beneficial **outcomes.** An example of a program is a 10-session cognitive behavioral intervention (the program) to reduce children's symptoms of posttraumatic stress disorder (the outcome) resulting from exposure to violence. Another example is a 15-minute Web-based education tool (the program) to teach older adults about the risks of alcohol drinking (the outcome).

Evaluation researchers use scientific methods to assess the process, outcomes, impact, or costs of programs and to provide new knowledge about social behavior. Program processes refer to the staff, activities, materials, and methods that are used to accomplish the outcomes. Assessing the process includes evaluating the characteristics of the program's leadership, the adequacy of the in-service training the staff receives, the appropriateness of newly configured classrooms and offices, the effectiveness of the length of each unit of instruction, and the technological and other resources available.

Evaluations that focus on the program (What happens? Who is responsible? What does the program look like?) rather than on the

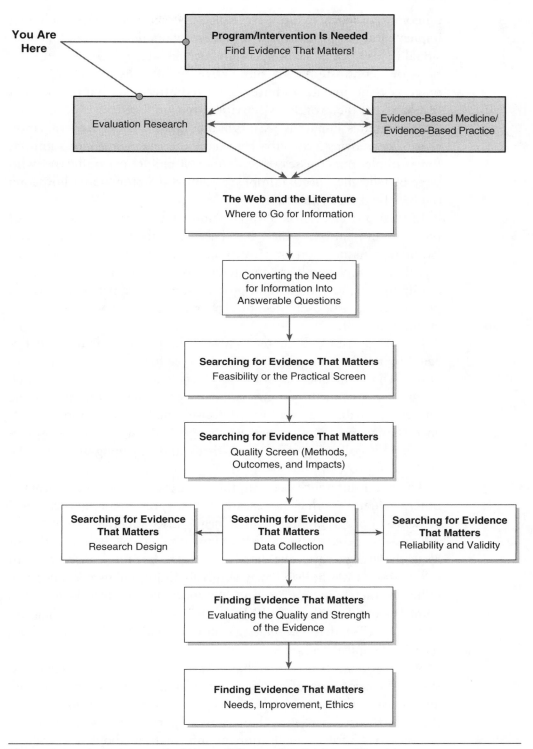

Figure 1.1   Location on the Way to Discovering Evidence That Matters

outcomes of participation are called by various names including **implementation, process,** and **formative** evaluations. In some professional fields (e.g., education, community research), formative evaluations are contrasted with **summative** evaluations, which examine outcomes and impact and are completed after a substantial portion (if not all) of the program's activities are completed.

A program's **impact** is its magnitude and duration. An evaluation researcher studying a cognitive behavioral therapy intervention's impact, for example, might assess the number of children (magnitude) who were beneficially affected (improvement in symptoms) and how long the benefits lasted (duration).

Evaluation research is a subdivision of the much larger field of program evaluation, which has been described by the American Evaluation Association or AEA (www.eval.org) as a profession composed of persons with varying interests, potentially encompassing but not limited to the evaluation of programs, products, personnel, policy, performance, proposals, technology, research, theory, and even of evaluation itself.

Evaluation research shares many of the purposes that are delineated by the AEA in connection with other forms of program evaluation. These include bettering products and practices, personnel, programs, organizations, governments, consumers, and the public interest; contributing to informed decision making and more enlightened change; precipitating needed change; and empowering all stakeholders by collecting data from them and engaging them in the evaluation process.

The main difference between the evaluation researcher and many other evaluators is that the researcher insists on obtaining the "best" evidence of program merit, which means strict adherence to the highest possible research standards. Many evaluators have a different focus than the research evaluator and tend to be more concerned with other aspects of the job, such as precipitating change or engaging others in the evaluation process. As you will see later, the research emphasis overlaps that of EBM's, which is defined by its explicit use of the "best" evidence in making decisions, evidence that comes from basic and clinical research.

When evaluators do **research,** they are participating in diligent and systematic processes of inquiry aimed at discovering, interpreting, and revising information about programs and interventions (terms that will be used here interchangeably). Research is also a term that is used to describe a collection of information about a particular subject, and it is associated with the **scientific method**. The scientific method is a set of techniques for investigating phenomena and acquiring new knowledge of the natural and social worlds, based on observable, measurable evidence.

The scientific method is also characterized by the belief that a study's activities must be objective so that the scientist cannot bias the interpretation of the results or change the results outright. Another basic expectation is that the researcher will make available complete documentation of the data and the methodology for careful scrutiny by other scientists and researchers, thereby allowing them the opportunity to duplicate and verify the results. Enabling this replication of results is a scientific and an ethical imperative.

In fact, the field of **ethics**, also called moral philosophy, is directly associated with scientific research. Ethics involves systematizing, defending, and recommending concepts of right and wrong behavior. Because evaluations always include human participants, the evaluator must demonstrate that the study design attends to ethical principles and respects participants' privacy, ensures that the benefits of participation are maximized, and provides all participants with equal access to the benefits. The criteria for including and excluding participant must be justified, and there must be a sufficient number of participants so that a program has a chance to prove itself. Also, the data collection and analysis must be appropriate and valid. Research that is not sound is unethical in itself because it results in misleading or false conclusions that, when applied, may result in harm.

Evaluation researchers rely on the scientific method, a characteristic they share with all social researchers who strive for the "truth." The main difference is that evaluation researchers study the effects of programs and interventions on participants whereas other social scientists most typically do not. More often than not, other social researchers focus on studies that describe relationships and predict events.

Example 1.1 gives samples of evaluation and other types of social research.

Evaluation research can mimic other social research when it is designed to provide new knowledge about human behavior as well as to provide evidence of program effectiveness. Research objectives C and D in Example 1.1, for example, which are research objectives, might also be achieved in connection with an evaluation study. Objective C, for example, might be achieved in connection with a program to improve children's ability to cope with pain. The achievement of objective D might occur as part of an evaluation of a program to train nurses and mental health nurse assistants to deal with seriously mentally ill hospitalized patients.

Example 1.1   Evaluation Research: Yes? No?

A. **Research Objective:** To investigate the effectiveness of acupuncture compared with sham acupuncture and with no acupuncture in patients with migraine.

Is this objective likely to be consistent with evaluation research purposes?

Answer: Yes. The researchers compare three interventions: acupuncture, sham acupuncture, and no acupuncture. (No acupuncture is considered an "intervention" in this case because the absence of acupuncture does not mean the absence of anything at all. The no acupuncture group may be on medication or other forms of therapy.)

B. **Research Objective:** To determine the effectiveness of an abuse-prevention curriculum designed to empower women with mental retardation to become effective decision makers.

Is this objective likely to be consistent with evaluation research purposes?

Answer: Yes. The intervention in this study is an abuse-prevention *curriculum.*

C. **Research Objective:** To clarify the concepts of coping with pain and quality of life (QoL) and to present a literature review of the strategies that children with recurrent headaches use to cope with their pain, the impact of recurrent headaches on children's QoL, and the influence of personal characteristics (such as age, family support) on headache, coping, and QoL in children.

Is this objective likely to be consistent with evaluation research purposes?

Answer: No. The researchers are not planning to analyze the process, outcomes, impact, or cost of a program or intervention.

D. **Research Objective:** To describe nurses' and mental health nurse assistants' perceptions of advantages and disadvantages of working on a psychiatric ward with a locked entrance door.

Is this objective likely to be consistent with evaluation research purposes?

Answer: No. The researchers are not planning to analyze the process, outcomes, impact, or cost of a program or intervention.

Although every discipline has its own specialized methodology and terminology, most evaluation researchers and other scientists begin their inquiries by asking **research questions** and proposing specific hypotheses as explanations of events. A research question is the objective of the evaluation, the uncertainty that the evaluator wants to diminish. Research questions often begin with a general concern. For example,

Can an educational program designed by and for teens reduce alcohol-related risks in adolescents?

Questions like these are usually refined even more so as to guide evaluation planning. For example,

How frequent is teen drinking in this county?

How willing are teens to participate in the design of a program to reduce alcohol-related risks?

How willing are teens to participate in an experimental study to reduce alcohol-related risks? The study's main activities will take place after school hours.

A research question is sometimes translated into one or more hypotheses. A hypothesis is a suggested explanation of a set of events, an explanation that is usually based on whether a relationship does not (or does) exist between these events. A typical evaluation hypothesis concerns the relationship between people who participate in a program and those who do not. Sample hypotheses for a program to reduce symptoms of depression among children in schools are given in Example 1.2.

Example 1.2   Two Sample Hypotheses for a Program to Reduce School Children's Symptoms of Depression

---

1. Students who receive a brief standardized program that is delivered by school mental health clinicians on school campuses will have significantly fewer self-reported symptoms of depression, and fewer reports of psychosocial dysfunction by parents at the 3-month assessment, than students who are randomly assigned to receive another program.

2. Improvement in symptoms of depression will not be translated into significant improvements in the classroom behavior as reported by teachers.

Hypotheses are tested in experimental studies. Does the relationship hold up under intense scrutiny? A controlled experiment generally compares the outcomes obtained from an experimental group against those from a control group, which is practically identical to the experimental group except for the one aspect (the experimental program) whose effect is being tested.

⚠ **CAUTION:** Research consumers should always check each study's research questions, objectives, and hypotheses to ensure that the outcomes and the study participants are relevant to their clients' needs. You many come upon evidence that supports the merits of a program that aims to achieve objectives like yours (e.g., reduce symptoms of depression) but that comes from a population (children) unlike yours (adults). It is also possible that claims of effectiveness are based on a population that interests you but that the outcomes (e.g., reduce symptoms) are not the ones of primary interest to you (e.g., provide knowledge about options for treatment).

A sample experimental study is outlined in Example 1.3. In the example, you will see that the experimental and control programs differ but that the objectives, outcomes, and participants do not. The idea of an experiment is that, if benefits are found over time in the experimental group, then it is fair to reason that they are due to the experimental program and not to group particularities (e.g., greater or lesser motivation to reduce risks).

Example 1.3   An Experimental Study to Reduce Alcohol-Related Risks: Comparing Experimental and Control Programs, Objectives, Participants, and Expected Outcomes

Program	Objectives	Participants	Expected Outcomes
Teen Alcohol Risk Reduction Program	Reduce risks of alcohol drinking	16 to 21 years of age Report drinking at least one alcoholic beverage in the past 4 weeks No history of alcohol or drug abuse	Risks are reduced as measured by Alcohol Risk Measure scores
Schools' Usual Alcohol Education	Reduce risks of alcohol drinking	16 to 21 years of age Report drinking at least one alcoholic beverage in the past 4 weeks No history of alcohol or drug abuse	Risks are reduced as measured by Alcohol Risk Measure scores

Not all evaluations are experimental. Some are **observational.** In observational research, the researcher takes a relatively passive role and does not introduce a new program but observes an already existing one. For example, a researcher who wants to find out why some teens are at risk for alcohol-related problems while others are not may interview students, some of whom participated in an alcohol risk reduction program about a year ago. The researcher would then analyze the interview data to uncover factors (e.g., participation in a program, age, family history of drinking) that predict risk. One question this researcher is likely to ask: "Do students who participated in the program have the same, greater, or lower risks than students who did not participate?" Observational studies are generally not as preferable as experimental ones because the researchers have no control over the criteria for participation in the program or other aspects of the program's design or implementation.

Evaluations that use the scientific method are able to provide accurate answers to questions such as the following. Have all planned program outcomes been achieved? What are the resources that are needed for the program to achieve its outcomes? Have all program participants benefited from the achievement? How long must participants wait for benefits to occur? How long do the program's effects last? Do the benefits of the program outweigh the risks to individuals? Do the benefits of program participation outweigh the costs to the public? What difference does the program make when compared to a logical alternative program?

Collecting information about the program and its costs and effects on participants is at the heart of evaluation. Data collection includes (1) identifying the **variables** that will be measured. A variable is a term given to a thing, or a certain value, that may change, such as the knowledge, performance, attitudes, or behaviors that describe the program participants' characteristics before and after being in the program. Data collection also involves (2) selecting, adapting, or creating measures like surveys and tests; (3) demonstrating the reliability (consistency) and validity (accuracy) of the measures; (4) administering the measures so that the rights of "human subjects" are respected; (5) "scoring" or assigning a value to the results; and (6) interpreting the score. Evaluators are old hands at the science that underlies the validation of measures of important and often difficult to assess factors, such as quality of life and well-being.

Evaluations often result in voluminous amounts of data that require careful management. Data management includes data entry and storage and requires thinking about methods of ensuring the accuracy of entry and setting up a system for ensuring confidentiality.

Evaluation data analysis can be extremely complex and include **quantitative** and **qualitative** methods. Quantitative methods rely on mathematical and statistical models. Qualitative methods involve investigating participants' opinions, behaviors, and experiences from their point of view and using logical induction. Most evaluation *research* relies heavily on quantitative methods to answer research questions and test hypotheses.

Evaluations are almost always conducted in "real life" situations in which some eligible people may not participate in all of the program's activities, others may participate in competing activities, and still others may drop out. That is why evaluations are sometimes referred to as **effectiveness** rather than **efficacy** studies, which are done under ideal conditions. Inability to control the environment and implement perfect research designs have led evaluation researchers to find ways of shoring up study validity by developing and improving upon existing research methods (e.g., propensity score analysis to control for baseline differences in study groups). These research innovations are increasingly being used for the same reason by other social scientists and health researchers.

- Evaluators are always on the lookout for new research methods. They are not shy, and they often borrow from other fields without asking for permission. Do not be surprised if you find ideas in evaluation research that come from disciplines as diverse as psychology, health services research, clinical research, sociology, communications, economics, and epidemiology, to name a few. In fact, one of the skills research consumers should acquire is how to evaluate the research from other fields upon which evaluation studies rely. In Chapter 6, for example, we will review methods for assessing whether the outcome measures that evaluators choose are reliable and valid.

- Evaluation researchers sometimes look to **clinical trials** for ways of analyzing data. Clinical trials are evaluations of medical and surgical treatments, drugs, and other interventions that are conducted in health care settings like clinics and hospitals. The outcomes investigated in clinical trials may be medical (e.g., reductions in blood pressure), psychosocial (e.g., improvements in health-related quality of life), and economic (e.g., which of two equally effective programs costs less).

Example 1.4 provides two **abstracts** of evaluation studies. An abstract is an abbreviated version of the objectives, methods, findings, and conclusions of a much larger report. For now, you do not have

Example 1.4   Evaluation Research in the Abstract

1. An Evaluation of an Intervention to Reduce Alcohol-Related Risks and Problems in Older Adults (Fink, Elliott, Tsai, & Beck, 2005)

   Objectives: To evaluate whether providing physicians and older patients with personalized reports of drinking risks and benefits and patient education reduces alcohol-related risks and problems.

   Design: Prospective comparison study.

   Setting: Community primary care.

   Participants: Twenty-three physicians and 665 patients aged 65 and older.

   Intervention: Combined report, in which 6 physicians and 212 patients received reports of patients' drinking classifications and patients also received education; patient report, in which 245 patients received reports and education, but their 5 physicians did not receive reports; and usual care.

   Measurements: Assessments at baseline and 12 months later to determine patients' nonhazardous (no known risks), hazardous (risks for problems), or harmful (presence of problems) classifications using the Computerized Alcohol-Related Problems Survey (CARPS). The CARPS contains a scanned screening measure and scoring algorithms and automatically produces patient and physician reports and patient education.

   Results: At baseline, 21% were harmful drinkers, and 26% were hazardous drinkers. The patient report and combined report interventions were each associated with greater odds of lower-risk drinking at follow-up than usual care (odds ratio=1.59 and 1.23, respectively, $P<.05$ for each). The patient report intervention significantly reduced harmful drinking at follow-up from an expected 21% in usual care to 16% and increased nonhazardous drinking from 52% expected in usual care to 58%. Patients in the combined report intervention experienced a significantly greater average decrease in quantity and frequency.

   Conclusion: Older primary care patients can effectively reduce their alcohol consumption and other drinking risks when given personalized information about their drinking and health.

   SOURCE: Fink, Elliott, Tsai, and Beck (2005).

2. A Psychological Intervention for Children With Symptoms of Posttraumatic Stress Disorder (Stein et al., 2003)

   Context: No randomized controlled studies have been conducted to date on the effectiveness of psychological interventions for children with symptoms of posttraumatic stress disorder (PTSD) that has resulted from personally witnessing or being personally exposed to violence.

(Continued)

Example 1.4 (Continued)

Objective: To evaluate the effectiveness of a collaboratively designed school-based intervention for reducing children's symptoms of PTSD and depression that has resulted from exposure to violence.

Design: A randomized controlled trial conducted during the 2001–2002 academic year.

Setting and Participants: Sixth-grade students at 2 large middle schools in Los Angeles who reported exposure to violence and had clinical levels of symptoms of PTSD.

Intervention: Students were randomly assigned to a 10-session standardized cognitive-behavioral therapy (the Cognitive-Behavioral Intervention for Trauma in Schools) early intervention group (n = 61) or to a wait-list delayed intervention comparison group (n = 65) conducted by trained school mental health clinicians.

Main Outcome Measures: Students were assessed before the intervention and 3 months after the intervention on measures assessing child-reported symptoms of PTSD (Child PTSD Symptom Scale; range, 0–51 points) and depression (Child Depression Inventory; range, 0–52 points), parent-reported psychosocial dysfunction (Pediatric Symptom Checklist; range, 0–70 points), and teacher-reported classroom problems using the Teacher-Child Rating Scale (acting out, shyness or anxiousness, and learning problems; range of subscales, 6–30 points).

Results: Compared with the wait-list delayed intervention group (no intervention), after 3 months of intervention, students who were randomly assigned to the early intervention group had significantly lower scores on symptoms of PTSD (8.9 vs. 15.5, adjusted mean difference, −7.0; 95% confidence interval [CI], −10.8 to −3.2), depression (9.4 vs. 12.7, adjusted mean difference, −3.4; 95% CI, −6.5 to −0.4), and psychosocial dysfunction (12.5 vs. 16.5, adjusted mean difference, −6.4; 95% CI, −10.4 to -2.3). Adjusted mean differences between the 2 groups at 3 months did not show significant differences for teacher-reported classroom problems in acting out (−1.0; 95% CI, −2.5 to 0.5), shyness/anxiousness (0.1; 95% CI, −1.5 to 1.7), and learning (−1.1, 95% CI, −2.9 to 0.8). At 6 months, after both groups had received the intervention, the differences between the 2 groups were not significantly different for symptoms of PTSD and depression; showed similar ratings for psychosocial function; and teachers did not report significant differences in classroom behaviors.

Conclusion: A standardized 10-session cognitive-behavioral group intervention can significantly decrease symptoms of PTSD and depression in students who are exposed to violence and can be effectively delivered on school campuses by trained school-based mental health clinicians.

SOURCE: Stein, Jaycox, Kataoka., et al. (2003).

to worry about the validity of the measurements, the adequacy of the research design, or the interpretation of the statistics. (That will come later on!) The idea is to show you how the separate parts of evaluation research are assembled to describe programs and evidence of their effects.

The data analytic methods used in evaluation research almost always produce an estimate of the program's effect by contrasting outcomes among the experimental and control participants. The researcher starts off with the assumption that no difference exists between the groups (the **null hypothesis**), and uses statistical tests to challenge the assumption. When the research data are analyzed, the statistical tests determine the P value, the probability of seeing an effect as big as or bigger than that occurring in the study by chance, if the null hypothesis were true. The null hypothesis is rejected in favor of its alternative if the P value is less than some predetermined level, traditionally 1% (0.01) or 5% (0.05). This predetermined level is call α (alpha) or the level of statistical significance.

For example, suppose a study compares programs A and B in terms of their ability to improve functional status in older adults. The researcher starts off with the assumption that the two programs are equally effective and sets alpha at 0.05. That means the researcher has set 5% as the maximum chance of incorrectly rejecting the null hypothesis (that there is no difference). This 5% is the level of reasonable doubt that the researcher is willing to accept. If the null hypothesis is falsely rejected (there actually is no difference and the null is correct), this is called a **Type I error**. Failing to reject the null hypothesis (there really is a difference) is called a **Type II error** and referred to as β (beta).

There are many reasons for Type I and Type II errors; among them are unreliable measures of the outcomes, inadequate research designs, and inappropriate data analysis. That is, Program A may actually be different or better than B (or the other way around), but a poorly designed study with inaccurate measures will not be able to detect the difference!

As you can see in the second evaluation in Example 1.4, evaluation researchers sometimes report results in terms of **confidence intervals (CI)** rather than P value. A CI is a measure of the uncertainty around the main finding of a statistical analysis. The **odds** are a way of expressing the chance of an event, calculated by dividing the number of individuals in a sample who experienced the event by the number for whom it did not occur. For example, if, in a sample of 100, 20 people did not improve and 80 people improved, the odds of improving are 20/80, which equals ¼, 0.25, or 1:4.

An **odds ratio** is the ratio of the odds of an event in one group (e.g., the experimental group or "cases") to the odds of an event in another group (e.g., the control group or "controls").

To calculate the odds ratio, you count the number in each group that experiences an event or has a "risk factor." You then divide the odds of having the risk factor among people of interest—traditionally called "the cases"—by the odds of having the risk factor among the controls. (Risk factors are variables that increase the likelihood of disease or other bad outcomes. For instance, smoking is a risk factor for heart disease. The vocabulary—terms such as *cases*, *controls*, and *risk factors*—comes from studies of public health problems.)

The formula for calculating the odds ratio is as follows:

The Formula for the Odds Ratio: AB/CD

Risk Factor Present?		Control	Total
Yes	A	B	A + B
No	C	D	C + D
Total	A + C	B + D	N

Here's how researchers might use the odds ratio.

Suppose a researcher is interested in the relationship between not eating breakfast (the risk factor) and trouble adhering to a diet. The researcher asks this question: When compared to people who eat breakfast, what is the likelihood that people who do not will have trouble adhering to a weight-loss diet?

The researcher identifies 400 people who have trouble adhering to a diet and 400 who do not. She finds that among all people with problems, 100 did not eat breakfast and 300 did. Among people without problems, 50 did not eat breakfast. To compare the odds of problems between the two groups, the researcher put the data into a table.

Odds Ratio: Problems Keeping to a Diet

No Breakfast	Case	Control	Total
Yes	100	50	150
No	300	400	700
Total	400	400	800

The odds ratio is calculated as follows:

$$OR = AD/BC \text{ so that}$$

$$100(A) \times 400(D) / 50(B) \times 300(C) = 4000/1500 = 2.67$$

The odds of being exposed to the risk factor (no breakfast) is 2.67 higher for people who have problems adhering to a weight-loss diet than for people who do not have such problems. The answer to the question is that people who do not eat breakfast are 2.67 times more likely to encounter problems adhering to a diet than people who eat breakfast.

Estimates of unknown quantities, such as the **odds ratio** (cited in the first evaluation) comparing an experimental program with a control, are usually presented as a point estimate (such as a −3.4 difference in scores between groups) and a 95% confidence interval (e.g., −6.5 to −0.4 point difference in scores). This means that if someone were to keep repeating a study in other samples from the same population, 95% of the confidence intervals from those studies would contain the true value of the unknown quantity (in this case, the difference in scores).

Alternatives to 95%, such as 90% and 99% confidence intervals, are sometimes used. Wider intervals indicate lower precision; narrower intervals, greater precision. For example, researchers could have a 99% confidence interval that would mean that they are 99% confident that the true value will be between 12 and 1, and they could also have a 99% confidence interval that would mean they are 99% certain that the true value will be between 1.2 and 1. The narrower interval (between 1.2 and 1) indicates greater precision.

Many medical and health journals prefer reports of confidence intervals to *P* values because they provide a plausible range for the true value of the difference between groups.

Research consumers should be concerned with practical or clinical significance as well as with statistical significance when looking for evidence that matters. Practical significance reflects how much of an effect a client, physician, patient, student, or other program participant sees or finds useful. Assessing practical significance takes into account factors such as the size of the program's effect, the severity of the need being addressed, and the cost.

The practical significance of a program or treatment is based on external standards provided by practitioners, clients, customers, patients, or researchers. Unfortunately, little consensus currently exists in almost any field as to the criteria for these standards.

Practitioners and researchers in evidence-based medicine use several different methods to come up with standards of clinical significance that are useful in all types of evaluation research. One method EBM practitioners use involves estimating the number of patients who would have to receive a particular treatment to prevent just one from having a bad outcome over a particular time period. This estimate is called the number needed to treat (NNT). If, for instance, the number of patients needed for a treatment is 10, then the practitioner or clinician would have to give the treatment to 10 patients to prevent 1 patient from having the bad outcome over the defined period, and each patient who received the treatment would have a 1 in 10 chance of being a beneficiary. The best NNT is 1: every person treated benefits. Unfortunately, an NNT of 1 is rarely achieved, and even an NNT of 20 or 40 may be significant (McQuay & Moore, 1997).

Other methods used by evidence-based health practitioners to determine clinical significance include calculating the extent to which an experimental treatment increases the probability of a good outcome and reduces the probability of a bad one.

Because of the pragmatic nature of almost all evaluation research, none is immune to methodological flaws. The evaluator's challenge is to design and implement a study that results in findings and conclusions that are more accurate than they would have been with another sampling strategy, research design, outcome measure, or analytic method. The evaluation's strengths must be demonstrably greater than its limitations. In short, the highest quality evaluations are those that result in the best evidence.

Table 1.1 contains a list of evaluation reports that will give you an introduction to the contents and format of typical evaluation studies. Later on, we will address methods for assessing their quality.

So the Evidence Is Valid, but Does It Matter?

Evidence that matters is meaningful to its users as well as scientifically valid. Who are the users of evaluation research? What makes evidence meaningful? Evaluation users are the sponsors and funders of research, the individuals and communities who participate in the research, and the policy makers and others who decide on the adoption of programs and practices. Evaluation users are often known collectively as **stakeholders** or **decision makers**. As a consumer of evaluation research, you are a stakeholder.

Table 1.1 Sample Evaluation Reports and Where to Find Them

Belsky, J., Melhuish, E., et al. (2006). Effects of Sure Start local programmes on children and families: Early findings from a quasi-experimental, cross sectional study. *British Medical Journal, 332*(7556), 1476–1478.

Ciaranello, A. L., Molitor, F., Leamon, M., Kuenneth, C., Tancredi, D., Diamant, A. L., et al. (2006). Providing health care services to the formerly homeless: A quasi-experimental evaluation. *Journal of Health Care for the Poor and Underserved, 17*(2), 441–461.

Diamant, A. L., Brook, R. H., Fink, A., & Gelberg, L. (2001). Assessing use of primary health care services by very low-income adults in a managed care program. *Archives of Internal Medicine, 161*(9), 1222–1227.

Fink, A., Elliott, M. N., Tsai, M., & Beck, J. C. (2005). An evaluation of an intervention to assist primary care physicians in screening and educating older patients who use alcohol. *Journal of the American Geriatrics Society, 53*(11), 1937–1943.

Finn, J., Kerman, B., & LeCornec, J. (2005). Effects of a national indicated preventive intervention program. *Journal of Community Psychology, 33*(6), 705–725.

Fishbein, M., Hall-Jamieson, K., Zimmer, E., von Haeften, I., & Nabi, R. (2002). Avoiding the boomerang: Testing the relative effectiveness of antidrug public service announcements before a national campaign. *American Journal of Public Health, 92*(2), 238–245.

Fox, P. G., Rossetti, J., Burns, K. R., & Popovich, J. (2005). Southeast Asian refugee children: A school-based mental health intervention. *International Journal of Psychiatric Nursing Research, 11*(1), 1227–1236.

Hay, J., LaBree, L., Luo, R., Clark, F., Carlson, M., Mandel, D., et al. (2002). Cost-effectiveness of preventive occupational therapy for independent-living older adults. *Journal of the American Geriatric Society, 50*(8), 1381–1388.

Husler, G., Werlen, E., & Blakeney, R. (2005). Strengthening families with first-born children: Exploratory story of the outcomes of a home visiting intervention. *Research on Social Work Practice, 15*(5), 323–338.

Parrish, A. R., Oliver, S., Jenkins, D., Ruscio, B., Green, J. B., & Colenda, C. (2005). A short medical school course on responding to bioterrorism and other disasters. *Academic Medicine, 80*(9), 820–823.

Polaschek, D. L. L., Wilson, N. J., Townsend, M. R., et al. (2005). Cognitive-behavioral rehabilitation for high-risk violent offenders—An outcome evaluation of the violence prevention unit. *Journal of Interpersonal Violence, 20*(12), 1611–1627.

Runyan, C. W., Gunther-Mohr, C., Orton, S., Umble, K., Martin, S. L., & Coyne-Beasley, T. (2005). Prevent A Program of the National Training Initiative on Injury and Violence Prevention. *American Journal of Preventative Medicine, 29*(5S2), 252–258.

Rydholm, L., & Kirkhorn, S. R. (2005). A study of the impact and efficacy of health fairs for farmers. *Journal of Agricultural Safety and Health, 11*(4), 441–448.

Sheeran, P., & Silverman, M. (2003). Evaluation of three interventions to promote workplace health and safety: Evidence for the utility of implementation intentions. *Social Science and Medicine, 56*(10), 2153–2163.

Stein, B. A., Jacox, L. H., Kataoka, S. H., Wong, M., Tu, W., Elliott, M. N., & Fink, A. (2003). Mental health intervention for school children exposed to violence: A randomized controlled trial. *JAMA, 290*, 603–611.

Wells, K. B., Sherbourne, C., Schoenbaum, M., Duan, N., Meredith, L., Unutzer, J., et al. (2000). Impact of disseminating quality improvement programs for depression in managed primary care: A randomized controlled trial. *JAMA, 268*(2), 212–220.

Evaluators have traditionally advocated including stakeholders as part of the study team, sometimes inviting them early in the process to define the focus of the research and later on to help make certain the data being collected are valid and useful. Often, special techniques, such as community forums or interviews with key members of the community, are relied upon to make sure that evaluation considers high priority, culturally relevant concerns. More recently, the process of **participatory evaluation** has been extended by some evaluators to include stakeholders as partners in setting the evaluation agenda, doing all phases of the research including analyzing and reporting on the results. Because evaluation almost always takes place within a political and organizational context, it requires group skills, management ability, political dexterity, and sensitivity to multiple stakeholders.

An important development in health evaluation research is the call to health researchers to conduct practical clinical trials (Tunis, Stryer, & Clancy, 2003) in which the hypothesis and study design are developed specifically to answer the questions faced by decision makers. According to proponents of practical clinical trials, there are widespread gaps in evidence-based knowledge, and the existence of these gaps suggests that systematic flaws can be found in the production of scientific evidence, in part because there is no consistent effort to conduct clinical trials designed to meet the needs of decision makers. To remedy this situation, these proponents stress that clinical and health policy decision makers—namely, research users—will need to become more involved in all aspects of clinical research, including priority setting, infrastructure development, and funding.

We will cover some of the most commonly used methods to elicit the views and expectations of stakeholders later on (Chapter 8). Evaluation research reviewers will find these methods useful because they ensure the meaningfulness to their clients of the recommended selection of programs and practices.

Evidence-Based Medicine (EBM): Some History and Definitions

The History

Evidence-based medicine (EBM) has become a crucial and topical issue in modern health throughout much of the world. EBM is strictly defined as the conscientious, explicit, and judicious use of current best evidence in making decisions about the care of individual patients. A more expansive definition includes health programs, practices, and policies in the decision-making process.

Testing medical interventions for safety and effectiveness in an experimental manner has probably existed for many hundreds of years. Among the first recorded evaluations is one that dates back to biblical times. Daniel of Judah compared the health effects of a vegetarian diet (the intervention) with those of the Royal Babylonian diet (control group) over a 10-day period. The Book of Daniel (1:15–16) records the findings:

> At the end of the ten days their appearance was better and their bodies healthier than all the young men who had been eating the royal delicacies. So the warden removed their delicacies and the wine from their diet and gave them a diet of vegetables instead.

Leonardo da Vinci wrote in his *Notebooks* (1508–1518) that

> Those who are enamored of practice without science are like a pilot who goes into a ship without rudder or compass and never has any certainty where he is going. Practice should always be based upon a sound knowledge of theory. (1.20)

According to Sackett, Straus, Richardson, Rosenberg, and Haynes (2000), five of the originators of EBM and the authors of an extremely influential textbook, the roots of EBM lie in Chinese medicine. In the reign of the Emperor Qianlong (1711–1799), a method known as "kaozheng" (practicing evidential research) was apparently practiced in relation to Confucian medical texts. Sackett, Straus, Richardson, Rosenberg, and Haynes also identify the ideas of EBM with postrevolutionary Paris clinicians, at least one of whom rejected the pronouncements of authorities that vivisection was good for cholera.

It was only in the twentieth century, however, that EBM really evolved to affect almost all fields of health care and policy. Professor Archie Cochrane, a Scottish epidemiologist, through his book *Effectiveness and Efficiency: Random Reflections on Health Services* (1972) and subsequent advocacy, was responsible for the increasing acceptance of the concepts behind evidence-based practice. The explicit methodologies used to determine "best evidence," however, were largely established by the McMaster University research group led by David Sackett and Gordon Guyatt. The term "evidence-based medicine" first appeared in the medical literature in 1992 in a paper by Guyatt, Cairns, Churchill, et al.

The Definitions: Research Evidence,
Clinical Expertise, and Patient Values

Sackett, Straus, Richardson, Rosenberg, and Haynes (2000) define EBM as the integration of best research evidence with clinical expertise and patient values.

The *best* **research evidence** is clinically relevant research, often from the basic sciences of medicine but especially from patient-centered clinical research. Patient-centered clinical research is analogous to evaluation research particularly in its advocacy and use of experimental methods to test effectiveness, impact, and cost. EBM is concerned not only with evidence that matters about interventions and programs but also addresses needs for information pertaining to diagnosis, prognosis, and prevention.

New evidence from clinical research both invalidates previously accepted tests and treatments and replaces them with new ones that are more powerful, more accurate, more efficacious, and safer. For example, stomach ulcers were once thought to be the result of stress or eating spicy foods. Generations of ulcer sufferers drank gallons of milk, avoided certain foods, and tried to stay calm. In 2005, two Australian physicians won a Nobel Prize for their work showing that most stomach ulcers and gastritis were caused by colonization with a bacterium called *helicobacter pylori* and not by stress or spicy food, as had been assumed before. Now, stomach ulcer patients are often treated with antibiotics (Marshall & Warren, 1984).

Giving up firmly held beliefs in the face of new evidence is challenging to say the least. As another example, consider one of the most unshakeable tenets of many health care practitioners, namely, that if patients are educated and made to be active partners in the treatment of their disease, their ability to take care of their disease should improve dramatically. Even this belief has been challenged by the evidence.

To evaluate the effectiveness of patient education in diabetic patients, a team of researchers (Sanchez et al., 2005) enrolled 200 patients who were treated at Duke University Hospital for acute coronary syndrome (ACS), a condition characterized by blockages in coronary arteries that prevent oxygen-rich blood from nourishing the heart, which can lead to chest pain and possibly heart attack. At enrollment, each patient took a standardized test that measured his or her knowledge related to diabetes. Patients were then ranked as either high-scoring or low-scoring.

The researchers found that, for diabetics, improved disease knowledge alone did not translate into improved blood sugar control, cholesterol levels, weight management, or mortality rates. They concluded that, while education may be important, other health care delivery variables must be addressed to reduce the risks of diabetic patients dying of heart disease, the main cause of death for these patients.

Clinical expertise means the ability to use clinical skills and past experience to rapidly identify each patient's unique health state and diagnosis, his or her individual risks and benefits of potential interventions, and his or her personal values and expectations.

Patient values are the unique preferences, concerns, and expectations that each patient brings to a clinical encounter and that must be integrated into clinical decisions if they are to serve the patient. EBM supporters and consumers believe that, when these three elements are integrated, clinicians and patients form a diagnostic and therapeutic alliance that optimizes clinical outcomes and quality of life.

Figure 1.2 is a graphic representation of the evidence-based medicine paradigm.

The figure suggests that clinical decisions must include consideration of the patient's clinical and physical circumstances to establish what is wrong with his or her health and what treatment options are available. Next, the options must be tempered by research evidence concerning their effectiveness and efficiency. Third, given the likely consequences associated with each option, the clinician must consider

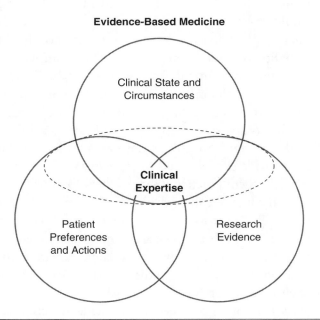

Evidence-Based Medicine

Clinical State and Circumstances

Clinical Expertise

Patient Preferences and Actions

Research Evidence

Figure 1.2   The Evidence-Based Medicine Paradigm

SOURCE: Sackett, D. L., Straus, S. E., Richardson, W. S., Rosenberg, W., & Haynes, R. B. (2000). *Evidence-based medicine: How to practice and teach EBM* (3rd ed.). New York: Churchill and Livingstone. Reprinted by permission of D. L. Sackett.

the patient's preferences and likely actions (in terms of which interventions she or he is ready and able to accept). Finally, clinical expertise is needed to bring these considerations together and recommend treatment that is agreeable to the patient. Put another way, EBM merges the science and art of medicine.

EBM has had a major impact on medicine, nursing, and other health professions in the United States and throughout the world. The application of the principles of EBM to all professions associated with health care, including purchasing and management, is referred to as evidence-based health care (Sackett et al., 2000). The principles have influenced thinking in nearly all the helping professions because of demands from the community and from program sponsors for evidence that matters. Outside of a strictly medical context, say in social work, criminology, criminal justice, education, or psychology, EBM is considered to be the parent discipline of evidence-based practice or EBP.

EBM practitioners have focused much of their intellectual effort on developing methods for grading the **quality** and rating the **strength** of a body of evidence (Lohr, 2004). The quality of each study's evidence depends on factors such as the characteristics of its research design, the adequacy of the sample size, the composition of the participants, and the validity of the outcomes. The strength of the evidence can only be determined if multiple studies are available. A strong body of evidence should meet three criteria: quality, quantity, and consistency. The quality of evidence is often a summation of the direct grading of the quality of individual studies. The quantity of evidence reflects the magnitude or impact of the effects (benefits and harms). The consistency of results reflects the extent to which studies report findings that reflect effects of similar magnitude and direction.

Because of the complexity of applying evidence-based research findings to clinical care, medical groups have created journals and online resources that provide practice guidelines, reviews of research, and bibliographies to help them practice EBM. Centers for EBM in a range of specialties exist throughout the world. The Centre for Evidence-Based Medicine (www.cebm.utoronto.ca) continually updates EBM resources, and the Agency for Healthcare Research and Quality (www.ahrq.gov) provides many useful tools. Despite these aids, however, many EBM practitioners find that they are like other consumers in needing to learn how to do their own research evaluation. Many medical schools anticipate this need and offer evidence-based medicine courses to teach students to identify individual and synthesized research studies and evaluate their quality. In fact, as the call for evidence increases, other fields, including nursing, education, and psychology, are introducing similar courses.

Evaluation researchers and EBM practitioners share similar objectives. They both count on the experimental method to provide evidence that matters and agree on the need to incorporate values and expectations into treatments, practices, and programs. Despite their many similarities, some EBM practitioners differ from evaluation researchers in at least one main use of their research results. In EBM, each physician's clinical expertise is used as the basis of judgments for applying research findings to the care of *individual* clients. That is, EBM physicians are presented with research findings on groups of people (such as diabetic patients or substance abusers), and they must translate the research into evidence-based care for individual patients. EBM physicians ask questions like these: Do the findings of this research apply to this individual? Is my patient so different from the study participants that the findings do not apply?

Evaluation consumers and other stakeholders who work outside of the direct clinical encounter concentrate on analyzing evidence to make decisions about the applicability of programs for *groups* of clients. They are not primarily concerned with translating research findings into options for individual care. Their job is to translate research that has included one group of people (such children exposed to violence or substance abusers) into recommendations regarding evidence-based programs and practices for another. Their questions are more likely to be like these: Do the findings of this research apply, *on average,* to the institutions and communities (such as schools, prisons, counties) in my setting? Are the people in my setting so different from participants in the study that the findings do not apply?

The techniques in this book are for stakeholders and other consumers of research who are mainly concerned with identifying programs to meet the needs of institutions, communities, and society. The book also advocates the acceptance of EBM's principle of incorporating client values into decisions about the choice of programs, and these values are represented by the common good.

Getting It Done: The Steps to EBM

EBM practice is comprised of five steps (Sackett et al., 2000) that are common to all evaluation consumption:

1. Convert the need for information into answerable questions. This step is often considered to be the hardest for EBM practitioners to accomplish. Any clinical situation can raise a very large number of questions, and selecting the most pertinent can be challenging. It is also difficult to state questions simply because the concepts involved in clinical settings are often very complex. Well-formulated questions are essential, however, in devising strategies that are likely to direct practitioners to the data they need to get answers.

Evaluation researchers and consumers also need to learn how to convert their information needs into questions. Researchers must discover how to ask answerable questions about outcomes, impact, and costs. Consumers or evaluators of research must ask questions about the quality of the research and its relevance to clients.

2. **Track down the best evidence to answer the questions.** Evidence databases are emerging in many fields, and, when available, they can be a primary source of information for the program seeker. But they are not always available, comprehensive, and current. To be complete, evidence databases need to be regularly updated—an enormous and costly task. Because databases may be two or three years behind the published literature, it is not uncommon for the evaluation consumer to have to rely upon individual studies or syntheses of many studies that are published in journals or made public online. Thus, to be certain that you have all available information, you, as a research consumer, need to acquire skills for searching the literature and also for applying systems to grade the quality and rate the strength of evidence.

3. **Critically appraise the evidence for validity and impact.** Once one or more potentially suitable programs are identified through evidence databases or the literature or both, here are the next questions: How valid is the evidence for the effectiveness of these programs? Does the evidence support a large and important impact? An accurate evaluation of validity requires the consumer to become knowledgeable about the basic foundations of research in order to be able to grade a study's quality.

4. **Integrate the critical appraisal with experience and understanding of values.** A really great study may produce evidence that matters about a program that has had an impact on very small numbers of people. Program seekers must find ways to determine from stakeholders how large the impact must be. What proportion of the population should receive benefits? What is the acceptable amount of time for benefits to be manifest? To endure?

5. **Evaluate one's own effectiveness and efficiency in executing steps 1–4 and seek ways to improve both next time.** Evaluation may be as specific as analyzing performance with respect to asking questions or searching for evidence, or it may pertain to the extent to which the EBM process made a difference in the processes or outcomes of care.

EBM and EBP: Perfect or Not So?

Almost nothing in health or social science is perfect, so, in a way, this is an unfair question because you know the answer already: EBM is not perfect. Among the limitations of practicing EBM is the relative shortage of consistently high quality research that meets the needs of many consumers. With time, faith in the approach, and financial support, this situation may be corrected. Perhaps a more important limitation than the shortage of evidence is that evidence that matters is not available regarding the outcomes of practicing EBM and EBP. Sackett et al. (2000) point out that no investigative team or research granting agency has yet overcome the problems of sample size and follow-up that such an evaluation of EBM requires. Also, ethical concerns exist because to conduct a scientific evaluation means having a control group that would be denied access to evidence-based treatment (so that the outcomes could be compared to the experimental group that would be given the evidence-based treatment). Sackett et al. (2000) point out, however, that many other studies have found that patients who received evidence-based interventions have better outcomes than those who do not, so that is a good start.

Getting It Together: Evaluation Research, EBM/EBP, and the Research Consumer

The research consumer is someone who works in the helping professions such as social work, education, psychology, nursing, public health, or occupational health and who has been given the assignment to find **evidence-based** (or **research-based**) programs and practices that are likely to work with a given population in a particular setting. Evaluation research and EBM are comprised of principles and methods that, when used in combination, improve the likelihood that the program that research consumers select will be pertinent and trustworthy.

Evaluation research has been around for decades and has experience designing and assessing programs to improve the public's education and well-being. EBM has developed systems for identifying programs and evaluating their quality and rating the strength of their evidence. Both evaluation research and EBM emphasize the importance of placing the evidence in the context of client or patient values and preferences.

Table 1.2 shows the relationship among the evaluation researcher, EBM practitioner, and research consumer.

Table 1.2   Evaluation Research, EBM, and the Research Consumer: Compare and Contrast

	Evaluation Research	Evidence-Based Medicine and Practice	Evaluating Research: The Consumer
Objective	Produce valid evidence about the process, outcomes, impact, and costs of programs and interventions.	Identify evidence that matters (valid, meaningful, and with consistent impact) to provide the best possible clinical care.	Identify high quality evidence-based programs that meet client needs, values, and expectations.
Methods	Use scientific method to design studies, collect information, and analyze and interpret data. Add a participatory dimension to ensure that evidence obtained is evidence that matters (meets needs, values, and expectations of stakeholders).	Use prespecified and transparent systems for grading the quality and rating the strength of the evidence. Use the best evidence available to select options for treatment and incorporating patient values and expectations.	Identify clients' needs, values, and expectations. Identify high quality programs. Match clients' values and high quality programs.
Ethical Concerns	Respect participants' rights to privacy and to have an understanding of the risks and benefits of participation.	Respect participants' rights to privacy and to have an understanding of the risks and benefits of participation.	Make certain that ethical concerns have been addressed by the researchers. Understand the limits of evaluation research and systems for rating its quality when selecting programs to meet clients' needs.

Figure 1.3 is a graphic representation of the evaluation consumer's role. As you can see from the figure, research consumers and the public they serve constitute an alliance that is analogous to the EBM practitioners' with patients. The figure also suggests that, in selecting programs, research consumers should identify institutional, community, and societal needs first. Next, the choice of programs must be tempered by the best research evidence concerning their effectiveness.

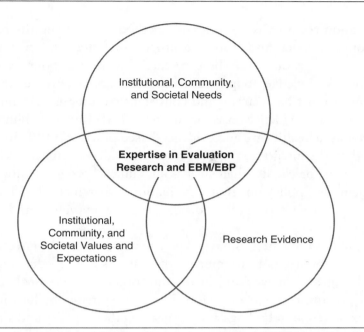

Figure 1.3 Practicing Research: Discovering Evidence That Matters

The basis for analyzing the research evidence rests on principles derived from evaluation research and EBM. Third, the research consumer must consider the client's values and expectations in weighing the evidence. Finally, expertise in evaluating research is needed to bring these considerations together.

Summary of Chapter 1: Evaluation Research and Evidence-Based Practice Partnership

Words to Remember

abstracts, clinical trials, confidence interval, control group, controlled experiment, effectiveness, efficacy, ethics, evaluation research, evidence that matters, experimental group, experimental studies, formative evaluation, hypotheses, impact, implementation evaluation, null hypothesis, number needed to treat, observational research, odds ratio, outcomes, *P* value, participatory evaluation, practical clinical trials, practical significance, process, program, qualitative, quantitative, research, research consumer, research ethics, research-based, research questions, scientific method, study quality, study strength, summative evaluations, Type I error, Type II error, variables

Evaluation research is a systematic method of assessing the **process, outcomes, impact,** and **costs** of a **program** or **intervention.** Scientific evaluations produce the **best research evidence** about programs and new knowledge about social behavior. For research evidence to **matter,** it must be accurate and consistent with its users' values and expectations. **Evidence-based medicine (EBM)** and its siblings, **evidence-based health care** and **evidence-based practice (EBP),** are exemplified by the integration of best research evidence, clinical expertise, and patient or client values in making clinical, programmatic, management, and policy decisions. Evaluation research and EBM overlap in their insistence on best evidence tempered by values and professional experience.

Evaluation researchers have expertise in analyzing the effectiveness and safety of programs to improve the public's health, education, and well-being and in working in organizational and political settings. EBM practitioners have developed explicit systems for locating and analyzing research findings and for grading their quality and strength. The **research consumer's** ability to obtain pertinent and reliable information that matters is strengthened by understanding and applying the methods and experiences that characterize both disciplines.

The Next Chapters

The next chapters build on evaluation research and EBM principles to focus on methods of identifying effective and useable programs, grading the quality and rating the strength of evidence that supports effectiveness, summarizing the results, and finding out about the values and expectations of research consumers and other users.

Chapter 2 discusses where to look for programs and how to ask the right questions.

Exercises

1. Explain whether each of these is an evaluation study or not.

   a. **Research Objective:** The purpose of the study was to evaluate a randomized culturally tailored intervention to prevent high-HIV-risk sexual behaviors for Latina women residing in urban areas.

   b. **Research Objective:** To determine the efficacy of a spit tobacco (ST) intervention designed to promote ST cessation and discourage ST initiation among male high school baseball athletes.

   c. **Research Objective:** To study drivers' exposure to distractions, unobtrusive video camera units were installed in the vehicles of 70 volunteer drivers over 1-week time periods.

2. Read the abstract of an evaluation of a home visiting program to prevent child abuse and neglect. Then answer the questions below.

Abstract: Preventing Abuse and Neglect of Children

Objectives: To assess the impact of home visiting in preventing child abuse and neglect in the first 3 years of life in families identified as at risk of child abuse through population-based screening at the child's birth.

Methods: This experimental study focused on Hawaii Healthy Start Program (HSP) sites operated by three community-based agencies. From 11/1994 to 12/1995, 643 families were enrolled and randomly assigned to intervention and control groups. Child abuse and neglect were measured by observed and self-reported parenting behaviors, all hospitalizations for trauma and for conditions where hospitalization might have been avoided with adequate preventive care, maternal relinquishment of her role as primary caregiver, and substantiated CPS reports. Data were collected through annual maternal interviews (88% follow-up each year of all families with baseline interviews); observation of the home environment; and review of CPS, HSP, and pediatric medical records.

Results: HSP records rarely noted home visitor concern about possible abuse. The HSP and control groups were similar on most measures of

(Continued)

(Continued)

> maltreatment. HSP group mothers were less likely to use common corporal or verbal punishment (AOR=.59, p=.01), but this was attributable to one agency's reduction in threatening to spank the child. HSP group mothers reported less neglectful behavior (AOR=.72, .02), which related to a trend toward decreased maternal preoccupation with problems and to improved access to medical care for intervention families at one agency.
>
> **Conclusions:** The program did not prevent child abuse or promote use of nonviolent discipline; it had a modest impact in preventing neglect. Possible targets for improved effectiveness include the program's implementation system and model.
>
> SOURCE: Duggan, McFarlane, Fuddy, et al. (2004).

Now that you have read the abstract, do the following:

    a. Describe the intervention
    b. Name the main outcomes that were studied
    c. Formulate at least two hypotheses based on a reading of the study's objectives

3. Define at least 6 characteristics of evaluation research.

4. Define the main characteristics of EBM/EBP.

5. In what ways are evaluation research and EBM similar? In what ways are they different?

6. How does evaluation research differ from other social research?

7. How is evaluation research like other social research?

8. Explain how the research consumer combines methods from research and EBM/EBP.

9. Compare these four definitions of evaluation.
    • Evaluation research is a systematic method of assessing the process, outcomes, impact, and costs of a program or intervention. Scientific evaluations produce the best research evidence about programs and new knowledge about social behavior. For research evidence to matter, it must be accurate and helpful to the evaluation's users.
    • The key to a successful program or project is evaluation. Evaluation provides formative feedback that helps guide a

program as it is being implemented. It also provides summative data that clearly demonstrate that the program is accomplishing its stated goals and objectives. Without effective evaluation, the program staff may fail to document important impacts the program has on its participants. It may also fail to recognize how different components in the program are affecting the participants or participating institutions. In an era of limited resources for educational programs, those programs that can document their success in having an impact on their participants and in using resources efficiently will be at an advantage for ongoing funding. (American Physiological Association, 2002)

- The purpose of evaluation is to produce information about the performance of a program in achieving its objectives. In general, most evaluations are conducted to answer two fundamental questions: Is the program working as intended, and why is this the case? Research methods are applied to answer these questions and to increase the accuracy and objectivity of judgments about the program's success in reaching its objectives. (Grembowski, 2001)

- The generic goal of most evaluations is to provide "useful feedback" to a variety of audiences including sponsors, donors, client-groups, administrators, staff, and other relevant constituencies. Most often, feedback is perceived as "useful" if it aids in decision-making. But the relationship between an evaluation and its impact is not a simple one—studies that seem critical sometimes fail to influence short-term decisions, and studies that initially seem to have no influence can have a delayed impact when more congenial conditions arise. Despite this, there is broad consensus that the major goal of evaluation should be to influence decision-making or policy formulation through the provision of empirically driven feedback. (Trochim, 2006)

Further Reading

Web Sites

Project ALERT is administered by the BEST Foundation for a
Drug-Free Tomorrow—http://www.projectalert.best.org.
For more information or for training, contact
BEST Foundation
725 S. Figueroa St., Suite 1615
Los Angeles, CA 90017
800-ALERT-10

Online Evaluation Resource Library—http://oerl.sri.com (accessed
August 2007)

The Online Evaluation Resource Library (OERL) is a library that
has a collection of plans, instruments, and reports that have been
used to conduct evaluations of projects funded by the Directorate for
Education and Human Resources (EHR) of the National Science
Foundation (NSF). OERL also contains glossaries of evaluation terminology, criteria for best practices, and scenarios illustrating how
evaluation resources can be used or adapted.

2

The Research Consumer as Detective

Investigating Program and Bibliographic Databases

Research consumers in search of evidence-based programs often find themselves faced with the daunting task of finding ones that are effective and pertinent. No single repository of programs exists, and to find appropriate programs and practices, you will need specialized investigative skills.

The first chapter of this book examined the foundations of evaluation research and evidence-based medicine and practice as a first step toward getting evidence that matters about programs and practices. This chapter discusses how to find program databases and establish their quality. It also introduces the research consumer to the **research literature review**, focusing on the identification of online articles databases and other sources of program information. The research review is a systematic, explicit, and reproducible method for identifying, evaluating, and synthesizing one or more studies or reports that make up an existing body of completed and recorded work produced by researchers, scholars, and practitioners about programs. It is a relatively new approach that owes a great deal to EBM practitioners.

After reading this chapter you will be able to

- Develop a plan for identifying evidence-based program databases
- Evaluate the quality of evidence-based program databases
- List alternatives to the Web for identifying and evaluating evidence-based programs

(Continued)

(Continued)

- Learn the eight tasks required in conducting a research literature review
- Choose an online bibliographic database that is likely to result in articles on evaluated programs
- Use the PICO method to formulate questions to focus a literature review search
- Create key words from research questions
- Use Boolean operators (e.g., and, or, not) when searching the research literature
- Learn the characteristics of search terms other than key words including authors, titles, journals, date of publication, etc.
- Identify sources other than the Web and bibliographic databases to learn about evaluated programs and practices

Figure 2.1 shows your location on the way to discovering evidence that matters.

Looking in All the Right Places: Finding the Evidence

Research consumers often have to do extensive detective work to find appropriate and effective programs and practices. Evaluated programs and practices can be found in the literature and on the Web, and their number is growing daily. Suppose you are looking for research-based programs to prevent family violence. There is no doubt that you can find them, but you will have to search several sites if your aim is to be comprehensive. Once you find the sites, your detective work is still far from complete because the sites may differ in their standards of effectiveness. Cautious research consumers have to be prepared to compare and assess standards across sites. Moreover, it takes a while for Web sites to be updated, so thorough research consumers will need to investigate recently published studies. This means learning to search and evaluate the quality of the literature and the strength of the evidence. Fortunately, thanks to EBM/EBP, consumers are in a better position to do this than ever before.

The difficulty in finding evidence-based programs is compounded by the fact that some practitioners and their funders believe that

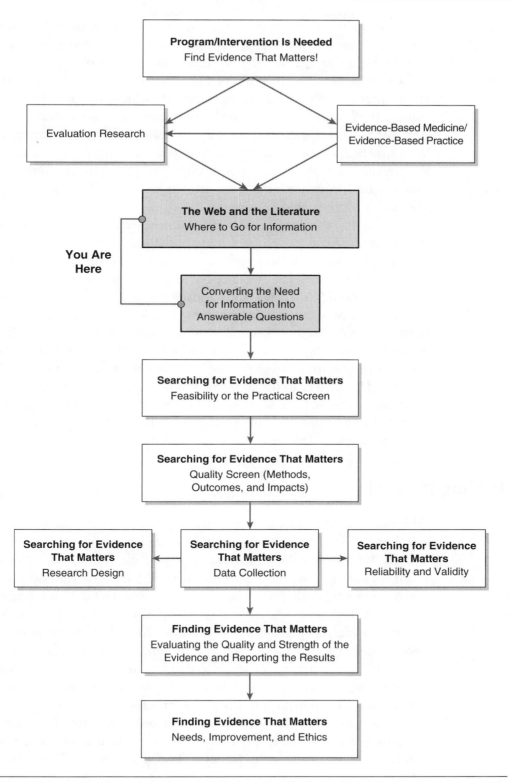

Figure 2.1   Location on the Way to Discovering Evidence That Matters

you risk more waiting to evaluate "commonsense" approaches than you gain from moving forward. Others believe that scarce resources should be spent on services and not on evaluation (or not on "research"). Because their financial supporters require an "evaluation," they comply by preparing a report, which, in some cases, is hundreds of pages. These detailed reports tend to contain descriptive and anecdotal information, which is of marginal use to consumers who need high quality evaluative information on program performance. As a result, one of the major problems confronted by consumers is how to find evidence-based practices in the face of a shortage of scientifically conducted evaluations.

Considering the debates over effectiveness standards and, in some instances, over the value of evidence-based practices and evaluation research, it is not surprising that much sleuthing becomes necessary if you are to find pertinent evidence-based programs.

Where should wary research consumers begin to look for evidence-based programs? Which criteria should be used in deciding if program evidence has been gathered according to high quality research standards? The answer to the first question about places to look for programs is threefold: the Web, the literature, and your colleagues. The answer to the second question about research standards requires you to acquire basic skills in evaluating research quality so that you can apply your own standards. To learn more about the answers to each of these questions, read on!

Trolling the Web

Although evidence-based programs are still relatively scarce in a number of fields, a growing number of agencies and professional groups are heeding the call to support and disseminate these programs. These groups have formulated evaluation criteria and have hired experts to study programs and make recommendations regarding which ones have scientific evidence of effectiveness. The results are increasingly being made available on the Web. As mentioned before, disagreements over the specific standards of effectiveness exist within and among program compilers and database creators, but their Web sites are definitely good places for the research consumer detective to begin the search for programs.

Let us start with the Web in the search for effective programs. Suppose you are looking for a program to prevent adolescent violence, aggression, and delinquency. The Center for the Study and

Prevention of Violence at the University of Colorado maintains an excellent and easy to use Web site that contains a compendium of evaluated programs. The Web address is www.colorado.edu. Enter "Blueprints for Violence" into the search area.

Once you are in the site, you will find a list of programs and the criteria for labeling them as a Blueprint model program (meets highest standards) or a Blueprint promising program (meets many of the standards). You will also find a description of the standards. If you want, you can select a program to meet your needs by using drop-down menus to describe the risk factors of concern to you (e.g., family, school), audiences (e.g., special needs), program type (mentoring, community policing), and strength of evidence (model or promising program).

Other emerging program database sites are listed in Table 2.1. The list is not intended to be comprehensive nor can we guarantee the accuracy of the addresses because of the rapidity with which Web addresses are known to disappear. The list is designed to facilitate your sleuthing by showing you the sorts of information that people are gathering about programs and to illustrate the kinds of information that you can reasonably expect as the number of databases available on the Web increases.

The Web is an excellent source of information about programs and practices. You have probably learned quite early on not to trust everything you read just because it is in print or comes from a supposedly authoritative source. Apply the same vigilance to the Web-based data.

Table 2.1   Evidence-Based Program Databases: A Very Partial List

The Cochrane Collaboration (www.cochrane.org) is an international not-for-profit and independent organization, dedicated to making up-to-date, accurate information about the effects of healthcare readily available worldwide. It produces and disseminates systematic reviews of healthcare interventions and promotes the search for evidence in the form of clinical trials and other studies of interventions. The major product of the Collaboration is the Cochrane Database of Systematic Reviews, which is published quarterly as part of The Cochrane Library. Although designed for health care, research consumers in many fields will find a wealth of information on many diverse topics including HIV/AIDS, tobacco cessation programs, and parent training programs. You can obtain study abstracts for free, but must pay for full reviews unless your institution assumes the costs or you live in certain countries including Denmark, Sweden, Australia, New Zealand, or England.

(Continued)

Table 2.1 (Continued)

The Promising Practices Network (PPN) Web site (www.promisingpractices.org) high-lights programs for children, youth, and families. PPN states that its target audiences are decision makers and practitioners rather than parents or researchers. The site's program information comes from a range of fields, rather than just one (such as violence, drugs, or education).

The What Works Clearinghouse is maintained by the U.S. Department of Education Institute of Education Sciences Web site (www.w-w-c.org). The Clearinghouse collects, screens, and identifies studies of the effectiveness of educational interventions (programs, products, practices, and policies) and produces reports on interventions that cover topics like these: elementary school math, middle school math, beginning reading, character education, preventing high school drop out, preschool children's school readiness, elementary school language learning, adult literacy.

The Campbell Collaboration (C2) (www.campbell.org) is an international effort whose mission is to prepare, maintain, and make accessible systematic reviews of studies on the effects of interventions. The focus is on education, crime and justice, social welfare, and other behavioral and social arenas. C2 maintains two databases, a Social, Psychological, Education, and Criminological Trials Registry, a prospective register of trials that are under-way, and a database covering C2 Reviews of Interventions and Policy Evaluations. The information is collected or produced by international experts within the C2 Education, Social Welfare, Crime, and Justice, and Methods Coordinating Groups.

Other Databases Include

Juvenile Justice Evaluation Center: Evidence-Based Programs
   www.jrsa.org/jjec/resources/evidence-based.html

The Center for Evidence-Based Practice: Young Children With Challenging Behavior
   http://challengingbehavior.fmhi.usf.edu

National Center for Mental Health Promotion and Youth Violence
   www.promoteprevent.org/resources/

School Dropout Prevention Best Practices
   www.colorado.gov/bestpractices/schooldropoutprevention/evidence.html

Web Resources in the Public Domain for Evidence-Based Social Work . . . Program Evaluation
   www.lib.umich.edu/socwork/rescue/ebsw.html

Resource Center for Adolescent Pregnancy Prevention's ReCAPP: Evidence-Based Programs
   www.etr.org/recapp/programs/effectiveprograms.htm

SAMHSA Model Programs: Substance Abuse and Mental Health Services Administration's (SAMHSA) National Registry of Evidence-Based Programs and Practices (NREPP)
   www.modelprograms.gov

Here are some cautionary tales:

 CAUTION: The standards of proof—the evidence—in support of any given program frequently differ from one group to another. Most important, they may differ from your standards in significance and quality. Some Web sites do not provide links to the research that provides their evidence. Other sites refer you to unpublished reports that may be difficult to locate. It is extremely important that you check the validity of each program's evidence for yourself.

 CAUTION: New measures of behavior and statistical techniques are constantly being added to the evaluation research inventory. Make sure the studies cited to justify effectiveness are up to date. Have the databases themselves been recently updated?

 CAUTION: Even good Web sites may not cover topics or programs that interest you. Web sites are discontinued without notice, and new ones appear—also without notice. As part of the consumers' detective work, you have to be prepared to search anew each time you plan to adapt or adopt a new program or service.

 CAUTION: Insistence on evidence-based programs is relatively new. Good program evaluations take years. You may have to search more than just the online databases to find them.

Use this checklist when searching the Web for evidence-based programs:

Checklist for Web Searches: Finding Evidence-Based Programs

- ✓ Check the date that the database was last updated. If it is more than three years old, use alternative sources of information about programs and practices. Check the literature for newly published research. Check government Web sites for programs still under development.
- ✓ Check the standards of evidence used to evaluate program effectiveness to make sure that they agree with yours.
- ✓ Review the original research articles and reports used to justify the selection of a program or practice as a model. These documents will offer greater insights into the program's characteristics than the summaries provided by most databases.
- ✓ Make sure congruence exists between your highest priorities and the topics and approaches encompassed by programs that appear promising to you.

Other Places, Other Programs: Expanding the Search ___

In addition to the Web, research consumers have many options in their search for programs. They include

- Research institutes and "think-tanks"
- Government agencies
- Public and private nonprofit charitable funds and trusts
- Colleagues at the workplace
- Colleagues at professional organizations
- The literature
- Journal articles
- Reports
- Systematic literature reviews of evaluated programs

Many national and international research institutes evaluate and support evidence-based programs. Among them are the RAND Corporation and the Research Triangle Institute in North Carolina.

Government agencies are also a source of information on programs. A major funder of programs and evaluations in the United States is the National Institutes of Health (NIH). The NIH is comprised of institutes such as the National Cancer Institute, the National Institute of Child Health and Development, the National Institute of Alcohol Abuse and Alcoholism, and the National Institute of Mental Health. The NIH maintains a database of all funded studies called "Computer Retrieval of Information on Scientific Projects" (CRISP), and these can be found at http://crisp.cit.nih.gov/. Because the work done by these institutes is world class, you can use their multiple databases to learn about new research methods and tools as well as the principles of learning, health behavior, and social and organizational structure and quality.

The U.S. Department of Education also maintains a Web site (www .ed.gov) that has links to other related sites including the Institute of Educational Sciences and the National Center for Educational Statistics. Table 2.2 contains examples of the U.S. Department of Education's services that may be of assistance.

Almost all U.S. states have extensive links to evidence-based resources. The New York State Office of Mental Health (www.omh.state.ny.us), for example, offers links to sites such as

- Evidence-Based Practices and Quality Improvements for Organizations
- Evidence Based Practices Resource and Information Centers
- Evidence-Based Practices Resources for Personal Digital Assistants (PDAs)

Table 2.2   A Government Agency's Assistance With Programs

- National Center for Education Evaluation and Regional Assistance (NCEE)
  An overview of the National Center for Education Evaluation and Regional Assistance. NCEE is responsible for conducting rigorous evaluations of the impact of federal programs, synthesizing and disseminating information from evaluation and research, and providing technical assistance to improve student achievement. http://ies.ed.gov/ncee/

- Policy and Program Studies Services (PPSS)
  Overview of Policy and Program Studies Service. PPSS analyzes policy, directs policy development for legislative proposals and program reauthorizations, conducts program evaluations, and provides technical expertise in formula development, modeling, forecasting, and trends analysis. http://www.ed.gov/about/offices/list/opepd/ppss/index.html

- New Directions for Program Evaluation at the U.S. Department of Education (April 2002)
  Describes effort to shift ED program evaluation away from compliance toward research and evaluation focused on results and the effectiveness of specific interventions. http://www.ed.gov/news/pressreleases/2002/04/evaluation.html

---

- Government Agencies: Federal, State, Local
- Practice Guidelines
- Searching the Evidence-Based Practices Literature
- Cultural Competency and Evidence-Based Practices
- National Recipient and Family Resource
- Specific Evidence-Based Practices Web Resources
  - Home-Based Crisis Intervention
  - Post Traumatic Stress Disorder Treatment

Where else can a consumer go to find evidence-based practices and programs? Every professional society (such as the American Educational Research Association or the American Sociological Association) has a Web site with lists of officers and other participants. Contact these people and ask for assistance in finding good programs and practices. These organizations also publish papers as do research organizations like RAND and CRESST. Ask for the papers and conference reports (if they are not immediately available on the Web). Also, contact the main charitable foundations or trusts in your region. Some may sponsor the development and evaluation of programs or know of other foundations that do.

An excellent Web site for best practices (and many other things as well) is the Utica Public Library: www.uticapubliclibrary.org/non-profit/ outcomes.html. At that site (accessed in August 2007), you will find additional sites to consults including

Best Practices for Nonprofits: Whatcom Council of Nonprofits http://www.wcnwebsite.org/practices/index.htm

Contentbank Best Practices http://www.contentbank.org

Federal Resources for Educational Excellence http://www.ed.gov/ free/index.html

UPS Best Volunteer Practices http://www.community.ups.com/ philanthropy/toolbox.html

National Governors Association Center for Best Practice http:// www.nga.org/center/

Effective Practices for Service Programs http://www.national serviceresources.org/epicenter/

America Connects Consortium: Sustaining, Capacity Building, Program Design and Evaluation links http://www.america connects.net/resources/

Benton Foundation Library http://www.benton.org/library

Community Information Best Practices http://www.si.umich.edu/ helpseek/BestPractices/index.html

> **CAUTION:** Relying on search engines to identify collections of evaluated programs is probably a waste of time. Search engines produce pages of information of variable quality that must be sorted through. If none of the above resources works (or the one that looks good has disappeared by the time you read this), contact appropriate departments in school districts, universities, social agencies, and research institutes for information. Search engines should be used to locate databases only when all else fails. Program databases may be unavailable in some fields.

One of the most important resources for information on programs is the literature. The literature includes published and unpublished reports and studies. Consumers use the literature in at least two ways. The first is to identify reports of new programs. A second use is to verify that programs found on the Web or recommended by individuals or agencies are pertinent and valid. The consumer, you recall, is supposed to have a high index of suspicion—like a good detective. Even if you trust the recommending source, you should be prepared to check on the primary source.

More on the uses and contents of the literature is yet to come. Read on!

_____ The Literature: The Research Consumer's Support

The foundation of evidence-based practice is scientifically obtained evidence about effectiveness. Most research consumers simply do not have the time or the resources to do their own evaluation research. Instead they rely on published and unpublished evaluation reports—the **research literature**—to guide them in program selection.

Because you are unlikely to conduct your own research and will rely upon studies conducted by others, you must become armed with the skills to evaluate the quality of these studies and the strength of their evidence. There is nothing new in telling you that you cannot always believe what you read. What is new is that, as someone who is responsible in whole or in part for selecting programs, you must be able to support the likelihood that they will work. This support will often come from the research literature.

A **review of the research literature** is different from a thorough reading of a journal article. It is a highly systematic, explicit, and reproducible method for identifying, evaluating, and synthesizing one or more studies or reports about programs, studies that make up the existing body of completed and recorded work produced by researchers, scholars, and practitioners. Research literature reviews are often called **systematic reviews.**

Most consumers of research-based programs tend to focus on reviews of the literature in their own fields. This is often a mistake. There are few really well-done evaluation studies in any single discipline on any single topic. Why miss out on insights from other fields? A comprehensive search is usually better than a restrictive one.

Research literature reviews can be contrasted with more subjective examinations of recorded information. When doing a research review, you systematically examine all sources and describe and justify what you have done. This enables someone else to duplicate your methods and to determine objectively whether or not to accept the results of the review. That way, when you state, "This program is effective and here are the reasons," someone else will be able to follow the logic of your selection.

In contrast to research reviews, **narrative literature reviews** are often idiosyncratic. Narrative reviewers tend to choose articles and reports without giving reasons for the selection, and they may give equal credence to good and poor studies. The results of narrative reviews are often based on a partial examination of the available literature, and their findings may be inaccurate or even false.

The Consumer as Reviewer: Eight Literature Reviewing Tasks

A research literature review follows a very specific protocol and can be divided into eight tasks:

1. *Learning about bibliographic and article databases, Web sites, and other sources.* A bibliographic database is an online collection of articles, books, and reports. The bibliographic databases of interest in research reviews contain full reports of original studies.

2. *Framing research questions.* A research question is a precisely stated question that guides the review. You need to be precise in order to focus the search.

3. *Selecting databases, Web sites, and other sources.* Once the research consumer has identified the question, the next step is to select the sources of information that are likely to provide the most accurate answers.

4. *Choosing a search strategy.* A search strategy relies on the words and phrases that you use to get appropriate articles, books, and reports. These descriptors come from the words and concepts that make up the research questions, and you use a particular grammar and logic to conduct the search.

5. *Applying practical screening criteria.* Preliminary literature searches always yield many articles, but only a few are relevant. You screen the literature to get at the relevant articles by setting criteria for inclusion into and exclusion from the review. Practical screening criteria include factors such as the language in which the article is printed, the setting of a study, and its funding source, as well as whether the study is likely to provide information about the programs you need for the population you are serving. We will discuss

this literature review activity as well as steps 5 through 8 in subsequent chapters.

6. *Applying methodological and special study screening criteria.* These include standards for evaluating scientific quality, the adequacy of a study's coverage, and its ethical integrity.

7. *Doing the review.* Reliable and valid reviews involve using a standardized method, often a printed or online form, for abstracting data from articles, training reviewers (if more than one) to do the abstraction, monitoring the quality of the review, and pilot testing the process to be sure it works.

8. *Synthesizing the results.* Research literature review results may be synthesized qualitatively or quantitatively. Qualitative syntheses present the review's findings by examining effect sizes and trends across several studies and relying upon the reviewers' experience and the quality and contents of the available literature to produce evidence that matters. A special type of quantitative synthesis—a meta-analysis—involves the use of statistical methods to combine the results of two or more studies.

_____ Choosing an Online Bibliographic Database

Reviews of the literature depend upon data from five main sources: online public (PubMed) and private (NexisLexis, ClNAHL, and EMBASE) bibliographic databases; specialized bibliographic databases (Cochrane database of systematic reviews, government reports, and collections maintained by professionals in law, business, and the environment); manual or hand searches of the references in articles; and expert guidance. Remember: The databases that are relevant to literature reviews are those that contain articles or studies. They are called **bibliographic or article databases**.

Everyone with an Internet connection has free access to much of the world's scientific, social scientific, technological, artistic, and medical literature—thanks to the U.S. government that supports it, the scientific community that produces it, and the schools and public and private libraries that purchase access to bibliographic databases and other sources of information. The U.S. National Library of Medicine at the National Institutes of Health, for example, maintains the best site for published medical research. This site is called MEDLINE/PubMed, and access is free from any electronic device with an Internet connection. All original studies include structured abstracts of each study's objectives, design, and conclusions; many studies are also available in their entirety. To get to MEDLINE, go to www.nlm.nih.gov and click on "Health Information." Another option is to go to the U.S. government's Web site: www.FirstGov.gov. This site also directs you to other databases including ERIC (Educational Resources Information Center). The National Library of Education (www.ed.gov/NLE) maintains ERIC (www.eric.ed.gov). If you forget these Web addresses, go to any search engine and enter PubMed, MEDLINE or ERIC.

University and other libraries, including public libraries, usually provide free access to hundreds of government, nongovernment, and private bibliographic databases.

A very small list of available databases is given in Table 2.3 to give you an idea of the range that is available.

How does the reviewer determine which online databases may be relevant in reviewing a particular research topic? Some, like PsycINFO or MEDLINE have names that describe their content (psychology and medicine, respectively). Other articles databases like TOXLINE (studies of air pollution and the biological and adverse effects of drugs among other things), EMBASE (pharmaceutical

Table 2.3   Online Bibliographic Databases: A Small Sample

AGELINE	JSTOR
Anthropology Plus	LexisNexis Academic
ArticleFirst	LexisNexis Congressional
BIOSIS Previews	Los Angeles Times (current; 1985–)
CANCERLIT	MathSciNet
Chicano	MLA Bibliography
CINAHL	New York Times (current; 1999–)
Contemporary Women's Issues	NLM Gateway
Dissertation Abstracts International	PapersFirst
EMBASE	PsycINFO
ERIC via Cambridge Scientific	PubMed
Abstracts	Science Citation Expanded Index
ERIC via FirstSearch/OCLC	SciFinder Scholar
Ethnic NewsWatch	Social Sciences Citation Index
GenderWatch	Social Services Abstracts
GeoRef	Sociological Abstracts
Government Printing Office	TOXLINE
Handbook of Latin American	Wall Street Journal (current; 1985–)
Studies	Web of Science
History of Science, Technology, and	
Medicine	

literature), and CINAHL (nursing and allied health) have names that are not obvious. You need to check out the databases whose names are not familiar to you.

Each library usually has a list of databases by subject area such as psychology or medicine. If you are unsure about the contents of a specific database, ask your librarian for information, or go directly to the site to find out what topics and resources it includes.

How do you select among bibliographic databases? It all depends upon your topic and study questions. For example, if you are interested in finding out what the literature has to say about the best way to teach reading to young children, then a database listing research in education, such as ERIC, is clearly an appropriate place to start. However, if you are interested in finding out about interactive reading programs, then a computer and information technology database may also be relevant. It helps to be precise about what you want and need to know, so you can choose all relevant databases.

A Note on Online or Electronic Journals

An increasing number of journals are appearing online without a print version. For example, the Public Library of Science (PLoS) is a nonprofit organization of scientists and physicians committed to making the world's scientific and medical literature a freely available public resource. Everything this group publishes is freely available online for reading, downloading, copying, distributing, and using (with attribution) any way you want. The American Educational Research Association (AERA) has a special interest group that maintains a site with links to journals that are freely accessible and available in many languages (http://aera-cr.asu.edu/ejournals/).

What Are Your Questions?

Did you ever use a search engine or bibliographic database to get information on a specific topic only to find that the results included hundreds of pages and thousands of nonsensical entries? If so, you are definitely not alone. Why does this happen? One reason can be traced to the methods used by the search engine's administrators to create and organize the listings. These methods are proprietary and not usually available for review by the public. But another important reason is that most people lack the special skills needed to perform efficient searches. Even though many search engines and most bibliographic databases are fairly user-friendly, most searches tend to be extremely broad, so the results include a great deal of related and unrelated information. Because the consumer will inevitably need to search the literature for evidence-based programs and practices, searching skills are an essential part of the job.

Searching skills begin with a request for information. This request is often referred to as a research question. For this purpose, a research question contains four components: the population or problem of concern; the intervention, practice, or program you hope to find; a comparison program; and the hoped-for outcomes. This formulation is derived from evidence-based medicine practices and is called **PICO**:

P = Problem/People targeted

I = Intervention (another term for practice or program)

C = Comparison intervention

O = Outcome

Examine these examples (Example 2.1) of three relatively nonspecific and specific questions using the PICO formulation.

Example 2.1   Specific and Nonspecific Questions and the Use of PICO

Topic 1: Care for Diabetic Patients

Less specific

Research Question A: How can we improve care for diabetic patients?

More specific

Research Question B: How well does interactive computer technology compare to written educational materials in improving quality of life when used as part of a comprehensive treatment plan for primary care patients with Type 2 diabetes?

Comment

Question B is more specific than A because it specifies the population (patients with Type 2 diabetes), type of program being sought (interactive computer technology), a comparison program (written educational materials), and the desired outcomes (improved quality of life).

P = Primary care patients with Type 2 diabetes

I = Interactive computer technology

C = Written educational materials

O = Improved quality of life

Topic 2: Preventing School Drop Out

Less specific

Research Question A: Which programs successfully prevent students from dropping out of school?

More specific

Research Question B: When compared with one another, which drop out prevention programs prevent high school students from dropping out of school before they graduate?

Comment

Question B is more specific because it specifies the persons for whom a program is sought (high school students), describes the type of program being sought (drop out prevention), contains a comparison (programs are compared to one another), and specifies the hoped-for outcome (graduation).

> P = High school students
>
> I = Drop out prevention
>
> C = Programs are compared to one another (the nature of the programs is not specified)
>
> O = Graduation

Topic 3: Alcohol Use and Health

Less specific

Research Question A: What programs are available to reduce the risks of alcohol-related problems in older adults?

More specific

Research Question B: When compared to physician education, how does patient education compare in reducing the risks of alcohol-related problems in persons 65 years of age and older?

Comment

Question is B is more specific because it defines the people being considered (persons 65 years of age and older), the type of program being sought (patient education), a comparison program (physician education), and the hoped-for outcome (reduction in risks of alcohol-related problems).

> P = Primary care patients who are 65 years of age and older
>
> I = Patient education
>
> C = Physician education
>
> O = Reduction in risks of alcohol-related problems

Research Questions and Descriptors and Key Words _____

When you go to an online bibliographic database, you should be armed with a research question. When stated precisely, a research question has the benefit of containing the words the reviewer needs to begin an online search. These words or search terms are often referred to as **key words, descriptors,** or **identifiers**.

Consider this question (Research Question 3B on page 49): When compared to physician education, how does patient education compare in reducing the risks of alcohol-related problems in persons 65 years of age and older?

From the question, you can see that the important words—key words—include *physician education, patient education, risks of alcohol-related problems 65 years of age and older.*

What key words are suggested based on the wording of Questions 1B and 2B (page 48)?

1. *Primary care patients with Type 2 diabetes, interactive computer technology, written educational materials, quality of life*

2. *High school students, drop out prevention, graduation*

Just knowing the basic key words is a start and a good one, but it is not always enough, unfortunately. For instance, suppose you are reviewing drop out prevention programs in order to find out which after-school programs work best to prevent high school students from dropping out before they graduate. You decide to use PsycINFO for your review because it is an online bibliographic database dealing with subjects in education and psychology. You also search the database using the exact phrase "drop out prevention" and are given a list of 210 articles. You find that the articles contain data on "graduation," but not all pertain to high school students. To narrow your search and reduce the number of irrelevant studies, you decide to combine "drop out prevention" with "high school graduation," and you find that your reviewing task is reduced to 36 articles. However, on further investigation, you find that not all of the 36 articles include data on effectiveness. So, you decide to further narrow the search by adding a new term "evaluation." Then you find that the reviewing task is reduced to a mere 13 articles. This seems like a manageable number of articles to review. This story has a point: As you proceed with your search, you may have to do some refining.

But consider this: Fewer articles are not always optimal. If your search is very narrow, you may miss out on some important ideas!

Your search may be overly restricted because you chose the key words based on your research question, but others who are interested in the same topic may have a different vocabulary.

One way to make sure you have covered all the bases is to check your key words or search terms with those used by authors of articles you trust and in articles of relevance. Did you include all the terms in your search that they included? The good news is that you can find out by checking the citations because all online citations include search terms.

Let's consider programs to prevent elder abuse. The research question is "When compared to one another, which programs have been shown to be effective in preventing elder abuse as indicated by fewer reports of abuse to county social services?" (P = Elderly people; I = All preventive programs; C = Compare all programs with each other; O = Fewer reports to country social services).

Example 2.2 illustrates a modified citation for articles on elder abuse programs from a search of Social Services Abstracts. Descriptors are terms used by Social Services Abstracts as part of its bibliographic indexing system or thesaurus.

Example 2.2   Social Services Abstracts: Descriptors to Enhance Search for Programs to Prevent Elder Abuse

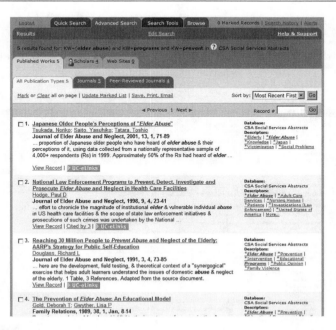

Additional search terms that may be added to your original search—based on the descriptors given in the search results—include *family violence, nursing homes, educational programs, and so on.*

Even More Search Terms: Authors, Titles, Title Words, and Journals and Then Some—Limiting the Search

You can search for programs and studies by asking for specific authors, titles of articles, words that you expect to be in the title (perhaps you forgot the exact title), and journals. Sometimes this is a useful way to identify key words and descriptors.

Searching by specifics—authors and titles—also limits or narrows your search. Narrowing your search can be especially useful if you are not doing an inclusive review. Other methods of narrowing the search include specifying the type of research design (e.g., clinical trials or randomized trials—more about these later), age groups (e.g., preschool child 2–5 years, child 6–12 years, or adolescent 13–18 years), language, date of publication, and whether the subjects of the study are male or female.

Most bibliographic databases facilitate your work by providing menus and drop-down lists of commonly used terms. For example, suppose you want to review the literature on programs to prevent alcohol misuse in adolescents. MEDLINE will let you "limit" the search by providing you with options for type of study design you want to review, in what languages, and for which ages or gender. Example 2.3 illustrates how this search appears in MEDLINE, while

Example 2.3   Search for Programs to Prevent Alcohol Use in Adolescents: PubMed

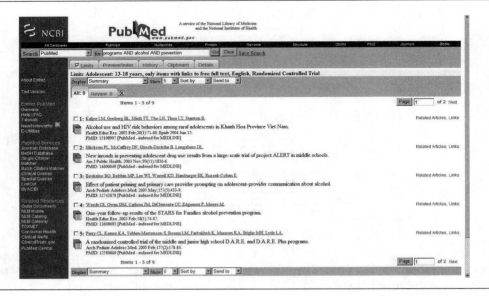

Example 2.4 illustrates how the same search appears in another database, PsycINFO. For the MEDLINE search, we added these limits: "Adolescent: 13-18 years, only items with links to free full text, English, Randomized Controlled Trial."

Example 2.4   Search for Programs to Prevent Alcohol Use in Adolescents: PsycINFO

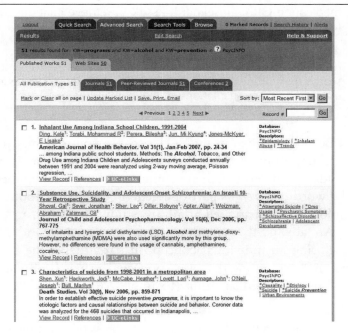

Notice that the two databases produce different articles, although if you continue on to look at the entire set of results, no doubt you will find some overlaps. It is critical, therefore, if you want to be comprehensive in your search for programs, to rely on more than one database.

How Do You Ask for Information? Searching With Boolean Operators

Literature review searches often mean combining key words and other terms with words such as AND, OR, NOT. These three words are called **Boolean operators.**

Look at these three examples of the use of Boolean logic (Example 2.5).

Example 2.5   Examples of Boolean Logic

1: AND

depression AND medication: Use AND to retrieve a set of citations in which each citation contains all search terms. The terms can appear in any order—"medication" may appear before "depression."

2: OR

medication OR counseling: Use OR to retrieve citations that contain at least one of the specified terms.

3: NOT

depression NOT children: Use NOT to exclude terms from your search. This search finds all citations containing the search term "depression" and then excludes from these citations all that contain the word "children."

Be careful when using NOT because you may inadvertently eliminate important articles. In Example 2.6, number 3, articles about children and depression are eliminated, but so are studies that include the word *children* as part of a general discussion about depression. If children are mentioned at all, the study is omitted.

An advanced method of using AND, OR, and NOT involves enclosing an individual concept in parenthesis; the terms inside the parentheses, terms that are connected using the Boolean operators, will be processed as a unit (Example 2.6).

Example 2.6   Searching PubMed for Articles on Depression and Counseling and Depression and Medication

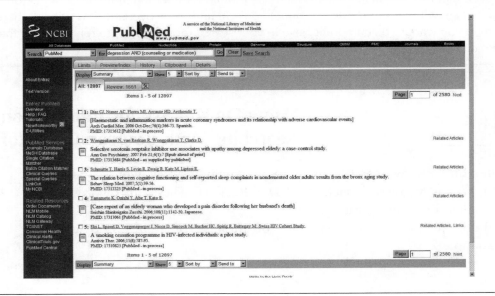

Example 2.6 presents an efficient method of searching that is called nesting. The computer will search for any articles on depression AND counseling as well as for any articles on depression AND medication. If both counseling and medication are studied in a single article about depression, the computer will be able to identify it.

Not all bibliographic databases require you to capitalize AND, OR, and NOT. Check the "advance search" function to make certain you are using the correct syntax and punctuation. Each search engine has its own peculiarities. Also, many have other functions that are helpful in making a search more efficient. One such function, a "wildcard" (often *), is used to shorten the number of words with a common root. For example, the term "agoraphob*" can be used to search for "agoraphobic" or "agoraphobia," while the term "*therapy" can be used to locate research dealing with "psychotherapy" or "pharmacotherapy."

 CAUTION: Initial key-word searches can lead to hundreds of articles. In all probability, you will need to review the titles and abstracts of each article that you identify in this first pass to assess their potential relevance. Use the key words displayed in relevant articles to continue your search. Some bibliographic databases provide links to other articles. Some of these may be pertinent and may offer clues to other key words.

 CAUTION: Limit your use of key words to two or three at a time. Use the bibliographic databases' advanced functions to restrict your initial search by language (e.g., English only), by type of journal (e.g., clinical journal), and by publication date (e.g., within the last year).

Pausing During the Search

When your search is no longer fruitful, review your collection of literature. Check the entire list for quality and comprehensiveness. Get assistance from someone who is interested in the topic or has worked in the field. Ask questions: Are all important investigators or writers included on the list? Have any major studies been excluded?

Supplementing the Online Search

Is the following statement true or false?

An experienced literature reviewer only needs access to the Internet to do a comprehensive literature review.

The answer is "false." Experienced literature reviewers must know how to locate databases and use the correct language and syntax to identify key words, subjects, titles, and so on to identify pertinent studies. However, search processes are far from uniform or perfect, the databases and study authors may not use search terms uniformly (especially true with new topics), and even the most proficient reviewers may neglect to find one or more studies regardless of how careful they are. Additionally, a reviewer may, in actuality, have access to just a few databases. Also, some studies may be in progress and not yet ready for publication. Finally, some potentially important studies may never get published.

The following checklist summarizes the main reasons for supplementing computer searches of the literature with searches using other data sources.

Checklist: Reasons to Supplement Electronic Searches

✓ Indication that many important studies are in progress or complete but not published

✓ Few acceptable studies are available

✓ Lack of uniformity across databases and fields in terminology

✓ Reason to believe that your electronic search is not comprehensive because you do not have access to all databases

Where do you go when being online is insufficient? Consider the following supplemental sources:

- Review the reference lists in high quality studies
- Talk to colleagues and other experts (including authors of articles that interest you)
- Review major government, university, and foundation Web sites

Reviewing References

After many, many hours of searching, you may fail to uncover all there is to know about a topic. This can easily happen if you rely on just one or two databases. Compare the results from MEDLINE and PsycINFO in Examples 2.3 and 2.4. As you can see, each provides a different array of articles.

One way to avoid missing out on important studies is to review the references in noteworthy articles. Noteworthy articles are those that are standard in your field or done by a researcher you trust. You do not necessarily need to retrieve the article to do this because some databases (like PsycINFO and Sociological Abstracts) provide a list of searchable references as part of the citation (if you ask for it).

Listen in on this conversation between a frustrated reviewer and a more experienced colleague to get a feeling for how references in articles can help provide coverage for a literature review.

Searching the References: A Conversation Between an Experienced and a Frustrated Reviewer

Experienced Reviewer (ER): I have been reviewing your list of references and notice that you do not include any reference to the CONSUMER program, which teaches young adults how to be better consumers.

Frustrated Reviewer (FR): I did a search of ten databases and asked specifically for CONSUMER. How did I miss that program?

ER: Very simple. CONSUMER is a new program, and its evaluation hasn't been published anywhere.

FR: If nothing about it is published, how can I be expected to find it?

ER: If you had reviewed the references in my study of the young adult consumer, you would have found it. I knew about the study, and I asked the principal investigator to tell me about it. Although no paper has been published, the U.S. government funded the evaluation, and so I was able to get a copy of the final report. You can download the final report from www.nixx.cdd.gov.

FR: I wonder how many other studies I may have missed because I didn't study the references.

ER: I wonder too.

Is Everything Worthwhile Published?

Unpublished literature has two basic formats. The first consists of documents (final reports that are required by funding agencies, for example) that are written and available in print or online—with some detective work—from governments and foundations. The evaluation report discussed in the conversation between the experienced and frustrated reviewer (immediately above) is an example. But some studies do not get published at all.

Although some unpublished studies are most certainly terrible or are the products of lazy researchers, some important ones are neither.

These studies are not published because their conclusions are unremarkable or even negative, and journals tend to publish research with positive and interesting findings.

Much has been written about the effects of failing to publish studies with negative findings. The fear is that, because only exciting studies with positive results are published and less provocative studies with negative or contrary findings are not published, some programs look more effective than they really are. That is, if Reading Program A has one positive study and two negative ones, but we only get to know about the positive one, then program A will appear to be effective, although it may not be. This phenomenon—publication of positive findings only—is called publication bias.

The general rule in estimating the extent of publication bias is to consider that, if the available data uncovered by the review are from high quality studies and reasonably consistent in direction, then the number of opposite findings will have to be extremely large to overturn the results.

Calling All Experts

"Experts" are individuals who are knowledgeable about the main topic addressed in the literature search. You can find experts by examining the literature to determine who has published extensively on the topic and who is cited often. You can also ask one set of experts to nominate another. Experts can help guide you to unpublished studies and work in progress.

They may also help interpret and expand upon your review's findings. They help answer questions like these: Do my literature review findings apply to everyone or just a particular group of people? How confident can I be in the strength of the evidence? What are the practical or clinical implications of the findings? The research consumer should consider techniques such as the Delphi, nominal group, focus group, and RAND/UCLA Appropriateness Method in bringing experts together to assist in the identification and evaluation of studies, articles, and evidence. You will encounter these techniques in greater detail in Chapter 8.

Example 2.7 contains a selection from a review of the literature on interventions to identify and treat women who experience interpersonal violence.

Example 2.7   A Portion of a Literature Review of Interventions for Violence Against Women

This article systematically reviews the available evidence for strategies applicable in the primary care setting to identify and treat women who experience interpersonal violence (IPV). For this review, IPV was defined as physical and psychological abuse of women by their male partners, including sexual abuse and abuse during pregnancy. The systematic review focused on the effectiveness of interventions to prevent IPV, including all comparative studies evaluating interventions to which a primary care clinician could refer a patient. These studies included interventions for women, batterers, and/or couples. The type of comparison group could be a no intervention control, a usual care control, or a group receiving an alternate intervention for study purposes. In the case of physical, sexual, and emotional violence, the primary health outcomes (i.e., changes in disease morbidity or mortality) are those related to physical and psychological morbidity of abuse; however, these data often are not available. Thus, self-reported incidence of abuse is often used as the primary outcome in these studies.

Data Sources

MEDLINE, PsycINFO, CINAHL, HealthStar, and Sociological Abstracts were searched from the respective database start dates to March 2001 using appropriate database-specific key words such as *domestic violence, spouse abuse, sexual abuse, partner abuse, shelters,* and *battered women,* among others. The reference lists of key articles were hand searched. Both primary authors reviewed all titles and abstracts according to the study selection criteria (see "Study Selection" below) to arrive at a final pool of articles for review. Also included were relevant articles from after the search end date and those articles identified by external reviewers.

Comment

This review relies on 5 online databases and a hand search of the reference lists of key articles. The investigators also reviewed articles that were relevant even if they appeared after the end date of their search. Finally, "experts," that is, external reviewers, were also relied upon for articles. The key words empirically related to the consequences of intimate partner violence. The research question for this review is

P = Women in the primary care setting who experience intimate partner violence (IPV)

I = Interventions for women, batterers, and/or couples

C = No intervention control, usual care control, or a group receiving an alternate intervention for study purposes

O = Self-reported incidence of abuse

SOURCE: Wathen and MacMillan (2003).

Summary of Chapter 2:
The Research Consumer as Detective

Words to Remember

Boolean operator, descriptor, identifier, key word, narrative literature review, online bibliographic or article databases, online or electronic journals, PICO, research literature review

Research consumers often have to do extensive detective work to find appropriate and effective programs and practices. Evidence-based programs are still relatively scarce in a number of fields, but a growing number of agencies and professional groups are heeding the call to support and disseminate these programs. These groups have formulated evaluation criteria and have hired experts to study programs and make recommendations regarding which ones have scientific evidence of effectiveness. The results are increasingly being made available on the Web.

When consulting online program databases, be sure to check the date that the database was last updated. If it is more than three years old, you should probably supplement your search with a review of the literature and government sites that support evaluation research. Also, check the standards of evidence used to evaluate program effectiveness to make sure that they agree with yours. Next, review the original evaluation articles and reports used to justify program choices. Make sure congruence exists between your highest priorities and the topics and approaches encompassed.

In addition to the Web, research consumers have many options in their search for programs. They include

- Research Institutes and "Think-Tanks"
- Government Agencies
- Public and Private Nonprofit Charitable Funds and Trusts
- Colleagues at the Workplace
- Colleagues at Professional Organizations
- The Literature

A **research literature review** is a highly systematic, explicit, and reproducible method for identifying, evaluating, and synthesizing one or more studies or reports that make up the existing body of completed and recorded work about programs, work produced by researchers, scholars, and practitioners. In contrast to research reviews, **narrative**

literature reviews tend to be idiosyncratic. Narrative reviewers are inclined to choose articles and reports without justifying why they are selected, and they may give equal credence to good and poor studies.

Systematic literature reviews involve eight key steps: (1) learning about the available bibliographic or article databases, Web sites, and other sources; (2) framing the research question to focus the review; (3) selecting databases; (4) developing a search strategy; (5) applying practical screening criteria; (6) applying methodological and nonmethodological screening criteria; (7) doing the review, which means abstracting preselected information in a reliable way; and (8) synthesizing the results.

Searching skills begin with a request for information. This request is often referred to as a "research" question. For this purpose, a research question contains four components: the population or problem of concern; the intervention, practice, or program you hope to find; a comparison program; and the hoped-for outcomes. This formulation is called **PICO**:

P = Problem/People targeted

I = Intervention (another term for practice or program)

C = Comparison intervention

O = Outcome

When you go to an online bibliographic database, you should be armed with a research question. When stated precisely, a research question has the benefit of containing the words the reviewer needs to begin an online search. These words or search terms are often referred to as **key words, descriptors,** or **identifiers**. Literature review searches often mean combining key words and other terms with words such as **AND, OR,** and **NOT**. These three words are called **Boolean** operators.

The Next Chapters

The next chapters examine how to sort through the research literature. **Chapter 3** discusses the practical screen through which you put articles and reports to make sure that that they are available to you and, if they are, that they are usable because they are pertinent to your client's needs. The remainder of the chapter discusses how to evaluate the quality of the literature and summarize the findings.

Exercises

1. You have been asked to find research-based programs to teach reading, and your colleague has been asked to do the same for programs to prevent high school drop out. You and your colleague decide to see if there are any existing evidence-based program databases to help you find both types of programs. How would you go about finding the databases?

2. A research consumer at a social service agency has discovered a database that specializes in evidence-based programs to prevent elder abuse, a topic of special importance to the agency. The consumer notes that the database is updated yearly, and the standards of evidence used to evaluate program effectiveness appear convincing. Before recommending any of the programs to the agency, the consumer wants to be certain that the programs have been rigorously evaluated. Unfortunately, no links to the original evaluations can be found, although the site provides an extensive bibliography. When the consumer goes to check the sources online, she finds that she does not have free access to them, and the agency cannot afford to buy the access. What should the consumer do?

3. Which of the following are typical research literature review tasks?
   a. Applying practical screening criteria
   b. Submitting a detailed protocol to an ethics committee
   c. Summarizing the findings in a protocol
   d. Evaluating the scientific quality of the review

4. Read the list of topics below and name at least one article or bibliographic database that might provide you with information on that topic.

   Topics:
   a. Reducing risky health behaviors in adolescents
   b. Improving science education in elementary schools
   c. Reducing symptoms of anxiety in older adults confined to wheelchairs
   d. Promoting health literacy

5. Frame questions for a literature review using the PICO method for each of the following topics.
   a. Preventing accidents in the home
   P = Older adults
   I = Web-based instruction

      C = Printed materials

      O = Fewer home-based falls

  b. Fostering parenting skills

      P = First-time parents

      I = Small group sessions every week for ten weeks

      C = Once a month home visits by a social worker for five weeks

      O = Better parenting skills (e.g., playing with child; learning what to do if child cries often)

  c. Enhancing community involvement in school activities

      P = Community leaders

      I = Ads on local television stations

      C = Electronic newsletter to community leaders

      O = Significant increase in membership in Parent-School Organization (PSO)

  d. Improving health literacy

      P = People 75 years of age and older

      I = Pharmacist

      C = Clinic Health Educator

      O = Knowledge of name, dosage, and purpose of medications

6. Using each research question that you just created, select key words that can be used to guide a literature search.

7. Use Boolean operators to conduct a search for literature to answer these research questions.

  a. How does an online educational program compare to printed materials in reducing the number of home-based falls in older adults?

    Key words: Web; aged 65 +; printed materials; education; falls; program; evaluation; evaluation research; English

  b. How do home visits and small group sessions compare in fostering parenting skills in first-time parents?

    Key words: home visits; small groups; parenting; program evaluation; evaluation research; English

8. In addition to key words, what other terms can be used to guide a literature search?

9. Name three sources of information about programs and practices NOT including databases of articles or bibliographic citations and other Web databases.

Further Reading

In addition to PICO, readers may find two other systems useful in guiding the formulation of questions to focus a literature search. These include POET (Patient-Oriented Evidence That Matters) and COPES (Client-Oriented, Practical Evidence Search).

3

The Practical Research Consumer

This chapter aims to maximize the efficiency with which you identify potentially useful research articles. It begins by discussing the practical screen, which consists of criteria to sift through the bombardment of articles that often result from even the most careful searches. Among the criteria are language, research design, program characteristics, outcome measures, research sponsorship, and the characteristics of the report or article. For consumers who are concerned with the costs of programs—and we all should be in times of scarce and rationed resources—the chapter also provides guidance in screening programs for information on program costs and their relation to the achievement of outcomes.

After reading this chapter, you will be able to

- Identify the components of the two practical literature review screens
  - Language, research design, the program and its comparison, data collection dates and duration, and sponsorship
  - Outcomes, participants, settings
- Become familiar with four methods of comparing program outcomes
- Differentiate cost-effectiveness from cost-benefit and cost utility as measures of economic outcomes
- Recognize that evaluation reports differ from statistical surveys and other program reports

Figure 3.1 shows your location on the way to discovering evidence that matters.

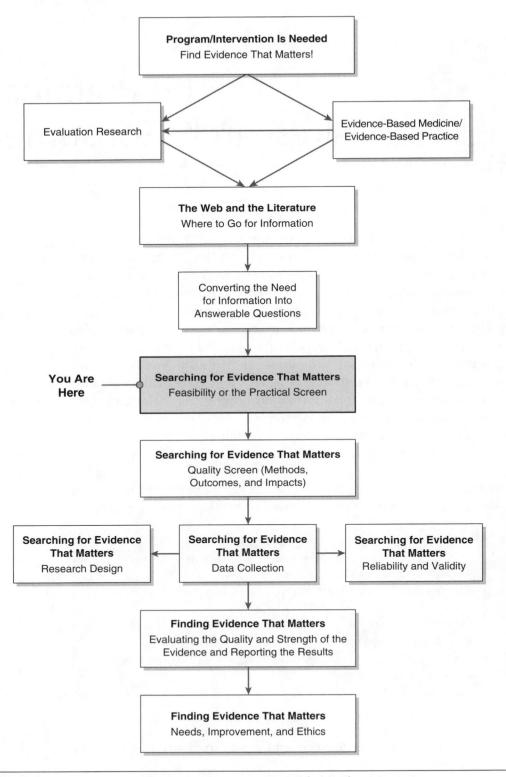

Figure 3.1   Location on the Way to Discovering Evidence That Matters

The Research Consumer's Practical Side

Not all reports and articles that are labeled evaluation studies are actually evaluations, and not all evaluations are equally valid. How can researcher consumers distinguish the high quality evaluation studies from the others? This chapter starts the process by discussing the first of two screens that help consumers sift through the countless number of documents that are available through specialized article databases and on the Web.

The first literature review screen is primarily practical, and you use it to identify studies that are appropriate for you to review in greater detail. The second screen is for quality, and it helps narrow the search to the best available studies. Here is the arithmetic:

Literature Review Arithmetic

Practical Screen → Research that is feasible to review

Quality Screen → Research that is valid because it is scientifically sound and pertinent

Practical Screen + Quality Screen → Research containing evidence that matters

---

The Practical Screen, Part 1: Language, Design, the Program, Timeliness, and Sponsorship

The **practical screen** consists of criteria that an article or report absolutely must achieve if it is to be included in the literature review. The criteria include attention to the language of the article or report, the study design, the nature of the program and its participants, the date of publication, and the study's funding source. Not everyone has the same practical criteria, but we all have some. Here is a checklist of the most common:

Checklist of Criteria to Make Research Literature Reviews Practical: The Practical Screen

---

✓ Publication Language

Excellent practices may be described in many languages. If you are unable to review articles about these practices because of your language skills, you may be missing out. Obtaining access to translators may not be possible, however, and so you may decide to live with a less comprehensive review than you might have otherwise.

<u>Example of Practical Screening Criterion: Language</u>

Include only studies in English and Spanish

✓ Journal or Origin of Publication

You may prefer certain journals or sources of information because you trust them.

<u>Example of Practical Screening Criterion: Journal or Source of Publication</u>

Include all education journals

Include only government reports

Include the most influential journals in this field

Exclude foundation reports

✓ Author

Certain authors or investigators are influential in a particular field. You may choose to insist that these people's work be part of any review because to omit their ideas means automatically ignoring significant information.

<u>Example of Practical Screening Criterion: Author</u>

Include all articles by Wendy Adams

Include all articles by Wendy Adams written after 2006

✓ Setting

If a report describes a practice that is performed in a setting like yours, it may have more meaning to you than one that takes place in a less familiar environment. You may decide only to include studies that occur in settings like yours.

<u>Example of Practical Screening Criterion: Setting</u>

Include all studies that take place in community health settings

Exclude all studies that take place in community social service centers

✓ Program/Practice Characteristics

If you have a specific requirement for a program or practice, then you should only review articles or reports of programs with those characteristics. Among the most important considerations may be the social or behavioral theory upon which the program is founded.

Examples of Practical Screening Criterion: Program/Practice Characteristics

Program's theoretical foundations

Include all programs that are built on cognitive behavioral therapy

Exclude all programs that are psychodynamically based

Other program characteristics

Staff:

Include all programs that are teacher-led
Exclude all programs that are learner-initiated

Resources:

Exclude all programs requiring teacher training by the program developers or other specially trained in-service personnel

Program Duration:

Include programs that require 10 sessions or less

✓ Research Design

A whole chapter will be devoted to the subtleties of research design because of its importance to the selection of high quality research. For this first practical pass at the literature, we are only interested in your overall preference for a type of study. Later on, we will evaluate how well the study was designed and implemented.

Research designs are typically divided into two categories: experimental and observational. **Experimental research designs** involve the collection of information to compare two or more groups, one of which participates in a new program while the other does not. An example of an experimental design is the randomized controlled trial in which the groups are constituted at random, which means that chance dictates which participants receive the experimental program.

In **observational research designs,** the variables of interest are observed rather than controlled. An example of an observational design is the prospective cohort in which a large group of people (e.g., all children in Head Start) is observed over a long period of time (e.g., 10 or more years). The purpose of the study is to describe what happens to the children in terms of important factors. How many graduate from high school, for instance. Of the high school graduates, how many go to college?

<u>Example of Practical Screening Criterion: Research Design</u>

Include only randomized trials

OR

Include randomized trials AND quasi-experimental designs

✓ Date of Publication

The publication date is important if you want to restrict your search to articles before or after a certain date.

<u>Example of Practical Screening Criterion: Publication Date</u>

Include only studies published from January 1, 2007, to December 31, 2007

Exclude all studies published before December 31, 2007

✓ Dates of Data Collection

Data collection refers to the information that is gathered to find out about the achievement of each outcome. For example, a survey of social workers' job satisfaction is one type of data collection, while a review of medical records to find out if patients' health has improved is another type.

   Some articles may be published within the past few years but rely on data from an earlier period. The research consumer must decide on the earliest period of data collection that is acceptable.

<u>Example of Practical Screening Criterion: Date of Data Collection</u>

Include only studies that collected their data from 2006 to the present

Exclude studies that do not give precise dates of data collection

✓ Duration of Data Collection

Some studies take place over a few weeks while others go on for years. If you are interested in identifying a program that lasts a relatively short time and for which limited effects can be expected, then you may be content with short data collection periods. Some study outcomes, like quality of life or the costs of preventing violence or illness, take longer periods of time to assess, and you would expect longer data collection periods.

<u>Example of Practical Screening Criterion: Duration of Data Collection</u>

Include only studies whose data collection continues for at least 12 months after completion of the program

✓ Content (Topics, Variables)

If the report or article does not specifically deal with your topic, you will probably want to exclude it from your review.

Example of Practical Screening Criterion: Content

Include only studies that focus on primary prevention of family violence

Exclude studies that focus on secondary or tertiary prevention of family violence

Exclude studies that focus on treatment

✓ Source of Financial Support

Research is funded by governments, philanthropic agencies, and private institutions and companies. If the funder has a stake in a study's outcomes, and the findings are positive, then the results may give the appearance of being compromised, or they may actually be compromised. A **conflict of interest** is a situation in which someone in a position of trust, such as a researcher, practitioner, or policy maker, has competing professional or personal interests. This competition can make it difficult to be impartial. Conflicts can be political, social, or economic. For example, a conflict of interest might occur if a researcher were related to someone on the funder's Board of Trustees, had previously done consultation work for the research funder, or had a proprietary interest in the program or intervention under study. Some journals, particularly in the medical field, require investigators to indicate if they have conflicts of interest and, if they do, to state what they are. Although a statement on its own does not eliminate the conflict, it provides the research consumer with information that can be used in evaluating the credibility of the study's findings.

Example of Practical Screening Criterion: Source of Financial Support

Exclude all studies whose funders have a financial interest in the outcomes

Exclude all studies in which conflict of interest information is missing

A literature review may use some or all types of practical screening criteria as illustrated in Example 3.1.

Example 3.1   Practical Screening Criteria: Using Inclusion and Exclusion Criteria

---

Example 1: Quality of Life

To identify articles in English pertaining to measures of quality of life we used three sources of information: The U.S. Social Functioning Bibliography (which cites 1,000 articles), MEDLINE (National Library of Medicine), and PsycINFO (American Psychological Association). We limited candidate articles to those having the term "quality of life" in their titles. From these candidate articles, we selected only those that were published from 2006 to the present and that also described or used at least one questionnaire. We excluded letters, editorials, and reviews because these are not really studies at all. We also excluded articles that were not written in English, French, Russian, Danish, or Spanish, all of which we had the resources to translate. We also excluded reports that dealt primarily with methodology or policy or whose principal investigator listed a conflict of interest pertaining to the study's funder. We then reviewed the list of articles and restricted our selection to 15 prominent journals. Here is a summary of the inclusion and exclusion criteria:

Inclusion Criteria	*Type*
Term "quality of life" in titles	Content
Published from 2006 to the present	Publication date
Described or used at least one questionnaire or instrument	Content
English, French, Russian, and Danish	Publication language
In one of 15 prominent journals (actual names given)	Journal

Exclusion Criteria	*Type*
Letters, editorials, review articles	Research design
Articles that deal with research design, measure development, or policy	Content
Articles whose principal investigator lists a conflict of interest with the study's funder	Source of financial support

Example 2: Child Abuse and Neglect

We examined evaluations of programs to prevent child abuse and neglect that were conducted from 2006 through 2008. In our selection, we did not distinguish between types of abuse (such as physical or emotional) and neglect (such as emotional or medical), intensity, or frequency of occurrence. Only evaluations of programs that were family based, with program operations focused simultaneously on parents and children rather than just on parents, children, childcare professionals, or the community, were included. We excluded studies that aimed to predict the causes and consequences of abuse or neglect or to appraise the effects of programs to treat children and families after abuse and neglect had been identified. We also excluded essays on abuse, cross-sectional studies, consensus statements, and methodological research, such as the development of a new measure of abuse, and studies that did not produce judgments of program effectiveness. Here is a summary of the inclusion and exclusion criteria:

Inclusion Criteria	Type
Evaluations of programs to prevent child abuse and neglect	Content
Conducted from 2006 through 2008	Duration of data collection
Family-based programs: focus simultaneously on parents *and* children	Content

Exclusion Criteria	Type
Studies aiming to predict the causes and consequences of abuse or neglect	Content
Evaluations of programs to treat child abuse and neglect	Content
Essays on abuse, cross-sectional studies, consensus statements, and studies that do not produce judgments of effectiveness	Research design
Methodological research, such as the development of a new measure of abuse	Content

The Practical Screen, Part 2: Outcomes and Participants

Now that you have eliminated the studies and reports that you cannot use at all (because you cannot read them, they are out of date, they take place in a setting that bears little resemblance to yours, and so on), you need to go through the studies that remain to make sure they contain pertinent and valid information on outcomes and participants. Ask these questions: Does the evaluation provide information on topics of concern to my clients? If so, was effectiveness evaluated in a sample of people who are likely to be representative of my clients?

Effectiveness Is a Comparative Concern: Outcomes

A program's effectiveness is found in its **outcomes**. An outcome is a result such as reading test scores, quantity and frequency of alcohol use, self-efficacy, quality of life, health status, recidivism rate, symptoms of depression, job skills, and costs. Beneficial outcomes are improvements, e.g., higher reading test scores or lower rates of harmful alcohol use. Outcomes are also called **dependent variables**.

By definition, a program or practice is effective only if it produces equal or better outcomes than a comparable alternative. A comparable alterative is a program or practice that is designed to or has achieved a beneficial outcome with similar participants under similar circumstances.

The comparison between outcomes for participants and nonparticipants can be made using a variety of methods as shown in Table 3.1.

As you can see, at least four methods of comparison were possible:

1. Select experimental and comparison groups at random from all potentially eligible participants using standard statistical software. The experimental group gets a special program, but the comparison may not get it at all. In the example, the comparison group is only guaranteed that it will see a film related to the topic of violence.

2. Select experimental and wait-list comparison groups at random from all potentially eligible participants using standard statistical software. Participants are randomly assigned to each of the two groups. The comparison group also gets the program.

3. Use a volunteer experimental group and a large sample on which data were collected previously and stored in a publicly accessible database. In this example, the large sample—the comparison group—is a nationally representative sample. There is no possibility that the comparison group will get the program.

4. Use a volunteer experimental group only. In this case, the experimental group is its own comparison. That is, it is compared to itself from time to time.

Which of these comparison methods is best? By best, we mean that the method produces more accurate information than the other methods. Based on the limited amount of information given in the scenarios, 1 and 2 are likely to be better methods of comparison than 3 or 4. The reason is that the evaluators have much tighter control over events in 1 and 2. The evaluators decide who is in the experimental and comparison groups and on the nature of the program.

In scenario 3, the evaluator has no sway over who is included in the comparison group. In fact, the comparison group—even if it is

Table 3.1   One Scenario and Four Methods of Comparing Outcomes

Scenario:

Young people who are exposed to persistent violence in their communities may subsequently experience symptoms of depression. The Community Centers Movement (CCM) has decided to screen all teens that come to its neighborhood clinics over a 12-month period to identify a sample who have witnessed violence and also have symptoms of depression.

Over the 12-month period, the CCM identified 300 teens. One of the following takes place:

1. CCM evaluators use standard statistical software to assign 150 of the 300 teens at random to one of two groups. The first group, the experimental group, consists of participants who join a 6-week counseling program that is administered by trained psychiatric social workers. The second group is asked to watch a film on community violence and then to discuss its effects. The two groups are compared before and after the programs (counseling versus film). Before the programs, both groups are equally symptomatic. CCM evaluators hypothesize that, after each group receives its respective program, the counseling group's depressive symptoms will decrease significantly when compared to the film-watching group's symptoms. If the evaluators are correct, the 150 teens in the film group will be offered the counseling program at the conclusion of the evaluation.

2. CCM evaluators use standard statistical software to assign 150 of the 300 teens at random to one of two groups. The first, the experimental group, consists of participants who join a 6-week counseling program that is administered by trained psychiatric social workers. The second, the "comparison" group, is put on a waiting list. At the end of the 6 weeks, the comparison group receives the counseling program. The evaluators have three hypotheses: (1) At baseline (before the experimental group is counseled), the groups will not differ in their symptom scores; (2) After 6 weeks, the experimental group will have better scores than the wait-list group; (3) After 12 weeks (that is, at the conclusion of the wait-list group's counseling) the experimental group's 6-week scores and the wait-list group's 6-week scores will not differ.

3. CCM evaluators invite 300 eligible teens to participate in a 6-week counseling program. The Office of Mental Health has a large database consisting of depression scores that were obtained from a nationally representative sample of teens. The evaluators hypothesize that, before the counseling program, CCM teens will have worse scores than the national sample but that after it, CCM teens will obtain scores that do not differ from the rest of the nation.

4. Every year for 3 years, the evaluators follow 150 teens who volunteered to participate in a counseling program for their depressive symptoms. The evaluators hypothesize that the 150 teens will maintain their improved scores over time.

nationally representative—may be quite different in important ways from a group that is specifically created to participate in a program. For instance, in the hypothetical example above, members of the program group may differ from the national group in the quantity and frequency of violence exposure, the type of violence they experience, and demographic characteristics such as age, income, or race and ethnicity. These characteristics are called independent variables. They are considered independent because they are extraneous to potential program effects. For example, no program can change a person's education or gender or the amount of violence to which he or she has been exposed: These factors are independent or free of the program. They are called variables because they are measurable factors, characteristics, or attributes of an individual or system that might be expected to vary over time or between individuals.

Why use an already existing database for comparison purposes? Researchers sometimes rely on existing databases for "normative" data because analyzing existing data is relatively inexpensive when compared to collecting data on one's own. Also, a really sound database is often viewed as a gold standard for comparison purposes. Statistical databases like those maintained by the U.S. National Center on Health Statistics, the National Health Interview Survey, and the U.S. Census are often invaluable tools in evaluation research. You just have to be careful that the norm and the new group are enough alike so that comparing them produces meaningful results.

The problem with the comparison method of scenario 4 is that volunteers may be very different from the "typical" person who may benefit from a program. They may be more motivated to change, for example.

Without a comparison group, you cannot tell if the volunteers were affected by just the program or by external events. You can improve the design of the study by adding a second group that is also observed over a three-year period. Ideally, the second group would be selected at random from all who are eligible to begin with. That is, its members, too, would have witnessed violence and have symptoms of depression. Suppose the evaluation found that students receiving the program had better outcomes. In that case, because people were assigned to groups at random, the evaluator would have little reason to assume that one group had more interfering events (more exposures to violence, say) than the other.

Studies with very large samples (much larger than the 150 to 300 described in these examples) that are observed over many years using relatively consistent methods can provide invaluable data. The Nurses' Health Study, the Physicians' Health Study, and the Framingham Heart Study are three examples of very large (tens of thousands of people), long-term studies that have influenced the world's thinking on health and medical care. Studies like these are unique and scarcely represented in other fields. In order for studies like this to succeed, they need extraordinarily careful planning, commitment over time, and funding.

 CAUTION: The choice of the comparison group is as important as the choice of the experimental group. A weak comparison group, one whose program is unlikely to succeed anyway, will bias the research findings in favor of the experimental group.

 CAUTION: Perfect selection and assignment of experimental and comparison groups do not on their own guarantee sound research. Many other factors must be considered. Among them are the composition and size of the sample who participate, the program's objectives and implementation, the timing and validity of the measures used to collect information, and the appropriateness of the data analysis.

The previous examples give little information on these factors. Which measures of depression are being used? Are they valid for teens? Why was the six-week program chosen? What is the evidence that it is beneficial for teens? What methods were used to compare groups and measure change over time? These questions (and others) must be answered to get a fair estimate of effectiveness.

Population Matters

You can only measure how effective a program is for a specific group of people, for a defined population. The defined population is specified by the researcher. For instance, suppose you find an evaluation of an educational program that convinces you that program participants achieve desired exercise levels. You must then ask these questions: Who are the "participants"? Suppose they are men and women between the ages of 21 and 65 years of age. If you plan to use the program with older (greater than 65 years of age) or younger (20 years of age and younger) people, you cannot be at all certain that the program will work for you. In fact, if your population and circumstances do not match those of the research, you have to either conduct a new evaluation in your setting or find another, more pertinent program.

Does this mean that, if a research user's end purpose deviates even a little from a program's objectives, methods, or settings, the results will be different? Must users conduct a separate evaluation every time they modify a program to meet the client's needs? These are tough questions to answer because, at present, we really do not know the answers. To provide an accurate response, we would need to study the effects on outcomes and effectiveness of changing program components within and across a diverse group of programs and participants. Some of you may choose to do this, assuming you have the resources.

Rather than conduct still more studies and evaluations, many evaluation researchers and consumers are taking to heart a more pragmatic approach in which more diverse groups of people are included into studies to maximize their applicability to as many people and places as possible. Like so many ideas that guide the development and evaluation of research-based practices, this one comes from medical research. Practical evaluations are also referred to as practical or pragmatic clinical trials (Glasgow, Magid, Beck, Ritzwoller, & Estabrooks, 2005; Tunis, Stryer, & Clancy, 2003). The idea is to develop programs that have effects in the real world, and that means evaluating programs and practices in real-world rather than lab and laboratory-like settings. Consider these two evaluation researchers:

A Tale of Two Evaluation Researchers

Restrictive Evaluator: I am evaluating a program to improve older adults' knowledge of how two different medications may interact with each other and have adverse effects. To be eligible for our study, participants must be 65 years of age and older, take five or more medications at least once a week, and have visited the clinic at least twice in the past twelve months. Participants must also live within ten miles of the clinic and be willing to attend a one-hour educational session at the clinic four times a month for three months. People will be excluded from the evaluation who have a serious psychiatric (e.g., schizophrenia) or medical illness (e.g., congestive heart failure), who smoke, or who do not have access to reliable e-mail to keep track of their medication use.

Inclusive Evaluator: I am also evaluating a program to improve older adults' knowledge of medication interactions. To be eligible for our study, participants must be 65 years of age and older and take at least two medications at least once a week. We will accept all participants who are willing to attend a one-hour educational session at the clinic four times a month for three months.

What are the advantages and limitations of each approach: the restrictive versus the inclusive?

A Tale of Two Evaluation Researchers: Continued

Restrictive Evaluator

Advantage: If the findings are positive, the restrictive evaluator can confidently characterize the population for whom the program is most likely to work: people 65 years of age and older, who take at least five medications, visited the clinic twice in last twelve months, have no serious mental or physical illness, have access to e-mail, live within ten miles of the clinic, and are willing to attend a one-hour educational session at the clinic four times a month for three months.

Disadvantage: The findings will be precise, but they will probably apply to a very specific population who may represent only a small proportion of people at the clinic or anywhere else. Identifying and enrolling people who meet the criteria for inclusion into the evaluation and who also do not meet the exclusion criteria may take the evaluator a great deal of time, costing money and delaying the publication of the results.

Inclusive Evaluator

Advantage: The inclusive evaluator has set broad criteria for inclusion into the program. Because of this, the pool of people who may qualify for participation is likely to be greater than the pool available to the restrictive evaluator. Research shows that over half of all adults who are 65 years of age and older take at least one or two medications for their health problems (including high blood pressure or high cholesterol). Fewer older adults take three or more medications, and even fewer take five or more. Access to a relatively large pool of recruits shortens the study's timeline and facilitates the production of timely information. Moreover, the "generalizability" of the findings—the extent to which they apply to the types of people who generally come to the clinic—is enhanced by including a diverse group of people.

Disadvantage: The criteria for participation are so general that the findings may be difficult to interpret. Suppose the evaluation found that, on average, the program achieved its objectives. The evaluator must still ask questions to discover details: Did all people benefit, or did some people benefit so much more than others that they drove up the average score? For example, did people who were "healthier" do much better than those who were less healthy? The restrictive evaluator excluded the least healthy (those with serious psychiatric or medical illnesses) from the program, so at least the research consumer knows from the start that the program may not apply to this population.

Money Matters

Suppose the research consumer identifies two programs that achieve similar outcomes. Which criteria should be used to select between them? One consideration should be the relative costs of the two programs. How do you choose between one program that is more effective than another but that also costs more? The answers to these questions about costs can be obtained using economic evaluation methods. Table 3.2 defines four of the major methods used in analyzing the comparative outcomes and costs of programs (Drummond, Richardson, O'Brien, Levine, & Heyland, 1997).

Table 3.2   Four Methods of Comparing Outcomes and Costs

Cost-Effectiveness Analysis: Programs are cost-effective when they save costs and offer equal or better outcomes than the alternative. A program is cost-effective when no other program is as effective at lower cost.

 CAUTION: A program does not have to achieve all of its outcomes to be cost-effective but it *must* cost less than its competition. Programs are also cost-effective when they save costs and offer equal or better outcomes than the alternative.

Cost-Benefit Analysis: Programs have value when their benefits (expressed in monetary terms) are equal to or exceed their costs.

 CAUTION: It is often difficult to express program benefits in monetary terms. For example, how does one go about placing a financial value on years of life saved, reductions in family violence, prevention of drug and alcohol abuse, or other similar planned social program outcomes?

Cost Minimization Analysis: This is a type of cost-effectiveness analysis in which Programs A and B have identical outcomes and the goal is to determine which one has the lower costs.

Cost Utility Analysis: This is a type of cost-effectiveness analysis in which the outcomes of Program A and B are weighted by their value or quality and measured by a common metric such as "quality of life years." Quality of life years or QALYs is a measure that encompasses both the quantity or duration of life and its quality. For instance, an operation may gain a patient 10 years of life but result in physical impairment. A QALY measure takes into account the number of years of life saved (say, 10) in conjunction with the quality of the saved years (a value judgment). The goal of the analysis using a metric like QALY is to determine which program produces the most quality-adjusted life years at lower cost.

Program sponsors (such as the board of a nonprofit trust or foundation) have been increasing their demands for economic evaluations of social and health programs. Their justification is based on the realization that resources for programs are scarce, the resources have alternative uses, people have different needs, and we never have enough resources to satisfy everyone's needs. The application of cost-effectiveness measures to meet one group's needs over another's has ethical implications. For instance, the elderly, the mentally ill, children with special needs, and others may be excluded from access to certain programs because they are not expected to benefit a great deal from them, a particular problem when the programs are expensive. Moreover, people with special needs have traditionally been excluded from research because they are not "interesting" enough, do not yield reliable data (because they have multiple complex problems), or are not able to participate in research. As a result, the available data may be insufficient to measure the effectiveness, let alone the cost-effectiveness, of any given program for these groups. Critics of the use of economic evaluation also point out that what is "effective" sometimes differs between clinicians and researchers. If so, then what is "cost-effective" will likewise differ.

Program Activities and Resources

Evaluation reports are obliged to include information on program activities and the resources needed to accomplish them. Program activities are all those "processes" that are done to and for the target audience in pursuit of the program's outcomes. For example, in a program designed to train volunteers to help in evacuating people from their homes during a hurricane, one activity might consist of a three-hour training session in how to pack essentials for a family of four that will last up to three days in a shelter. The training session is to be done by already trained program staff. The activity is the training session, and the resource is access to three hours of a trained staff member's time.

 CAUTION: Economic evaluations are scarce—actually nonexistent—in many fields.

Evaluation Report or Something Else?

Evaluation reports result in appraisals of practice or program effectiveness. Evaluations depend on a specific research question, and they must be designed to answer that question through valid data collection, analysis, and interpretation. It is not uncommon to find articles and reports that claim to be evaluative although they are actually compilations of statistics or the findings of surveys, focus groups, interviews, and so on.

Statistical information on its own is relatively neutral. In deciding upon best practices, however, you need to know if the statistics are presented primarily to describe or to support an appraisal of program effectiveness. A simple description is not what you want. Consider this:

Contrasting Description and Evaluation

Question: How many children received healthy snacks at midmorning?

Descriptive Answer: Three hundred children received healthy snacks at midmorning.

Evaluation Question: Was the program effective in providing children with healthy midmorning snacks?

Evaluation: When compared to children who were randomly selected to be in Program X, children in our program received significantly more healthy snacks at midmorning. Put another way, 300 children in our program received healthy snacks compare to 132 in the other program. This difference was statistically significant using the ABC test. (A "good" evaluator would include the actual statistical results here.)

The description consists of the number of children receiving healthy snacks at midmorning. The evaluation produces a judgment based on a statistical comparison between two randomly constituted groups. (At this point in the review process, we are not concerned with how well the groups have been randomized or whether the statistical test and its findings are appropriate. We will need to address these concerns later in the reviewing process.)

Question: How many participants enjoyed their participation in the research?

Survey Result: Half of the participants (50%) said that they enjoyed participating in the research.

Evaluation Question: Did we meet our standards for promoting enjoyment among participants?

Evaluation: Based on previous years, we set a standard for enjoying program participation. We anticipated that at least 65% of participants would state they were satisfied. We found that 50% reported that they enjoyed participating in the study. We concluded that the program had not met the standard we set.

If a report does not answer evaluation questions, then it is not, properly speaking, an evaluation report. An additional illustration may clarify this point.

Suppose you are the head of a school district that is looking for a program to reduce its high drop out rate. Suppose also that you search the Dropout Prevention database maintained by the (hypothetical) Division of Education and come up with these two reports:

Reports on TRUST and MENTOR: Two Programs to Reduce School Drop Out Risks

Report 1. The TRUST program provided mentors to over 300 high school students. We compared TRUST to a similar program called MENTOR, which served fewer than 250. TRUST mentors spent at least 3 hours each month with each student. MENTOR mentors spent 1. We can expect that TRUST students will remain in school at a greater rate than MENTOR students.

Report 2. Program TRUST provides mentors to high school students to reduce their risks of dropping out before graduation. Mentors are expected to spend an average of 3 hours each month with students. Students in 10 of the district's high schools are randomly assigned to participate in one of two programs: TRUST or MENTOR. The evaluation asked these questions: When, compared to MENTOR, does participation in TRUST reduce the risk of dropping out? The evaluators designed a study to compare the proportion of at risk TRUST students with the proportion of at risk MENTOR students. Over a 24-month period of observation, the evaluators found that, when compared to students in the program TRUST, students in MENTOR had a 2.5 times greater risk of dropping out. The evaluators concluded that TRUST achieved its objective of reducing the risk that high school students will drop out.

The first bit of information is purely statistical. It tells you how many mentors were provided to students in TRUST and MENTOR and how much time the mentors devoted to their jobs. You cannot tell from the information whether either program is effective in reducing the risk of dropping out, even though the *evaluators make the claim* that it is likely to be effective. Presumably, the claim is based on the larger number of students being served and the greater amount of time spent by the TRUST mentors. But, suppose the mentors in TRUST are not as well trained as those in MENTOR? If that is the case, the amount of time spent with the student may not matter; in fact, spending more time may even be harmful. For instance, untrained mentors may have inaccurate or misleading information about the consequences of dropping out, where additional prevention assistance may be obtained, or other important facts.

The second bit of information about the TRUST program describes the evaluation question (Does program participation reduce the risk of dropping out?) and the answer (It does). The statistics in this case (comparing proportions of those at risk in the programs TRUST and MENTOR) are given expressly for the purpose of answering the evaluation question.

> ⚠ **CAUTION:** Just providing statistical data is insufficient. To evaluate an intervention or program, a report or article or summary must provide answers to a research or evaluation question. Do not be misled by reports that only describe the participants, their opinions, or the amount of resources spent on them. Also beware of claims of effectiveness based on just looking at the numbers (rather than designing a study to analyze them). It is often tempting to support any program that purports to help a large number of needy people. However, unless the program is properly designed and implemented and also supported by evidence of its effectiveness, you simply cannot tell whether the participants are benefiting. Maybe the program is indeed beneficial, but without evidence, how do you know? Perhaps some other program is more effective, while another is equally as effective but less costly.

Are Evaluation Reports All There Is?

Research consumers may use many other types of research to better understand the methods or findings of evaluation research. For instance, research consumers who are interested in reading programs may review the latest research on how children learn to read. Similarly consumers who are thinking of implementing health literacy programs may spend time examining measures of health literacy to better understand those used in evaluation studies.

Use the following checklist when putting together the practical screen.

Checklist for Expanding the Practical Literature Review Screen

- ✓ Is this an evaluation report or something else?

- ✓ Does the report meet all the selected practical criteria?

- ✓ Are outcomes carefully defined?

- ✓ Are appropriate study outcomes compared?

- ✓ Are the study participants likely to be similar to the group of interest to my setting?

- ✓ Are the characteristics of the comparison group similar to those of the experimental group?

- ✓ Is information provided on costs, effectiveness, and benefits?

Summary of Chapter 3: The Practical Research Consumer

Words to Remember

conflict of interest, cost-benefit, cost-effective, cost minimization, cost utility, dependent variables, experimental research design, observational research design, outcomes, practical screen

The **practical screen** consists of criteria that an article or report absolutely must pass through to be eligible for review. The screen typically consists of the article's or report's publication language; the study's author and design; the publication date; the dates and duration of data collection; and the program's outcomes, content, settings, and participants.

Evidence-based programs make differences in **outcomes**. An outcome is a measurable result such as reading test scores, quantity and frequency of alcohol use, self-efficacy, quality of life, health status, recidivism rate, symptoms of depression, job skills, and costs. Beneficial outcomes are improvements: higher reading test scores or decreases in harmful alcohol use, for example. Outcomes are **dependent variables**.

Some evaluations study the costs of achieving program outcomes. There are four common types of cost evaluations. Programs are **cost-effective** when they save costs and offer equal or better outcomes than the alternative. A program is cost-effective when no other program is as effective at lower cost. Programs have value when their benefits (expressed in monetary terms) are equal to or exceed their costs (**cost-benefit**). **Cost minimization** analysis is a type of cost-effectiveness analysis in which Program A and B have identical outcomes and the goal is to determine which one has the lower costs. A **cost utility** analysis is also a type of cost-effectiveness analysis, but, in this case the outcomes of Program A and B are weighted by their value or quality and measured by a common metric such as "quality of life years" or QALYs.

Evaluation reports result in appraisals of program effectiveness. Evaluations depend on a specific research question, and they must be designed to answer that question through valid data collection, analysis, and interpretation. It is not uncommon to find articles and reports that claim to be evaluative although they are actually just compilations of statistics or the findings of surveys, focus groups, interviews, and so on.

The Next Chapters

Now that you have screened the literature and discovered research that appears promising, the next step is to evaluate its quality. The next three chapters deal with methodological quality, specifically, with understanding research design and data collection so that you can evaluate their validity.

Exercises

1. Read the following five statements and tell if you agree or disagree with each or if you do not have sufficient information to agree or disagree.

Statement	Agree, Disagree, Cannot Tell (Not Enough Information)		
1. If a report provides detailed descriptive statistical information about a program (such as the number of people who participated in the program, how many of them benefited, and the duration of the program), that is proof that the program is effective.	Agree	Disagree	Cannot Tell
2. To qualify as an effective program, you need at least one of these: data on how program participants' outcomes compare to nonparticipants'; comparable outcome data from established databases; long-term data on outcomes for one or more groups of people.	Agree	Disagree	Cannot Tell
3. Once you find an effective program, it doesn't matter if you change parts of it to meet your needs as long as you stay true to the program developer's intentions.	Agree	Disagree	Cannot Tell
4. Effective programs are usually less costly than ones that are of unproven effectiveness.	Agree	Disagree	Cannot Tell
5. Evaluation reports do not need to include information on program activities such as staff training and monitoring of quality and adherence to the study's implementation because such information is not needed to arrive at a conclusion about a program's effectiveness.	Agree	Disagree	Cannot Tell

2. Describe the practical criteria used in this review.

Does a Fetus Feel Pain?

This literature review examines whether a fetus feels pain and, if so, whether safe and effective techniques exist for providing direct fetal anesthesia or analgesia in the context of therapeutic procedures or abortion.

We systematically searched PubMed for English-language articles focusing on human studies related to fetal pain, anesthesia, and analgesia. Included articles studied fetuses of less than 30 weeks' gestational age or specifically addressed fetal pain perception or nociception. Articles were reviewed for additional references. The search was performed without date limitations and was current as of June 6, 2005.

---

3. Read the program description below. Provide this information about the program from its description.
   - Official name of the program
   - Characteristics of target population
   - Characteristics of comparison group
   - Data on the outcomes that are being compared
   - How the program is implemented
   - Duration of each activity
   - Duration of the program
   - Resources needed to perform each major activity (e.g., number of counselors and in-service trainers; amount of time needed for training and monitoring of quality; financial resources required to purchase computers, books, and access to proprietary bibliographic databases)
   - Information on costs, cost-effectiveness, or cost-benefit

---

Program Description

The Cognitive-Behavioral Program for Veterans with Trauma or CBV is designed for use by veterans who have symptoms of posttraumatic stress syndrome, commonly called PTSD. The evaluation of CBV was funded by the Federal Office of Veterans' Affairs.

CBV uses cognitive behavioral therapy (CBT), is offered in ordinary primary mental health care clinics, and relies on a small group format (five–eight veterans per group). The primary outcome is scores on a well-known Trauma Inventory (a reference is cited here). There are ten small group sessions, and, in each, a set of CBT techniques is introduced to the veterans. The instructional methods are a mixture of didactic presentation and reliance on worksheets during and between sessions. The veterans are required to do homework. Homework assignments are developed collaboratively between the veteran and the clinician in each session and are reviewed at the beginning of the next session.

A sample of five of the ten sessions is given below. For more detail, please go to www.CBV.edu.

Session 1

   Introduction of group members, confidentiality, and group procedures
   Explanation of treatment using case examples
   Discussion of reasons for participation (kinds of stress or trauma)

Session 2

   Education about common reactions to stress or trauma
   Relaxation training to combat anxiety

Session 3

   Thoughts and feelings (introduction to cognitive therapy)
   Fear thermometer
   Linkage between thoughts and feelings
   Combating negative thoughts

Session 4

   Combating negative thoughts

Session 5

   Avoidance and coping (introduction to real-life exposure)
   Construction of fear hierarchy
   Alternative coping strategies

Before the formal evaluation, CBV had been pilot tested for feasibility and acceptability (reference is cited here). The current CBV program was implemented on a continuous basis from the late autumn through the spring of the 200X-200Y by two full-time and one part-time psychiatric social worker from the Veterans Affairs Mental Health Services Unit. The groups most often met once a week at a time mutually agreed upon at the end of each session. Most groups met during the late afternoon.

Clinicians received two days of training and weekly group supervision from the clinician investigators (names of investigators are listed here). The clinicians followed a treatment manual to ensure that the program was uniformly administered. Clinicians were granted some flexibility to meet the specific needs of the participants in the group.

4. Which type of economic evaluation was probably performed?

An Economic Analysis of Programs to Care for Mentally Ill Patients

Evaluators interviewed 40 mentally ill patients who were given hospital-based home care and 40 who received conventional outpatient follow-up. The interviews covered topics like disease maintenance behavior, psychotic symptoms, social function, service satisfaction, and cost. The cost for each patient was the sum of costs for all direct mental health services. The evaluators found that the costs of the hospital-based home care model were lower than those of conventional outpatient follow-up and that, over a one-year period, hospital-based home care was associated with improvements in mental health, social outcomes, and satisfaction with services. Policy makers may consider the improved outcomes and the lower costs in the hospital-based home care program revealed in this analysis as they allocate resources and develop policy for the care of mentally ill patients.

SOURCE: Tsai, Chen, and Yin (2005).

---

5. Read the following description of a literature review and answer the questions below.

This article systematically reviews the available evidence for strategies applicable in the primary care setting to identify and treat women who experience interpersonal violence (IPV). For this review, IPV was defined as the physical and psychological abuse of women by their male partners, including sexual abuse and abuse during pregnancy. The systematic review focused on the effectiveness of interventions to prevent IPV, including all comparative studies evaluating interventions to which a primary care clinician could refer a patient. These studies included interventions for women, batterers, and couples. The type of comparison group could be a no intervention control, a usual care control, or a group receiving an alternate intervention for study purposes. In the case of physical, sexual, and emotional violence, the primary health outcomes (i.e., changes in disease morbidity or mortality) are those related to the physical and psychological morbidity of abuse; however, these data often are not available. Thus, self-reported incidence of abuse is often used as the primary outcome in these studies.

---

a. What are the outcomes that concern the reviewer?

b. Which comparison groups are acceptable?

4

The Designing Research Consumer

Chapter 3 discussed the range of practical criteria that can be used to assemble accessible and pertinent evaluation studies. This chapter is concerned with beginning the process of evaluating study quality.

High quality evaluation research uses the scientific method to investigate the effectiveness of programs and practices. Some evaluation studies are of higher quality than others, and the research consumer must learn to distinguish among them. One important index of quality is the rigor of the study's research design. This chapter discusses the most commonly used experimental and observational research designs and explains criteria for evaluating their quality.

After reading this chapter, you will be able to

- Describe the characteristics of commonly used evaluation research designs including
  - Randomized controlled trials with concurrent and wait-list control groups (e.g., randomizing individuals and clusters or groups; blinding)
  - Quasi-experimental designs with concurrent control groups (including matching; propensity score analysis)
  - Time-series designs (e.g., pretest-posttest and interrupted time-series)
  - Observational designs including cohorts, case controls, and cross-sectional surveys
- Describe an evaluation's main objective based on a summary of its report and also describe how participants were assessed for inclusion and exclusion, name the evaluation research design, and briefly summarize the findings
- Write up the results comparing an experimental and a control group when provided with a table of data

(Continued)

(Continued)

> - Name the threats to internal and external validity in evaluation reports
> - When given an excerpt from an evaluation report, list the variables or "covariates" that the researchers controlled for statistically to prevent them from confounding the results.

Figure 4.1 shows your location on the way to discovering evidence that matters.

Research Design: Creating the Structure

An **evaluation's research design** is its structure. At its most stingy, the structure consists of the new program that is to be compared to the alternative, participants who are assigned to be part of the new program *or* the alternative, and a schedule of measurements (e.g., before program participation and immediately after). Unfortunately, evaluation research design does not have a standard vocabulary, and so consumers have to be multilingual. **Baseline** information, for example, is sometimes called **pretest** data. Both terms refer to information collected about study participants before the program begins. Another set of terms includes **independent** versus **predictor** variables. Both refer to factors, such as gender and age, that are not expected to change because of the program. The program itself is a special type of independent variable, one that is "manipulated" by the researcher.

The reason for the inconsistency in word usage can be traced, often, to the different terms assigned to these concepts within various disciplines. In education, for example, data obtained before a program begins are called pretest data. This makes sense because schools and students are used to testing, particularly to achievement testing. It is not surprising, therefore, that data on program outcomes in educational evaluations are called posttest data. In other fields, however, testing in the usual sense is rare, so an alternative vocabulary has emerged. In the health disciplines, for example, preprogram information is often called baseline data, and data collected after are referred to as postprogram or outcome data.

Evidence that matters comes from studies that use many different research designs. Evidence-based practice does not fret over the terms "qualitative" or "quantitative" research design because it is primarily concerned with the design's rigor. Many researchers in all fields agree

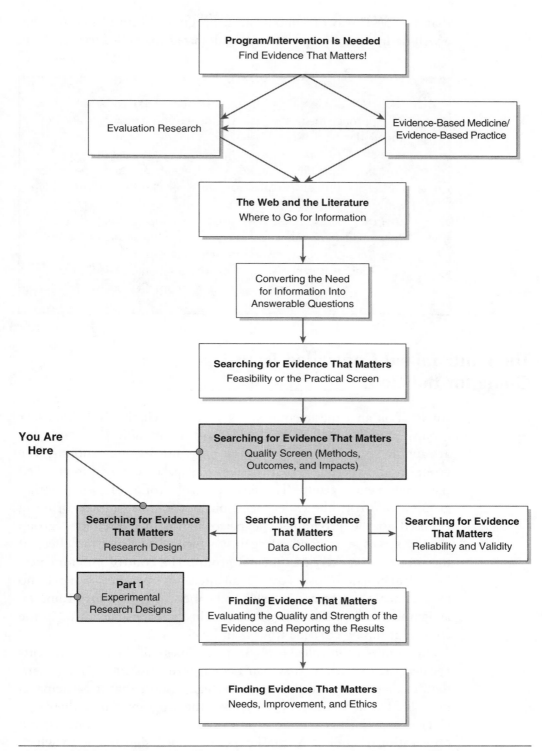

Figure 4.1   Location on the Way to Discovering Evidence That Matters

that the "best" way of demonstrating program effectiveness is through a well-designed and implemented **randomized controlled trial** or **RCT**.

⚠ **CAUTION:** Scientific evaluations, exemplified by a well-done RCT, produce the best research evidence about programs and new knowledge about social behavior. A poorly designed and implemented RCT produces invalid findings. Just calling a study an RCT does not automatically produce evidence that matters. The design must adhere to strict standards. But even the best research evidence may not matter unless it is consistent with its users' values and expectations. Evidence-based medicine (EBM) and its siblings, evidence-based health care and evidence-based practice (EBP), are characterized by the integration of best research evidence, clinical expertise, and patient or client values in making clinical, programmatic, management, and policy decisions.

The Randomized Controlled Trial: Going for the Gold

An RCT is an experimental study in which eligible individuals or groups of individuals (e.g., schools or communities) are assigned at random to receive one of several programs or interventions. The group in an experiment that receives the specified program is called the **experimental group**. The term **control group** refers to another group assigned to the experiment, but not for the purpose of being exposed to the program. The performance of the control group usually serves as a standard against which to measure the effect of the program on the experimental group. The control program may be typical practice ("usual care"), an alternative practice, or a placebo (a treatment or program believed to be inert or innocuous). **Random assignment** means that people end up in the experimental or in the control group by chance rather than by choice.

Randomized controlled trials are sometimes called **true experiments** because, at their best, they can demonstrate causality. That means that, in theory at least, the researcher can assume that if participants in an RCT achieve desirable outcomes, the program caused them.

True experiments are often contrasted with quasi experiments, and observational studies. A **quasi-experimental design** is one in which the control group is predetermined (without random assignment) to be comparable to the program group in critical ways, such as being in the same school or eligible for the same services. In **observational designs,** the evaluator does not intervene. He or she studies the effects of already existing programs on individuals and groups (e.g., a **retrospective cohort study, historical analysis,** or **summative evaluation** of programs like Head Start or the Welfare to Work Program of the U.S. government). Observational designs are sometimes called descriptive.

True and quasi-experimental designs aim to link programs to outcomes, while observational studies are used to illuminate the need for programs, learn about their implementation, and clarify the findings of current evaluations by applying lessons learned from previous research.

The RCT is considered the gold standard of research designs because it is the only one that can be counted on to rule out inherent participant characteristics that may affect the program's outcomes. Put another way, if participants are assigned to experimental and control programs randomly, then the two groups will probably be alike in all important ways before they participate. If they are different afterwards, the difference can be reasonably linked to the program.

Suppose the evaluators of a workplace literacy program hope to improve workers' writing skills. They recruit volunteers to participate in a six-week writing program and compare their writing skills to those of other workers who are, on average, the same age and have similar educational backgrounds and writing skills. Suppose also that, after the volunteers complete the six-week program, the evaluators compare the two groups' writing and find that the experimental group performs much better. Can the evaluators claim that the literacy program is effective? Possibly. But the nature of the design is such that you cannot really tell if some other factors that the evaluators did not measure are the ones that are responsible for the apparent program success. The volunteers may have done better because they were more motivated to achieve (that is why they volunteered), have more home-based social support, and so on.

A better way to evaluate the workplace literacy program is to (1) randomly assign all eligible workers (e.g., those who score below a certain level on a writing test) to the experimental program and to an alternative control program and then to (2) compare changes in writing skills over time. With random assignment, all the important factors (such as motivation and home support) are likely to be equally distributed between the two groups. Then, if the scores are significantly different in favor of the experimental group, the evaluators will be on firmer ground in concluding that the program is effective (Table 4.1).

Table 4.1   An Effective Literacy Program Based on RCT Results: An Imaginary Example

	Random Assignment to Experimental Literacy Program	*Random Assignment to Control Program*
Average baseline or pretest writing scores	Same score as control group	Same score as experimental group
Average postprogram or posttest writing scores	Significant improvement in scores	Scores remain unchanged from baseline

Conclusion: The experimental literacy program is effective.

In sum, RCTs are quantitative, comparative, controlled experiments in which investigators study two or more programs, interventions, or practices in a series of eligible individuals who receive them in random order. Another name for the randomness with which participants receive programs is **random allocation.** To find out more about the exalted status of the RCT and how to keep it pure, read on!

Randomized Controlled Trial or True Experiment: Variations on a Theme

Two commonly used randomized control designs are

1. Concurrent controls in which two (or more) groups are randomly constituted, and they are studied at the same time (concurrently). Concurrent controls are sometimes called parallel controls.

2. Wait-list controls in which one group receives the program first and others are put on a waiting list; if the program appears to be effective, participants on the waiting list receive it. Participants are randomly assigned to the experimental and wait-list groups.

Concurrent Controls: Do It at the Same Time

Here is how evaluation researchers design randomized controlled trials with concurrent groups.

1. First the researcher appraises the eligibility of the potential participants.
   - Some people are excluded because they did not meet the inclusion criteria or they did meet the exclusion criteria.
   - Some eligible people decide not to participate. They change their mind, become ill, or are too busy.

2. The remaining potential participants are enrolled in the evaluation study.

3. These participants are randomly assigned to the experiment or to an alternative (the control).

4. Participants in the experimental and control groups are pretested, that is, compared at baseline (before program participation) when possible. They are always compared (posttested) after participation.

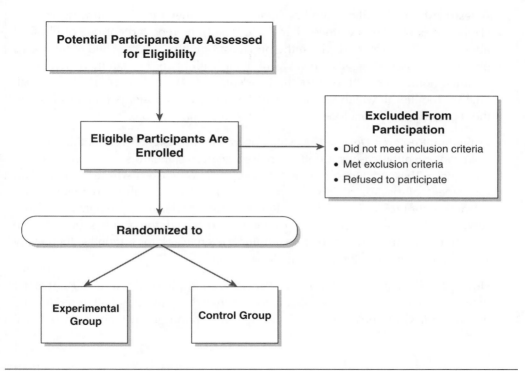

Figure 4.2   Randomized Control Trial With Concurrent Controls

Example 4.1 illustrates three randomized controlled trials with concurrent controls.

Wait-List Control: Do It Sequentially

With a **wait-list control** design, both groups are assessed for eligibility, but one is randomly assigned to be given the program now—the experimental group—and the other—the control—is put on a waiting list. After the experimental group completes the program, both groups are assessed a second time. Then the control receives the program and both groups are assessed again (Figure 4.3).

Example 4.1   Three RCTs With Concurrent Controls

1. **Evaluating Home Visitation by Nurses to Prevent Child Maltreatment in Families Referred to Child Protection Agencies**

   Objective: Recurrence of child maltreatment is a major problem, yet little is known about approaches to reduce this risk in families referred to child protection agencies. Since home visitation by nurses for disadvantaged first-time mothers has proven effective in the prevention of child abuse and neglect, the researchers investigated whether this approach might reduce the recurrence of maltreatment.

   Assessment for Eligibility: Families were eligible if they met the following criteria: (1) the index child was younger than 13 years, (2) the reported episode of physical abuse or neglect occurred within the previous 3 months, (3) the child identified as physically abused or neglected was still living with his or her family or was to be returned home within 30 days of the incident, and (4) families were able to speak English. Families in which the abuse was committed by a foster parent, or in whom the reported incident included sexual abuse, were not eligible.

   Evaluation Research Design: The evaluators randomly assigned 163 families to control or intervention groups. Control families received standard services arranged by the agency. These included routine follow-up by caseworkers whose focus was on assessment of risk of recidivism, provision of education about parenting, and arrangement of referrals to community-based parent education programs and other services. The intervention group of families received the same standard care plus home visitation by a public-health nurse every week for 6 months, then every 2 weeks for 6 months, then monthly for 12 months.

   Findings: At 3-years' follow-up, recurrence of child physical abuse did not differ between groups. However, hospital records showed significantly higher recurrence of either physical abuse or neglect in the intervention group than in the control group.

   SOURCE: MacMillan, Thomas, Jamieson, et al. (2005).

2. **Evaluating Therapy for Depressed Elderly People: Comparing a Holistic Approach to Medication Alone**

   Objective: To find out whether recovering the ability to function socially takes a different course with integrative, holistic treatment than it does with medication alone.

   Assessment for Eligibility: To be included, participants had to be female; aged 65–75; living at home; and disturbed by symptoms such as sadness, lack of drive, and reclusion. Grounds for exclusion were the need for personal assistance in any of four key activities of daily living (bathing, dressing, walking inside the house, and transferring from a chair); significant cognitive impairment with no available proxy; diagnosis of a terminal illness, psychosis, or bipolar disorder; the current use of antidepressants or psychotherapy; and plans to change residence within the next four months.

Evaluation Research Design: A randomized trial in which the randomization was arranged so that half the women would be treated with antidepressants, social therapy, sports therapy and psychotherapy, while the other half—the control group—would be treated only with medicine.

Findings: Both forms of therapy did afford a relatively rapid reduction of depressive symptoms. The integrative treatment not only led to a quicker reduction in depression, however, but was also the only one that led to a significant improvement in the ability to function socially.

SOURCE: Nickel, Nickel, Lahmann, et al. (2005).

3. Evaluating a Health Care Program to Get Adolescents to Exercise

Objective: Many adolescents do not meet national guidelines for participation in regular, moderate, or vigorous physical activity; for limitations on sedentary behaviors; or for dietary intake of fruits and vegetables, fiber, or total dietary fat. This study evaluated a health care–based intervention to improve these behaviors.

Assessment for Eligibility: Adolescents between the ages of 11 and 15 years were recruited through their primary care providers. A total of 45 primary care providers from 6 private clinic sites in San Diego County, California, agreed to participate in the study. A representative group of healthy adolescents seeing primary care providers was sought by contacting parents of adolescents who were already scheduled for a well-child visit and by outreach to families with adolescents. Adolescents were excluded if they had health conditions that would limit their ability to comply with physical activity or diet recommendations.

Evaluation Research Design: After baseline measures but before seeing the provider, participants were randomized to either the Patient-Centered Assessment and Counseling for Exercise + Nutrition (PACE+) program or to a sun protection control condition.

Findings: Compared with adolescents in the sun protection control group, girls and boys in the diet and physical activity program significantly reduced sedentary behaviors. Boys reported more active days per week. No program effects were seen with percentage of calories from fat consumed or minutes of physical activities per week. The percentage of adolescents meeting recommended health guidelines was significantly improved for girls for consumption of saturated fat and for boys' participation in days per week of physical activity. No between-group differences were seen in body mass index.

SOURCE: Patrick, Calfas, Norman, et al. (2006).

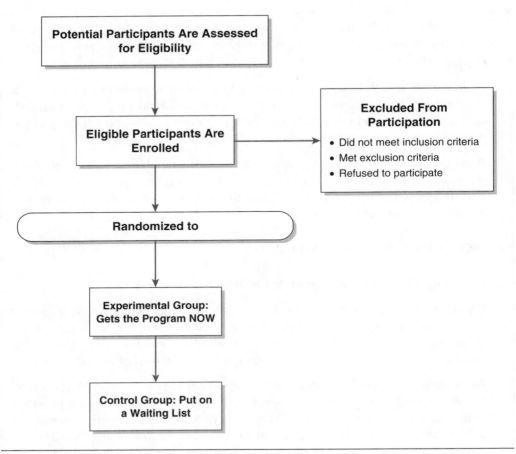

Figure 4.3   Randomized Controlled Trial Using a Wait-List Control

Comparing outcomes with a wait-list control is timed differently from the timing used to compare outcomes for concurrent controls. Here are the steps:

1. Compare Group 1 (experimental group) and Group 2 (control group) at baseline (the pretest). If random assignment has "worked," the two groups should not differ from one another.

Question: What prevents the researcher from finding any differences between groups?

Answer: Random assignment means that chance will make sure that all-important characteristics that might affect program outcomes are evenly distributed between and among groups. No group will contain older or more self-confident or hostile or loving people than any other, for example.

2. Give Group 1—the experimental group—the program.

3. Assess the outcomes for Groups 1 and 2 at the end of the program. If the program is "working," expect to see a difference in outcomes favoring the experimental group.

4. Give the program to Group 2.

5. Assess the outcomes a second time. If the program is working, Group 2 should catch up to Group 1 (Figure 4.4), and both should have improved in their outcomes.

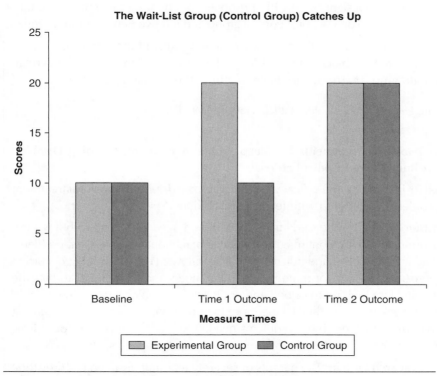

Figure 4.4 Evaluating Effectiveness With a Wait-List Control

Example 4.2 has three illustrative wait-list control evaluation designs.

A wait-list control design (sometimes called "switching replications" or "delayed treatment" designs) has the advantage of allowing the evaluator to compare experimental and control group performance on the same program. It is sometimes difficult to find or implement an alternative control program that is equal to or better than the new program. Further, the new program may be designed to fill a gap in the availability of programs, and no comparable program may

Example 4.2   Three RCTs With Wait-List Controls

---

1. **Evaluating a Methadone Maintenance Treatment in an Australian Prison System**

   Objective: To determine whether methadone maintenance treatment reduced heroin use, syringe sharing, and HIV or hepatitis C incidence among prisoners.

   Assessment for Eligibility: Male inmates were eligible to participate if they (1) were assessed as suitable for methadone maintenance by a detailed interview with medical staff who confirmed they had a heroin problem; (2) were serving prison sentences longer than four months at the time of interview; and (3) were able to provide signed informed consent.

   Evaluation Research Design: All eligible prisoners seeking drug treatment were randomized to methadone or a wait-list control group and followed up after four months.

   Findings: Heroin use was significantly lower among treated than control subjects at follow-up. Treated subjects reported lower levels of drug injection and syringe sharing at follow-up. There was no difference in HIV or hepatitis C incidence.

   SOURCE: Dolan, Shearer, MacDonald, Mattick, Hall, and Wodak (2003).

2. **Evaluating Two Brief Treatments for Sleep Problems in Young Learning Disabled Children: A Randomized Controlled Trial**

   Objective: To investigate the efficacy of a media-based, brief behavioral treatment of sleep problems in children with learning disabilities.

   Assessment for Eligibility: The study included children aged 2–8 years with any form of severe learning disability, confirmed by a general practitioner. Severe sleep problems were defined according to standardized criteria as follows: (1) night waking occurring three or more times a week for more than a few minutes and the child disturbing the parents or going into their room or bed and/or (2) settling problems occurring three or more times a week with the child taking more than one hour to settle and disturbing the parents during this time. These problems needed to have been present for at least three months and not be explicable in terms of a physical problem such as pain.

   Evaluation Research Design: The parents of severely learning disabled children took part in a randomized controlled trial with a wait-list control group. Face-to-face delivered treatment was compared to usual care, and a booklet-delivered treatment was compared to usual care.

   Findings: Both forms of treatment (face-to-face and booklet) were almost equally effective compared with the controls. Two thirds of children who were taking over 30 minutes to settle five or more times per week and waking at night for over 30 minutes four or more times per week improved on average to having such settling or night waking problems for only a few minutes or only once or twice per week. These improvements were maintained after six months.

   SOURCE: Montgomery, Stores, and Wiggs (2004).

---

3. Evaluating a Mental Health Intervention for Schoolchildren Exposed to Violence: A Randomized Controlled Trial

Objective: To evaluate the effectiveness of a collaboratively designed school-based intervention for reducing children's symptoms of posttraumatic stress disorder (PTSD) and depression that has resulted from exposure to violence.

Assessment for Eligibility: Sixth-grade students at two large middle schools in Los Angeles who reported exposure to violence and had clinical levels of symptoms of PTSD using standard measures.

Evaluation Research Design: Students were randomly assigned to a ten-session standardized cognitive-behavioral therapy (the Cognitive-Behavioral Intervention for Trauma in Schools) early intervention group or to a wait-list delayed intervention comparison group conducted by trained school mental health clinicians.

Findings: Compared with the wait-list delayed intervention group (no intervention), after three months of intervention, students who were randomly assigned to the early intervention group had significantly lower scores on symptoms of PTSD, depression, and psychosocial dysfunction. At six months, after both groups had received the intervention, the differences between the two groups were not significantly different for symptoms of PTSD and depression.

SOURCE: Stein, Jaycox, Kataoka, et al. (2003).

---

actually be available at all. Finally, the nature of the design means that everyone receives the program, and, in some circumstances, this may be an incentive for everyone to participate fully.

Wait-list control designs are particularly practical when programs are repeated at regular intervals, as they are in schools with a semester system. Students, for example, can be randomly assigned to Group 1 or Group 2, with Group 1 participating in the first semester. Group 2 can then participate in the second semester. The design is especially efficient in settings that can wait for results. Doing evaluation research is difficult enough, however, without having to conduct the same study twice!

Wait-list control designs are also reliant upon having the experimental group cease its improvement at the time of program completion. If improvement in the experimental group continues until the control group completes the program, then the effects of the program on the control group may appear to be less spectacular than they actually were. To avoid this confusion, some investigators advocate waiting for improvement in the experimental program to level off (a "wash out" period) and to time the implementation of the control program accordingly. However, the amount of time needed for the effect to wash out is usually unknown in advance.

Doing It Randomly

Randomization is considered to be the primary method of ensuring that participating study groups are probably alike at baseline, that is, before they participate in a program. The idea behind randomization is that if chance—which is what random means—dictates the allocation of programs, all important factors will be equally distributed between and among experimental and control groups. No single factor will dominate any of the groups, possibly influencing program outcomes. That is, each group will be as smart, as motivated, as knowledgeable, as self-efficacious, etc. as the other to begin with. As a result, any differences between or among groups that are observed later, after program participation, can reasonably be assigned to the program rather than to the differences that were there at the beginning. In researchers' terms, randomized controlled trials result in unbiased estimates of a program's effects.

How does random assignment work? Table 4.2 describes a commonly used method and some considerations.

Table 4.2   Random Assignment in Evaluation Research

1. An algorithm or set of rules is applied to a table of random numbers, which are usually generated by computer (although tables of random numbers are sometimes used in small studies). For instance, if the research design includes an experimental and a control group and an equal probability of being assigned to each, then the algorithm could specify using the random number 1 for assignment to the experimental group and 2 for assignment to the control group—or vice versa. (Other numbers are ignored.)

2. As each eligible person enters the study, he or she is assigned one of the numbers (1 or 2).

3. The random assignment procedure should be designed so that members of the research team who have contact with the study participants cannot influence the allocation process. For instance, random assignments to experimental or control groups can be placed in advance in a set of sealed envelopes by someone who will not be involved in opening them. Each envelope should be numbered (so that all can be accounted for by the end of the study). As a participant comes through the system, his or her name is recorded, the envelope is opened, and then the assignment (1 or 2) is recorded next to the person's name.

4. It is crucial that the researchers prevent interference with randomization. Who would tamper with assignment? Sometimes, members of the research team may feel pressure to ensure that the most "needy" people receive the experimental program. One method of avoiding this is to ensure that tamper-proof procedures are in place. If the research team uses envelopes, they should ensure the envelopes are opaque (so no one can see through them) and sealed. In large studies, randomization is done off site.

Variations on how to actually conduct the random allocation of participants and programs certainly exist. As described in the checklist below, the research consumer should look for adherence to certain principles regardless of the specifics of the method reported in a particular evaluation study.

Checklist of Basic Principles of Study Group Randomization

✓ Study team members who have contact with participants should not be part of the allocation process. If possible, do randomization off site.

✓ Make sure that assignment, once it is made, is not readily available to evaluation team members.

✓ Use a table of random numbers or a computer-generated list of random numbers. Develop a method for selecting the first number.

Doing It in Clusters

In some situations, it may be preferable for evaluators to randomly assign **clusters** of individuals (such as families or communities) rather than individuals on their own to the experimental or control groups. In fact, randomization by cluster may be the only feasible method of conducting an evaluation in many settings. Evaluations that use clusters to randomize are variously known as field trials, community-based trials, or cluster randomized trials.

Compared with individually randomized trials, cluster randomized trials are more complex to design and require more participants to obtain equivalent statistical power and more complex analysis. This is because observations on individuals in the same cluster (say, children in a classroom) tend to be interrelated by potentially **confounding** (confusing) factors. For example, students in a classroom are about the same age, may have the same ability, and will have similar experiences. Consequently, the actual sample size is less (one classroom) than the total number of individual participants (25 students). The whole is less than the sum of its parts! Example 4.3 contains an example of random assignment by cluster. In this example, the cluster comprises colleges.

Example 4.3   A College-Based Smokeless Tobacco Program for College Athletes

---

Objective: The purpose of this study was to determine the effectiveness of a college-based smokeless tobacco cessation intervention that targeted college athletes. Effectiveness was defined as reported cessation of smokeless tobacco use in the previous 30 days.

Assessment for Eligibility: Current users of smokeless tobacco (use more than once per month and within the past month) were eligible for the study. A total of 16 colleges with an average of 23 smokeless tobacco users in each were selected from lists of all publicly supported California universities and community colleges. Half the participants were selected to be urban and half to be rural; all had varsity football and baseball teams. One-year prevalence of cessation among smokeless tobacco users was determined by self-report of abstinence for the previous 30 days.

Evaluation Research Design: The occurrence of smokeless tobacco use was calculated for each athlete using information from a questionnaire given to them at baseline. Colleges were then matched by pairs so that the level of smoking was approximately the same in each of the individual colleges paired. One college from each pair was randomized to receive the program, while the other college in the pair received no program.

Findings: In both groups, 314 students provided complete data on cessation. Cessation frequencies were 35% in the program colleges and 16% in the control colleges. The program effect increased with level of smokeless tobacco use.

SOURCE: Walsh, Hilton, Masouredis, Gee, Chesney, and Ernster (1999).

Please note the following: Data on the outcome (cessation of smokeless tobacco use in the previous 30 days) were collected from individual students, but randomization was done by college—not by student. Is this OK? The answer depends upon how the evaluation deals with the potential problems caused by randomizing with one unit (colleges) and analyzing data from another (students).

Research consumers must make certain that evaluators provide information as to whether or not baseline characteristics are balanced among clusters and individuals. The evaluators in Example 4.3 sought to achieve balance (that is, equivalence) among universities (the clusters) by including only public universities and junior colleges in California. They aimed for equivalence in smoking levels among students within each university by pairing up universities in terms of their students' smoking levels and randomly assigning pair members to the experimental or control group.

In addition to descriptive information on methods used to ensure equivalence, the research consumer is also entitled to proof that the process worked and that, after it was over, the groups were indeed equivalent. The consumer should look for the information on the statistical methods that the evaluators used and for a statement like the following:

> Of 273 children with asthma in this cohort, 42.1% were female, 41.7% were African-American, and the average age was 8.2 years. The baseline characteristics for Program and non-Program groups were quite similar in terms of demographics, enrollment, and asthma comorbidity. Compared with the Program group, the non-Program group had a significantly higher percentage of females and "other race" children, but significantly less Managed Care Organization enrollment and less allergy comorbidity. (Guo, Jang, Keller, McCracken, Pan, & Cluxton, 2005)

Despite all efforts, chance may dictate that the two groups differ on important variables at baseline. Bad luck! Statistical methods may be used to "correct" for these differences, but it is usually better to anticipate the problem. Methods are available for helping chance along.

Enhancing Chance

Small to moderate sized RCTs can gain power to detect a difference between experimental and control programs (assuming one is actually present) if special randomization procedures are used to balance the numbers of participants in each (**blocked randomization**) and in the distribution of baseline variables that might influence the outcomes (**stratified blocked randomization**).

Why are special procedures necessary if random assignment is supposed to take care of the number of people in each group or the proportion of people in each with certain characteristics? The answer is that, by chance, one group may end up being larger than the other or differing in age, gender, and so on. Good news: This happens less frequently in large studies (with a thousand or more participants). Bad news: The problem of unequal distribution of variables becomes even more complicated when groups or clusters of people (schools or families) rather than individuals are assigned. In this case, the evaluator has little control over the individuals within each cluster, and the number of clusters (over which he or she does have control) is usually relatively small (e.g., 5 schools or 10 clinics). Some form of constraint such as stratification is almost always recommended in RCTs in which allocation is done by cluster.

Two commonly used methods for ensuring equal group sizes and balanced variables are blocked randomization and stratified blocked randomization as described in Table 4.3.

Table 4.3   Enhancing Chance: Blocked and Stratified Blocked Randomization

Blocking or balancing the number of participants in each group

Randomization is done in "blocks of predetermined size." For example, if the block's size is six, randomization proceeds normally within each block until the third person is randomized to one group, after which participants are automatically assigned to the other group until the block of six is completed. This means that in a study of 30 participants, 15 will be assigned to each group, and in a study of 33, the disproportion can be no greater than 18:15.

Stratification or balancing important predictor (independent) variables

Stratification means dividing participants into segments. Participants can be divided into differing age groups (the stratum) or gender or educational level, for example. In a study of a program to improve knowledge of how to prevent infection from HIV/AIDS, having access to reliable transportation to attend education classes is a strong predictor of outcome. It is probably a good idea to have similar numbers of people who have transportation (determined at baseline) assigned to each group. This can be done by dividing the study sample at baseline into participants with or without transportation (stratification by access to transportation), and then carrying out a blocked randomization procedure with each of these two strata.

Example 4.4 illustrates how these techniques have been applied in program evaluations.

Example 4.4   Enhancing Chance by Using Special Randomization Procedures

1. We randomly allocated families to control or intervention groups using a computer program sequence generated by our statistician, *blocked* after every eight allocations. We aimed to do secondary analyses within the intervention group, albeit with modest power, on the basis of the number of nurse visits. Therefore, to increase the numbers in the intervention group, toward the end of recruitment, we randomly allocated families using a 5-to-3 ratio (5 intervention families to 3 controls). Randomization was stratified by the age of the index child—i.e., younger than 4 years and 4 to 12 years—since evidence exists indicating that preschool children are at increased risk for recurrence of physical abuse and neglect. Group assignment was placed in numbered sequential sealed envelopes.

2. Group allocation was based on *block randomization.* A sequential list of case numbers was matched to group allocations in blocks of ten by randomly drawing five cards labeled "control" and five cards labeled "treatment" from an envelope. This procedure was repeated for each block of ten sequential case numbers. The list of case numbers and group allocation was held by a researcher not involved in recruiting or interviewing inmates. The trial nurses responsible for assessing, recruiting, and interviewing inmates had no access to these lists. Once an inmate had been recruited and interviewed, the study nurse contacted the Central Randomization System via a mobile telephone to ascertain the inmate's group allocation.

3. After the baseline period, patients meeting the inclusion criteria were *randomly stratified by center* (block size 12 not known to trial centers) in a 2:1:1 ratio (acupuncture: sham acupuncture: waiting list) using a centralized telephone randomization procedure (random list generated with Program Sample 2.0).

Doing It Blindly

In some randomized studies, the participants and investigators do not know which participants are in the experimental or the control groups: This is the double-blind experiment. When participants do not know, but investigators do, this is called the **blinded** trial. Participants, people responsible for program implementation or assessing program outcomes, and statistical analysts are all candidates for being blinded.

Experts in clinical trials maintain that blinding is as important as randomization in ensuring valid study results. Randomization, they say, eliminates **confounding variables** or **confounders** before the program is implemented—at baseline—but it cannot do away with confounding variables that occur as the study progresses. A **confounding variable** is an extraneous variable in a statistical or research model that affects the dependent variables but has either not been considered or has not been controlled for. For example, age, educational level, and motivation may be confounders in a study that involves adherence to a complicated intervention.

Confounders can lead to a false conclusion that the dependent variables are in a causal relationship with the independent or predictor variables. For instance, suppose research shows that drinking coffee (independent or predictor variable) is associated with heart attacks (the dependent variable). One possibility is that drinking coffee causes heart attack. Another is that having heart attacks causes people to drink more coffee. A third explanation is that some other confounding factor, like smoking, is responsible for heart attacks and is also associated with drinking coffee. We will save a discussion of how to handle baseline confounders for later in this chapter.

Confounding during the course of a study can occur if participants get extra attention or the control group catches on to the experiment. The extra attention or changes in the control group's perceptions may alter the outcomes of a study. One method of getting around and understanding the biases that may result in unblinded studies is to "standardize" all program activities and to monitor the extent to which the program has been implemented as planned.

Wary research consumers should pay special attention to the biases that may have occurred in randomized controlled studies without blinding. Expect the evaluator to report on the program's implementation and the extent to which any deviations from standard program procedures may have affected the outcomes.

Example 4.5 contains examples of blinding used in RCTs.

Example 4.5   Blinding in RCTs

Example 1. The Researcher Is Blinded

Seventy-five opaque envelopes were produced for the initial randomization and lodged with an independent staff member. Each contained a slip of paper with the word "conventional," "booklet," or "control" (25 each). The randomization was performed by this staff member selecting an envelope for each participant immediately after the initial assessment meeting with parents. For the re-randomization of the control crossover group this process was repeated with a second batch of 26 envelopes, half each with the word "conventional" or "booklet." The researcher conducting the study was therefore blind to the nature of the treatment allocated until after the posttreatment assessment. Following that point, both participant and researcher were aware of the treatment group to which they had been randomized.

Example 2. Patients and Evaluators Are Blinded

This study was a randomized, multicenter trial comparing acupuncture, sham acupuncture, and a no-acupuncture waiting list condition. The additional no-acupuncture waiting list control was included because sham acupuncture cannot be substituted for a physiologically inert placebo. Patients in the acupuncture groups were blinded to which treatment they received. Analysis of headache diaries was performed by two blinded evaluators. The study duration per patient was 28 weeks: 4 weeks before randomization, the baseline; 8 weeks of treatment; and 16 weeks of follow-up. Patients allocated to the waiting list received true acupuncture after 12 weeks and were also followed up for 24 weeks after randomization (to investigate whether changes were similar to those in patients receiving immediate acupuncture).

CAUTION: Despite their potential for absolute scientific virtue, you cannot assume that evaluations that are labeled RCTs meet high standards or that they automatically guarantee access to evidence that matters. At the minimum, valid conclusions also depend on careful study planning, adherence to a study protocol, a representative sample, adequate sample size, accurate and timely data collection, and appropriate statistical analysis and interpretation of data. A high quality research design is just one component of the mix. (We will discuss each of the others in later chapters.)

RCTs are generally expensive, time-consuming, and tend to address very specific research questions. They should probably be saved for relatively mature programs and practices, that is, those that previous research suggests are likely to be effective. Previous research includes large pilot studies and other randomized trials. Except for drug trials and other types of medical research, research consumers outside the health field can expect to find only a few relevant RCTs in their fields and even fewer that meet all criteria for scientific validity (double blinded, for example).

Despite an important advantage over other types of evaluation designs—specifically, their ability to establish that Program A is likely to have *caused* Outcome A—their requirement for "control" sometimes gives them a bad name. Some researchers and practitioners express concern over the fairness of excluding certain groups and individuals from participation or from receiving the experimental program. Others question the idea of regarding humans as fit subjects for an "experiment" and of obtaining good information from quantitative or statistically oriented research. To some extent, these are personal or ethical concerns and are not inherent weaknesses of the RCT design itself. Nevertheless, it is certainly reasonable to expect researchers to explain their choice of design in ethical as well as methodological terms. In Example 4.6, the evaluators of a program to provide respite care for homeless patients, a cohort study, defend themselves in this way:

Example 4.6   Statement by the Evaluators of a Study of Respite Care for Homeless
                   Patients Regarding the Ethics of Their RCT

Finally, a randomized control trial is needed. Although the available demographic data, clinical variables, and baseline utilization data were similar in our respite care and usual care study groups, it is possible that unmeasured variables, including differential rates of substance use or psychiatric illness, may have confounded our results. *Some might argue that a randomized trial would be unethical, given the obvious humanitarian virtues of respite care. But a randomized trial would be no less ethical than the current status quo in the United States, where respite care is available only to some, not all, homeless people* [italics added]. Now is the time for such a trial, given the results of the present study, the financial distress of many U.S. hospitals, and the unmet needs of our country's homeless people.

SOURCE: Buchanan, Doblin, Sai, and Garcia (2006).

The evaluators understand that some people believe that if you have an intervention or program that is perceived to be humanitarian (such as respite care), you should not conduct an experiment in which some people are necessarily denied services. The investigators counter by arguing that some homeless people do not have access to respite care anyway. The evaluators also point out that evaluation research that takes the form of a randomized trial can help clarify the results of their study by providing information on unmeasured factors like differential rates of substance use or psychiatric illness.

Quasi-Experimental Evaluation Designs

Quasi-experimental evaluations are characterized by nonrandomized assignment to groups or by conducting a series of measures over time on one or more groups.

Nonrandomized Controlled Trials: Concurrent Controls

Nonrandomized controlled trials are a type of quasi-experimental design. In fact, the term quasi experiment is often synonymous with the term nonrandomized control trial and defined as a design in which one group receives the program and one does not, the assignment of participants to groups is not controlled by the researcher, and assignment is not random.

Quasi-experimental, nonrandomized controlled trials rely on participants who (1) volunteer to join the study, (2) are geographically close to the study site, or (3) conveniently turn up (at a clinic or school) while the study is being conducted. As a result, people or groups in a quasi experiment may self-select, and the evaluation findings may not be unbiased because they are dependent upon participant choice rather than chance.

Quasi-experimental evaluation researchers use a variety of methods to ensure that the participating groups are as similar to one another as possible (equivalent) at baseline or before "treatment." Among the strategies used to ensure equivalence is one called **matching**. Previously, we saw the matching approach applied to the randomized trial of a smokeless tobacco program for college athletes (Example 4.3).

Matching requires selecting pairs of participants or clusters of individuals who are comparable to one another on important confounding variables. For example, suppose a researcher was interested in comparing the acuity of vision among smokers and nonsmokers. One method of helping to ensure that the two groups are balanced on important confounders requires that, for every smoker, there is a non-smoker of the same age, sex, and medical history.

Matching can effectively prevent confounding by important factors like age and sex for individuals. The strategy's implementation can be relatively expensive, however, because finding a match for each study participant is sometimes difficult and often time consuming.

Other techniques for allocating participants to study groups in quasi experiments include assigning each potential participant a number and using an alternating sequence in which every other individual (1, 3, 5, etc.) is assigned to the experimental group and the alternate participants (2, 4, 6, etc.) are assigned to the control. Another option is to assign groups in order of appearance so, for example, patients who attend the clinic on Monday, Wednesday, and Friday are in the experimental group, and those attending on Tuesday, Thursday, and Saturday are assigned to the control. To prevent certain types of patients (e.g., those who can only come on a certain day) from automatically being in one or other of the groups, the procedure for assignment can be reversed after some number of days or weeks.

Illustrations of nonrandomized, quasi-experimental designs with concurrent groups are given in Example 4.7.

Well-done quasi-experimental designs have many desirable features. They can provide information about programs when it is inappropriate or too late to randomize participants. (In reality, it is not uncommon to find evaluators who are called in late in the game rather than during the program planning process.) Another desirable characteristic of quasi experiments is that, when compared to RCTs, their settings and participants may more accurately reflect the messiness of the real

Example 4.7   Quasi-Experimental Design: Concurrent Groups

---

1. Reducing Injuries Among Teen Agricultural Workers

Objective: To test an agricultural safety curriculum [Agricultural Disability Awareness and Risk Education (AgDARE)] for use in high school agriculture classes.

Assessment for Eligibility: A total of 21 schools (1,138 agriculture students) from Kentucky, Iowa, and Mississippi participated in the program.

Evaluation Research Design: Schools in each state were grouped geographically to improve homogeneity in agricultural commodities and production techniques and then assigned randomly to either one of two intervention groups (A or B) or the control group. Fourteen schools were assigned to the intervention arms, and seven schools were assigned to the control group.

Findings: Students who participated in AgDARE scored significantly higher in farm safety attitude and intent to change work behavior than the control group. School and public health nurses, working together with agriculture teachers, may make an effective team in reducing injuries among teen agricultural workers.

SOURCE: Reed and Kidd (2004).

2. Contraceptive Practices Among Rural Vietnamese Men

Objective: To test a social-cognitive intervention to influence contraceptive practices among men living in rural communes in Vietnam.

Assessment for Eligibility: There were 651 married men from 12 villages in two rural communes (An Hong and Quoc Tuan) in the An Hai district of Hai Phong province in Vietnam. Interviewers visited each household in the selected villages and sought all married men aged 19–45 years who had lived with their wives in the same house during the three months prior to the study. The inclusion criteria were as follows: the wife was currently not pregnant, the couple did not plan to have a child in the next six months, they currently did not use condoms consistently for family planning, and the wives currently did not use the pill consistently for family planning.

Evaluation Research Design: Villages were chosen as the primary unit for intervention. From each of the two communes, three villages were chosen for intervention and three as controls. The intervention villages were separated from control villages by a distance of 2–3 km. Participants in both study groups were assessed, using interviewer-based questionnaires, prior to (baseline) and following the intervention (posttest).

Findings: There were 651 eligible married men in the 12 villages chosen. A significant positive movement in men's stage of readiness for IUD use by their wife occurred in the intervention group. There were no significant changes in the control group. Compared to the control group, the intervention group showed higher pros, lower cons, and higher self-efficacy for IUD use by their wife as a contraceptive method. Interventions based on social-cognitive theory can increase men's involvement in IUD use in rural Vietnam and should assist in reducing future rates of unwanted pregnancy.

SOURCE: Ha, Jayasuriya, and Owen (2005).

world—that is, the research consumer's world. The RCT requires strict control over the environment, and to get that control, the evaluator has to be extremely stringent with respect to the research question being posed and who is included and excluded from study participation. Messiness is unwelcome. As a result, RCT findings may apply to a relatively small population in constrained settings.

Nonrandomized designs are sometimes chosen over randomized ones in the mistaken belief that they are more ethical than randomized trials. The idea behind the ethical challenge is that, if the evaluation researcher suspects that Program A is better than Program B, then how (in ethical terms) can he or she allocate Program B to innocent participants? In fact, evaluations are only ethical if they are designed well enough to have a strong likelihood of producing an accurate answer about program effectiveness. There are many cases in which programs that were presumed effective turned out not to be so after all. (See the NIH Conference on Youth Violence discussed in Chapter 1 for examples of favorite programs that do not hold up to rigorous evaluation.) We have to assume that the evaluator has no evidence that Program A is better than B to start with because, if he or she had proof, then the evaluation would be unnecessary.

Some researchers and practitioners also think that quasi experiments are less costly than RCTs, but this has never been proven. Poor studies, whether RCTs *or* quasi experiments, are costly when they result in misleading or incorrect information, which may delay or even prevent participants from getting needed services or education.

Good quasi experiments are difficult to plan and implement and require the highest level of research expertise. Many borrow techniques from RCTs including blinding. Many others use sophisticated statistical methods to enhance confidence in the findings.

The most serious potential flaw in quasi-experimental designs without random assignment is that the groups in the experimental and control programs may differ from one another at baseline so that the program cannot have a fair trial. Therefore, in evaluating quasi experiments, the consumer must focus on the evidence provided by researchers that either no difference in groups existed to begin with or the appropriate statistical methods were used to control for the differences.

Time-Series Designs

Time-series designs are **longitudinal** studies that enable the researcher to monitor change from one time to the next. They are sometimes called repeated measures analyses. Debate exists over whether time-series designs are research or analytic designs.

Self-Controlled or Pretest-Posttest Designs

In a simple self-controlled evaluation design (also called pretest-posttest only design), each participant is measured on some important program variable and serves as his or her own control. Participants are usually measured twice (at baseline and after program participation), but they may be measured multiple times afterward as well. For example, suppose parishioners participate in a program to improve community service activities. To evaluate the program, the parishioners might be surveyed three times: before starting a program to find out about their attitudes toward community service, immediately after their participation in a one-year program to find out the extent to which their attitude changed, and at the end of two years to ascertain if the change is sustained. Because a control group is not part of the design, participants' innate characteristics such as age, gender, and motivation are eliminated as confounding variables.

However, the absence of confounding variables is not a sufficient basis to use pretest-posttest time-series designs. Among their disadvantages are that participants may become excited about taking part in an experiment and this excitement helps motivate their good performance. Further, between the pretest and the posttest, they may mature physically, emotionally, and intellectually and become more interested in the program. Finally, self-controlled evaluations may be affected by historical events, including changes in program administration and policy.

Because of their limitations, self-controlled time-series designs are not considered experimental designs (some researchers call them pre-experimental rather than quasi-experimental), and they are only appropriate for pilot studies or preliminary feasibility studies. Studies of this type aim to determine if the program can be implemented in the desired setting and if it is at all reasonable to hypothesize that it achieves its objectives. Example 4.8 shows a pretest-posttest time-series design used for this purpose.

Example 4.8   Pretest-Posttest Time-Series Design: A Pilot Test of a Cognitive-Behavioral Program for Women With Multiple Sclerosis

---

Objective: The purpose of this quasi-experimental study was to evaluate the effectiveness of a cognitive-behavioral intervention for women with multiple sclerosis (MS).

Assessment for Eligibility: Thirty-seven adult women with MS participated in a group-based program titled "Beyond MS," which was led by master's-prepared psychiatric nurses.

> **Evaluation Research Design:** Perceived health competence, coping behaviors, psychological well-being, quality of life, and fatigue were measured at four time periods: 5 weeks before the beginning of the intervention, immediately before the program, at the end of the 5-week program, and at a 6-month follow-up.
>
> **Findings:** There were significant improvements in the participants' perceived health competence, indices of adaptive and maladaptive coping, and most measures of psychological well-being from pretest to posttest. The positive changes brought about by this relatively brief program were maintained during the 6-month follow-up period.

SOURCE: Sinclair and Scroggie (2005).

Time-series designs of this type are used primarily because they are convenient: The evaluation team can find one group of volunteers, but a control group is not available or is beyond the team's financial means to assess, so researchers use what they can in the study.

Historical Controls

Some researchers make up for the lack of a readily available control group by using a **historical control**. With traditional historical controls, investigators compare outcomes among participants who receive a new program with outcomes among a previous group of participants who received the standard program. An illustration of the use of historical controls is given in Example 4.9.

Time-series designs can also be improved by adding more measurements for a single group of participants before and after the program (in a single time-series design) and adding a control (in a multiple time-series design).

Interrupted or Single Time-Series Designs

The **interrupted or single time-series** design without a control group (hence, the "single") involves repeated measurement of a variable (e.g., reported crime) over time, encompassing periods both before and after implementation of a program. The goal is to evaluate whether the program has "interrupted" or changed a pattern established before the program's implementation. For instance, an evaluation using an interrupted times-series design may collect quarterly arrest rates for drug-related offenses in a given community for two years before and two years following the implementation of a drug enforcement task force. The evaluation's analysis would

Example 4.9   Historical Controls: Use and Impact of an eHealth System by
                    Low-Income Women With Breast Cancer

Objective: To examine the feasibility of reaching underserved women with breast cancer and determine how they use the system and what impact it had on them.

Assessment for Eligibility: Participants included women recently diagnosed with breast cancer whose income was at or below 250% of the poverty level and were living in rural Wisconsin (n = 144; all Caucasian) or Detroit (n = 85; all African American).

Evaluation Research Design: Historical Control: A comparison group of patients (n = 51) with similar demographics was drawn from a separate recently completed randomized clinical trial.

Findings: When all low-income women from this study are combined and compared with a low-income control group from another study, the Comprehensive Health Enhancement Support System [CHESS]) group was superior to that control group in 4 of 8 outcome variables at both statistically and practically significant levels (social support, negative emotions, participation in health care, and information competence). We conclude that an eHealth system like CHESS will have a positive impact on low-income women with breast cancer.

SOURCE: Gustafson, McTavish, Stengle, et al. (2005).

focus on changes in patterns before and after the introduction of the program. In a multiple time-series design, multiple interrupted observations are collected before and after a program is launched. The "multiple" means that the observations are collected in two or more groups.

Time-series designs are complex evaluation designs requiring many observations of outcomes and, in the case of multiple time-series designs, the participation of many individuals and even communities. Their complex analysis has led some researchers to assert that they are really data analytic strategies.

Observational Designs

In **observational evaluation designs,** researchers conduct studies with existing groups of people or use existing databases. They do not intervene, which is to say, they do not introduce programs. Among the observational designs that are used in evaluation research are cohorts, case controls, and cross-sectional surveys.

Cohort Designs

A **cohort** is a group of people who have something in common and who remain part of a study group over an extended period of time. In public health research, cohort studies are used to describe and predict the risk factors for a disease and the disease's cause, incidence, natural history, and prognosis. They tend to be extremely large studies.

Cohort studies may be **prospective** or **retrospective**. With a prospective design, the direction of inquiry is forward in time while, with a retrospective design, the direction is backward in time.

Prospective Cohort Design

Example 4.10 contains an abstract of The National Treatment Improvement Evaluation Survey, a longitudinal study of a national sample of substance abuse treatment programs that had received federal treatment improvement demonstration grants in 1990–1991 (the cohort). Treatment programs and their clients across 16 states completed highly structured lay-administered interviews between July 1993 and November 1995. Administrative interviews elicited information from senior program administrators that focused on program finances and staff configuration, including the primary measure of interest and whether the program had staff designated as case managers.

Example 4.10   Prospective Cohort Design: Case Managers as Facilitators of Medical and Psychosocial Service Delivery in Addiction Treatment Programs

---

Objective: To examine whether having designated case management staff facilitates delivery of comprehensive medical and psychosocial services in substance abuse treatment programs.

Assessment for Eligibility: Clients from long-term residential, outpatient, and methadone treatment modalities.

Research Design: A prospective cohort study of 2,829 clients admitted to selected substance abuse treatment programs.

Findings: Availability of designated case managers increased client-level receipt of only two of nine services, and exerted no effect on service comprehensiveness compared to programs that did not have designated case managers. These findings do not support the common practice of designating case management staff as a means to facilitate comprehensive services delivery in addiction treatment programs.

SOURCE: Friedmann, Hendrickson, Gerstein, and Zhang (2004).

High-quality prospective or longitudinal studies are expensive to conduct, especially if the researcher is concerned with outcomes that are relatively rare or hard to predict. Studying rare and unpredictable outcomes requires large samples and numerous measures. Also, researchers who do prospective cohort studies have to be on guard against loss of subjects over time or **attrition** or **loss to follow-up**. For instance, longitudinal studies of children are often beset by attrition because, over time, they lose interest, move far away, change their names, or are otherwise unavailable. If a large number of people drop out of a study, the sample that remains may be very different from the one that was originally enrolled. The remaining sample may be more motivated or less mobile than those who left, for example, and these factors may be related in unpredictable ways to any observed outcomes.

When reviewing prospective cohort studies, make sure that the researchers address how they handled loss to follow-up or attrition. Ask these questions: How large a problem was attrition? Were losses to follow-up handled in the analysis? Were the study's findings affected by the losses? If answers to any of these questions are not forthcoming, then confidence in the quality of the evaluation must be diminished.

Because of the difficulties and expense of implementing prospective cohort designs, many cohort designs reported in the literature tend to be retrospective. Retrospective cohort designs use existing databases to identify cohorts; they may do an analysis of the data that already exist in the database or collect new data. A sample retrospective cohort design that identifies the cohort and collects new data is illustrated in Example 4.11.

Example 4.11   Retrospective Cohort Design: Tall Stature in Adolescence and Depression in Later Life

---

Objective: To examine the long-term psychosocial outcomes for women assessed or treated during adolescence for tall stature.

Assessment for Eligibility: Women assessed or treated for tall stature identified from the records of Australian pediatricians were eligible to participate.

Research Design: Retrospective cohort study in which women treated for tall stature were traced using electoral rolls and telephone listings. Once found, the women were contacted by mail and invited to complete a postal questionnaire and computer assisted telephone interview. Psychosocial outcomes were measured using the depression, mania, and eating disorders modules of the Composite International Diagnostic Interview (CIDI), the SF-36, and an index of social support.

> **Findings:** There was no significant difference between treated and untreated women in the prevalence of 12 month or lifetime major depression, eating disorders, or scores on the SF-36 mental health summary scale or the index of social support. However, compared with the findings of population-based studies, the prevalence of major depression in both treated and untreated tall girls was high.

SOURCE: Bruinsma, Venn, Patton, et al. (2006).

Retrospective cohort designs have the same strengths as prospective designs. Like them, they can establish that a predictor variable (such as being in a treatment program) precedes an outcome (such as depression). Also, because data are collected before the outcomes being assessed are known with certainty, the measurement of variables that might predict the outcome (such as being in a program) cannot be biased by prior knowledge of which people are likely to develop a problem (such as depression).

Case-Control Designs

Case-control designs are generally retrospective. They are used to explain why a phenomenon currently exists by comparing the histories of two different groups, one of which is involved in the phenomenon. For example, a case-control design might be used to help understand the social, demographic, and attitudinal variables that distinguish people who, at the present time, have been identified with frequent headaches from those who do not currently have frequent headaches. The researchers in a case-control study like this want to know which factors (e.g., dietary habits, social arrangements, education, income, or quality of life) distinguish one group from the other.

The cases in case-control designs are individuals who have been chosen on the basis of some characteristic or outcome (such as frequent headaches). The controls are individuals without the characteristic or outcome. The histories of cases and controls are analyzed and compared in an attempt to uncover one or more characteristics that are present in the cases and not in the controls.

How can researchers avoid having one group decidedly different from the other, say healthier or smarter? Some methods include randomly selecting the controls, using several controls, and carefully matching controls and cases on important variables.

Example 4.12 uses a sophisticated sampling strategy to compare the role of alcohol use in boating deaths.

Example 4.12   Alcohol Use and Risk of Dying While Boating

Objective: To determine the association of alcohol use with passengers' and operators' estimated relative risk of dying while boating.

Assessment for Eligibility: A study of recreational boating deaths among persons aged 18 years or older from 1990–1998 in Maryland and North Carolina (n = 221) provided the cases, which were compared with control interviews obtained from a multistage probability sample of boaters in each state from 1997–1999 (n = 3,943). Persons aged 18 years or older from 1990–1998 in Maryland and North Carolina (n = 221) were compared with control interviews obtained from a multistage probability sample of boaters in each state from 1997–1999 (n = 3,943).

Research Design: Case-control study

Outcome Measures: Estimated relative risk of fatality associated with different levels of blood alcohol concentration (BAC) among boaters: Each control boat was approached and the operator was asked to participate in the study. The operator was interviewed and asked to provide details on the boat and the boat's activities in the past hour. Next, the operator and up to two randomly selected passengers (18 years) were asked to complete a short self-administered questionnaire that included questions on general health and demographic characteristics. Last, the operator and the selected passengers were asked to provide a breath sample for alcohol testing by a handheld breathalyzer (CMI Intoxilyzer D-400R; CMI Inc., Owensboro, Kentucky). The interviewer also recorded information about the boat, number of passengers, evidence of alcohol use, apparent sobriety of the operator, and refusals.

Findings: Drinking increases the relative risk of dying while boating, which becomes apparent at low levels of blood alcohol concentration and increases as blood alcohol concentration increases. Prevention efforts targeted only at those operating a boat are ignoring many boaters at high risk. Countermeasures that reduce drinking by all boat occupants are therefore more likely to effectively reduce boating fatalities.

SOURCE: Smith, Keyl, Hadley, et al. (2001).

In this study, a complex random sampling scheme was employed to minimize bias among control subjects and maximize their comparability with cases (e.g., deaths took place in the same location).

Epidemiologists and other health workers often use case-control designs to provide insight into the causes and consequences of disease and other health problems. Reviewers of these studies should be on the lookout for certain methodological problems, however. First, cases and controls are often chosen from two separate populations. Because of this, systematic differences (such as motivation and cultural beliefs) may exist between or among the groups that are difficult to anticipate, measure, or control, and these differences may influence the study's results.

Another potential problem with case-control designs is that the data often come from people's recall of events, such as asking women to discuss the history of their physical activity or asking boaters about their drinking habits. Memory is often unreliable, so the results of a study that depends upon memory may result in misleading information.

Cross-Sectional Designs

Cross-sectional designs result in a portrait of one or many groups at one period of time. They are sometimes called descriptive or pre-experimental designs. Following are three illustrative uses of cross-sectional designs (Example 4.13).

Example 4.13   Cross-Sectional Designs

1. Refugees are interviewed to find out their immediate fears and aspirations.
2. A survey is mailed to consumers to identify perceptions of the quality of the goods and services received when ordering by catalogue.
3. A community participates in a Web survey to find out its needs for health services.

The major limitation of cross-sectional studies is that, on their own and without follow up, they provide no information on causality: They only provide information on events at a single, fixed point in time. For example, suppose a researcher finds that girls have less knowledge of current events than boys. The researcher cannot conclude that being female somehow causes less knowledge of current events. The researcher can only be sure that, in *this* survey undertaken at *this* particular time, girls had less knowledge than boys did.

To illustrate this point further, suppose you are doing a literature review on community-based exercise programs. (See Example 4.14.) You are specifically interested in learning about the relationship between age and exercise. Does exercise decrease with age? In your search of the literature, you find this report.

Example 4.14   A Report of a Cross-Sectional Survey of Exercise Habits

In March of this year, Researcher A surveyed a sample of 1,500 people between the ages of 30 and 70 to find out about their exercise habits. One of the questions he asked participants was, "How much do you exercise on a typical day?" Researcher A divided his sample into two groups: People 45 years of age and younger and people 46 years and older. Researcher A's data analysis revealed that the amount of daily exercise reported by the two groups differed with the younger group reporting 15 minutes more exercise on a typical day.

Example 4.15   A Cross-Sectional Survey of Two Groups of Parents With Tourette's
                    Disorder

Researchers examined the mental health and caregiver burden in parents of children
with Tourette's Disorder compared with parents of children with asthma. They surveyed
parents at Tourette's Disorder and pediatric asthma hospital outpatient clinics. The survey consisted of measures of parent mental health (General Health Questionnaire
[GHQ]-28) and caregiver burden (Child and Adolescent Impact Assessment) scores. Of
the parents of children with Tourette's, 76.9% had mental health distress on the GHQ-
28 compared with 34.6% of the parents of children with asthma; this effect remained
significant after taking into account demographic variables (like age and education).
Parents of children with Tourette's also experienced greater caregiver burden.

Based on this summary, does amount of exercise decline with age?
The answer is that you cannot get the answer from Researcher A's
report. The decline seen in a cross-sectional study like this one can
actually represent a decline in exercise with increasing age, or it may
reflect the oddities of this particular sample. The younger people in
this study may be especially sports minded, while the older people
may be particularly adverse to exercise. As a reviewer, you need to
figure out which of the two explanations is better. One way you can
do this is to search the literature to find out which conclusions are
supported by other studies. Does the literature generally sustain the
idea that amount of exercise always declines with age? After all, in
some communities the amount of exercise done by older people may
actually increase because, with retirement or part-time work, older
adults may have more time to exercise than do younger people.

Suppose you are interested in finding out how parents of children
with Tourette's Disorder and parents of children with asthma compare
in their mental health and burden of care giving. Can you get the information you need from the cross-sectional survey in Example 4.15?

It is difficult to tell from the example if the differences in mental
health found by the researchers are due to the nature of Tourette
parents' care-giving burden or to something else entirely. It is possible, for example, that the particular group of Tourette parents might
have significant mental health problems regardless of their children's
illness. The reviewer needs more information about the two study
samples and how they were selected in order to make a decision as to
the validity of the researchers' findings.

Cross-sectional surveys are also used to describe a study's sample
each time it is measured. Example 4.16 shows how two cross-sectional
studies can be used to depict pretest (baseline) and postprogram data.

Example 4.16   Cross-Sectional Study Results: Baseline and Postprogram Data

Table 1: Clinical and Demographic Characteristics of Participants at Baseline		
	Mean (SD)	
Characteristics	Earty Intervention (n = 61)	Delayed Intervention (n = 65)
Age, y	11.0 (0.3)	10.9 (0.4)
Female, No. (%)	33 (54)	38 (58)
Child report		
Symptoms of PTSD, score*	24.5 (6.8)	23.5 (7.2)
Symptoms of depression, score†	17.6 (10.8)	16.7 (7.3)
No. of violent events experienced‡	2.9 (2.1)	2.7 (2.2)
No. of violent events witnessed‡	5.8 (2.2)	6.1 (2.2)
Any violence involving a knife or gun, No. (%)‡	44 (72)	52 (80)
Parent report§		
Psychosocial dysfunction	19.1 (9.4)	16.2 (8.1)
Teacher report		
Acting out problems	11.3 (7.0)	10.6 (5.5)
Shyness/anxiousness problems	10.2 (4.1)	11.0 (5.1)
Learning problems	13.8 (7.3)	12.7 (7.0)
Parent demographics		
Education, y	8.3 (3.6)	8.6 (4.2)
Married, No. (%)	48 (79)	45 (70)
Employed, No. (%)	25 (41)	31 (48)
Household income < $15,000, No. (%)	22 (36)	28 (44)

Abbreviation: PTSD, posttraumatic stress disorder.
*Child PTSD Symptom Scale (range, 0.51).
†Child Depression inventory (range, 05.2).
‡Life Event Scale.
§Pediatric Symptom Checklist (range, 0.70).
Teacher Child Rating Scale (range for subscales, 6.30).

Comment: The enrolled sample of 126 students had substantial levels of exposure to violence and symptoms of PTSD. The mean number of violent events in the previous year experienced by the students was 2.8, and the mean number witnessed by the students was 5.9. The mean percentage of students who reported experiencing or witnessing violence involving a knife or gun was 76%. The mean CPSS score was 24.0, indicating moderate to severe levels of symptoms of PTSD. The mean CDI score was 17.2. The early intervention and delayed intervention groups did not show significant differences in baseline values.

SOURCE: Stein BD, Jaycox LH, Kataoka SH, et al. A mental health intervention for schoolchildren exposed to violence: A randomized controlled trial. *JAMA*. Aug 6 2003;290(5):603–611. Reprinted by permission of the American Medical Association.

(Continued)

Example 4.16 (Continued)

Post-Stroke Informal Care Characteristics	Stroke Unit (n=148)[*]	Stroke Team (n=147)	Domiciliary Care (n=140)
Received care, n (%)	94 (63.5)	98 (66.7)	100 (71.4)
Time care was received, week	26.93 (21.13)	21.44 (20.61)	19.48 (20.13)
From co-residents, hours			
Personal care per week	2.14 (3.71)	1.03 (2.18)	2.38 (4.01)
Transport per week	0.87 (2.35)	0.70 (1.51)	0.67 (1.12)
Meal preparation per week	1.74 (3.58)	0.66 (2.14)	1.11 (2.65)
Housework per week	1.15 (2.49)	0.75 (1.68)	1.12 (2.22)
DIY per week	0.11 (0.50)	0.09 (0.33)	0.17 (0.62)
Gardening per week	0.29 (0.81)	0.17 (0.58)	0.39 (0.94)
Shopping per week	0.62 (1.03)	0.42 (0.85)	0.56 (0.88)
Outings per week	2.68 (15.82)	1.33 (8.99)	0.24 (0.79)
Socializing per week	32.28 (39.67)	28.56 (39.69)	39.74 (41.95)
Total per average week	41.88 (50.53)	33.71 (44.35)	46.38 (48.15)
Total over 12 months	1312.19 (2177)	718.11 (6778)	899.18 (1760)
From nonresidents, hours			
Personal care per week	0.03 (0.22)	0.12 (0.67)	0.26 (1.50)
Transport per week	0.27 (0.62)	0.33 (0.74)	0.34 (0.93)
Meal preparation per week	0.07 (0.39)	0.16 (0.79)	0.31 (1.58)
Housework per week	0.22 (0.80)	0.24 (0.72)	0.29 (1.35)
DIY per week	0.18 (0.45)	0.12 (0.38)	0.12 (0.41)
Gardening per week	0.07 (0.35)	0.08 (0.38)	0.09 (0.59)
Shopping per week	0.25 (0.62)	0.42 (0.82)	0.88 (8.45)
Outings per week	0.20 (0.56)	0.49 (2.91)	0.16 (0.67)
Socializing per week	2.83 (8.30)	3.07 (8.96)	2.35 (8.36)
Total per average week	4.13 (10.45)	5.03 (11.54)	4.79 (16.51)
Total over 12 months	114.51 (409)	127.44 (348)	79.70 (283)
Total over 12-month assessment period from co-residents and nonresidents	1435.63 (2278)	845.55 (1549)	978.88 (1749)

Values are mean ± SD.

[*]n = 147 for some components of the data for this group because 1 patient had incomplete data. DIY indicates do it yourself (home maintenance/improvement).

Comment: There were no significant between-group differences in proportions of patients requiring hospital admission after the initial episode, patients admitted to institutional care, or patients receiving informal support. Although the stroke team group received less informal care in total per week from co-residents than other groups, the difference was not significant. However, they received significantly less help with personal care compared with the stroke unit (P=0.016) and domiciliary care (P=0.003) groups and less help with meal preparation than the stroke unit group (P=0.004). Stroke unit patients received more informal care (mean, 1436 hours) than stroke team patients (846 hours; P=0.025).

SOURCE: Patel, Knapp, Perez, Evans, and Kalra (2004).

_____ Observational Designs and Controlled Trials

Observational data can be useful adjuncts to randomized, controlled trials and quasi experiments. They can assist the evaluator in determining whether effectiveness under controlled conditions translates into effective treatment in routine settings. Also, some problems simply do not lend themselves to a randomized, controlled trial. For instance, when they studied the effects of cigarette smoking on health, it was impossible for evaluators to randomly assign some people to smoke while assigning others to abstain. The only possible design was an observational one, albeit one that involved decades of observing hundreds of thousands of people all over the world.

The case for observational studies over RCTs is suggested (somewhat humorously) in the following study reported in the _British Medical Journal_ (Smith & Pell, 2003):

The investigators in the study aimed to determine whether "parachutes are effective in preventing major trauma related to gravitational challenge." To find out, they reviewed all the randomized controlled trials they could find in Medline, Web of Science, EMBASE, and the Cochrane Library databases. They also reviewed appropriate Internet sites and citation lists. To be included, a study had to discuss the effects of using a parachute during free fall. The effects were defined as death or major trauma, defined as an injury severity score > 15.

Despite their diligence and scientific approach to the review, the investigators were not able to find any randomized controlled trials of the effectiveness of parachute intervention. They concluded that as with many interventions intended to prevent ill health, the effectiveness of parachutes has not been subjected to rigorous evaluation by using randomized controlled trials. The investigators point out that this is a serious problem for hard-line advocates of evidence based medicine who are adamantly opposed to the adoption of interventions evaluated by using only observational data. To resolve the problem, the investigators recommend that the most radical protagonists of evidence based medicine organize and participate in a double blind, randomized, placebo controlled, crossover trial of the parachute. They further conclude that individuals who insist that all interventions need to be validated by a randomized controlled trial need to come down to earth with a bump.

The Bottom Line: Internal and External Validity

When consumers search for evidence that matters, they are looking for evaluations that provide scientific proof that Program A causes Outcome A. They are also concerned that, if Program A causes Outcome A, two other factors are true: (1) the population and settings of the program evaluation are relevant to those in which the tested program will be used, and (2) their research clients can afford to implement the program. For example, consider a team of school officials who are planning to adopt a program to improve mathematical reasoning for sixth graders. The team has scant resources for inservice training for its teachers. Suppose also that the team identifies an RCT of a math program for sixth graders that has really great evidence that participants improve their math reasoning scores. The evaluators, who are in another state, insist that, for the program to work outside the experimental setting, prospective users need special training. In this example, the resource-poor school officials may have to forgo the program because they cannot afford to implement it as planned, and, without standardized implementation, the outcomes may not be achieved.

Concern over well-designed evaluations and relevant programs and outcomes is related to the twin concepts of internal and external validity. The ability to make accurate inferences about a program's outcomes and effectiveness (Program A caused Outcome A) is called **internal validity**. **External validity** refers to the extent to which the design produces results that are applicable to other programs, populations, and settings. Another term for external validity is **generalizability**.

Internal Validity Is Threatened

Just as the best laid plans of mice and men (and women) often go awry, evaluations, no matter how well planned, lose something in their execution. We have seen that randomization may not produce equivalent study groups, for example, or people in one study group may drop out more often than people in the other. Factors such as less than perfect randomization and attrition can "threaten" or compromise an evaluation's validity. The most common threats (also known as biases) have been categorized decades ago by Campbell and Stanley. Table 4.4 contains a list of common **threats to internal validity**.

Table 4.4   Threats to Internal Validity

Threat to Internal Validity	*Definition*	*Explanation*
Selection of participants	Biases result from the selection or creation of groups that are not equivalent. Selection can interact with history, maturation, and instrumentation.	Either the random assignment did not "work," or attempts to match groups or control for baseline confounders was ineffective. As a result, groups can be distinguished by being more affected by a given policy, more mature, and more affected by differential administration and content of the baseline and postprogram measures.
History	Unanticipated events occur while the evaluation is in progress.	A change in policy or a historical event may affect participants' behavior while they are in the program. For instance, the effects of a school-based program to encourage healthier eating may be affected by a healthy eating campaign on a popular children's television show.
Maturation	Processes (e.g., physical and emotional growth) occur within participants inevitably as a function of time.	Children in a three-year school-based physical education program mature physically.
Testing	Taking one test has an effect upon the scores of a subsequent test.	After a three-week program, participants are given a test. They recall their answers on the pretest, and this influences their responses to the second test. The influence may be positive (they learn from the test) or negative (they recall incorrect answers).
Instrumentation	Changes in a measuring instrument or changes in observers or scorers cause an effect.	Evaluator A makes slight changes between the questions asked at baseline and after the conclusion of the program. Evaluator B administers the baseline measures, but Evaluator A administers the posttest measures.

(Continued)

Table 4.4 (Continued)

Threat to Internal Validity	Definition	Explanation
Statistical regression	This effect operates when participants are selected on the basis of extreme scores and regress or go back toward the mean (e.g., average score) of that variable.	Only people at great risk are included in the program. Some of them inevitably "regress" to the mean or average "score." Regression to the mean is a statistical artifact, i.e., due to some factor or factors outside of the study.
Attrition	This is the differential loss of participants from one or more groups on a nonrandom basis.	Participants in one group drop out more frequently than participants in the others or are lost to follow-up.
Expectancy	A bias is caused by the expectations of the evaluator or the participants or both.	Participants in the experimental group "expect" special treatment, while the evaluator "expects" to give it to them (and sometimes does). *Blinding* is one method of dealing with expectancy. A second is to ensure that a standardized process is used in delivering the program.

External Validity Is Threatened

Threats to external validity are most often the consequence of the way in which participants or respondents are selected and assigned. For example, respondents in an experimental situation may answer questions atypically because they know they are in a special experiment; this is called the **"Hawthorne" effect**. External validity is also threatened whenever respondents are tested, surveyed, or observed. They may become alert to the kinds of behaviors that are expected or favored. Sources of external invalidity are included in Table 4.5.

External validity is dependent upon internal validity. Evaluation findings cannot be generalized to other populations and settings unless we first know if these findings are due to the program or to other factors.

Randomized controlled trials with double blinding have the greatest chance of being internally valid—assuming that their data collection and analysis are also valid. As soon as the evaluator begins

Table 4.5   Threats to External Validity

Threat	Definition	Explanation
Interaction effects of selection biases and the experimental treatment	This threat occurs when an intervention or program and the participants are a unique mixture, one that may not be found elsewhere. This threat is most apparent when groups are not randomly constituted.	Suppose a large company volunteers to participate in an experimental program to improve the quality of employees' leisure time activities. The characteristics of the company (some of which—like leadership and priorities—are related to the fact that it volunteered for the experiment) may interact with the program so that the two together are unique; the particular blend of company and program can limit the applicability of the findings.
Reactive effects of testing	These biases occur when a baseline measure interacts with the program, resulting in an effect that will not generalize.	Two groups of students participate in an ethics program evaluation. Group 1 is given a test before watching a film, but Group 1 just watches the film. Group 1 performs better on a posttest because the pretest sensitizes them to the program's content, and they pay more attention to the film's content.
Reactive effects of experimental arrangements or the Hawthorne effect	This effect can occur because participants know that they are participating in an experiment.	Sometimes known as the Hawthorne effect, this threat is caused when people behave uncharacteristically because they are aware that their circumstances are different. (They are being observed by cameras in the classroom, for instance, or they have been "chosen" for an experiment.)
Multiple program interference	This bias results when participants are in other complementary activities or programs that interact.	Participants in an experimental mathematics program are also taking physics class. Both teach differential calculus.

to deviate from the strict rules of an RCT, threats to internal validity begin to appear. Example 4.17 illustrates a sample of the threats to validity found in evaluation reports. These inevitably diminish confidence in a program's evidence of effectiveness.

Example 4.17   Threats to Internal and External Validity: Reducing Confidence in the
                   Evidence of the Effectiveness of Four Programs

---

1. Evaluating a Health Care Program to Get Adolescents to Exercise

An additional concern in interpreting results is the potential impact on our findings
of measurement reactivity in which self-reported behavior is influenced by the measurement process itself. Repeated assessments of the target behaviors as well as extensive surveys on thoughts and actions used to change behaviors (not described in this
article) could have motivated and even instructed adolescents in both conditions to
change behaviors, and control participants reported improvements in several diet and
physical activity behaviors [*reactive effects of testing*]. Measurement effects have been
demonstrated in studies promoting physical activity through primary care settings, and
this also may occur with diet assessment.

SOURCE: Patrick, Calfas, Norman, et al. (2006).

2. Evaluating a Mental Health Intervention for Schoolchildren Exposed to Violence: A Randomized Controlled Trial

The CBITS intervention was not compared with a control condition such as general
supportive therapy, but rather with a wait-list delayed intervention. As a consequence,
none of the informants (students, parents, or teachers) were blinded to the treatment
condition. It is possible that the lack of blinding [*expectancy*] may have contaminated
either the intervention or assessments. School staff and parents may have provided
more attention and support to students who were eligible for the program while they
were on a waiting list; alternatively, respondents may have been more likely to report
improvement in symptoms for those students whom they knew had received the intervention. Using blinded evaluators is an important step for the future, to provide an
objective rating of outcomes. . . .

Further research also is needed to determine if our findings would be replicated in
nonurban and non-Latino populations and to examine the intervention's effectiveness in
alternative settings treating large numbers of children, such as pediatric clinics, adolescent medicine clinics, and community mental health centers [*potential lack of generalizability due to study's taking place in specific settings and with specific populations*].

SOURCE: Stein, Jaycox, Kataoka, et al. (2003).

3. HIV-Risk-Reduction Intervention Among Low-Income Latina Women

Individuals lost to follow-up (n = 112) differed from those who received at least one
session of the intervention (n = 292) [*attrition; generalizability*] with respect to age
(younger), ethnicity (Puerto Rican), years in the United States (slightly more years
in United States), education (completed 1 more year), marital status (less likely to be
married), insurance source (more likely to have insurance), and acculturation (more
non-Hispanic acculturation) [*selection*].

SOURCE: Peragallo, Deforge, O'Campo, et al. (2005).

> **4. Tall Stature in Adolescence and Depression in Later Life**
>
> Another possibility is that the assessment or treatment procedures predisposed women to depression either because it medicalized the issue of their height or because of the intrusiveness of the assessment and treatment [*reactive effects of testing and of experimental arrangements*] and its effect on adolescent girls. In this study, there was evidence that women who reported a negative experience of assessment or treatment procedures were significantly more likely to have a history of depression than women who did not, which is consistent with other studies.
>
> SOURCE: Bruinsma, Venn, Patton, et al. (2006).

Access to the highest quality RCTs does not guarantee that research consumers will find their results relevant. RCTs ask very specific research questions and focus on explicitly defined settings and populations. Concern over lack of clinical relevance has led a growing number of evidence-based medicine researchers to advocate "practical" or "pragmatic trials" that loosen up some of the requirements of RCTs. For example, some recommend the use of a broad sample rather than a stringently defined one to more accurately represent the mixture of people that actually come to clinical settings. However, too much flexibility may compromise internal validity. The challenge for research consumers is to find evaluation studies that provide an acceptable balance between internal and external validity.

An accurate evaluation report will always describe threats to its validity, sometimes called limitations, in the discussion or conclusions section. Unfortunately, many evaluation reports do not list all of the threats, nor do they indicate how these threats affect findings. The following checklist consists of questions that research consumers should consider asking when evaluating a study's internal and external validity.

Checklist of Questions to Consider Asking When Evaluating Internal and External Validity in Program Evaluations

✓ If the evaluation has two or more groups, is information given on the number of people in each group who were eligible to participate?

✓ If the evaluation has two or more groups, is information given on the number in each group who agreed to participate?

✓ If the evaluation has two or more groups, is information given on the number in each group who were assigned to groups?

✓ If the evaluation has two or more groups, is information given on the number in each group who completed all of the program's activities?

✓ Were reasons given for refusal to participate among participants (including personnel)?

✓ Were reasons given for not completing all program or evaluation activities?

✓ Did any historical or political event occur during the course of the evaluation that may have affected its findings?

✓ In long-term studies, was information given on the potential effects on outcomes of physical, intellectual, and emotional changes among participants?

✓ Was information provided on concurrently running programs that might have influenced the outcomes?

✓ Was there reason to believe that taking a preprogram measurement affected participants' performance on a postprogram measurement? This problem might arise in evaluations of programs that take a few weeks or require only a few sessions.

✓ Was there reason to believe that changes in measures or observers may have affected the outcomes?

✓ Did the evaluators provide information on whether or not observers or people administering the measures (e.g., tests or surveys) were trained and monitored for quality?

✓ If participants were chosen because of special needs, did the evaluators discuss how they dealt with regression toward the mean?

✓ Did the evaluator provide information on how evaluators ensured that the program was delivered in a standardized manner?

✓ Were participants or evaluators blinded to the intervention? If not, did the evaluators provide information on how the outcomes were affected?

The Problem of Incomparable Participants: Statistical Methods to the Rescue

Randomization is designed to reduce disparities between experimental and control groups by balancing them with respect to all characteristics (such as participants' age, sex, or motivation) that might affect a study's outcome. With effective randomization, the only difference between study groups is whether they are assigned to receive an experimental program or not. The idea is that, if discrepancies in outcomes are subsequently found by statistical comparisons (for example, the experimental group improves significantly), they can be attributed to the fact that some people received the experiment while others did not.

In observational and nonrandomized evaluation studies, the researcher cannot assume that the groups are balanced before they receive (or do not receive) a program or intervention. In observational studies, for example, measured participant characteristics are obtained before, during, and after program participation, and it is often difficult to determine exactly which characteristics are baseline variables. Also, there frequently are unmeasured characteristics that are not available, inadequately measured, or unknown. But if the participants are different, then how can the evaluator who finds a difference between experimental and control outcomes separate the effects of the intervention from differences in study participants? One answer is to consider taking care of potential confounders during the data analysis phase using statistical methods like analysis of covariance and propensity score methods.

Analysis of Covariance

Analysis of covariance (ANCOVA) is a statistical procedure that results in estimates of intervention or program effects "adjusted" for participants' background (and potentially confounding) characteristics or **covariates** (such as age, gender, educational background, severity of illness, type of illness, motivation, and so on). The covariates are included explicitly in a statistical model.

Analysis of covariance "adjusts" for the confounder by assuming (statistically) that all participants are equally affected by the same confounder, say age. That is, the ANCOVA can provide an answer to this question: If you balance the ages of the participants in the experimental and control groups so that age has no influence on one group versus the others, how do the experimental and control groups compare? The ANCOVA "removes" age as a possible confounder at baseline.

The choice of covariates to include in the analysis comes from the literature, preliminary analysis of study data, and expert opinion on which characteristics of participants might influence their willingness to participate and benefit from study inclusion.

Example 4.18 illustrates the use of ANCOVA to balance the age and sex of bipolar patients in a study of impulsivity. Impulsivity is a part of a larger group of personality predispositions such as extraversion, sensation seeking, and a lack of inhibitory behavioral controls.

Example 4.18   ANCOVA in a Study of Trait Impulsivity in Patients With Mood Disorders

---

Background: Impulsivity is a key component of the manic behavior of bipolar disorder and is reported to occur in bipolar patients as a stable characteristic, i.e., a trait. Nevertheless, impulsivity has not been widely studied in depressed bipolar patients. We assessed impulsivity in depressed and euthymic bipolar and unipolar patients and healthy controls. We hypothesized that bipolar subjects would have higher levels of trait impulsivity than the comparison groups.

Methods: Twenty-four depressed bipolar, 24 depressed unipolar, 12 euthymic bipolar, and 10 euthymic unipolar patients, as well as 51 healthy subjects were evaluated with the Barratt Impulsiveness Scale (BIS). Analysis of covariance with age and sex as covariates was used to compare mean group differences.

Results: Depressed bipolar, euthymic bipolar, and depressed unipolar patients did not differ and showed greater impulsivity than healthy controls on all of the BIS scales. Euthymic unipolar patients scored higher than healthy controls only on motor impulsivity.

Limitations: Higher number of past substance abusers in the bipolar groups, and no control for anxiety and personality disorders, as well as small sample sizes, limit the reach of this study.

Conclusions: This study replicates prior findings of stable trait impulsivity in bipolar disorder patients, and extends them, confirming that this trait can be demonstrated in depressed patients, as well as manic and euthymic ones. Trait impulsivity may be the result of repeated mood episodes or be present prior to their onset; either way it would influence the clinical presentation of bipolar disorder.

Comment: The evaluators are asking this question: If all patients were balanced on all baseline confounders or covariates such as age, gender, etc., would differences exist in impulsivity? Impulsivity is the dependent variable.

SOURCE: Peluso, Hatch, Glahn, et al. (2007).

Propensity Score Methods

The propensity score for an individual is the probability of being given the experimental intervention or program depending upon the individual's background characteristics. Put another way, the propensity score is a measure of the likelihood that an individual would have been given the experimental program based on his or her background characteristics. Mathematically, the propensity score is the probability (between 0 and 1) that a participant is in the experimental group given his or her background characteristics.

A propensity score is frequently estimated by using logistic regression in which the experimental program variable (participated yes or no) is the outcome, and the background characteristics (15 years of age and under; 16 years and older), not the study outcomes (improved workplace literacy or better quality of life), are the independent or predictor variables in the model. The model would then include age as a predictor of participation. For example, a propensity score analysis could be used to find out if participants who are 15 years of age and under are more or less likely to be in the experimental program than participants who are 16 years and older.

The goal of a propensity score analysis is to create subgroups of study participants who are similar across a broad range of confounding variables or covariates, and then to test the program effect within those groups. That is, within homogenous subgroups (such as all older participants or all teens at risk for school drop out) the evaluator compares the outcomes of those who did and did not receive the program. For example, using a propensity score analysis, the evaluator of a school drop out prevention program's effectiveness could compare the drop out rate among high risk students who participated in the program with the rate of high risk students who did not.

The advantage of the technique is that the evaluator can include all relevant covariates, no matter how many are identified. Unfortunately, identifying the covariates is not always easy because although it is axiomatic that there are always many of them, no one knows exactly how many and what they are. Research consumers should raise their index of suspicion regarding the choice of confounders or covariates in evaluations that use propensity score analysis or ANCOVA.

An example of the use of propensity score analysis is given in Example 4.19.

As a rule, it is better for researchers to account for confounders when they are designing the study than to wait until after the study is complete and they are doing the statistical analysis. For instance, researchers can use matching techniques (described earlier) to create groups. Of course, matching has problems, too, including difficulties in finding matches. Unfortunately, however, statistical methods like ANCOVA may not be the answer to the problem of confounders either; studies have shown that these methods may not be able to remove all the confounders adequately.

Example 4.19   Evaluating SAFE Homes for Children With the Help of Propensity
                   Score Analysis

Objective: To evaluate the SAFE Homes (SH) program, a short-term group care program
for children between 3 and 12 years of age who enter care for the first time. The program aims to improve case outcomes by consolidating resources to facilitate assessment and treatment planning.

Assessment for Eligibility: Children were included in the sample if (a) the removal was
the first placement for the child; (b) they entered out-of-home care between the dates
(inclusive) of April 1, 1999, and December 31, 2000; and (c) they were between the
ages of 3 and 12 years old at the time of entry into care. Children were excluded from
the sample if (a) their case record was incomplete; (b) access to the case record was
denied for security reasons because the case involved relatives of department employ-
ees; or (c) foster care children (FC) had siblings that had previously gone through SH
services in another community.

Evaluation Research Design: Propensity score matching to control for hidden bias in
treatment group assignment. The one-year outcomes of 342 children who received SAFE
Home services and 342 matched foster care (FC) control children were compared. The
684 subjects were selected from a larger pool of 909 subjects using propensity score
matching. An original cohort of 909 subjects was divided into five groups according to
propensity score quintile to create five groups of subjects with similar risk and maltreatment history profiles. When there was an excess of children from one group included in
a quintile, subjects from the other group were randomly removed so that the final
sample included an equal number of SH and FC cases in each quintile. This resulted in
a reduction of the original cohort of 909 to a sample of 684 propensity score matched
subjects, with the two groups now statistically indistinguishable on each of the 16 case
characteristics included in the propensity score.

Findings: Prior to the initiation of the SAFE Homes program, 75% of the children who
entered care in the state experienced three or more placements in the first year. The
outcomes of both the SH and FC cases were significantly improved over pre–SAFE
Home state statistics. The FC group, however, had comparable or better outcomes on
most variables examined. In addition, the total cost for out-of-home care for the
children in FC was significantly less, despite the fact that the two groups spent similar
amounts of time in care (average time in care: 7 months).

SOURCE: DeSena, Murphy, Douglas-Palumberi, et al. (2005).

Designing evaluation research and analyzing data are complex, interrelated tasks. Research consumers must acquire statistical expertise or
access to it to ensure fair and effective assessments of each study's methods and the resulting evidence.

Summary of Chapter 4:
The Designing Research Consumer

Words to Remember

analysis of covariance, ANCOVA, attrition, baseline, blinding, blocked randomization, case-control study, cluster, cohort, concurrent controls, confounding variables, control group, covariates, cross-sectional, evaluation research design, experimental design, experimental group, external validity, Hawthorne effect, historical analysis, independent variable, instrumentation, interactive effects of selection bias, internal validity, interrupted time-series design, longitudinal, loss to follow-up, matching, multiple program interference, nonrandomized controlled trials, power, predictor, pretest, pretest-posttest design, posttest, propensity score, prospective, quasi-experimental design, random allocation, random assignment, randomization, randomized controlled trial, RCT, reactive effects of experimental arrangements, reactive effects of testing, retrospective, statistical regression, stratified blocked randomization, summative evaluation, threats to internal and external validity, time-series design, true experiments, wait-list controls

1. **Randomized controlled trials** can provide evidence that programs cause results. Strict rules regarding randomization and blinding must be followed.

2. **Quasi-experimental designs** can provide evidence that matters if the evaluator can demonstrate that participating groups do not differ before program implementation. Statistical methods (e.g., propensity score analysis) can compensate for the inability to randomize.

3. **Observational designs** (excluding quasi-experimental designs) can be used to provide information on events that have already occurred (e.g., retrospective cohorts) and on current status (e.g., cross-sectional survey of baseline performance).

4. When evaluating an evaluation study, keep in mind that research design is just one, albeit major, factor to consider in rating overall methodological quality. Other factors include fidelity to the program's protocol, the reliability and validity of data collection, and the appropriateness of the statistical methods.

5. An evaluation must be **internally valid** to be **generalizable** or **externally valid**. An internally valid (e.g., a high quality RCT) produces evidence that matters, however, only *if* its target population, settings, and interventions are applicable.

6. In observational and nonrandomized evaluation studies, selection is always a potential confounder. Thus, the researcher cannot assume that the study groups are balanced before they receive a program or intervention. **Analysis of covariance** and **propensity score methods** are statistical techniques to help understand and control for the bias. **Analysis of covariance (ANCOVA)** is a procedure that results in estimates of intervention or program effects "adjusted" for participants' background characteristics or **covariates.** The covariates are included explicitly in a statistical model.

7. The **propensity score** for an individual is the probability of being treated conditional on the individual's background characteristics. A propensity score is frequently estimated by using logistic regression in which the intervention variable is the outcome and the background characteristics are the independent or predictor variables in the model.

8. The research consumer must be prepared to find ways to evaluate the adequacy of any statistical techniques that are used to minimize selection bias and enhance internal validity.

The Next Chapter

Chapter 5 covers the methods evaluation researchers use to collect information. Among the measures that Chapter 5 covers are **self-administered surveys** (e.g., paper-and-pencil or online surveys) with forced choices or open-ended questions; achievement tests; **record reviews** (e.g., school, prison, and medical records; films; or diaries); observations (unobtrusive and participant); interviews; **large databases** and **data sets** from previous studies; **vignettes**; and physical examinations.

Exercises

1. Find the following two articles. Describe their main objective, describe how participants were assessed for inclusion and exclusion, name the evaluation research design, and briefly summarize the findings.

   Article 1. Guo, J. J., Jang, R., Keller, K. N., McCracken, A. L., Pan, W., & Cluxton, R. J. (2005). Impact of school-based health centers on children with asthma. *Journal of Adolescent Health, 37*(4), 266–274.

   Article 2. Linde, K., Streng, A., Jurgens, S., et al. (2005). Acupuncture for patients with migraine: A randomized controlled trial. *JAMA, 293*(17), 2118–2125.

2. Read the following baseline information, and write a paragraph describing the findings:

Table: Baseline Characteristics of Smokeless Tobacco (ST) Users by Group

	Control (n = 166)		Intervention (N = 141)	
	n	*%*	*n*	*%*
Years in high school				
Senior	46	27.7	41	29.1
Junior	57	34.3	57	40.4
Sophomore	48	28.9	24	17.0
Freshman	15	9.0	19	13.5
Smoking status				
Current	20	12.1	15	10.7
Former	33	20.0	28	20.0
Never	112	67.9	97	69.3
Confidence in ability to quit				
None/a little	65	39.4	49	35.5
Somewhat	27	16.4	31	22.5
Very	73	44.2	58	42.0
Frequency of ST use				
Daily	77	46.4	54	39.1
Weekly	56	33.7	45	32.6
Monthly	33	19.9	39	28.3
Time till first ST use after walking				
≤5 min	14	8.6	7	5.2
6-30 min	34	21.0	13	9.7
>30 min-3 h	33	20.4	34	25.4
>3 h	81	50.0	80	59.7
Type of ST typically used				
Dip or dip and chew	141	86.0	126	93.3
Chew only	23	14.0	9	6.7

SOURCE: Walsh MM, Hilton JF, Masouredis CM, Gee L, Chesney MA, Ernster VL. Smokeless tobacco cessation intervention for college athletes: results after 1 year. *Am J Public Health.* Feb 1999;89(2):228–234. Reprinted with permission from the American Public Health Association.

3. Name the threats to internal and external validity in the following two study discussions.

   1. *The Role of Alcohol in Boating Deaths (Smith, Keyl, Hadley, et al., 2001)*

      Although many potentially confounding variables were taken into account, we were unable to adjust for other variables that might affect risk, such as the boater's swimming ability, the operator's boating skills and experience, use of personal floatation devices, water and weather conditions, and the condition and seaworthiness of the boat. Use of personal floatation devices was low among control subjects (about 6.7% of adults in control boats), but because such use was assessed only at the boat level and not for individuals, it was impossible to include it in our analyses. . . . Finally, although we controlled for boating exposure with the random selection of control subjects, some groups may have been underrepresented.

   2. *Violence Prevention in the Emergency Department (Zun, Downey, & Rosen, 2006)*

      The study design would not facilitate a blinding process that may provide more reliable results. . . . The study was limited by those youth who were excluded, lost to follow-up, or had incomplete documents. Unfortunately, the study population has significant mobility and was commonly unavailable when the case managers attempted to interview them. The study was limited by the turnover of case managers.

      Note: In addition to the "limitations" discussed above, the evaluators cite other study problems. For example, the evaluators say, "This study and the results noted were limited by the duration of case management and follow-up to 6 months. Perhaps, a longer period of at least 1 year may produce improved results." They also state, "All of the components of the evaluation tool, except for Future Expectations and Social Competence, were validated, but the combination has not been."

4. Describe the advantages and limitations of commonly used evaluation research designs including
   - Randomized controlled trials with concurrent and wait-list control groups
   - Quasi-experimental or nonrandomized designs with concurrent control groups
   - Time-series designs
   - Observational designs including cohorts, case controls, and cross-sectional surveys

5. List the covariates reported in the excerpts taken from this study.

   The Effectiveness of a Community-Based Intervention for Parents to Help Reduce Conduct Problems in Clinically Referred Children (Gardner, Burton, & Klimes, 2006) *

   > **Design**: Randomised controlled trial, follow-up at 6, 18 months, assessors blind to treatment status.
   >
   > **Participants**: 76 children referred for conduct problems, aged 2–9, primarily low-income families, randomised to treatment vs. 6-month wait-list group. Retention was 93% at 6 months, 90% at 18 months.
   >
   > **Interventions**: Webster-Stratton Incredible Years video-based 14-week group programme, teaches cognitive-behavioural principles for managing behaviour, using a collaborative, practical, problem-solving approach.
   >
   > **Primary outcomes**: Child problem behaviour by parent-report and home-based direct observation; secondary outcomes include observed positive and negative parenting; parent-reported parenting skill, confidence, and depression.
   >
   > **Analysis**: *T*-tests for continuous, and chi-sq for categorical, variables revealed no significant differences between groups at baseline on demographic factors, parent-reported parenting skills, depression, or child behaviour problems. However, since there was some variation between groups, particularly on observational measures, we controlled for baseline scores when analysing intervention effects, using ANCOVA, with baseline scores as covariates for each corresponding post-intervention score.

   *This study is from the UK, and the spelling (e.g., randomised vs randomized) is left as the authors intended.

6. List the variables used in the propensity score analysis discussed in the excerpts from the following research report.

   A Propensity Score Analysis of Brief Worksite Crisis Interventions After the World Trade Center Disaster (WTCD): Implications for Intervention and Research (Boscarino, Adams, Foa, & Landrigan, 2006)

   > Because our study was a population-based observational design, we statistically controlled for selection bias as the result of observable factors by matching intervention cases to controls using a propensity score method. In this study, variables for the propensity score were those potentially

related to receiving worksite interventions and included demographic factors, exposure to WTCD events, residential location, treatment history, etc. . . .

To control for potential bias, study matching variables in our study included age, gender, marital status, level of education, household income, race/ethnicity, immigrant status, language spoken, borough of residence, exposure to WTCD events, history of mental health treatment, history of depression, and having experiences a peri-event panic (PEP) attack during the WTCD.

5

The Research Consumer Reviews the Measures

$\mathbf{E}$ valuation researchers collect information from their study's participants by relying on **measures** of process, impact, outcomes, and costs. This chapter discusses measures that are commonly used by evaluators and reviews their advantages and limitations. Among the measures the chapter examines are **self-administered surveys** (paper-and-pencil and online surveys) with forced choices or open-ended questions; achievement tests; **record reviews** (e.g., school, prison, and medical records; films; and diaries); observations (unobtrusive and participant); interviews; large **databases** and **data sets** from previous studies; **vignettes**; and physical examinations. The chapter also compares quantitative and qualitative data collection and the reasons for using multiple measures to study a single concept.

Research consumers should examine data collection measures to determine if they are the most reasonable method of obtaining information about the concept being studied. For instance, to measure social interaction among elementary school children, a researcher may find structured observations more appropriate than asking children or their families about friends and after-school activities. You, the consumer, however, may prefer interviews to observations.

Another reason research consumers need to examine an evaluation's measures is to better understand the characteristics of the data that are collected. Participants who answer yes or no to a question about whether they read at least one book a month, for example, provide a different type of data from those who state the exact number of books they read in a month. This chapter discusses the different types of data (e.g., categorical for yes and no versus continuous for the exact number) that may result as a consequence of measurement type.

After reading this chapter, you will be able to

- Identify the multiple measurement types that are appropriate for answering evaluation questions, measures that include
  - Self-administered surveys (paper-and-pencil and online surveys) with forced choices or open-ended questions
  - Forced-choice achievement tests
  - Record reviews (e.g., school, prison, and medical records; films; and diaries)
  - Observations (unobtrusive and participant)
  - Interviews
  - Large databases and data sets from previous studies
  - Vignettes
  - Physical examinations
- Understand the advantages and limitations of typically used evaluation measures
- Distinguish between qualitative and quantitative data collection
- Identify the role of content analysis in quantitative and qualitative data collection
- Understand the reasons for using multiple measures in a single evaluation
- Distinguish between categorical, ordinal, and continuous responses
- Identify the measures cited in evaluation reports

Figure 5.1 shows your location on the way to finding evidence that matters.

Evaluation's Main Measures

Data collection is the core of evaluation research. The evaluator must collect information on all study variables, including the characteristics and achievements of the program and all its constituent parts, in order to produce any evidence at all. The quality of that evidence, and whether the evidence matters, is part two of the story.

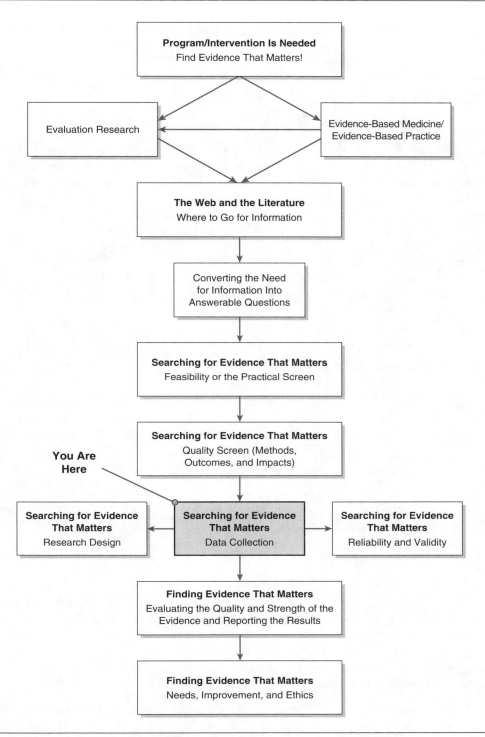

Figure 5.1   Location on the Way to Discovering Evidence That Matters

Evaluation data can be obtained from many sources. Consider the options for data collection in the following two studies:

Options for Data Collection in Two Evaluations

Evaluation 1. Improving Middle School Students' Knowledge of Chemistry

The evaluator asks: When compared to two other districts, has participation in this district's new in-service chemistry teacher education resulted in a statistically and practically meaningful improvement in knowledge over a 12-month period among middle school students in the district?

Here are the potential data collection needs and measures for Evaluation 1.

Potential Data Collection Needs	Potential Measures
1. Children's chemistry knowledge	1. Achievement tests
2. Other child-related variables that may affect children's knowledge such as previous exposure to chemistry classes; scores on other science tests; attitudes toward science	2. School records; student surveys
3. Family-related variables (e.g., mother is a chemist) that may affect children's knowledge	3. Parent surveys
4. School-related variables (e.g., support for chemistry labs and clubs) that may affect children's knowledge	4. Observations of school facilities; administrative staff surveys
5. Teacher's knowledge of content of in-service classes	5. Achievement tests
6. Teacher's adherence to principles taught in the in-services course	6. Classroom observations
7. Teacher's attitudes toward satisfaction with the principles and methods of the in-service course	7. Teacher surveys

Evaluation 2. Quality of Life

The evaluator asks: When compared to the traditional program, does participation in the Center for Healthy Aging improve older persons' quality of life by expanding their social contacts?

Here are the potential data sources for Evaluation 2.

Data Collection Needs	Potential Measures
1. Quality of life, specifically social contact	1. Surveys of participants to ask about nature and extent of social contacts; surveys of their families, friends, and health care providers; reviews of diaries kept by patients; observations of participants' weekly activities

Evaluation 1 is concerned with improvements in students' knowledge of chemistry as a result of teachers' participation in a district-wide in-service program. Evaluation 2 is interested in improvements in "quality of life." Improvements in knowledge and quality of life are the outcome or dependent variables. The programs (experimental versus control; traditional versus new) are the predictor or independent variables.

The Evaluation 1 researchers have identified additional independent variables—also called **covariates**—that may help predict or explain the outcomes. These include children's previous experience with chemistry and family and school support. Evaluation 1 has at least 5 variables that must be accounted for. Evaluation 2 has one outcome variable (quality of life as indicated by expanded social contact) but six potential data sources: surveys of patients, friends, families, and health care providers; diaries; and observations.

Before we discuss how to evaluate the technical quality of these measures, it is important to review the characteristics of the most commonly used evaluation data sources.

_____ Gathering the Data: Weighing the Options

Self-Administered Surveys

Self-administered survey questionnaires ask participants to answer questions or respond to **items** in writing ("paper-and-pencil") or online. Some paper-and-pencil surveys are mailed to participants, and others are completed on site, at a clinic or school, for example.

Survey items may be "open-ended," enabling the **respondent to** give the answer in her or his own words (Example 5.1).

Example 5.1   Open-Ended Question: Respondents Answer in Their Own Words

How courteous are the people who answer the telephone?

_____

_____

_____

_____

Example 5.2   Closed Question: Respondents Reply to a Set of Choices

The people who answer the phone are courteous.	
Circle one choice	
Definitely agree	1
Agree	2
Disagree	3
Definitely disagree	4

Survey items may take the form of statements or questions that give respondents choices for their answers (Example 5.2). This survey item type is referred to as a closed, closed-ended, or forced-choice question.

The majority of surveys used in effectiveness evaluations rely on questions that "force" participants to choose among alternatives. **Forced-choice** questions are efficient and reliable. Their efficiency comes from being easy to use, score, and enter as data. Their reliability is enhanced by the uniformity of data that results when the number of responses is limited (e.g., agree or disagree; frequently or infrequently; and so on).

Open-ended questions can offer insight into why people believe the things they do, but interpreting them can be extremely difficult unless they are accompanied by an elaborate coding system, and people are trained to classify the data they get within the system. This raises costs for busy evaluators, and, in large evaluations, even when certain data are collected, the results are often not reported.

Consider these two answers to a question from a survey of participants in an elementary school teaching program (Example 5.3).

It is not easy to compare A's and B's responses. Participant B lists the instructor as useful. Does this mean that the instructor is a useful resource in general, and how does this compare with Participant A's view that the instructor's lectures were useful? In other words, are A and B giving the same answer? Participant A says the textbook was useful. If the only text used in the program was titled *Teaching in the Classroom*, then A and B perhaps gave the same answer. But since the two recorded responses are different, some guessing or interpretation is necessary.

Participants A and B each mentioned something that the other did not: field experience and learning atmosphere. If these were equally important, then they could be analyzed individually. But suppose

Example 5.3   Open-Ended Question for Elementary School Teaching
Program

Question:	What were the three most useful parts of the program?
	_____
	_____
	_____
Answers:	Participant A
	Instructor's lectures
	The field experience
	Textbook
	Participant B
	Instructor
	Teaching in the classroom
	The most useful part was the excellent atmosphere for learning provided by the program.

neither was particularly significant from the perspective of the survey's users. Would they then be assigned to a category labeled something like "miscellaneous"? Categories called miscellaneous usually are assigned to all the difficult responses, and, before you know it, miscellaneous can become the largest category of all.

Although participants may find it easy to answer an open-ended question, the evaluator invariably finds that analysis and interpretation are quite complicated. As a result, open-ended question results are rarely reported. Instead, evaluators usually rely on questions like the one below in Example 5.4.

Scoring and analyzing the results of self-administered surveys with forced choices have become relatively easy. The responses can be scanned or entered manually into statistical databases. Online surveys can be programmed so that the responses are automatically entered into a database and some analyses can be performed instantly. From the evaluator's perspective, online surveys are efficient because they save paper, save the time needed for manual data entry (and the data entry errors that may go with it), and do away with the need to find storage space for completed forms. The evidence is not yet in, however, about which of the two survey types (paper-and-pencil or online surveys) attracts the most eligible participants, and both methods require careful planning and attention to confidentiality.

Example 5.4   Closed Questions for Elementary School Teaching Program

Question: How satisfied are you with each of the following parts of the program?

Parts of the Program	Circle one choice			
	Definitely Not Satisfied	*Not Satisfied*	*Satisfied*	*Definitely Satisfied*
The textbook, *Teaching in the Classroom*	4	3	2	1
The instructor's knowledge of subject matter	4	3	2	1
The practicality of lecture topics	4	3	2	1
The field experience	4	3	2	1
Other, specify	4	3	2	1

Advantages of Self-Administered Surveys (Questionnaires)

- Many people are accustomed to completing survey questionnaires regardless of where or how they are administered. This familiarity means that the evaluator will need to provide only minimal instruction, potentially saving time and improving efficiency.
- Mailed and online surveys can simultaneously reach large groups of people at relatively low cost.
  - o Online surveys can produce immediate findings for both the evaluator and participants. Participants like to compare their responses to other responses. The ability to do so is an incentive for some people to complete the survey.

Disadvantages

- Participants may not give truthful answers.
- If asked to recall events (e.g., "In the past four weeks, how often did you. . . . ?"), participants may not remember.
- The people who respond to surveys may be the ones who feel most strongly (really pleased or really angry). Persons with middle-of-the-road views may not want to bother with the survey.

- The self-administered survey's format is not suitable (and not really designed) for obtaining explanations of behavior or sensitive information.
- Without supervision, some participants may fail to answer some or even all questions because they do not understand them, even if they have no difficulty with the idea of a survey.
- Some people may have difficulty completing surveys especially if the reading level required is high or they are not interested, too busy, or ill.

An illustration of a self-administered survey's use in an evaluation is given in Example 5.5. In the example, the evaluators use self-administered questionnaires to measure loneliness among college freshmen.

Example 5.5   Using Self-Administered Surveys in an Evaluation: Accounting for Loneliness and Depression (Wei, Russell, & Zakalik, 2005)

This longitudinal study examined whether social self-efficacy and self-disclosure serve as mediators between attachment and feelings of loneliness and subsequent depression. Participants were 308 freshmen at a large midwestern university. The researchers measured attachment, feelings of loneliness, and subsequent depression. Loneliness was assessed with a short version of the UCLA (University of California, Los Angeles) Loneliness Scale, which is **a self-administered survey**. The UCLA Loneliness Scale has been designed to detect variations in loneliness in everyday life. The short form of the UCLA Loneliness Scale contains 10 items (5 positive [nonlonely] and 5 negative [lonely] items, which are randomly distributed in the instrument). Participants are asked to indicate on a scale ranging from 1 (never) to 4 (always) how often they feel as described in each item. Scores on the scale can range from 10 (lowest degree of loneliness) to 40.

 CAUTION: Self-reported data, the type that results from self-administered questionnaires, may differ markedly from the "truth." People may be unable to remember or unwilling to report information.

Forced-Choice Achievement Tests

The most commonly used method of collecting information on evaluation participants' educational accomplishment is the written forced-choice or multiple-choice achievement test. Written tests of this type measure knowledge, understanding, and application of theories, principles, and facts. To assess other kinds of learning, such as the evaluation of evidence or the synthesis of information from different sources, other methods, such as observation of performance or analysis of written papers and scientific studies, are more appropriate.

Most evaluations of educational programs rely to some extent on written multiple-choice achievement tests. An example (5.6) is given below.

Example 5.6   Multiple-Choice Question on an Achievement Test

---

What is the **best** source of information on an individual's eating habits?
Please circle one choice only.

Diaries 1
Vignettes 2
Telephone interviews 3
Online surveys 4
Mailed surveys 5

Advantages of Achievement Tests

- Almost all students are used to multiple-choice achievement tests and have similar expectations of them regardless of the students' field of learning, age, or other demographic factors.
- Years of experience with multiple-choice tests have resulted in extensive knowledge of their statistical properties. As a result, many standardized tests are available that enable the evaluator to compare findings across students who have differing backgrounds and experience. A lucky evaluator will not have to write new achievement test questions.
- Tests are the often the best method of measuring the knowledge that is supposed to result from a particular lesson or course of instruction.
- Multiple-choice tests are relatively easy to score and interpret.

Disadvantages

- Multiple-choice tests are not appropriate for measuring "higher" levels of knowledge, understanding, attitudes and values, actual behavior, or skills.
- Not all programs are geared to standardized tests or test questions. Developing new questions requires skill and costs money.

- Each test question must be carefully tested to ensure that it measures the concept it is supposed to measure. Some test questions measure ability to read rather than ability to reason thoughtfully about the correct answer.
- Some people are philosophically opposed to multiple-choice tests because they believe that they are misused and that they measure superficial knowledge. These people may refuse to answer some or all questions.

 CAUTION: Achievement tests are designed to measure knowledge. The relationship of improved knowledge to desirable changes in attitudes and behavior is far from linear. If you are interested in programs that assess changes in attitudes and behavior, look for other measurement types.

Record Reviews

Record reviews are analyses of an evaluation participant's documented behavior, such as their school or medical records. The documentation may be in print, online, or in audio or video form.

Evaluation records come in two types. The first type consists of records that are already in place (e.g., a participants' medical record). The second form of record is one that the evaluator may ask participants to develop specifically for a given program. For example, an evaluator of a nutrition education program may ask participants to keep a diary of how much food they consumed over a one-month period after they have completed their study participation.

Evaluators use existing records like medical and school records in retrospective cohort evaluations and to get baseline information for time-series designs. (For more information on these research designs, see Chapter 4.) For example, in an evaluation of a new reading program, the evaluators might examine participants' school records to obtain reading scores in the three years prior to a new program's introduction. If participation in the reading program indicates improvement, the evaluators can examine scores over time to determine if scores were going up anyway and whether the program sustained or accelerated this improvement.

Evaluators also use data from existing records because doing so reduces the burden that occurs when participants are required to complete evaluation surveys or achievement tests. In other words, existing records are **unobtrusive measures**. Why ask participants to spend their time answering questions when the answers are already available in their records? Birth date, gender, place of birth, and other demographic variables are often found in accessible records and need not be asked directly of participants.

Records are also relatively accurate repositories of behavior. For example, evaluators interested in the effects of a program on school attendance can ask students, teachers, or parents about attendance. But school records are probably more reliable because they do not depend on people's recall, and they are updated regularly. For the same reason, records are also good places to find out about actual practices. Which books were used? Check the bookstore's inventory and the library's records. Which treatments are usually prescribed? Check a sample of medical records. How many children were sent to which foster families? Check the foster agency files.

The main problems with using records are that they are not always accessible or understandable—even when electronic. If an evaluation uses more than one site (e.g., two hospitals or four states), the study team may have to learn how to access the data in each system and then create a mechanism for linking the data across systems. Also, coding practices vary, and it takes time to learn them.

Diaries are a special type of record in which people are specifically asked to record (e.g., in writing or on film) certain activities. Diaries are typically used in evaluations of programs involving diet, sleep, substance abuse, and alcohol use. People are notoriously inaccurate when asked to recall how much they ate or drank, but keeping a diary improves the quality of their information.

Example 5.7 describes the use of diaries in an evaluation of a combined dietary, behavioral, and physical activity program to treat childhood obesity. The researchers asked obese children to keep 2-day food records three times during the course of the study.

Example 5.7   Food Diaries and Obese Children (Nemet et al., 2005)

This evaluation examined the short and long term effects of a 3-month program among an experimental and control group of obese children. All children were instructed on how to keep a 2-day food record and were evaluated for understanding and accuracy through administration of a 24-hour recall before initiation of the study. Children kept three 2-day food records (at baseline, at the end of the 3-month program, and 1 year later). The food record data were reviewed by the project nutritionist and checked for omissions (for example, whether dressing was used on a salad listed as ingested with no dressing) and errors (for example, inappropriate portion size). All children completed the baseline, 3-month, and 1-year food records.

Advantages of Records

- Obtaining data from existing records can be relatively unobtrusive in that daily activities in schools, prisons, clinics, and so on need not be disturbed.
- Records are a relatively reliable storehouse of actual practice or behavior.
- If data are needed on many demographic characteristics (e.g., age, sex, insurance status), records are often the best source.
- Data obtained from records such as medical and school records reduce participants' research burden.

Disadvantages

- Finding information in records is often time consuming. Even if records are electronic, the researcher may have to learn how to use multiple systems and go through an elaborate process to gain access to them.
- The evaluator must be sure that the record review process is reliable and accurate. This may mean extensive training of staff and monitoring the quality of the review.
- Certain types of information are rarely recorded (e.g., functional or mental status; time spent with clients "after hours").
- Records do not provide data on the appropriateness of a practice or on the relationship between what was done by the practitioner (the process of care) and results (the outcomes of care).

An example of the use of achievement tests and records is given in an evaluation to study the effects of full-day and half-day kindergarten on children's academic outcomes (Example 5.8).

Example 5.8 Achievement Tests and Records: Full-Day and Half-Day Kindergarten

---

The purpose of this study was to evaluate the effects of full-day and half-day kindergarten on children's academic outcomes through 2nd grade (reading achievement, mathematic achievement, grade retention, special education referral, and school attendance). The following measures were compared: (1) 2nd grade reading and math scores from the Iowa Test of Basic Skills [*an achievement test*]; (2) whether or not participants had been retained in grade during the first 3 years of school; (3) whether or not participants had been referred for special education services during the first 3 years of school; and (4) kindergarten **attendance records.**

⚠️ **CAUTION:** Records are only as good as the information contained in them. Some may be incomplete (e.g., school or medical records may not contain the same information across all students or patients.) Others, like diaries, are self-reports and are subject to the same potential misrepresentations as self-administered surveys.

Observations

Observations are appropriate for describing the environment (e.g., the size of a classroom or the number, types, and dates of magazines in the office waiting room) and for obtaining portraits of the dynamics of a situation (e.g., a meeting between parents and teachers; children at play).

Observations take three basic forms. One is called **participant observation** because the researcher actually becomes part of the community being observed. An example would be a researcher who spends one month living among homeless people to better understand the challenges they face. Evaluation researchers rarely use participant observations because they are time consuming and expensive.

The second type of observation is called **in-person observation**. In-person observations are made by one or more trained observers who are actually present at the events of interest. Observations may be summarized by using checklists, notes, cameras, and audiotapes.

A portion of an example observation checklist is given in Example 5.9 (taken from www.teaching.berkeley.edu/observe.html, accessed April 2006).

A third type of observation, **the unobtrusive observation**, involves placing a camera or audiotape in a room or clinic or yard and letting it roll. If a technician is involved, he or she is not trained to be part of the evaluation study and does not participate in any way. After the events being observed are completed, members of the research team extrapolate ideas from the tapes or other recording devices. Extrapolation and coding for analysis takes a great deal of skill and requires special expertise. More than one extrapolator is essential to make certain that the analysis is comprehensive and accurate. Although rarely used on their own (too expensive to implement, difficult problems with ethics committees), unobtrusive observations can be used effectively to complement other measures.

An illustration of the use of unobtrusive observations is given in Example 5.10. The researchers in this example installed video camera units in cars to study drivers' exposure to distractions.

Example 5.9   Observation Checklist

This checklist is intended to help both those who are being observed and those who are observing. The focus is on the mechanics of the classroom interaction, not on the content of the course.

1. Physical Features
- seminar room
- medium sized lecture hall
- large lecture hall
- lighting
- position of seats
- doors (e.g., at front or back)
- blackboards, other equipment, podium
- general noise level (does room echo; is there street noise, air conditioning noise, etc.)
- ventilation (stuffy, cold, hot, etc.)

2. Traffic Flow
- where do students sit? in back? down front?
- disruptions if people come late? (having to find a seat in middle, squeaky doors, etc.)
- where are handouts placed?
- number who attended (compare to enrollment)
- is material handed out at beginning/end/how?

3. Preliminary Activities
- material on the board (outline of the day)
- interactions with audience while handing out material?

4. Beginning
- is there a real beginning or does it just start?
- does the beginning encourage audience, make them feel welcome?

5. The Main Event
- outline of what will be accomplished today?
- is lecture easy to follow (even if details of the subject matter aren't easily accessible to observer)?
- are there distinct sections?
- are there clear transitions between sections?
- summaries of points?
- time for questions?
- is lecture material read? are notes used? extensively?

(Continued)

Example 5.9 (Continued)

---

6. **Interaction With Audience**
   - eye contact? or reading or board work without reference to audience?
   - encourages questions? when? how?
   - how are questions handled? repeating them? can everyone hear all questions? are the answers clear?
   - are questions from students treated seriously or as interruptions?
   - asks questions? is it clear that they are questions to be answered?
   - is the interaction continuous/frequent/occasional/rare?

7. **Voice**
   - is it clear/loud enough for the room?
   - varied?
   - are important points properly emphasized?
   - other characteristics of the voice, e.g., does tone indicate interest in the subject/ in the audience/in . . . [audience's] questions?

SOURCE: Observation Checklist. Stephen K. Tollefson, Office of Educational Development, University of California, Berkeley (http://teaching.berkeley.edu/observe.html), 1993, 2006.

Example 5.10   Unobtrusive Observation: What Distracts Drivers? (Stutts et al., 2005)

Unobtrusive video camera units were installed in the vehicles of 70 volunteer drivers over 1-week time periods to study drivers' exposure to distractions. The video data were coded based on a detailed taxonomy of driver distractions along with important contextual variables and driving performance measures. Results show distractions to be a common component of everyday driving. In terms of overall event durations, the most common distractions were eating and drinking (including preparations to eat or drink), distractions inside the vehicle (reaching or looking for an object, manipulating vehicle controls, etc.), and distractions outside the vehicle (often unidentified). Distractions were frequently associated with decreased driving performance, as measured by higher levels of no hands on the steering wheel, eyes directed inside rather than outside the vehicle, and lane wanderings or encroachments.

Advantages of Observations

- Observations provide an opportunity to collect firsthand information.
- Observations can provide information that cannot be anticipated because the evaluator is present when the unforeseen occurs.

Disadvantages

- A very structured format and extensive training are required for dependable observations. Otherwise, it is possible that two people may witness the same event, but interpret it differently.
- Observations are labor intensive and time consuming.
- The observer (camera or human) can influence the environment being studied, and people can act differently from usual because they are being "watched." The best observations are ones in which people have consented to be watched but become unaware of the observer.

 CAUTION: People sometimes "see" what they look for. At least two trained observers are needed to guarantee reliable observations.

 All episodes to be observed have to be selected carefully so that they typify the phenomenon being observed.

Interviews

Interviews are conducted in person (with or without the assistance of a computer) and on the telephone and using electronic methods. They are particularly useful in studies involving people who have difficulty completing self-administered questionnaires because they have trouble seeing, writing, or reading. Some researchers use them when they want the in-depth information that personalizing a survey can bring. Because interviews involve direct personal contact, interviewers need to be carefully screened, trained, and monitored, and these are costly activities. In evaluation research, interviews almost always rely on preset questions and extensive interviewer training.

Example 5.11 is an excerpt from a sample telephone interview form.

Example 5.11   Portions of a Telephone Interview Form

Instructions: The purpose of this telephone interview is to determine to what extent the health care facility implements the Clinical Practice Guideline on Treating Tobacco Use and Dependence. Read the Introduction and survey questions as they are written. Circle the appropriate response to each question. *Do not read aloud items in capital letters.* For questions that ask for additional detail, please write the response clearly.

(Continued)

Example 5.11 (Continued)

Introduction

Hello. My name is _____(FIRST AND LAST NAME) and I am a volunteer for the _____ Drug Free Coalition. We are talking with heatlh care clinic administrators and providers about steps clinics are taking to implement the clinical practice guideline to treat drug use and dependence. Could I please speak with _____, or an administrator or a provider who is familiar with staff training and current clinical practice?

APPROPRIATE PERSON ANSWERS THE CALL

Hello. My name is _____(FIRST AND LAST NAME) and I volunteer for the Drug Free Coalition. Our coalition has worked with your facility in the past to help implement the Clinical Practice Guideline to treat alcohol use and dependence. We are talking with clinics to understand whether the guideline is being implemented. This interview should not take more than 10 minutes. Do you have time now to answer a few questions about the Clinical Practice Guideline?

IF NO: Can I make an appointment to call you back?

IF YES: Great. Thank you. Before I ask the first question, I would like to confirm the following: (GO THROUGH EACH ITEM IN THE BLUE BOX AND EITHER CONFIRM THE INFORMATION ALREADY WRITTEN DOWN OR ASK FOR IT WITH THE INDIVIDUAL YOU ARE SPEAKING WITH.)

1. **Clinic Name**

2. **Contact Name/Position**

3. **Does your clinic have a dedicated staff member, cessation champion or team that treats alcohol abuse and dependence?**

   YES   1
   NO   2
   DON'T KNOW   3

4. **Do providers at your facility receive formal training to implement the clinical practice guideline on treating alcohol abuse use and dependence?**

   YES   1
   NO   2
   DON'T KNOW   3

   Probe if yes: Please describe the type of formal training your providers receive:

   _____

   _____

   _____

   _____

5. Does your clinic have a system to identify patients who use alcohol?

YES   1
NO (SKIP TO QUESTION 7)   2
DON'T KNOW   3

Probe if yes: Please describe the system used to identify patients.

_____

_____

_____

_____

6. Is there anything else you would like to tell our project about the implementation of the clinical practice guideline?

_____

_____

_____

_____

Advantages of Interviews

- Interviews allow the evaluator to ask about the meaning of questions.
- Interviews can be useful in collecting information from people who may have difficulty reading or seeing.

Disadvantages

- Interviews are time consuming and labor intensive.
- Interviewers require extensive training and monitoring if they are to elicit accurate information in a timely manner.
- Special skills may be required to interpret responses that are off the record.

An example of an evaluation that used both interviews and observations is given in Example 5.12. In the evaluation, study team members interviewed parents and used a special observation form to analyze children's home environments.

Example 5.12   Interviews and Observations: Evaluating Head Start (Love et al., 2005)

Early Head Start, a federal program begun in 1995 for low-income pregnant women and families with infants and toddlers, was evaluated through a randomized trial of 3,001 families in 17 programs. Interviews with primary caregivers, child assessments, and observations of parent-child interactions were completed when children were 3 years old. In the parent interview, for example, the evaluators asked parents questions about their child's health using two measures: (a) a global rating of health status over the past year on the 5-point scale (1 = poor, 5 = excellent) and (b) a question from the Parent Services Interview that asks if the child had received immunizations since the last interview. The evaluators used the total score from the Home Observation for Measurement of the Environment (HOME) to assess the quality of stimulation and support available to a child in the home environment.

 CAUTION: Self-reported data, the type that results from interviews, may not reflect actual behavior.

Large Databases and Data Sets From Previous Studies

Governments, statisticians, and researchers compile data into **databases** to keep track of individuals and communities so as to describe and monitor health, education, and social services. Many nations and the United Nations also maintain large databases and provide statistical reports based on their contents. A database contains all the information collected on a population of people. A data set consists of a subset of information that was extracted from the database for a specific analytic purpose. A researcher who extracts the information on all persons 85 years of age and older from a database containing statistics on all people in the nation who are 65 years of age and older has created a data set.

Evaluators typically use large databases and data sets to help program planners understand the extent of need for a program and to set evaluation standards. For instance, suppose an evaluation team is asked to find out if an alcohol prevention program is needed for older adults and, if it is, to provide advice on evaluating its impact. Say that the team decides to go to the Center for Disease Control's Web site (www.cdc.gov) to gather data on the frequency of drinking in people who are 65 years of age and older. The team wants to know what the percentage of drinkers is and if it is changing (that is, getting "worse").

Once at the CDC site, the evaluation team clicks on *Surveillance*, then *Behavioral Risk Factor Surveillance System*, and then *Trends Data*. At *Trends Data*, the team uses the pull-down menu to get to *Alcohol Use: Chronic Drinking*. The researchers are next directed to a summary of the U.S. national statistics on chronic alcohol use. They then click on *Grouped by Age* to find a table of statistics and a graph of the results. They learn that the median percentage of persons 65 plus who are chronic drinkers increased to 2.7% in 2001 (the latest year for which figures were available in 2006) from 1.5% in 1997. This 1.8 times increase is rather hefty when considering the number of people involved in the increase. In addition, the number of older adults is going to increase over the next decades, so the problem is going to remain an important one.

Using the data from the CDC's survey, the evaluation team tells the program planners that chronic use of alcohol is a growing problem in older adults and that it is reasonable to consider developing and evaluating preventive programs. As a standard of effectiveness, the team suggests that any new program should aim to reverse the trend toward increasing chronic use. The program planners decide to investigate the characteristics of a program that is likely to achieve this aim.

Other sites that contain data sets and statistical summaries include The National Center for Health Statistics (NCHS), the National Library of Medicine (through its National Information Center of Health Services Research and Health Care Technology), and the U.S. Bureau of the Census. The National Center for Health Statistics has data sets that include a vital registration system (e.g., a reporting system for events such as deaths, fetal deaths, birth registrations, marriage registrations, divorce registrations, and abortions). These data are published in *Vital Statistics of the United States*.

Other databases that evaluators use that are of interest to research consumers are provided by the National Center for Education Statistics (NCES), located within the Institute of Education Sciences in the U.S. Department of Education. The NCES is the primary federal entity for collecting and analyzing data related to education. Its address is http://nces.ed.gov. The Social Statistics Briefing Room provides access to current federal social statistics. It provides links to information produced by a number of federal agencies. All of the information included in the Social Statistics Briefing Room is maintained and updated by the statistical units of those agencies. All the estimates for the indicators presented by the Federal Statistics Briefing Room are the most currently available values. Its address is http://www.white house.gov/fsbr/ssbr.html. Last, but certainly not least, is the U.S.

Department of Justice, Office of Justice Programs, Bureau of Justice Statistics at www.ojp.usdoj.gov. At the site, you can get information about crime and victims (e.g., victim and incident-based statistics), criminal offenders, homicide trends, reentry trends, international statistics, and so on.

Evaluators sometimes use data sets from previous studies to answer questions that they were unable to get to the first time around. For example, the researchers in a large heart disease prevention program called the Multiple Risk Intervention Trial (MRFIT) collected data on the smoking habits of wives of the participants. The reason they did this was to find out how wives' smoking status affected whether their husbands smoked. After the study was completed, one of the investigators realized that they had an opportunity to investigate the health effects of passive smoking. In fact, they found that heart disease was much more prevalent in nonsmoking men who were married to smoking wives when compared to similar nonsmoking men married to nonsmoking wives (Svendsen, Kuller, Martin, & Ockene, 1987).

Example 5.13 illustrates the use of an existing database, the Adult Disability Follow-Back Survey or DFS. The evaluation investigated whether home accommodations influenced the amount of human help provided to adults who use wheelchairs.

Example 5.13   Large Database: Home Accommodations and Adults Who Use
                    Wheelchairs (Allen, Resnik, & Roy, 2006)

The purpose of the study was to investigate whether home accommodations influence the amount of human help provided to a nationally representative sample of adults who use wheelchairs. The researchers analyzed data from the Adult Disability Follow-Back Survey (DFS), Phase II, of the Disability Supplement to the National Health Interview Survey (NHIS-D), an ongoing survey of the noninstitutionalized population. In 1994 and 1995, all survey participants completed the NHIS-D, Phase I, a supplemental questionnaire on disability designed to obtain national estimates of various types of disability in the general population. The Phase I questionnaire was then used as a screening device to determine eligibility for Phase II of the survey. Of the approximately 145,000 adults who participated in the NHIS-D, Phase I, 29,019 were selected for the DFS based on their responses to questions related to disability, chronic conditions, functional and sensory impairments, levels of health-service utilization, and receipt of disability benefits. The DFS was designed to yield in-depth information on disability-related issues, including transportation, employment, personal assistance needs, unmet needs, and use of health care and supportive services. The analytic sample for the study consisted of 899 adults aged 18 and older who reported using wheelchairs in the previous 2 weeks.

Advantages of Existing Databases and Data Sets

- Using existing data can be economical and relatively speedy because the evaluator does not have to collect new information.
- The information in an existing database can add new understandings to justify a program's need or explain a study's findings.

Disadvantages

- The selection of data to collect, the choice of persons from whom to collect, the quality of the data, and how data were recorded are all predetermined. For example, an evaluator who wanted actual grade level may have to "settle" for data such as "at grade level" and "not at grade level." It is conceivable that the evaluation questions and the data used to answer them are unevenly connected or even disconnected.

 CAUTION: Beware of Dueling Data Sets

Practically every day, the results of new studies using existing data are published and reported upon in monographs, journals, and newspapers. Many of these studies are on the same topic, but because data come from different sets of data, the results may differ.

In Example 5.14 (*New York Times*, April 19, 2006), two studies examined the U.S. high school drop out rate. The conclusions are somewhat similar, but the interpretations are different.

Example 5.14   Dueling Data Sets: Who Wins?

Nationwide, about 72 percent of the girls in the high school class of 2003—but only 65 percent of the boys—earned diplomas, a gender gap that is far more pronounced among minorities, according to a report being released today (April 19, 2006) by the Manhattan Institute (www.manhattan-institute.org).

The report, "Leaving Boys Behind: Public High School Graduation Rates," found that 59 percent of African-American girls, but only 48 percent of African-American boys, earned their diplomas that year. Among Hispanics, the graduation rate was 58 percent for girls, but only 49 percent for boys. Mr. Greene's findings are based on school districts' data that states report to the federal government. His findings have

---

(Continued)

Example 5.14 (Continued)

---

come under fire from other researchers, including Lawrence Mishel of the Economic Policy Institute (www.epinet.org). Mr. Mishel emphasizes that he, too, believes that African-American and Hispanic graduation rates are alarmingly low, but he says that Mr. Greene's work seriously exaggerates the problem.

In a recent opinion article in *Education Week* (March 8, 2006), Mr. Mishel estimates that 73 percent of African-Americans get high school diplomas. He bases his calculations on data from census surveys. He also cites studies from New York City and Florida finding graduation rates at least 10 percentage points higher than Mr. Greene finds. Mr. Mishel says high school graduation rates have been improving, especially among blacks. In contrast, Mr. Greene says graduation rates have been relatively flat for years.

The disagreement among the researchers is partly about different sets of data. It also mirrors political differences between the conservative Manhattan Institute, which favors school choice, and the liberal Economic Policy Institute, which has strong ties to unions.

"They're using two different types of data, and each has its own problems," said Claudia Goldin, a Harvard economics professor who does her own education research. "The truth lies somewhere in between."

Which of the two interpretations discussed in the *New York Times* article is correct? To answer the question somewhat objectively necessitates reviewing each of the reports to find the answers to questions like these:

- How did each study define African American and Hispanic? Did each data set use those terms exactly, or did the researchers have to combine categories (e.g., Cuban and Puerto Rican) to come up with them?
- How did each study define dropping out?
- How were African Americans, Hispanics, and dropouts identified in each data set? Was every student in each of the 50 states included in each study, or was a sample selected? If a sample, which sampling methods were used? Which states were included?
- How did each of the two studies handle information on gender, race/ethnicity, and drop out status that may have been missing from the data set?
- Did the final set of students "look" like students in the United States? That is, did the proportions of students in each study who were male and female, Hispanic and not Hispanic, African American and not African American resemble the proportions among U.S. students as a whole?
- Did the authors of each study present a clear picture of any limitations of their research, and, if there were any, how serious were they in terms of one's confidence in the findings?

Vignettes

A **vignette** is a short scenario that is used in collecting data in "what if" situations. Example 5.15 describes how a group of researchers explored the impact of a doctor's ethnicity, age, and gender on patients' judgments. Study participants are given one of eight photos of a "doctor" who varied in terms of ethnic group (Asian versus White), age (older versus younger), and gender (male versus female). Six general practices in South West London (England) took part and 309 patients rated the doctor in terms of the expected behavior of the doctor, the expected behavior of the patient, and the patient ease with the doctor.

Example 5.15   Vignettes: Influence of Physicians' Ethnicity, Age, and Gender (Shah & Ogden, 2006)

The researchers used a factorial design involving photographs of a doctor who varied in terms of ethnicity (White versus Asian), age (old versus young), and gender (male versus female). This required eight separate photographs. The age groups were defined broadly with "young" being doctors aged between 25 and 35 and "old" being doctors aged between 50 and 65. Patients were asked to rate the photograph in terms of expected behavior of the doctor, expected behavior of the patient, and patient ease with the doctor. Eight individuals were identified that fitted the required ethnicity, age, and gender criteria. Background features, lighting, hairstyle, expression, make up, etc. were kept as consistent as possible. Photographs were taken using a digital camera.

Participants were presented with one of the eight photographs followed by this statement: "Imagine that you have been feeling tired and run down for a while; you see this doctor for the *FIRST* time." They were then asked to rate the picture (doctor), using scales ranging from "not at all" *[1]* to "extremely" *[5]* in terms of three broad areas: expected behavior of the doctor, expected behavior of the patient, and expected ease of the patient.

Advantages of Vignettes

- Vignettes can be fun for participants to complete.
- Vignettes can be efficient. They enable the evaluator to vary important factors (e.g., age and gender) one factor at a time. Not every participant has to review a scenario with every factor as long as all participants review some factors and all factors are reviewed.

Disadvantages

- Producing vignettes requires technical and artistic (writing) skill if the results are to be convincing.

- The researcher cannot be certain that the responses accurately reflect the participant's true feelings or behavior.
- Sampling can get complicated when varying factors and participants.

> **CAUTION:** Vignettes are hypothetical. The scenarios they describe may never occur in the evaluation participant's life, and, even if they do, the participant may not act as indicated in the hypothetical setting. Vignettes are self-reports, not actual behavior.

Physical Examinations

Physical examinations are sometimes used in evaluations of drug and alcohol programs (e.g., urine tests), in programs to prevent violence in families and communities, and in programs to improve medical outcomes such as a reduction in blood pressure for people with hypertension. Many physical tests are reliable and have "norms" or standards against which to compare experimental and nonexperimental group performance.

When One Measure Is Not Sufficient Measurement _____

Most effectiveness evaluations use more than one measure because there are many variables. The measures serve four purposes:

1. To screen potential participants for inclusion and exclusion into the evaluation

2. To measure baseline variables such as demographics and other important covariates

3. To measure program implementation

4. To measure outcomes, impact, and costs

Evaluators may not include the results of all measurements in their report. In your role as a research consumer, you have to decide on the importance of information that is omitted from publication in reports and articles. For example, the evaluator may focus on how the outcomes were measured and not (from your perspective) adequately address the screening instrument or how information on adherence to the study was collected.

> **CAUTION:** Make certain that you are able to identify a measure for all variables that interest you.

Example 5.16 gives abbreviated examples of the use of multiple measures in evaluation studies.

Example 5.16   Multiple Measures in Evaluation Research

---

1. Gender Differences in Outcomes From Prison-Based Residential Treatment

The evaluators identified participants in residential drug abuse programs (RDAP) from 4 female and 16 male programs in minimum, low, and medium security prisons. All programs operational at the time were selected except those serving high-security inmates (not near release for follow-up purposes), those serving Immigration and Naturalization Service detainees, and those of only a 4-month duration. All individuals who were within 3 years of release at the time of admission were approached for participation in the evaluation project.

A total of 2,986 individuals were approached for interviews [**measure**] as part of the drug treatment program evaluation project. Of those individuals approached, 340 refused to participate. Logistic regression analyses demonstrated that neither age, race, ethnicity, history of violence, nor history of prior commitments predicted refusal to participate in the research, either for men or women. From the sample of 2,646 individuals with interview data, we excluded those who were not released from prison to supervision by a U.S. Probation officer because we did not have the post-release data needed to construct the outcome variables used in the analyses. Approximately 87% of the subjects were released to supervision [**measure**], thus providing a sample of 2,315. The sample comprised 1,193 treatment subjects and 1,122 comparison subjects. There were 1,842 male subjects and 473 female subjects.

There were 40 institutions from which comparison subjects were selected, 20 that offered residential treatment and 20 that did not but were of similar security levels to those that offered residential treatment (e.g., served similar populations). We identified individuals within 6 to 15 months of release at these 40 institutions who had not volunteered for RDAP and for whom it was too late in their sentence to volunteer. We administered a brief survey [**measure**] on history of drug use to a random sample of these individuals. Any individual who reported regular drug use (that is, use once per week for at least one month) was selected as a comparison subject because they would have met the minimal criteria for admission to RDAP at an earlier stage in their sentence.

(Continued)

Example 5.16 (Continued)

Inmate background information was obtained from automated data files [**measure**], interviews with research subjects [**measure**], and interviews with probation officers [**measure**] for all those subjects who agreed to participate in the evaluation.

Both outcome measures, the arrest dates and dates of substance use, came from the interview [**measure**] with the probation officer who reviewed his/her case file containing this information. Our outcome measure of recidivism consisted of the first occurrence of an arrest for a new offense or a sentence revocation during the first 3 years after release from custody [**measure**]. Our outcome measure of substance use was the first occurrence of evidence of substance use [**measure**], either of an illicit drug or alcohol during the 3-year post release period. Evidence of drug use was defined as a positive urinalysis test, a refusal to submit to a urinalysis test, an admission of drug use to the probation officer, or a positive breathalyzer test [**measures**]. When a person refused a urine test, the assumption was that he or she would have had a positive urine test result.

The Diagnostic Interview Schedule (DIS) interview) [**measure**] was used to obtain *DSM-III-R* (American Psychiatric Association, 1987) diagnoses of depression and anti-social personality. Post-release living situation information (living with a spouse, living with a common-law spouse, and living without a spouse) was obtained from interviews [**measure**] with probation officers.

SOURCE: Pelissier et al. (2003).

2. Secondary Prevention of Intimate Partner Violence

Despite the recognition of intimate partner violence (IPV) against women as a global health issue associated with significant morbidity and mortality, evidence-based treatment strategies for primary care settings are lacking. Because of this, the evaluators designed a study to assess the comparative safety behaviors, use of community resources, and extent of violence following two levels of intervention.

A demographic data form was [**measure**] used to document age, education, employment, self-identified race or ethnicity, and relationship to and cohabitation status with the abuser. Country of birth and degree of acculturation (for Hispanic women only) were measured on a 5-item scale that assesses preference for speaking English in a variety of settings [**measure**].

With the exception of demographics, acculturation, and safety behaviors, all instruments at baseline asked about violence and use of community resources during the preceding 12 months. For the safety behavior checklist, the women were asked, "Have you ever . . . ?" The interview [**measure**] took approximately 30 minutes. At 6, 12, 18, and 24 months, the woman was asked "Since the last time we talked, have you . . . ?"

The Safety Behavior Checklist [**measure**] is a 15-item safety survey developed by violence experts and is part of the March of Dimes protocol, first published in English and Spanish in 1994. The checklist was administered to assess use of safety behaviors and chart future adoption.

The Community Resources Checklist [**measure**] was designed to ask women whether they had used eight different types of community agencies for dealing with abuse: alcohol or drug treatment, battered women's groups, church or clergy, healthcare, legal services, police, shelter, or social services.

The Severity of Violence Against Women Scale (SAVAWS) is a 46-item instrument [**measure**] designed to measure threats of physical violence (19 items) and physical assault (27 items) (Reference is cited by authors here). Examples of behaviors that threaten physical violence are threats to destroy property, hurt the woman, or harm other family members. Examples of behaviors that represent physical violence are kicking, choking, beating up, and forced sex. For each item, the woman responds using a 4-point scale to indicate how often the behavior occurred (0 = *never*, 1 = *once*, 2 = *2–3 times*, 3 = *4 or more times*).

The Danger Assessment Scale is a 15-item questionnaire [**measure**] with a yes/no response format designed to assist women in determining their potential risk for becoming a homicide victim. . . . All items refer to risk factors that have been associated with homicide in situations involving abuse. Examples of risk factors include the abusers' possession of a gun, use of drugs, and threats of suicide by the abuser.

The Employment Harassment Questionnaire is an 8-item instrument [**measure**] taken from a recent report to Congress. (The questions are answered as *yes* or *no*.) Items include *repeated calls and/or visits to the worksite* and *preventing the woman from going to work*.

SOURCE: McFarlane et al. (2006).

Responses and Ratings: Choices for Participants and Evaluators

Some evaluation measures, such as self-administered questionnaires and interviews, require participants to respond to questions. Other measures, such as observations and reviews of records, require the evaluator to respond to questions as well. For example, the evaluation observer explicitly answers this big question: What do you see? In reviewing records, the evaluator answers another question: What do you find?

Most evaluation researchers use at least one measure that has preset or forced response choices regardless of who is responsible for producing the data. For instance, the observation checklist (Example 5.9) is a set of forced-choice questions that the evaluation team completes. Most evaluations only use or only report the results of measures that have preset choices. Some social scientists refer to data collected from these measures as **quantitative** because preset response choices produce results that can be quantified or enumerated.

Content Analysis

Qualitative data are collected from open-ended questions, observations, and reviews. The data may be summarized into individual narratives, or the content of the data may be analyzed to find common thoughts among the answers produced by groups of individuals. Individual narratives are not often reported in evaluation research, and research consumers will probably encounter very few.

The process of systematically reviewing, analyzing, and interpreting data from open-ended questions, observations, and records—from all types of human communication—is called **content analysis**. A content analysis relies on trained personnel to search the data for "themes" that consistently occur. Once a list of themes is compiled, they can be compared statistically.

In Example 5.17, the researchers describe the methods they use to identify the therapies discussed in popular magazines that teenage girls read. They categorize the information using a typology (e.g., lifestyle and biochemical therapies). The categories in content analysis are often referred to as **themes.**

Qualitative measures and strategies (like content analysis) are used throughout the evaluation cycle. For example, qualitative data are collected to help justify program development and evaluation. Some of the techniques discussed later in the book (Chapter 8), such as focus groups and public forums, produce qualitative data. Qualitative data are also used in evaluation research to provide testimony as to why a program succeeded (or failed).

A most important use of qualitative measures is in determining the **fidelity** with which a program is implemented or its **integrity.** Observers can visit some or a sample of program activities or they may view film or audiotapes of them as illustrated in Example 5.18.

Example 5.17   Content Analysis: Reviewing Editorials and Advertising

The researchers conducted a content analysis of editorial content and advertising from 3 categories of magazines: 5 teen targeted (*Seventeen, CosmoGirl!, Teen People, J-14, YM*), 5 black and Latina culturally targeted (*Ebony, Essence, Jet, Latina, People en Espanol*), and 3 young women's (*Glamour, Vogue, Cosmopolitan*). Six issues of each title published in 2007 were examined (78 issues in total). We used Kemper's typology (lifestyle, biochemical, bioenergetic, biomechanical) to categorize complementary and alternative medicine (CAM) therapies. [These are the qualitative "themes" that the researchers looked for in reviewing the content of each magazine.]

Example 5.18   Examining the Integrity of a Program (Stein et al., 2003)

The evaluators examined the integrity of the intervention as delivered by the clinicians compared with the [program] manual by having an objective clinician rater listen to randomly selected audiotapes of sessions and assess both the extent of completion of the session material and the overall quality of therapy provided. Using a scale developed for this intervention, completion of required intervention elements, including at least cursory coverage of the topic, varied from 67% to 100% across sessions, with a mean completion rate of 96%. On 7 items assessing quality, quality of sessions was moderate to high across sessions.

Not Quite Free to Choose: Data Collection With Preset Choices

It is not only *what* you ask but also *how* you ask participants to respond that matters. Evaluators may decide to record the presence or absence of an activity they observe, for instance, or they may be asked to indicate whether an activity's quality is excellent, good, fair, or poor. Participants may be asked to place their reading preferences in order of priority or they may be asked whether they agree or disagree that certain items reflect their preference, as in Example 5.19.

The responses to the questions posed to the evaluators and participants produce differing types of data. Question 1 for the evaluator results in a number, while question 2 produces a yes or no, and question 3 results in an ordered answer (the order goes from excellent to poor). The participants give a number in response to question 1, make a list of favorites in response to question 2, and order their responses (definitely a favorite to definitely not a favorite) for question 3. Together, the questions and the characteristics of the response choices produce the information on which evaluators base their conclusions about a program's process, outcomes, impact, or costs. Thus, deciding on the response choices is an important research consideration.

Example 5.19   Asking Questions in a Deliberate Way

For evaluators:

1. How many articles were reviewed?
   _____ Number of articles reviewed.

2. Please indicate if you witnessed any of the following activities. Make one choice for each.

(Continued)

Example 5.19 (Continued)

Activities	1. Yes	2. No
One person dominated the session	1	2
The therapist interrupted clients more than once	1	2
Clients interrupted each other at least three times in the first 15 minutes	1	2

3. Please rate the quality of each activity.
   Key:
   4 = Excellent
   3 = Good
   2 = Fair
   1 = Poor

Activity	Please circle one choice for each activity			
Client interaction	4	3	2	1
Therapist interaction	4	3	2	1
Therapist and client interaction	4	3	2	1
Appearance of clinic	4	3	2	1
Availability of appropriate community referrals	4	3	2	1

For participants:

1. Please give the number of books you have read in the past 7 days.
   _____ Number of books read in the past 7 days.

2. Please put your favorite books in order of preference. You most favorite book should be assigned "1." Your least favorite should be assigned "5."

	1 = Most favorite; 5 = Least favorite
Pride and Prejudice	
Tarzan	
Harry Potter and the Goblet of Fire	
Girl of the Limberlost	
The Da Vinci Code	

3. Each of the following books has been selected as a favorite by people between the ages of 18 and 25. Please indicate whether each listed book reflects your reading preference.
Key:
4 = Definitely a favorite; 3 = probably a favorite; 2 = probably not a favorite; 1 = definitely not a favorite; 9 = No opinion

	Please mark one choice for each listed book				
	Definitely a favorite	*Probably a favorite*	*Probably not a favorite*	*Definitely not a favorite*	*No opinion*
Pride and Prejudice	☐	☐	☐	☐	☐
Tarzan	☐	☐	☐	☐	☐
Harry Potter and the Goblet of Fire	☐	☐	☐	☐	☐
Girl of the Limberlost	☐	☐	☐	☐	☐
The Da Vinci Code	☐	☐	☐	☐	☐

Response Choices: Getting the Data From the Questions

Response choices are variously referred to as **rating** or **measurement scales** and **levels of measurement**. There are three basic measurement levels: **categorical, ordinal,** and **numerical.**

1. *Categorical Responses.* Categorical response choices force respondents to put answers into categories. The responses are sometimes called **nominal** because they ask people to "name" the groups to which they belong. Are you male or female? This is an example of a response question that places people into one of two named categories. Other ways of "categorizing" respondents include asking about religious affiliation, school last attended, last job held, or grocery store chain most commonly frequented, for example. These categories have no natural order. That is, in most cases attending X school last is no better or worse than attending Y school last. When only two choices are possible (e.g., male and female), the results are termed **dichotomous.** That is, gender is a dichotomous variable (Example 5.20).

Example 5.20   Categorical Responses

What is the newborn's gender? (Circle one)

Male 1
Female 2

Which *one* of the following best describes your occupation? (Mark [X] one choice.)

Program Evaluator	☐
Research Consumer	☐
School Administrator	☐
Public Health Nurse.	☐
Juvenile Justice Coordinator	☐
Psychiatric Social Worker.	☐

2. *Ordinal Responses.* Questions using ordinal response options offer responses with a built-in order. The order may be imposed (e.g., poor, fair, good, very good, excellent) or naturally occurring (Example 5.21):

Example 5.21   Ordinal Response

What is the highest level of education that you achieved? (Circle one)

Elementary school 1
Some high school 2
High school graduate. 3
Some college 4
College graduate 5
Postgraduate. 6

The **Likert scale** is frequently used to get ordinal responses. Typical examples of Likert scales are given in Example 5.22:

Example 5.22   Ordinal Rating Scales of the Likert Type

frequently	strongly approve
sometimes	approve
almost never	disapprove
	strongly disapprove
very favorable	definitely agree
favorable	probably agree
unfavorable	probably don't agree
very unfavorable	definitely don't agree

Ordinal responses may also be visual (Example 5.23).

Example 5.23   Ordinal Responses Presented Visually

Please describe how much you hurt right now. Point to the face that describes how much you hurt.

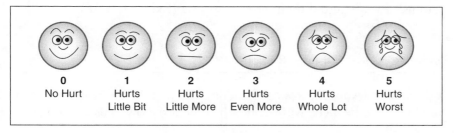

3. *Numerical Responses: Continuous and Discrete.* Continuous responses can have an infinite number of values (e.g., weight) as in Example 5.24.

Example 5.24   Continuous Response Options

What is your blood pressure? ____/____mm/Hg

How tall are you (in centimeters)? _____cm

Continuous measures may be visual. One type is called the visual analog scale. It consists of a line anchored by word descriptors (e.g., "no pain" and "very severe pain") used to assess a characteristic that ranges across a continuum of values (Example 5.25).

Example 5.25 Continuous Responses That Are Visual

Please place an "X" anywhere on the line to describe how much pain you have right now.

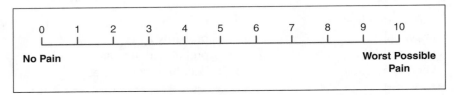

To ensure that the results are comparable, researchers must give all respondents the exact same scale, and the 10 points must be placed along a true continuum such as from 0 to 10 cm. That way, the exact location of the response can be assigned a number (e.g., 1 cm or 1.25 cm or 4.37 cm).

Numerical data may be discrete, and questions eliciting this data can ask for an actual number in response (Example 5.26)

Example 5.26 Discrete Responses

On days that you drank alcohol during the past 12 months, how many drinks of alcohol (beer, wine, and/or hard liquor) did you usually drink?

Five or more.	☐
Four	☐
Three	☐
Two	☐
One	☐

Response options must be chosen carefully. The distinctions between categorical, ordinal, and continuous measures determine the kinds of statistical treatments the evaluator can use.

Suppose a team of evaluators wants to compare satisfaction between participants in an experimental program with that of participants in a control program. If researchers measure satisfaction, say on a scale of 1 to 10, using a visual scale so that participants can put their responses any place along a line, then the evaluators can compute the average score in each group and compare the averages. But if the evaluators use categorical response options (yes, I am satisfied, or no, I am not), then they must make the comparison by using counts (number of yes and no answers in group 1 versus the number of each answer in group 2).

The statistical methods used to compare averages (e.g., average weight or average scores on an achievement test) differ from those used to compare counts. If the evaluators rely on ordinal response options (5 = *definitively satisfied* to 0 = *definitively not satisfied*), some may regard the data as continuous and compute averages (by adding all the 5s, 4s, etc. and dividing by the number of respondents) while others may choose to dichotomize the responses (selections of 3 or greater versus 2 or less) and compare counts (numbers of respondents falling into each category).

Response options also influence the quality of the data. For example, the results will be less than desirable if participants cannot read or understand the response choices, there are too many (or too few) choices, or people are unsure as to how to record their answers.

Coming up with a winning combination of questions and response options is a difficult task. The best measures go through extensive experimentation to ensure that they result in reliable and valid measures. Only reliable, valid measures can result in evidence that matters. The concepts of reliability and validity are so important that they will occupy their own entire chapter.

Table 5.1 describes some of the questions that evaluators are taught to ask before they decide to choose one measurement type over another.

Some of the criteria used in selecting an evaluation measure are practical (resources, ability to collect data in an ethical way) while others focus on acceptability (participants will complete all activities; users will have confidence in the results). In practice, this may mean that the evaluator's choice may be limited to feasibility and satisfactoriness, with the role of quality remaining unclear. For instance, suppose a superb but costly measure is available, but the evaluator, who is short of cash, chooses an alternative, less expensive measure. A compromise of this kind may reduce the quality of the evidence.

Table 5.1   Questions Asked by Evaluators When Selecting Measures

- Which variables are to be measured?
- Can I borrow or adapt a currently available measure for each variable, or must one or more measures be created?
- If appropriate measures are available, do I have the technical and financial resources to acquire and administer them?
- If none is available, do I have the technical skills, financial resources, and time to create them?
- Are participants likely to be able to fill out forms, answer questions, and provide information, etc. called for by the measures?
- In studies that involve direct services and use of information from medical, school, prison, and other confidential records, can I obtain permission to collect data in an ethical way?
- To what extent will users of the evaluation's results (e.g., practitioners, students, patients, program developers, policy makers, and sponsors) have confidence in the measures?

Summary of Chapter 5:
The Research Consumer Reviews the Measures _____

Words to Remember

categorical, content analysis, continuous measures, covariates, databases, data sets, dichotomous, discrete measures, forced-choice questions, in-person observation, instruments, items, levels of measurement, Likert scale, measurement scales, nominal, numerical, open-ended questions, ordinal, participant observation, program fidelity, qualitative, quantitative, rating scales, record reviews, respondent, self-administered survey questionnaires, unobtrusive measures, unobtrusive observation, vignettes

Data collection is the core of evaluation research. An evaluation without data is, in fact, incongruous. The evaluator must collect information on all study variables, including the characteristics and achievements of the program and all its constituent parts in order to produce any evidence at all.

The evaluator may use many differing methods to collect data. Self-administered survey questionnaires ask participants to answer questions or respond to **items** in writing ("paper-and-pencil") or online. The most commonly used method of collecting information on evaluation participants' educational accomplishment is the written forced-choice or multiple-choice achievement test. Evaluators also use records to obtain information. Records come in two forms. The first type consists of records that are already in place (e.g., a medical record). The second form of record is one that the evaluator may ask participants to develop specifically for a given program (e.g., an exercise log).

Observations are appropriate for describing the environment (e.g., the size of a classroom or the number, types, and dates of magazines in the office waiting room) and for obtaining portraits of the dynamics of a situation (e.g., a meeting between parents and teachers, children at play). Interviews are conducted in person (with or without the assistance of a computer) and on the telephone and using electronic methods. Governments, statisticians, and researchers compile data into databases or data sets to keep track of individuals and communities so as to describe and monitor health, education, and social services.

Physical examinations are sometimes used in evaluations of drug and alcohol programs (e.g., urine tests), in programs to prevent violence in families and communities, and in programs to improve medical outcomes such as a reduction in blood pressure for people with hypertension.

Some social scientists refer to data collected from measures using **forced choices** as **quantitative** because these measures produce results that can be quantified or enumerated. **Qualitative** data are collected from open-ended questions, observations, and reviews.

The process of systematically reviewing, analyzing, and interpreting data from open-ended questions and observations and from records—from all types of human communication—is called **content analysis.**

Response options are variously referred to as **rating** or **measurement scales** and **levels of measurement.** There are three basic measurement levels: **categorical, ordinal,** and **numerical.**

The Next Chapter

The next chapter discusses methods for determining the reliability and validity of each measure. A reliable measure is precise in that it produces almost the same value each time it is used. A valid measure accurately measures what it is supposed to.

Exercises

1. Locate the following evaluations and name the types of measures used in each.

   a. King, C. A., Kramer, A., Preuss, L., Kerr, D. C. R., Weisse, L., & Venkataraman, S. (2006). Youth-nominated support team for suicidal adolescents (version 1): A randomized controlled trial. *Journal of Consulting and Clinical Psychology, 74,* 199–206.

   b. Garrow, D., & Egede, L. E. (2006). Association between complementary and alternative medicine use, preventive care practices, and use of conventional medical services among adults with diabetes. *Diabetes Care, 29*(1), 15–19.

   c. Lieberman, P. M. A., Hochstadt, J., Larson, M., & Mather, S. (2005). Mount Everest: A space analogue for speech monitoring of cognitive deficits and stress. *Aviation Space and Environmental Medicine, 76,* 1093–1101.

2. Are the following variables categorical (nominal), ordinal, continuous, or discrete?

   a. Gender
   b. Age
   c. Education (year graduated)
   d. Education (college/no college)
   e. Number of cigarettes smoked each day
   f. Attitude toward school (always look forward, sometimes look forward, never look forward)
   g. Score on achievement test (greater than 51 points; 50 or less)
   h. Score on achievement test (1 = lowest score to 100 = highest score)

3. Are the following statements true or false?

	True	*False*
Most evaluations only report the results of measures with preset choices. Some social scientists refer to data collected from these measures as quantitative because they produce results that can be quantified or enumerated.		
Qualitative data are rarely collected from open-ended questions, observations, and reviews.		
A most important use of qualitative measures is in determining the fidelity with which a program is implemented.		
A content analysis relies on trained personnel to search the data for themes that commonly occur in the data.		

6 The Research Consumer Evaluates Measurement Reliability and Validity

Evidence that matters is collected from reliable, valid, responsive, and interpretable measures of program process, outcomes, impact, and costs. Put another way, for the research findings to count, they must come from measures that have the capacity to consistently and accurately detect changes in program participants' knowledge, attitudes, and behavior. This chapter discusses the characteristics of reliable and valid measures and the effects on design and measurement validity of incomplete or missing data.

After reading this chapter, you will be able to

- Distinguish between reliability and validity
- Identify the characteristics of reliability and validity including
  - Test-retest reliability, internal consistency, split-half, alternative form, and intra- and inter-rater reliability
  - Content, predictive, concurrent, and construct validity
- Distinguish among the characteristics of sensitivity, specificity, false positive, and false negative
- Interpret a chart that shows the flow of participants in evaluation studies from eligibility through data collection to data analysis
- Review how missing data are handled and assess the effects on reliability and validity

Figure 6.1 shows your location on the way to discovering evidence that matters.

Identifying acceptable measures that are **reliable, valid,** responsive, and interpretable is often easier said than done. Even standardized achievement tests, the backbone of the American (and many other countries') educational system and its evaluations, have numerous

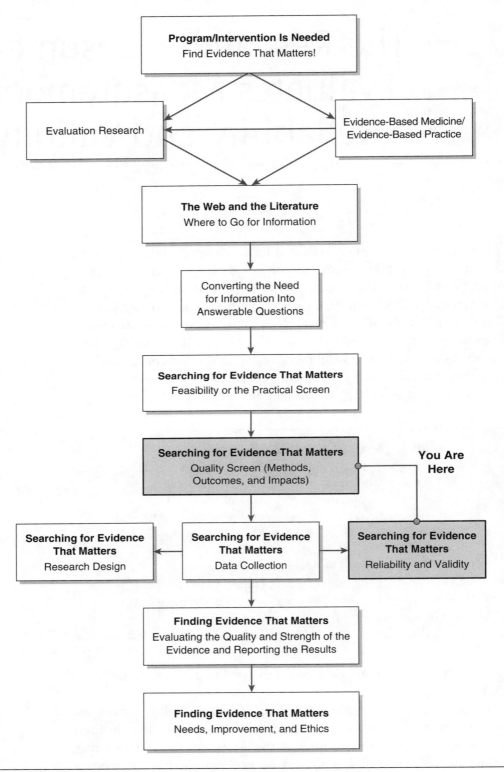

Figure 6.1   Location on the Way to Discovering Evidence That Matters

and vocal critics. Critics question the tests' dependability (reliability), cultural appropriateness (validity), effectiveness as a reflection of the nation's curriculum intentions (validity, responsiveness), and meaning (interpretability). Measurement only increases in complexity when it comes to assessing multidimensional concepts such as quality of life, mental health, parenting, citizenship, violence, social networks, and so on. These concepts are exactly the ones that tend to be of special concern to research consumers.

Much of the vocabulary that is associated with measurement comes from the field of **psychometrics**. Psychometrics is the discipline that is concerned with the theory and technique of psychological measurement, which includes the measurement of knowledge, abilities, attitudes, and personality traits. In recent years, psychometric methods have been applied to the panoply of measures found in evaluations of programs to improve health, education, and social welfare.

Because of the complexity of developing measures that result in "truth," the use of any measure is accompanied by error. **Measurement error** is a term used to describe the discrepancy between responses to a measure and the true value of the concept. Evidence that matters comes from measures that maximize truth and minimize error. Developing and finding such measures, as you can well imagine, is a big deal and requires hard work.

When you review research reports and articles, you will see that most of the measures that researchers use to collect data are adapted from other studies or adopted as is, with minimal, if any, change. Creating a measure from the beginning is tantamount to conducting a research study, and most researchers cannot afford to do both their study and a separate, preparatory one to develop a measure to collect their data. Some researchers (correctly) adopt measures but test them first in their own setting and revise accordingly. Even the revisions need to be retested (albeit on a relatively small group of people), just to be certain that the new measure is as effective as the old but more appropriate for the new setting.

The criteria used to select measures almost always focus first on an instrument's reliability and validity. The term "**instrument**" is often used interchangeably with the term "measure."

Reliability and Validity: A Team Approach

A reliable measure is, above all, a consistent one. A measure of quality of life, for example, is reliable if, on average, it produces the same information from the same people today and two weeks from now.

You need a measure to be reliable—to give you consistent results—but reliability alone is not enough. For instance, if the needle of a scale is five pounds away from zero at its start point (before there is any weight on the scale), I will always over-report my weight by five pounds. Is the measurement consistent? Yes, but it is consistently wrong! Is the measurement valid? No! In fact, it is incorrect. A measurement's validity refers to the degree to which it accurately measures the characteristic it is supposed to measure (e.g., my weight). A valid measure is also an accurate and consistent—or reliable—one. So if we want to understand validity, it helps to learn first about reliability.

Reliability

A reliable measure is reproducible and precise: Each time it is used it produces the same value. A beam scale can measure body weight precisely, but a questionnaire about good citizenship is likely to produce values that vary from person to person and even from time to time. A measure (e.g., of good citizenship) cannot be perfectly precise as its underlying concept is imprecise (e.g., because of differing definitions of good citizenship). This imprecision is the gateway to **random (chance) error**. Error comes from three sources: variability in the measure itself, variability in the respondents, and variability in the observer.

A measure can itself produce unreliable data if it is difficult to complete or improperly designed. For example, if a test's scoring boxes are difficult to fill in (e.g., too small or hard to see) or the scanning software is deficient, then unreliable data will result. The respondents may be the source of error if they are especially tired, not really motivated, or extremely anxious. If people in a dental clinic expecting a root canal are asked to complete a questionnaire, the responses they give about their current mood are likely to differ somewhat from the responses they might have given under less strained circumstances. Finally, the observer or administrator of the measure can also introduce error. An interviewer who treats respondents differently from day to day or does not follow a strict interviewing protocol, for example, can produce unreliable data because he or she is inconsistent.

How do you know if a measure is reliable and not subject to error? Researchers assess the reliability of measures in four ways as illustrated in Table 6.1.

Table 6.1   Four Ways of Assessing Reliability

Type of Reliability	How Assessed
Within measure	Test-retest, internal consistency, split-half
Between measures	Alternate form
Within observer	Intra-rater
Between observers	Inter-rater

Within Measure Reliability

Test-Retest Reliability

A measure has test-retest reliability if the **correlation** or **reliability coefficient** between the scores obtained each time the measure is used is high. A correlation is a numerical index that reflects the **linear relationship** (described by a straight line) between two numerical measurements made on the same group of people. A correlation coefficient—*r*—ranges from −1 to +1, with 0 indicating no relationship. The absolute value of the coefficient reflects the strength of the correlation so that a correlation of −.60 is stronger than a correlation of +.50.

Suppose students are tested twice: first in April and a second time in May. If the test is reliable, and no special program to change behavior was introduced, on average, the test scores should be pretty much the same both times. Their relationship should be nearly perfect or 1.0 (+1). But perfection is not possible, and two variables tested over time will differ to some extent because people differ from time to time (e.g., they are more tired at one time than at another) and the measures are not perfect to begin with. To find out the exact *r*, statisticians compute a **Pearson product-moment correlation coefficient**. Researchers (Landis & Koch, 1977) have set standards for interpreting the strength of the relationship between test and retest reliability (Table 6.2).

Table 6.2   Standards for Test-Retest Reliability

Correlation Obtained Between Test and Retest	Strength of Relationship
.00 to .20	Poor
.21 to .40	Fair
.41 to .60	Moderate
.61 to .80	Substantial
.81 to 1.0	Almost perfect

Researchers and research consumers should be looking for substantial or almost perfect test-retest reliability.

Another concern in estimating test-retest reliability is with the number of people who should be tested. In general, researchers have agreed that between 25 and 100 people is an acceptable sample size especially when the sample is part of a larger study. It is not uncommon for expert researchers to study and report on how a given measure performs with the participants in their study who, after all, are not usually identical to the participants with whom the measure was originally tested. This special testing is to make certain that the measure is reliable in the evaluation's setting.

Researchers usually discuss and justify measures in the "methods" section of their reports and articles. Sometimes, you will find a section devoted to "instruments" or to "main measures." Example 6.1 contains two slightly modified examples of the kind of write up a research consumer might see in a study of a measure's test-retest reliability.

Example 6.1   Establishing Test-Retest Reliability

---

1. An Instrument That Describes the Diverse Problems Seen in Milder Forms of Pervasive Developmental Disorder (PDD).

To examine test–retest reliability, 59 mothers completed the Children's Social Behavior Questionnaire (CSBQ) for the second time after an interval of approximately four weeks. The average age of their children was 9.03, with a standard deviation of 2.87. Test–retest reliability was established by means of Pearson r. For all scales, test–retest reliability was good (*actually almost perfect*) total score ($r = .90$); "not optimally tuned to the social situation" ($r = .89$); "reduced contact and social interest" ($r = .88$); "orientation problems in time, place, or activity" ($r = .82$); "difficulties in understanding social information" ($r = .80$); "stereotyped behavior" ($r = .80$), and "fear of and resistance to changes" ($r = .83$).

SOURCE: Hartman, Luteijn, Serra, and Minderaa (2006).

2. Development of a Short Form of the Workstyle Measure

Test–retest reliability was assessed by examining the correlation of the baseline short form total workstyle score with the short form total workstyle score from the surveys completed 3 weeks after the baseline assessment. This analysis indicated stable test–retest reliability with a correlation coefficient of $r = 0.88$, $P < 0.01$.

SOURCE: Feuerstein and Nicholas (2006).

Internal Consistency Reliability

Internal consistency is an indicator of the cohesion of the items in a single measure. That is, all the items in an internally consistent measure actually assess the same idea or concept. One example of internal consistency might be a test of two questions. The first statement says, "You almost always feel like smoking." The second question says, "You almost never feel like smoking." If a person agrees with the first and disagrees with the second, the test has internal consistency.

When reviewing evaluation reports that discuss internal consistency, you will come across terms like **Cronbach's alpha** and **Kuder-Richardson** **(KR)**. Table 6.3 lists these terms and briefly describes their meaning.

Table 6.3   Internal Consistency: Cronbach's Alpha and Kuder-Richardson (KR)

Term	Explanation
Cronbach's Alpha	Cronbach's **α** (alpha) reflects the extent to which a set of test items can be treated as measuring a single latent variable. Latent variables, as opposed to observable variables, are those variables that cannot be directly observed but are rather inferred from other variables that can be observed and directly measured. Examples of latent variables include attitudes toward school, self-efficacy, and quality of life. Cronbach's alpha can range between 0 and 1. A measure with an alpha .61 and above is usually considered to be internally consistent.
Kuder-Richardson (KR) Reliability	This reflection of internal consistency is like Cronbach's alpha except that it is used for measures in which questions can be responded to in only one of two ways (true/false or yes/no). Like alpha, Kuder-Richardson reliability can range from 0 to 1. An internally consistent measure would have a Kuder-Richardson reliability of at least .61 and above.

Example 6.2 gives excerpted samples of how an evaluator justifies the internal consistency of the measures included in a study.

Example 6.2   Justifying Measures' Internal Consistency

---

1. Secondary Prevention of Intimate Partner Violence

The Severity of Violence against Women Scale (SAVAWS) is a 46-item instrument designed to measure threats of physical violence (19 items) and physical assault (27 items). Examples of behaviors that threaten physical violence are threats to destroy property, hurt the woman, or harm other family members. Examples of behaviors that represent physical violence are kicking, choking, beating up, and forced sex. For each

---

(Continued)

Example 6.2 (Continued)

item, the woman responds using a 4-point scale to indicate how often the behavior occurred (0 = *never*, 1 = *once*, 2 = *2–3 times*, 3 = *4 or more times*). The possible range of scores was 0 to 57 for the threats of abuse and 0 to 81 for physical assault. Internal consistency reliability estimates for abused women have ranged from .89 to .91 for threats of abuse and .91 to .94 for assault. . . . For the present study, reliability, as measured by Cronbach's alpha, was .92 for both threats of abuse and physical assault.

The Employment Harassment Questionnaire is an 8-item instrument taken from a recent report to Congress . . . using studies of worksite harassment of women by intimate partners. The questions are answered as yes or no. Items include repeated calls and/or visits to the worksite and preventing the woman from going to work. The range of scores was 0 to 8. The instrument has a reported internal consistency of .76 . . . For the present study, reliability, as measured by Cronbach's alpha, was .87.

SOURCE: McFarlane, Groff, O'Brien, and Watson (2006).

2. The Self-Injury Questionnaire

The Self-Injury Questionnaire (SIQ) is a 30-item, self-report instrument, conceptualized from the trauma literature and tested initially in a community sample. The SIQ, based on . . . classification of self-injury, measures intentions for self-harm per method (overdose, cut, hang, etc.) across all four subscales (i.e., body alterations, indirect self-harm, failure to care for self, and overt self-injury). It measures the frequency, type, and functions of self-harm behaviors and their associations with histories of childhood trauma. The items represent eight conceptual themes for self-injurious behavior: regulation of feelings, regulation of realness, safety, communication with self, communication with others, fun, social influence, and regulation of body sensations. Cronbach alphas were also adequate for each of five subscales.

SOURCE: Santa Mina, Gallop, Links, et al. (2006).

NOTE: If the alphas are "adequate," they must be .61 and above.

Split-Half Reliability

To estimate **split-half reliability,** the researcher divides a measure into two equal halves (say by choosing all odd numbered questions to be in the first half and all even numbered questions to be in the second half). Then, using a technique called the **Spearman-Brown prediction formula,** the researcher calculates the correlation between the two halves. A correlation coefficient of .61 and above is considered acceptable for split-half reliability.

Example 6.3 gives an example of how split-half reliability is written up.

Example 6.3   Writing Up the Results of Split-Half Reliability

---

Note on Psychometric Properties of Playfulness Scales With Adolescents

In total, 105 female and 85 male high school students completed two scales designed to measure playfulness, the Playfulness Scale for Adults and the Adult Playfulness Scale, and two scales designed to measure creativity, the Similes Test and The Franck Drawing Completion Test. The playfulness scales exhibited high internal consistency and good construct validity. Cronbach alpha was .84 for the Playfulness Scale for Adults and .88 for the Adult Playfulness Scale, and split-half reliability was .79 (Spearman-Brown) and .79 (Guttman a variation of the Spearman-Brown) for the Adult Playfulness Scale and .87 (Spearman-Brown) and .86 (Guttman) for the Playfulness Scale for Adults. The 2-week test-retest reliability for the Playfulness Scale for Adults was .89, which compared favorably to the test-retest reliability of .84 previously reported for the Adult Playfulness Scale.

SOURCE: Fix and Schaefer (2005).

Between Measures Reliability

Alternate form reliability refers to the extent to which two instruments measure the same concepts at the same level of difficulty. Suppose students are given an achievement test before participating in a new computer skills class and then again two months after completing it. Unless the two tests are of equal difficulty, you cannot tell if better performance after the second administration represents performance on an easier test or improved learning. It is therefore crucial in longitudinal studies to use alternative measures that are interchangeable. The Pearson product-moment correlation coefficient is usually computed to determine alternate form reliability. Look for correlations of .61 and above.

When reviewing evaluations with longitudinal or time-series designs, look for evidence that the measures used at each point in time are equivalent.

Intra- and Inter-Rater Reliability

Intra-rater reliability refers to the extent to which an individual's observations are consistent over time. If you score the quality of 10 evaluation reports at time A, for example, and then rescore them two weeks later at time B, your intra-rater reliability will be perfect if the two sets of scores are in perfect agreement.

Inter-rater reliability refers to the extent to which two or more observers or measurements agree with one another. Suppose you and a coworker score the quality of 10 evaluation reports. If you and your coworker have identical scores for each of the 10 reports, your inter-rater reliability will be perfect.

A commonly used method for determining the agreement between observations and observers results in a statistic called *kappa,* defined as the agreement beyond chance divided by the amount of agreement possible beyond chance. What is a "high" kappa? By convention, a kappa > .70 is considered acceptable intra- or inter-rater reliability, but this depends highly on the researcher's purpose. Another rule is that K = 0.40 to 0.59 is moderate inter-rater reliability, 0.60 to 0.79 is substantial, and 0.80 is outstanding (Landis & Koch, 1977).

The kappa statistic can also be used in determining the agreement between the results of two measurements (as shown in Table 6.4).

Some researchers use the kappa in place of a correlation coefficient to measure test-retest reliability. That is, the kappa is used as a measure of agreement between scores taken at time A and scores in at a later time, time B (Table 6.5).

Table 6.4   Agreement Between Measures: Kappa

The Brief Health Services Questionnaire

This study examined the validity, utility, and costs of using a brief telephone-administered instrument, the Brief Health Services Questionnaire (BHSQ), for self-reported health care provider contacts relative to collection and abstraction of complete medical records. The study sample was 441 community-dwelling at-risk drinkers who participated in an 18-month longitudinal study. Agreement between BHSQ self-reports and abstracted provider contacts was good to very good for general medical (79% agreement, kappa = .50) and specialty mental health contacts (93% agreement, kappa = .62), but low for "other" miscellaneous health contacts (61% agreement, kappa = .04).

SOURCE: Booth et al. (2006).

Table 6.5   Kappa and Test-Retest Reliability

The test-retest reliability of PTSD diagnosis was moderate with a kappa of 55 using the retest sample of 65 children.

SOURCE: Foa et al. (2001).

Measurement Validity

Validity refers to the degree to which a measure assesses what it is supposed to measure. For example, a test that asks students to *recall* information is an invalid measure of their ability to *apply* information. Similarly, an attitude survey is not valid unless you can prove that people who are identified as having a positive attitude on the basis of their responses to Attitude Measure X are different in some observable way from people who are identified as having a negative attitude.

A measure must be reliable to be valid, but it may be reliable (such as the scale described previously which consistently reports 5 pounds too much weight) and invalid. All valid measures are reliable.

Measurement validity is not the same thing as either **internal validity** or external validity we discussed in connection with evaluation research design (Chapter 4). Internal validity is the extent to which the design and conduct of an evaluation are likely to have prevented bias so we can have confidence in the accuracy of the findings. External validity refers to the extent to which evaluation results provide a correct basis for generalizations to other people and circumstances. Measurement validity refers to the extent to which a measure or instrument provides data that accurately represent the concepts of interest.

Measurement validity is often thought of as having four dimensions: **content**, **predictive**, **concurrent**, and **construct**.

Content Validity

Content validity refers to the extent to which a measure thoroughly and appropriately assesses the skills or characteristics it is intended to measure. A depression scale may lack content validity if it only assesses the affective dimension of depression but fails to take into account the behavioral dimension. The trick in developing a measure with content validity is to be extremely knowledgeable regarding the theories underlying the concept being measured (e.g., depression) as well as regarding what research says about it.

Another dimension of validity is how a measure appears on the surface: Does it seem to cover all the important domains? Ask all the needed questions? This dimension is called **face validity**. Face validity is established by experts in the field who are asked to review a measure and to comment on its coverage. Face validity is the weakest type because it does not have theoretical or research support.

Criterion validity refers to the degree to which a measure correlates with an external criterion of the phenomenon being investigated. You can understand criterion validity better if you see that the term is a coverall term for **predictive** and **concurrent validity**.

Predictive Validity

Predictive validity refers to the extent to which a measure forecasts future performance (the criterion). A graduate school entry examination that predicts who will do well in graduate school (as measured, for example, by grades) has predictive validity.

Concurrent Validity

Concurrent validity is demonstrated when a new measure compares favorably with one that is already considered valid (the criterion). For example, to establish the concurrent validity of a new aptitude test, the researcher can administer the new and the older validated measure to the same group of people and compare the scores. Or, the researcher can administer the new test, and then compare the scores to experts' judgment. A high correlation between the new test scores and the criterion measure's—the older validated test—means the new test has concurrent validity. Establishing concurrent validity is useful when a new measure is created that claims to be shorter, cheaper, or fairer than an older one.

Construct Validity

Construct validity is established experimentally to demonstrate that a measure distinguishes between people who do and do not have certain characteristics. For example, a researcher who claims constructive validity for a measure of competent teaching will have to prove that teachers who do well on the measure are competent whereas teachers who do poorly are incompetent.

Construct validity is commonly established in at least two ways:

1. The researcher hypothesizes that performance on the new measure correlates with performance on one or more measures of a similar characteristic (**convergent validity**) and does not correlate with performance on measures of dissimilar characteristics (**discriminant validity**). For example, a researcher who is validating a new quality of life measure might posit that it is highly correlated ("converges") with another quality of life measure, a measure of functioning, and a measure of health status. At the same time, the researcher would hypothesize that the new measure does not correlate with (it "discriminates" against) selected measures of social desirability (the tendency to answer questions so as to present yourself in a more positive light) and of hostility.

2. The researcher hypothesizes that the measure can distinguish one group from another on some important variable. For example, a

measure of compassion should be able to demonstrate that people who are high scorers are more compassionate than low scorers, who are less compassionate. This requires translating a theory of and research on compassionate behavior into measurable terms, identifying people who are compassionate and who are unfeeling (according to the theory and research), and proving that the measure consistently and correctly distinguishes between the two groups.

When you review evaluation reports to assess the adequacy of their measures' approach to validity, you will find information on both reliability and validity, as in the illustrations in Example 6.4.

Example 6.4   Write-Ups of Reliability and Validity

---

1. Validating an Anger Scale in Sweden

In this study, the internal reliability and **construct validity** of the recently adapted Swedish version of the Novaco Anger Scale (NAS-1998-S), as well as its scale correlations with demographic and criminality variables, were investigated. **Construct validity** was established by assessing the correlation pattern of the scales of NAS-1998-S with concurrent scales of similar and distinct constructs. Ninety-five male violent prisoners, ranging in age from 18 to 67 years, participated. The results demonstrated good **internal reliability,** consistent **intra-scale relationships**, and appropriate **construct validity** of NAS-1998-S.

SOURCE: Lindqvist, Daderman, and Hellstrom (2005).

2. Comparing Three Measures of Violence

A four-item brief instrument, HITS (Hurt, Insulted, Threatened with harm, and Screamed at) is compared with two other previously validated measures: The Woman Abuse Screening Tool (WAST) and the Index of Spouse Abuse-Physical Scale (ISA-P). Cronbach's alpha was 0.76, 0.80, and 0.78 for the English version of HITS, ISA-P, and WAST, respectively. The Spanish version of HITS had lower internal consistency than ISA-P and WAST (0.61, 0.77, 0.80, respectively). However, when administered first and analyzed alone, the Spanish version of HITS had a reliability of 0.71. For the total sample, all three instruments showed good reliability.

The English interviews had similar reliability of all instruments regardless of whether participants completed HITS and WAST or ISA-P first. The Spanish interviews revealed that both presentations were similar in the reliability of ISA-P and WAST. However, compared to those who first answered the ISA-P, the reliability of HITS was higher for those who first answered HITS and WAST (Cronbach's alpha = 0.71 and 0.49, respectively). Presentation method was not significantly associated with total scores of HITS, ISA-P, and WAST, after controlling for demographic characteristics.

SOURCE: Chen, Rovi, Vega, Jacobs, and Johnson (2005).

Sensitivity and Specificity

Sensitivity and **specificity** are two terms that are used in connection with screening and diagnostic tests and measures to detect "disease." All research consumers working in the helping professions such as nursing and allied health, and some in the fields of social work and psychology, will encounter these terms.

Suppose a research consumer were interested in finding an effective program to prevent hazardous alcohol use. The consumer might come across a statement such as this in her literature review: "The Alcohol-Hazardous Drinking Index (AHDI) was 89% **sensitive** and 93% **specific** in identifying at-risk drinkers." **Sensitivity** refers to the proportion of people with disease who have a positive test result. Said another way, a sensitive measure will correctly detect disease (such as alcohol-related risk) among people who have the disease. A sensitive measure is a valid measure. What happens when people without the disease get a positive test anyway, as sometimes happens? That is called a **false positive**. Insensitive, invalid measures lead to false positives.

Specificity refers to the proportion of people without disease who have a negative test result. Measures with poor specificity lead to **false negatives**. They invalidly classify people as not having a disease (such as alcohol-related risk) when in fact they actually do.

A third term associated with sensitivity and specificity is **positive predictive value** (sometimes abbreviated as **PPV**). The PPV of a test is the probability that a person has the disease when restricted to those patients *who test positive* (as compared to those who have the disease). Finally, there is the **negative predictive value** (**NPV**), which is defined as the probability that the patient will not have the disease when restricted to all patients who test negative.

Examples of how these terms are used in evaluation reports are given in Example 6.5.

Needing It All or Just Needing Some of It: Reliability, Validity, Sensitivity, and Specificity

Research consumers are barraged with statistics on reliability and validity (and sometimes on sensitivity and specificity). Evaluation reports can be overwhelming to plough through under any circumstances, and, if you become overwhelmed, you may be tempted to just accept the researchers' word on the quality of their measures' reliability and validity. Passive acceptance of the researchers' evaluations and descriptions

Example 6.5   Sensitivity, Specificity, and Predictive Value

---

1. The Postpartum Bonding Questionnaire

Scale 1 (a general factor) had a sensitivity of 0.82 for all mother-infant relationship disorders. Scale 2 (rejection and pathological anger) had a sensitivity of 0.88 for rejection of the infant, but only 0.67 for severe anger. The performance of scale 3 (infant-focused anxiety) was unsatisfactory. Scale 4 (incipient abuse) selected only a few mothers, but was of some value in identifying those at high risk of child abuse. Revision of the thresholds can improve sensitivity, especially of scale 2, where a cut-off point of 12 = normal, 13 = high better identifies mothers with threatened rejection. These new cut-off points would need validation in another sample.

SOURCE: Brockington, Fraser, and Wilson (2006).

2. The Alcohol Use Disorders Identification Test—French Version

In total, 1,207 patients presenting to outpatient clinics (Switzerland, n = 580) or general practitioners' (France, n = 627) successively completed CAGE, MAST, and AUDIT self-administered questionnaires and were independently interviewed by a trained addiction specialist. AUDIT showed a good capacity to discriminate dependent patients (with AUDIT >=13 for males, sensitivity 70.1%, specificity 95.2%, PPV 85.7%, NPV 94.7% and for females sensitivity 94.7%, specificity 98.2%, PPV 100%, NPV 99.8%); and hazardous drinkers (with AUDIT >=7, for males sensitivity 83.5%, specificity 79.9%, PPV 55.0%, NPV 82.7% and with AUDIT >=6 for females, sensitivity 81.2%, specificity 93.7%, PPV 64.0%, NPV 72.0%).

SOURCE: Gache, Michaud, Landry, et al. (2005).

3. The Childhood Experience of Care and Abuse Questionnaire (CECA.Q)

When sensitivity and specificity of these higher cut-off scores were determined against the CECA interview, higher overall correct classification was achieved (average 80%) than with the previous cut-offs, and higher specificity or true negative rate (average 87%) but lower sensitivity or true positive rate (average of 60%).

SOURCE: Bifulco, Bernazzani, Moran, and Jacobs (2005).

---

can be a mistake. Despite the verbiage, some of the claims some researchers make some of the time may actually be irrelevant to you, while others may contain ambiguous if not misleading information.

As you go through a research article or report, make certain that the measures are concerned with the same outcomes that you are, that you agree with the researchers in terms of their definitions of the outcomes, and that, if given the choice, you would measure them in the same way. Measures of self-confidence, anger, quality of life, and so on are defined and measured differently depending upon their theoretical foundations and research base. When in doubt about a measure's background and theoretical and empirical rationales, go to the researchers' cited references. Remember that the data collected to measure process, impact, outcome, and cost are the foundation of the program evaluation's evidence. It is imperative that they be valid to produce evidence that matters.

You should also demand that the evaluator reports the exact statistical results (such as the test-retest correlation coefficient = 0.80) for each important measure. Do not accept statements such as "The interclass correlation was high" or "The construct validity was good when compared to the ABC Measure." If the language about a measure's validity is vague or unclear, or you are uncertain as to the adequacy of the evidence for choosing it for the evaluation, go to the original source (the one cited by the researcher) and make your own judgment.

 CAUTION: Always check the origins of the measures used in evaluating programs and practices that are in the running for adoption. Make sure that the measures have been rigorously evaluated before their use in the research.

Triangulation

In some evaluations, the researchers cannot find an appropriate measure of an important variable, and they do not have the resources to develop one. When researchers have difficulty finding one single measure to do the trick, they sometimes use multiple measures to collect data on a single outcome, with the expectation that, if the findings converge, then their confidence in the results will improve. Some researchers refer to the use of multiple measures as **triangulation**. Unless each of the measures is reliable and valid, however, and its contribution to the outcome is known, multiple invalid measures will not buy you much.

Reliability and Validity Within and Across Evaluations _____

There is a common misconception that, if an evaluator uses a previously validated instrument, he or she does not need to check the reliability and validity with his or her own data. Responsible evaluators must check an instrument's reliability and validity within the context of its use with their own participants, make any modifications necessary, report on the nature of the modifications, and discuss if and how these changes affected the reliability or validity of the measure. You will find this does not happen as often as desirable, and, when it does not happen, you must conclude that the evaluator is using a measure of unknown reliability and validity.

_____ Missing in Action: Where Are the Data?

Researchers collect data at numerous points throughout their study. Screening or assessment measures are used to determine who is and who is not eligible to participate. Baseline information is collected, and then the performance of the program is monitored by assessing progress and outcomes. Progress can be measured twice (say by comparing baseline performance and performance at the end of a program) or several times (say at baseline, six months after baseline, a year after baseline, at the end of program participation, and a year after that). Whether data are collected a few or many times, opportunities arise for program participants to refuse to complete some or all of a study's measures.

Researchers will tell you that complete data are rarely if ever obtained on all participants. In fact, experienced researchers will also tell you that they always anticipate that important data will be missing for some participants (especially in large and longitudinal evaluations). In practice, this means that researchers know that the possibility exists that participants who remain to the bitter end and complete all data collection tasks may very well differ from the dropouts and refusers. They may be more motivated to stay in for any number of reasons. They may be healthier, enjoy participating in research, have the time to participate, be grateful for the attention or the services, or be more highly educated, for example.

We have seen (in Chapter 4) that a loss of participants jeopardizes an evaluation's internal validity because it leaves behind a selected and possibly biased sample of participants. But it does something else, too. It prevents the program from being given a fair trial. If insufficient data are collected from an inadequate number of people, then the study may not be able to detect any program effects (assuming there are any) because it does not have the power to do so (a Type II error). A Type II error is analogous to a false negative because the evaluator concludes there is no difference between experimental and control program participants (the null hypothesis) when a difference actually exists. A Type I error is analogous to a false positive in that the evaluator concludes that a difference exists when one does not.

Researchers recognize all too well the seriousness of losing participants and data. Many plan ahead and enroll more participants in the study than the statisticians tell them they need to be able to detect true program differences. Some simply exclude missing data from the final analysis. If, for example, half the data were missing on a certain variable, such as quality of life or anxiety, the evaluator will simply exclude that variable from the final analysis.

Some researchers compensate for missing data through analytic methods. For example, they may fill in a "reasonable" value such as an average score for each participant who did respond. Suppose Participant A did not answer a survey question about his annual household income. To fill in the blank with a reasonable value, the evaluator can compute the average of all participants' responses to the question and use the average as the value for Participant A. The reasoning behind this approach is that Participant A is unlikely to deviate substantially from the average person in the study. This approach probably works, however, only if just a few respondents leave out a particular question, and if the evaluator has no reason to think that any given respondent is different, on average, from the others.

What happens if people drop out of the study and complete little or even none of the required data collection measures? Many evaluation researchers involved in medical clinical trials argue for the use of an **intention to treat analysis** (ITT), especially in randomized controlled trials. With this type of analysis, all **participants** are included in the study group to which they were allocated, whether or not they received (or completed) the **intervention** given to that group. Intention to treat analysis is thought to prevent **bias** caused by the loss of participants, which may disrupt the **baseline** equivalence established by randomization. Intention to treat analysis may underestimate the full effects of a program (because some people are included who did not receive the intended program). An alternative to ITT is per protocol analysis on participants who can be evaluated because they complete a certain portion of the program (such as 80%

of all activities) and produce a certain amount of data (such as 80% of all required data).

Loss of study information from attrition or refusal or inability to complete data collection can be a very serious problem for researchers and program developers. Statistical fixes exist, including some of the ones discussed above, but they are complex and controversial, and most researchers try to avoid the problem to begin with.

Circumstances certainly exist in which people drop out. For example, they may become extremely ill or victims of unexpected personal, legal, or financial difficulties. External catastrophic events (earthquakes or floods) or changes in program or evaluation funding may subvert a study. However, the research consumer should be skeptical about the quality of an evaluation study that cannot keep enough participants to come to reasonable conclusions based on the data that are collected.

Experienced researchers are realistic about the study's inclusion and exclusion criteria, train and monitor project staff to recruit and work with participants effectively, reimburse participants for spending their time to complete study activities, provide participants with readable updates on individual and study progress, ensure informed consent, and keep all information confidential.

In the Final Analysis, What Data Are Available?

When researchers plan their study, they anticipate collecting reliable and valid data from everyone who is eligible to join. Their dream is to collect complete information from everyone. But the reality is that some study participants drop out, do not complete the program, and do not complete all data collection activities. If the study is carefully planned and monitored for quality, the chances are that the dream and the reality will overlap and that sufficient data will be collected to produce evidence that matters.

Proponents of evidence-based medicine (www.consort-statement .org) and health (http://www.trend-statement.org/) suggest that a flow diagram accompany evaluation studies so that the research consumer can better understand the data collection and analysis pathway. A sample data collection flow chart is shown in Figure 6.2. As you can see, the chart is designed to help you visualize where in the research scheme of things participants dropped out and why the data analysis is on data collected from a smaller number of people than were eligible to begin with.

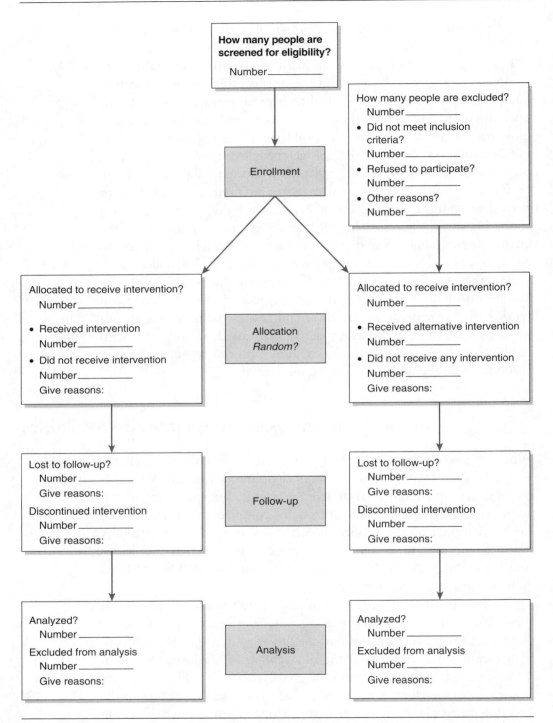

Figure 6.2   Data Collection Flow Chart: Who Is Eligible and Who Provides Data for Analysis?

SOURCE: Taken from www.consort-statement.org.

Outcomes With High Hopes Versus Reality That Modifies Them

Clinically and practically relevant outcomes that focus on factors like quality of life, gang violence, family coherence, knowledge, health, and well-being are often the most meaningful program outcomes. Achieving such lofty goals requires long-term and large studies. Although these are often the ideal, they may not always be possible to conduct. In practice, it is not uncommon for program developers and researchers to find that programs accomplish one or a few **proximate** outcomes rather than the hoped-for ultimate outcomes. Proximate outcomes are intermediate outcomes. They are chosen because they are meaningful in themselves and because previous research and clinical insight suggest that they are associated with the hoped-for outcome. For example, a reduction in the quantity and frequency of alcohol use can be considered a proximate outcome in a program to reduce alcohol-related problems (the ultimate outcome).

Table 6.6 describes the relationship between hoped-for and proximate outcomes.

Example 6.6 gives excerpts of evaluation summaries given on the Promising Practices Network (www.promisingpractices.org). As you can see from the information, each program's main goals may not have been demonstrated, but they all appear to have had some very good proximate outcomes.

The research consumer must decide if proximate outcomes are compelling evidence of program effectiveness. You may consider using consensus techniques or focus groups to help you decide on the value of the proximate outcomes in your setting (Chapter 8).

Table 6.6   Hoped-For Outcomes or Lofty Goals Versus Proximate Outcomes and Reality

---

Hoped-for outcome: Improvement in the quality of life

Program: Cognitive behavioral therapy

Participants: Children and adolescents who suffer frequent and severe headaches

Proximate outcome achieved by program participants: Decrease in symptoms of depression

Reason for choice of proximate outcomes: Depression influences headache prevalence (Bandell-Hoekstra et al., 2000). Cognitive behavioral therapy is effective in treating recurrent headache (Eccleston et al., 2003) in children as well as in decreasing their symptoms of depression (Stein et al., 2003).

Example 6.6   Measuring and Achieving Outcomes

---

1. The Program: Creating Lasting Family Connections

Creating Lasting Family Connections is a family-based program developed by the Council on Prevention and Education: Substances, Inc. (COPES) that attempts to reduce alcohol and other drug use among teenagers by increasing family resiliency and community connections. The program was first evaluated as a research project in 1988 under the title Creating Lasting Connections. Initially, as evaluated, parents of teenagers attended 42 to 56 hours of classes, and the teenagers attended 14 to 20 hours of classes, spread out over a six- to seven-month period. Parents' classes, divided into three modules, included training on substance abuse knowledge and issues, family management skills, and communication techniques. Teenagers joined their parents for the communication techniques module. Follow-up care was also provided for one year (up to six months after the end of training) through bimonthly telephone consultations and/or home visits. The program also attempted to increase community strength by involving community members in program implementation and participant recruitment.

The Outcomes

Direct Effects: Proximate Outcomes

 - Parents and teenagers made greater use of community services.
 - Parents' skills in communicating with their children improved.
 - Parents involved their children to a greater extent in setting rules relating to alcohol and other drug (AOD) use.

No Direct Effects

 - Use of alcohol and other drugs
 - Families' involvement in community activities

2. The Program: The Gang Resistance Education and Training (G.R.E.A.T.) Program

The Gang Resistance Education and Training (G.R.E.A.T.) program is a school-based curriculum facilitated by law-enforcement officers. The program's primary objective is to prevent delinquency, youth violence, and gang membership. The G.R.E.A.T. program was originally developed in 1991 by police officers from the Phoenix metropolitan area and agents of the Bureau of Alcohol, Tobacco, and Firearms. Since then, the gang prevention program has been replicated numerous times in cities across the country. By 1997, G.R.E.A.T. had been established in all 50 states and the District of Columbia with more than 2,400 participating officers.

The Outcomes

At initial post-test, there were *no significant differences* between the G.R.E.A.T. and comparison groups for gang membership, drug use, total delinquency, minor delinquency, person delinquency (e.g., assault, robbery, harassment), property delinquency (e.g., arson, auto theft, burglary, larceny), or status delinquency (e.g., school truancy, curfew violations, or running away from home).

As found from the longitudinal follow-up surveys, G.R.E.A.T. participants were *significantly less likely* to demonstrate property delinquency [*a proximate outcome*] while they were marginally less likely than the control group to have engaged in minor delinquency or to have exhibited higher scores on the measure of total delinquency. *No significant differences* were found between the groups for gang membership, drug use, person delinquency, or status delinquency.

NOTE: All italics are used for the purposes of explanation. This font is not in the original explanation of the program and its evaluation.

_____ Data Collection and Evidence That Matters

By now, you have undoubtedly realized that, when reviewing research, you must check methodological rigor as well as relevance. Methodological rigor is a concept that applies to the evaluation's design, sample, and measures. If the methods are inadequate or the data are insufficient, faulty evidence is produced, and this evidence does _not_ matter. If the methods are adequate but the participants, settings, and characteristics of the program are not relevant to your needs, than the evidence may be accurate and may matter to someone, but this evidence does _not_ matter to you!

The following checklist is a guide for the research consumer to use when evaluating the quality of the measures used to collect evidence about program effectiveness.

Checklist for Evaluating the Quality of Measures to Make Sure You Get Evidence That Matters

- ✓ Review each main measure to certify that you accept its theoretical underpinnings. Ask: Does each measure have content validity?

- ✓ Study each main measure in its entirety. Review the instructions, questions, and responses. The researcher should provide you with sufficient information (and links to the entire measure) so that you can reproduce the measure to better study each item.

- ✓ If the researcher has changed any important components of a measure (such as adding or eliminating questions or changing the response options) check to see if information is provided in the evaluation report on the reliability and validity of the newly constituted measure.

- ✓ If the researcher uses multiple measures, make certain that the reliability and validity of each is reported and that the contribution made by each measure to the study's findings is discussed.

- ✓ Make certain each measure used is valid for your setting before accepting the validity of the data derived from it. The data may have come from a measure that was tested and validated in a particular group of people (e.g., victims of community violence) and not be applicable to your group (e.g., victims of domestic violence).

✓ Always review the original studies cited by the researcher to assess how well reliability and validity were established in the first place. Reviewing original validation studies is especially important for studies of programs and practices that may be candidates for adoption.

✓ Do not assume that a measure that is used in superbly designed evaluation research has been validated in a rigorous manner. Methodologically interesting studies have been known to use mediocre measures!

✓ Follow the path of missing data to determine how missing information affects the validity of the study's findings. Missing data can compromise the evaluation's research design and prevent the program from being given a fair trial.

✓ Carefully review the adequacy with which the researchers handled missing data. If necessary, hire a statistics consultant to help you.

✓ Compare the program's goals and evidence of its outcomes. If differences exist, how important are they? Are proximate outcomes sufficient to constitute evidence that matters?

Summary of Chapter 6: The Research Consumer Evaluates Measurement Reliability and Validity _____

Words to Remember

alternate form reliability, concurrent validity, construct validity, content validity, convergent validity, correlation, correlation coefficient, Cronbach's alpha, discriminant validity, false negative, false positive, instrument, intention to treat analysis, internal consistency, inter-rater reliability, intra-rater reliability, kappa, Kuder-Richardson reliability, linear relationship, measurement error, negative predictive value, Pearson product-moment correlation, positive predictive value, predictive validity, proximate outcomes, psychometrics, random error, reliability coefficient, reliable, sensitivity, specificity, split-half reliability, test-retest reliability, triangulation, valid

A reliable measure is, above all, a consistent one. A measure of quality of life, for example, is reliable if, on average, it produces the same information from the same people today and two weeks from now. A reliable measure is reproducible and precise: Each time it is used it produces the same value.

Validity refers to the degree to which a measure assesses what it is supposed to measure. For example, a test that asks students to *recall* information is an invalid measure of their ability to *apply* information.

Content validity refers to the extent to which a measure thoroughly and appropriately assesses the skills or characteristics it is intended to measure. A depression scale may lack content validity if it only assesses the affective dimension of depression but fails to take into account the behavioral dimension.

Another dimension of validity is how a measure appears on the surface: Does it seem to cover all the important domains? Ask all the needed questions? This dimension is called **face validity**.

Criterion validity refers to the degree to which measurement is associated with an external criterion. It is a coverall term for predictive and concurrent validity because both involve comparing a measure to something else (the criterion).

Predictive validity refers to the extent to which a measure forecasts future performance. A graduate school entry examination that predicts who will do well in graduate school (as measured, for example, by grades) has predictive validity.

Concurrent validity is demonstrated when two measures agree with one another, or a new measure compares favorably with one that is already considered valid.

Construct validity is established experimentally to demonstrate that a measure distinguishes between people who do and do not have certain characteristics. For example, a researcher who claims construct validity for a measure of competent teaching will have to prove that teachers who do well on the measure are competent whereas teachers who do poorly are incompetent.

Sensitivity refers to the proportion of people with disease who have a positive test result. Said another way, a sensitive measure will correctly detect disease (such as alcohol-related risk) among people who have the disease. A sensitive measure is a valid measure. **Specificity** refers to the proportion of people without disease who have a negative test result. Measures with poor specificity lead to **false negatives**. They invalidly classify people as not having a disease (such as alcohol-related risk) when in fact they actually do.

A term associated with sensitivity and specificity is **positive predictive value** (sometimes abbreviated as **PPV**). The PPV of a test is the probability that a person has the disease when restricted to those patients *who test positive* (as compared to those who have the disease). Finally, there is the **negative predictive value,** which is defined as the probability that the patient will not have the disease when restricted to all patients who test negative.

When researchers have difficulty finding one single measure to do the trick, they sometimes use multiple measures to collect data on a single outcome. Some researchers refer to the use of multiple measures as **triangulation.**

It is not uncommon for program developers and researchers to find that programs accomplish one or a few **proximate outcomes** rather than the hoped-for ultimate outcomes. Proximate outcomes are intermediate outcomes. They are chosen because they are meaningful in themselves and because previous research and clinical insight suggest that they are associated with the hoped-for outcome.

The Next Chapters

The next chapter concentrates on how knowledge about research design and valid data collection can be used in grading the quality and evaluating the strength of the evidence produced by researchers. The final chapter focuses on methods of ensuring that research-based programs and practices meet user and decision maker needs in an ethical way.

Exercises

1. An evaluator's colleague decided to play a practical joke. The colleague came across a glossary of terms that the evaluator had prepared for a class she was teaching and altered some of the definitions. Now, the glossary contains some false statements and some true ones. You are the Good Samaritan and decide to correct the statements before the evaluator finds out she is the victim of a joke.

   Here are some of the statements from the glossary that the colleague altered. Your job is to put in the correct terms.

A measure has internal consistency reliability if the correlation or reliability coefficient between scores recorded at different times is high.

A commonly used method for determining the agreement between observations and observers results in a statistic called *alpha* defined as the agreement beyond chance divided by the amount of agreement possible beyond chance.

Content validity refers to the extent to which a measure thoroughly and appropriately assesses the skills or characteristics it is intended to measure.

Predictive validity is demonstrated when two measures agree with one another, or a new measure compares favorably with one that is already considered valid.

Construct validity is established experimentally to demonstrate that a measure distinguishes between people who do and do not have certain characteristics like fear of flying or good quality of life.

A sensitive measure will correctly detect disease (such as alcohol-related risk) among people who have the disease.

Specificity refers to the proportion of people without disease who have a negative test result.

Some researchers refer to the use of multiple measures as triangulation.

A Type II error is analogous to a false positive in that the evaluator concludes that a difference exists when one does not.

The null hypothesis postulates that no difference exists between experimental and control program participants.

With intention to treat analysis, outcomes between study groups are compared with every participant analyzed according to his or her randomized group assignment regardless of whether she received the assigned intervention or produced any data, under most circumstances.

In practice, it is not uncommon for program developers and researchers to find that programs accomplish one or a few proximate outcomes rather than the hoped-for ultimate outcomes. Proximate outcomes are intermediate outcomes.

---

2. Read the following excerpts from evaluation articles and determine which concepts of reliability and validity are covered.

   a. The self-administered questionnaire was adapted with minor revisions from the Student Health Risk Questionnaire, which is designed to investigate knowledge, attitudes, behaviors, and various other cognitive variables regarding HIV and AIDS among high school students. Four behavior scales measured sexual activity (4 questions in each scale) and needle use (5 questions); 23 items determined a scale of factual knowledge regarding AIDS. Cognitive variables derived from the Health Belief Model and Social Learning Theory were employed to examine personal beliefs and social norms (12 questions).

   b. All essays were reviewed by a single reviewer with expertise in the topic; a subset of 35 essays was reviewed by a second blinded expert. Rates of agreement for single items ranged from 81% ($k = .77$; $P < .001$) to 100% ($k = 1$; $P < .001$).

   c. The Child-Parent Checklist was given on October 1 to 250 parents. On October 10, 100 parents, a randomly selected subsample of the first group of parents, were sent the Checklist a second time. Seventy-eight parents returned the completed Checklist. Their time 1 and time 2 responses were compared for consistency.

3. Read the report of the following RCT:

   Wolchik, S. A., Sandler, I. N., Millsap, R. E., et al. (2002). Six-year follow-up of preventive interventions for children of divorce: A randomized controlled trial. *JAMA, 288*(15), 1874–1881.

   Then (a) list each outcome measure, and (b) describe its reliability and validity.

4. Read these two articles and compare each in terms of the adequacy of their data collection flow chart and discussion of how they handled missing data.

   MacMillan, H. L., Wathen, C. N., Jamieson, E., et al. (2006). Approaches to screening for intimate partner violence in health care settings: A randomized trial. *JAMA, 296*(5), 530–536.

   Riggs, N. R., Elfenbaum, P., & Pentz, M. A. (2006). Parent program component analysis in a drug abuse prevention trial. *Journal of Adolescent Health, 39*(1), 66–72.

7

Getting Closer

*Grading the Literature and Evaluating
the Strength of the Evidence*

A research literature review is a highly systematic and reproducible method of identifying, evaluating, and **synthesizing** one or more studies that make up the existing body of **recorded work** produced by researchers, scholars, and practitioners. This chapter discusses strategies to evaluate the **quality** of the literature and the **strength** of the evidence. The strategies rely on the knowledge you gained in Chapters 2 through 6.

Chapter 2 discussed how to locate and query article databases to find pertinent literature. Chapter 3 concentrated on the **practical criteria** that research consumers use to screen articles to ensure a manageable review. These criteria included factors such as the article's language and publication date and the relevance to clients and other decision makers of the study's outcomes, setting, and population. Chapters 4 through 6 discussed research methods, focusing on research design and collecting reliable and valid data.

In addition to addressing the quality of the literature and strength of the evidence, this chapter also discusses how to reliably abstract information from the literature and create charts and tables that facilitate analysis and the reporting of results. Finally, the chapter discusses two major types of systematic literature reviews, including meta-analysis, and examines ways of ensuring that the reviews meet the highest quality standards.

After reading this chapter, you will be able to

- Identify the extent to which a meta-analysis adheres to recommended principles
- Identify the limitations in design that may affect the validity of a study's conclusions and how much the conclusions matter
- Determine if two reviewers agree when abstracting the literature by computing and understanding kappa (a statistic used to express whether agreement between observers exceeds chance)

Figure 7.1 shows your location on the way to discovering evidence that matters.

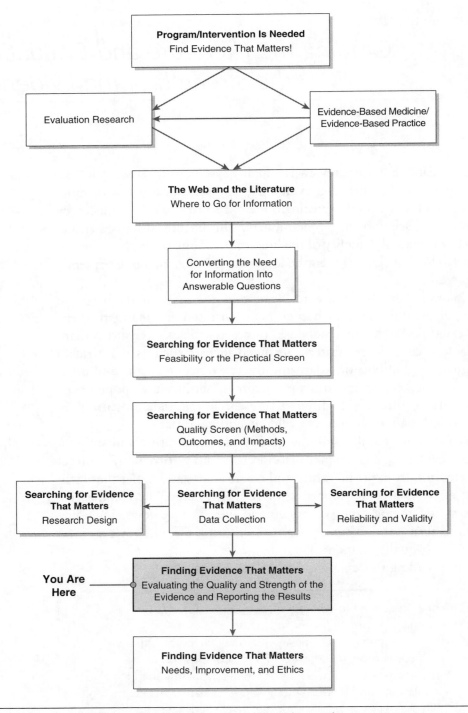

Figure 7.1   Location on the Way to Discovering Evidence That Matters

Doing It Right: Reviewing the Literature From Locating Articles to Reporting Results

Research consumers conduct literature reviews to learn about effective programs and practices and to evaluate the quality and strength of their supporting evidence. Doing a review means applying highly systematic, explicit, and reproducible methods for identifying, evaluating, and reporting on one or more studies, articles, or reports.

The research literature review process is depicted in Figure 7.2. You have already done all the work to get through the practical screen and are now ready to evaluate the quality of the literature that has passed through this screen.

The Spotlight Is on Quality

A research literature review begins with a focused question that is subsequently deconstructed into key words or other search strategies. The reviewer then applies a practical screen to sort through the abstracts and entire articles that result from the initial search. The practical screen includes language, date of publication, the relevance of the program's stated outcomes and theoretical foundations, the applicability of the setting and participants, and so on.

Some researchers distinguish between **methodological** and **non-methodological quality**. **Methodological quality** is the extent to which all aspects of a study's design and implementation combine to protect its findings against biases. A focus on methodological quality means intensively examining factors such as the scientific soundness of the research design and sampling strategy, measurement, and data analysis.

Evaluating **nonmethodological quality** means analyzing the clarity and relevance of the program's objectives, theoretical basis, and content; the trustworthiness of the research's funding source; and the adequacy of the resources, setting, and ethical considerations. Nonmethodological quality criteria are important because they are indicators of a program's potential pertinence and acceptability. Therefore, while high methodological quality produces valid evidence, high nonmethodological quality is necessary for the evidence to matter.

As you have surmised from reading previous chapters, research must adhere to numerous methodological standards if it is to be characterized as high quality. That brings us to the methodological screen. Must all standards be used for all studies?

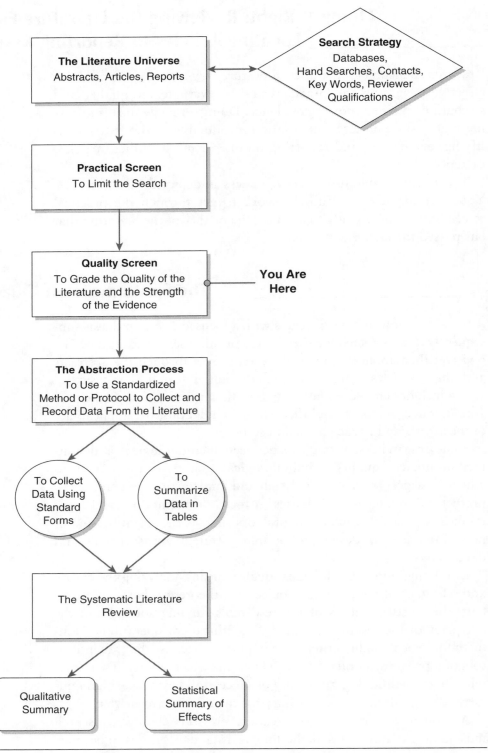

Figure 7.2   The Literature Reviewing Process

Here is an attempt to answer this question, an attempt presented as a discussion between two reviewers who are starting a literature review.

Reviewer 1: I think we should focus on whether the study's sample is any good and if its research design is internally and externally valid.

Reviewer 2: OK. What would you look for?

Reviewer 1: Well, I would read each study and ask questions: Was the sample randomly selected? Is the design internally valid? Externally valid?

Reviewer 2: Is that it?

Reviewer 1: What more do you want?

Reviewer 2: Well, I can think of a whole bunch of things. For instance, I wouldn't just be concerned with random sampling because sample size counts too. Also, I don't know how you would decide if a design was internally valid on the whole. Don't you need to ask specific questions? Is this design subject to maturation, selection, history, instrumentation, statistical regression, or history? If more than one group is included in the research, are the participants randomly assigned to each? Are participants blinded to which intervention they are in? Are participants measured over time? If so, is the number of observations explained? Justified? Shall I go on?

Reviewer 1: There is no need to go on. I can see you know about research design and data collection, but I am not sure that all of the questions you raise are relevant to this particular literature review. For example, I doubt that we will find any blinded studies. We are relying primarily on nonrandomized research. Also, I am not certain we have the resources to answer all of your questions. We have at least 55 studies to review, and each review takes an hour under usual circumstances. Moreover, we plan on having two people review each article, and, if they disagree on any aspect of the review, a third person will be called in to adjudicate. So you can see that we need at least two full weeks of personnel time to do the review, and we have already spent three weeks going through the process of identifying and obtaining access to the 55 studies. That comes to a total of 5 personnel weeks.

Reviewer 2:   Literature reviews are really time consuming and very expensive. Let us examine each criterion to see how important it is to our review.

Reviewer 1:   I have another idea. I came across a method for organizing our examination. It was developed by the U.S. Agency for Healthcare Research and Quality (AHRQ). AHRQ plays a major role in evidence-based practice through its Evidence-Based Practice Center program.

Reviewer 1 is correct in calling attention to the time and expense of doing reviews. Although very good systems for grading the quality of evidence are readily available to them, many reviewers sometimes waste time and money trying to come up with one of their own.

In 1999, the U.S. Congress directed AHRQ to analyze systems to rate the strength of the scientific evidence underlying health care practices, research recommendations, and technology assessment. AHRQ commissioned the Evidence-Based Practice Center at Research Triangle Institute International–University of North Carolina to produce a report that would describe systems that rate the quality of evidence in individual studies or grade the strength of entire bodies of evidence and provide guidance on the best practices in the field of grading evidence (West, King, Carey, et al., 2002).

The researchers reviewed the literature and the Web and relied upon experts to help them uncover and compare systems. They specified desirable domains and, of those, they chose domains considered absolutely critical for a grading scheme. Table 7.1 lists the domains

Table 7.1   Domains for Evaluating the Quality of RCTs and Observational/ Nonrandomized Studies

Randomized Controlled Trials	*Observational/Nonrandomized Studies*
Study question	Study question
Study population	Study population
Randomization	*Comparability of participants*
Blinding	*Exposure or program/intervention*
Interventions	*Outcome measures*
Outcomes	*Statistical analysis*
Statistical analysis	Results
Results	Discussion
Discussion	*Funding or sponsorship*
Funding or sponsorship	

SOURCE: Adapted from West, S., King, V., Carey, T. S., Lohr, K. N., McKoy, N., Sutton, S.F., et al. (2002). *Systems to rate the strength of the evidence.* Rockville, MD: Agency for Healthcare Research and Quality, Department of Health and Human Services.

(e.g., study population) that comprise the criteria for evaluating quality of individual RCTs and observational or nonrandomized studies. The critical domains are italicized.

RCTs: CONSORTing With the Best

As you can see from Table 7.1, for RCTs, an adequate statement of the study question is a *desirable* domain that a grading scheme should cover, but adequate descriptions of the study population, randomization, and blinding are *critical* domains that a grading scheme must cover.

To help the research consumer in evaluating the quality of research *reports*, that is, to begin to grade the extent to which reports adequately cover each domain, proponents of evidence-based medicine have developed the Consolidated Standards of Reporting Trials (**CONSORT**) consisting of standards for *reporting* on randomized controlled trials in health and medicine (www.consort-statement.org). The statement is available in several languages and has been endorsed by prominent medical, clinical, and psychological journals.

CONSORT consists of a checklist and flow diagram to help improve the quality of reports of randomized controlled trials. It offers a standard way to report evaluation research. The checklist includes items, based on evidence, that need to be addressed in the report; the flow diagram provides readers with a clear picture of the progress of all participants in the research, from the time they are randomized until the end of their involvement. The intent is to make the experimental process more clear, so consumers of RCT data can more appropriately evaluate its validity for their purposes. Since the CONSORT statement first appeared, it has been revised to account for the fact that, in some situations, it is preferable to randomly assign *groups* of individuals (such as families or medical practices) rather than individuals to experimental and comparison groups. Now, new items appear on the CONSORT checklist to account for cluster randomization (Campbell, Elbourne, & Altman, 2004).

Although the CONSORT statement was intended for reporting RCTs, it has been used to guide reviewers in evaluating the quality of RCTs. Reviewers focus on the critical domains identified by AHRQ and ask questions about the adequacy with which they are reported using CONSORT requirements. Example 7.1 shows the form such a questionnaire might take.

Example 7.1 A Sample Questionnaire to Obtain Information on a Report of an RCT's Adherence to Critical Quality Domains

Instructions. Answer every question for each article/report by placing a check in the appropriate column: Yes, No, or NA (Not applicable). Please record the page number or numbers that contain the information on which you based your answer. Comments should be recorded when necessary in the last column.

Domain Specified as Critical by AHRQ	Quality Question Based on CONSORT Requirements	Yes	No	NA	Page #s	Comments
Study population including eligibility, recruitment, settings, sample size	1. Are eligibility criteria for individual and groups or clusters of participants (e.g., individuals, clinics, schools) explicitly defined by the researchers?					
	2. Do the researchers clearly describe their methods for recruiting participants for the study (e.g., volunteered, were referred)?					
	3. Is a detailed description provided for each of the settings (e.g., schools, clinics, prisons) in which participants were recruited?					
	4. Is a detailed description provided for each of the settings (e.g., schools, clinics, prisons) in which data were collected?					
	5. Do the researchers describe in detail how sample size was determined (e.g., a formal calculation)?					
Randomization including generating and implementing the random allocation sequence as well as who generated the sequence, enrolled participants, and assigned them to groups	6. Do the researchers specify the method of generating the allocation sequence (e.g., random number table; computer-generated list)?					
	7. If the research used blocking or stratification, was it described adequately?					
	8. Do the researchers describe in detail how they implemented the random allocation sequence (e.g., numbered envelopes) clarifying whether					

	the sequence was concealed until programs were assigned?
	9. If the random allocation was done in clusters (e.g., schools, communities), is adequate information provided on the equivalence of the groups at baseline? If not, is an adequate description given of how the differences were handled?
	10. Are the people who prepare the random generation and those who assign study participants to experimental and control groups the same or different people?
Blinding (being kept unaware of the assigned intervention)	11. Were the Intervention participants (e.g., students, parents, teachers, patients, doctors, data analysts) blinded to the program to which they were assigned? (Name which of these were blinded.)
	12. Do the researchers thoroughly describe the experimental programs?
Programs/Interventions	13. Do the researchers provide an adequate explanation of the choice of comparison or control programs?
	14. Do the researchers thoroughly describe the comparison programs?
	15. Do the researchers measure the extent to which experimental and comparison programs are implemented as planned—their fidelity?

(Continued)

Example 7.1 (Continued)

Domain Specified as Critical by AHRQ	Quality Question Based on CONSORT Requirements	Yes	No	NA	Page #s	Comments
Outcomes including their importance and measurement	16. Do the researchers clearly define all important outcomes?					
	17. Do the researchers describe the methods used to collect data?					
	18. Are the measures/instruments reliable? Valid?					
Statistical analysis (comparing outcomes in experimental and control groups)	19. Do the researchers describe the smallest unit that is being analyzed to evaluate the program (e.g., individual, group, community)?					
	20. If the unit of analysis (e.g., student, patient) is different from the unit of random assignment (e.g., schools, hospitals), is the analytic method used to account for this discrepancy described and justified?					
	21. Do the researchers adequately describe their choice of analytic methods?					
	22. Do the researchers describe how they handle missing data?					
	23. Do the researchers name the statistical software they used?					
	24. Do the researchers describe the number of people in the experimental and comparison programs who dropped out before the study's end or were not included in the analysis? The number of withdrawals in both groups must be given along with a description of the reasons for withdrawal.					

222

Note that the questionnaire in Example 7.1 uses an "on-off" scale. Researchers either describe how they handle missing data or they do not, for example. There is no room for responses such as "almost always," "sometimes," "almost never." Some reviewers may prefer these more graded response options.

 CAUTION: The CONSORT statement consists of guidelines for *REPORTING* the results of RCTs. If studies are incompletely or inaccurately documented, they are likely to be downgraded in quality (fairly or unfairly).

 CAUTION: This sample questionnaire (Example 7.1) contains selected items based on the *critical* domains identified by AHRQ for Randomized Controlled Trials (RCTs; West et al., 2002). Other domains—research questions, results, discussion—are considered desirable, and the reviewer may want to collect data on them as well as on the results, discussion, and funding domains.

 CAUTION: When you use a questionnaire to grade a study's quality, all key terms contained in it must be defined. For example, terms such as "clearly describe," "adequately," "justify," and "not applicable" must be defined, and so must terms such as reliability and validity.

To Agree or Disagree: Defining Terms

Consider the following items from the grading questionnaire in Example 7.1.

Do the researchers thoroughly describe the experimental programs?

Do the researchers thoroughly describe the comparison programs?

For the purposes of the review, what constitutes a "thorough" description? Such terms must be defined. A sample definition is given in Example 7.2.

Example 7.2   A Sample Definition of a Thorough Program Description

---

A thorough description of a program (experimental or comparison) includes information on the

1. Theoretical foundations of the program

2. Findings of previous research regarding the program

3. Specific units of program content

4. Duration of individual segments or units of the program

5. Duration of the entire program

6. Program's distinguishing activities

7. Settings in which the program took place

8. Administration of each program activity

9. Fidelity with which the program is implemented according to plan

---

Example 7.3 contains a "thorough" description of a program designed to reduce symptoms of posttraumatic stress disorder and depression in children exposed to violence. The program's description is thorough because it meets all of the criteria in Example 7.2.

Example 7.3   An Example of a Thorough Program Description

The numbers in brackets refer to the following criteria for a thorough program description.

1. Theoretical foundations of the program

2. Findings of previous research

3. Specific units of program content

4. Duration of individual segments or units of the program

5. Duration of entire program

6. Program's distinguishing activities

7. Settings in which the program took place

8. Administration of each program activity

9. Fidelity with which the program is implemented according to plan

The intervention was a 10-session CBT group called the Cognitive-Behavioral Intervention for Trauma in Schools (CBITS), [1] which was designed for use in an inner-city school mental health clinic with a multicultural population. [7] (See the box below for a description of the program units.) [3] The CBITS intervention incorporates CBT skills in a group format (five–eight students per group) [6] to address symptoms of PTSD, anxiety, and depression related to exposure to violence. Generally, in each session, a new set of techniques was introduced by a mixture of didactic presentation, age-appropriate examples, and games to solidify concepts, and individual work on worksheets happened during and between sessions. [6] The techniques taught to the students were similar to those used in other CBT groups for individuals with PTSD. The CBITS intervention emphasizes applying techniques learned in the program to the child's own problems. Homework assignments were developed collaboratively between the student and the clinician in each session and were reviewed at the beginning of the next session [6].

Cognitive-Behavioral Intervention for Trauma in Schools (CBITS)

Session 1

Introduction of group members, confidentiality, and group procedures

Explanation of treatment using stories

Discussion of reasons for participation (kinds of stress or trauma)

.

.

.

.

Session 10

Relapse prevention and graduation ceremony

The CBITS intervention was implemented on a continuous basis from the late autumn through the spring of the 2001–2002 academic year [5] by one part-time and two full-time psychiatric social workers from the LAUSD Mental Health Services Unit. [8] The groups most often met once a week. Students were excused from one class period to attend the group sessions, which lasted one class period. [4] Clinicians consulted with school administrators and liaison staff to determine when to conduct the group sessions. The sessions often were offered at different times each week so that they could be conducted during study halls and other

---

(Continued)

Example 7.3 (Continued)

nonacademic periods when possible, and to minimize the number of times a student would miss the same academic class. **[6]**

The CBITS intervention previously had been pilot tested for feasibility and acceptability; a pilot study using the CBITS intervention manual and format is reported elsewhere. **[2]** School clinicians received two days of training for application of the intervention and weekly group supervision from the clinician investigators (B.D.S., L.H.J., S.H.K.). **[6]** The school clinicians followed a treatment manual to ensure that the application of the intervention was standardized across clinicians. However, they had some flexibility to meet the specific needs of the students in the group.

We examined the integrity **[9]** of the intervention as delivered by the clinicians compared with the CBITS manual by having an objective clinician rater listen to randomly selected audiotapes of sessions and assess both the extent of completion of the session material and the overall quality of therapy provided. Using a scale developed for this intervention, completion of required intervention elements, including at least cursory coverage of the topic, varied from 67% to 100% across sessions, with a mean completion rate of 96%. On seven items assessing quality, quality of sessions was moderate to high across sessions.

SOURCE: Stein, Jaycox, Kataoka, et al. (2003).

 CAUTION: Understanding a program's implementation, particularly the extent to which it is administered as planned, is essential in understanding the program's outcomes. Research consumers should look for evidence that the implementation was monitored so that any conclusions about the program pertain to the program planners' intentions and not to interpretations of those intentions by people in the field. In recognition of the importance of monitoring program implementation, "fidelity" scales are becoming available for evaluators to use with selected evidence-based programs. For example, several scales may be found at the New York State Office of Mental Health's Web site (www.omh.state.ny.us).

Observational or Nonrandomized Studies: TREND and Quality

Many public health interventions are observational or nonrandomized controlled trials, sometimes called field trials, community-based studies, or practical clinical trials. The AHRQ critical domains for nonrandomized trials (Table 7.1) include comparability of participants, exposure or program/intervention, outcome measures, and statistical analysis.

To address these domains, the American Public Health Association has issued the **TREND** (**T**ransparent **R**eporting of **E**valuations with **N**onrandomized **D**esigns) statement (Des Jarlais, Lyles, & Crepaz, 2004). Example 7.4 is representative of a questionnaire based on the TREND statement that might be used to find out about the presence or absence of certain aspects of each critical domain specified by AHRQ.

Many of the questions used to grade RCTs may also apply to nonrandomized trials and vice versa. For example, questions about the program description and methods of handling missing data apply to both research design categories.

Scoring and Grading: Distinguishing Good From Poor Quality

Reviewers sometimes "score" each article and then, based on the score, assign a grade. Here are three commonly used grading and scoring methods:

1. **Assign a point for each quality criterion that is met, sum the points, and set a cut-off score for high quality.** For instance, the questionnaire in Example 7.2 consists of 23 questions. A scoring system can be set up in which an article must achieve a score of (say) 21 yeses or more in response to the questionnaire if it is to receive a high quality grade. This approach assumes that an article can still be high quality if it fails to meet just one or two criteria.

The Quality of Rating Form (QSRF; Gibbs, 2003) is an example of a scoring system. The system has been designed so that the best effectiveness studies score the highest. The QSRF has 18 items for assessing quality. It asks the rater to evaluate such factors as the clarity of the program's description, whether or not participants are randomly assigned, the extent to which the groups are equal before the program, and if the participants were randomly selected for study inclusion. All terms (such as *randomness* or *equality* of experimental and control group) are defined. Studies that achieve scores close to 100 are the ones considered to have the highest quality.

The Cochrane Collaboration (www.cochrane.org) provides its reviewing handbook and glossary online for free. The handbook contains the most comprehensive scoring system available.

Example 7.4 A Questionnaire to Obtain Information on a Report of a Nonrandomized Trial's Adherence to Critical Quality Domains

Domain Specified by AHRQ	Quality Questions Based on the TREND Statement	Yes	No	NA	Page #s	Comments
Comparability of participants	1. Do the researchers provide data on study group equivalence at baseline? 2. If baseline differences exist, is information given on the statistical methods used to take those differences ("control for") into account?					
Program/Intervention	3. Do the researchers thoroughly describe the experimental programs? 4. Do the researchers provide an adequate explanation of the choice of comparison or control programs? 5. Do the researchers thoroughly describe the comparison programs?					
Outcome measures	6. Are all important outcomes considered? 7. Do the researchers provide information on the size and precision of effects for main outcomes and intermediary or proximal outcomes? 8. Do the researchers summarize all important adverse events or unintended effects?					
Statistical analysis	9. Do the researchers discuss the statistical methods used to compare study groups for the primary outcomes? 10. Do the researchers describe statistical methods for additional analyses such as subgroup analyses and adjusted analyses? 11. Do the researchers describe methods for imputing missing data?					

Some evidence-based practitioners assert that you should use grading systems cautiously. According to them, almost all systems assume that research consists of discrete activities and that poor performance of one or two activities may have little or no bearing on the quality of the remainder. Scientific research is, however, an amalgamated set of activities, and failure to meet high standards in one domain is likely to diminish the validity of all. The grading approach is easy to implement and understand, but it must be used with care.

2. **Weigh one or more criteria more heavily than others**. A reviewer can assume that each article absolutely must attain satisfactory performance on one or several specific criteria to be assigned a high quality score. For instance, reviewers may decide that to receive a high quality grade, a study must (without exception) meet two criteria: (1) describe the procedures for randomization and (2) describe, in both the experimental and comparison groups, the number of participants who withdrew and the reasons they withdrew. If a study meets only one of these two criteria, regardless of which one, the study is downgraded.

3. **Assign all criteria equal weight, and assume that all high quality studies must achieve all criteria, that is, get a perfect score**. This is a very stringent approach to grading, and it may be difficult to enforce especially if good (but not perfect) studies are downgraded or eliminated from consideration.

At present, there is no research comparing the validity of one methodological quality scoring and grading system over the other. The following is a checklist of activities that should occur in applying any system.

Checklist for Scoring and Grading a Study's Methodological Quality

- ✓ Decide on all the factors that are important standards of high quality such as randomization, thorough program descriptions, and appropriate and effectively reported statistical analysis.

- ✓ Select a scoring system (e.g., all study participants must be randomized, all participants must be included in the analysis regardless of whether or not they completed all data collection activities).

- ✓ Define all key terms (e.g., reliable data collection) in advance of the review.

✓ Create a questionnaire or other template for recording the information abstracted from the literature review.

✓ Review 5 to 10 articles to test the reviewing process. If necessary, revise the process. Be sure to anticipate the need for revisions, which can take time and use up resources.

✓ Decide if the reviewers should be "blinded" to the authors' names or institutions. Some experts believe that removing names removes the temptation to favor one's friends or reject one's enemies. The evidence on the value of blinding in reducing such bias is ambiguous.

✓ All reviewers should jointly review 5 to 10 articles. The articles can be the same as those used in the first round. Each article should be discussed among reviewers after it is reviewed. Reviewers must agree on the meaning and answer to each item on the questionnaire. In cases of disagreement, another person not directly involved in the review should adjudicate. This person should understand the objectives of the review and be trained to do literature reviews.

✓ Begin the review in earnest when the reviewers are confident that they are likely to agree on the meaning of all concepts (e.g., what constitutes an "adequate" program description, the definition of validity).

✓ Monitor the quality of the review. Ask reviewers to jointly re-review every fifth or tenth article to ensure that each has been consistent in his or her responses and that the reviewers agree on the responses. Alternatively, ask an uninvolved person—the "gold standard"—to do a review of every fifth or tenth article. If only one reviewer is doing the review, that person should randomly select 3 articles from the first 10 he or she reviewed and review them again one week after the first review. If inconsistencies are found in the joint or individual review, check the definitions of all terms and, if necessary, retrain the reviewers.

Quality, Quantity, and Consistency = Strength of Evidence

The U.S. AHRQ defines the strength of the evidence as a combined index of its *quality, quantity,* and *consistency.* The quality of evidence is a sum of the grading of the individual articles. The quantity of evidence is the magnitude of effects. The consistency of results reflects the extent to which the research findings consist of effects of similar magnitude and direction.

The **U.S. Preventive Services Task Force (USPSTF)** is an independent panel of experts in primary care and prevention that systematically reviews the evidence of effectiveness and develops recommendations for clinical preventive services. The USPSTF is now under the auspices of AHRQ. In making its recommendations, the USPSTF grades by combining assessments of quality, quantity, and consistency of evidence.

The USPSTF's quality grading system is similar to that used by health authorities in Canada and the United Kingdom. Level I, the highest quality, consists of evidence obtained from at least one properly randomized controlled trial. The next level, II, is divided into three parts. Level II–1 is evidence that is obtained from well-designed controlled trials without randomization. Level II–2 consists of evidence obtained from well-designed cohort or case-control analytic studies—preferably from more than one center or research group. And Level II–3 is evidence obtained from multiple time-series studies with or without the intervention. Dramatic results in uncontrolled experiments (such as the results of the introduction of penicillin treatment in the 1940s) can also be regarded as Level II evidence. The weakest evidence is Level III, which consists of opinions of respected authorities, based on their clinical experience; descriptive studies and case reports; and reports of expert committees.

The USPSTF grades its recommendations according to one of five classifications (A, B, C, D, and I) reflecting the strength of evidence and magnitude of net benefit (benefits minus harms). Table 7.2 describes the grading system.

The Center for the Study and Prevention of Violence (CSPV) at the University of Colorado at Boulder (www.colorado.edu/cspv/blue prints) also combines quality and quantity grades in selecting its model "Blueprints" programs. There are five criteria for program selection: (1) evidence of a deterrent effect with a strong research design, (2) sustained effects, (3) multiple site replications, (4) analysis of mediating factors, and (5) cost versus benefits.

Evidence of a deterrent effect with a strong research design is, according to the CSPV, the most important of the selection criteria. The CSPV believes that providing sufficient quantitative data to document effectiveness in preventing or reducing violent behavior requires the use of evaluation designs that provide reasonable confidence in the findings (e.g., experimental designs with random assignment or quasi-experimental designs with matched control groups).

Table 7.2   The U.S. Preventive Services Task Force (USPSTF), Recommendations and
the Strength of the Evidence

A.—The USPSTF strongly recommends that clinicians provide [the service] to eligible patients. *The USPSTF found good evidence that [the service] improves important health outcomes and concludes that benefits substantially outweigh harms.* **Good:** Evidence includes consistent results from well-designed, well-conducted studies in representative populations that directly assess effects on health outcomes.

B.—The USPSTF recommends that clinicians provide [this service] to eligible patients. *The USPSTF found at least fair evidence that [the service] improves important health outcomes and concludes that benefits outweigh harms.* **Fair:** Evidence is sufficient to determine effects on health outcomes, but the strength of the evidence is limited by the number, quality, or consistency of the individual studies; [their] generalizability to routine practice, or [the] indirect nature of the evidence on health outcomes.

C.—The USPSTF makes no recommendation for or against routine provision of [the service]. *The USPSTF found at least fair evidence that [the service] can improve health outcomes but concludes that the balance of benefits and harms is too close to justify a general recommendation.*

D.—The USPSTF recommends against routinely providing [the service] to asymptomatic patients. *The USPSTF found at least fair evidence that [the service] is ineffective or that harms outweigh benefits.*

I.—The USPSTF concludes that the evidence is insufficient to recommend for or against routinely providing [the service]. *Evidence that the [service] is effective is lacking, of poor quality, or conflicting, and the balance of benefits and harms cannot be determined.* **Poor:** Evidence is insufficient to assess the effects on health outcomes because of [the] limited number or power of studies, important flaws in their design or conduct, gaps in the chain of evidence, or lack of information on important health outcomes.

The CSPV also argues that, although one criterion of program effectiveness is that the program demonstrates success by the end of the treatment phase, it is also important to demonstrate that these program effects endure beyond treatment and from one developmental period to the next. Designation as a Blueprints program requires a sustained effect at least one year beyond treatment, with no subsequent evidence that this effect is lost. Further, CSPV believes that replication is an important element in establishing program effectiveness and understanding what works best, in what situations, and with whom. Some programs are successful because of unique characteristics in the original site that may be difficult to duplicate in another site (e.g., having a charismatic leader or extensive community support and involvement). Replication establishes the strength of a program and its prevention effects and demonstrates that it can be successfully implemented in other sites.

Finally in the selection of Blueprints model programs, two additional factors are considered: whether a program conducted an analysis of mediating factors and whether a program is cost-effective. The Blueprints Advisory Board looks for evidence that change in the targeted risk or protective factors mediates the change in violent behavior. They assert that this evidence clearly strengthens the claim that participation in the program is responsible for the change in violent behavior, and it contributes to our theoretical understanding of the causal processes involved. Finally, to be a model program according to CSPV, a program must have reasonable costs, which should be less or no greater than the program's expected benefits. Highly priced programs are difficult to sustain when competition is high and funding resources low. Implementing expensive programs that will, at best, have small effects on violence is counterproductive.

The Promising Practices Network (PPN)—www.promisingpractice .net—is also concerned with quality and strength of the evidence. Usually, the PPN assigns proven program status only after a randomized control trial, although it will accept some quasi-experimental designs. The sample size of the evaluation must exceed 30 in each experimental group, i.e., more than 30 in the treatment group and more than 30 in the comparison group. In addition, the PPN requires evidence of a substantial effect size (at least one outcome is to be changed by at least 20%, 0.25 standard deviations—a measure of the deviation from the mean or average—or more). Finally, a proven program must show at least one outcome with a substantial effect that is statistically significant at the 5% level.

The Centre for Health Evidence also takes into account the quality and strength of the evidence in deciding whether or not to adopt a treatment. According to the Centre, high quality research answers "yes" to all of these questions:

Was the assignment of patients to treatments randomized?

Were all patients who entered the trial properly accounted for at its conclusion?

Was follow-up complete?

Were patients analyzed in the groups to which they were randomized?

Were patients, health workers, and study personnel "blind" to treatment?

Were the groups similar at the start of the trial?

Aside from the experimental intervention, were the groups treated equally? (Centre for Health Evidence, 2007)

The Centre is also concerned with what the results actually were and asks these evaluative questions: How large was the treatment effect? How precise was the estimate of the treatment effect? Finally, the Centre wants to know if the results can be applied to patient care (Centre for Health Evidence, 2007): Were all clinically important outcomes considered? Are the likely treatment benefits worth the potential harms and costs? In other words, is the intervention worth the effort that physician and patient must put into it? For example, suppose research shows that a particular intervention is associated with a 25% reduction in the risk of death. The Centre notes that although this may sound quite impressive, the intervention's impact may nevertheless be minimal.

The impact of a treatment is related not only to its relative risk reduction but also to the risk of the adverse outcome it is designed to prevent. This is where the concept of **number needed to treat** comes in (Chapter 1). The number needed to treat or NNT is the number of patients who need to be treated to achieve one additional favorable outcome. The Centre notes that, before deciding on an intervention, practitioners must consider the patients' risk of the adverse event if left untreated. For relative risk reduction (the proportional reduction in rates of bad outcomes between experimental and control participants), the higher the probability that a patient will experience an adverse outcome if we don't treat, the more likely the patient will benefit from treatment, and the fewer the number of patients needed to treat to prevent one event. Thus, both patients and clinical efficiency benefit when the number needed to treat to prevent an event is low. Physicians and other health care providers might not hesitate to treat even as many as 400 patients to save one life if the treatment was cheap, easy to apply and comply with, and safe. In reality, however, many treatments are expensive, and many carry risks.

The Evidence Makes the Grade: Time for Abstraction _____

The reviewer has been concentrating on whether or not research evidence makes the grade. In the cases where it does, the review can move to the next step: reading the articles and reports and extracting information from them. This is called the abstraction process. Figure 7.3 shows where abstraction fits into the literature review.

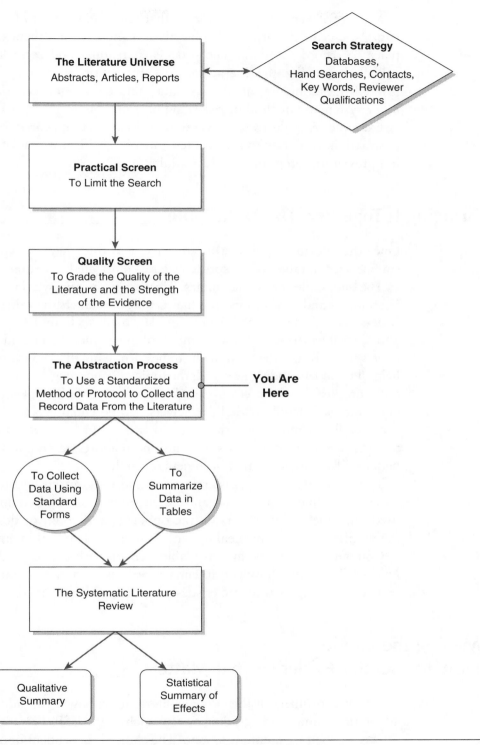

Figure 7.3   Abstracting Information From the Research Literature

Most reviewers rely on a "form" that tells them what to look for (e.g., "Describe the program's objectives") and provides them with a place to record the data. The process of reading and recording is called **abstracting** the literature. An abstraction form may be a printed questionnaire, an Access data table or spreadsheet, or any other systematic method of recording information.

Example 7.5 illustrates several questions that appeared on an abstraction form used to review literature on the effectiveness of alcohol prevention programs in older adults.

Bringing It Together: The Data Table

Once the information is abstracted onto the forms, they are typically summarized in tables or on spreadsheets as illustrated in Example 7.6.

The data tables are visual guides. They assist the reviewer in reporting findings and conclusions, and they enable consumers to evaluate the reviewer's logic. Data Table 1 in Example 7.6 allows both the reviewer and consumer to count the number of men and women in each reviewed study and the total in all studies. Knowing the total sample is helpful in understanding how well the topic of counseling programs for older drinkers has been covered and in evaluating the size of the program's impact. Similarly, both reviewers and potential program users can visually examine the variables addressed by the literature in order to determine if the ones of interest have been addressed and, if not, to better understand areas that need new research.

The data tables also assist reviewers and users in visualizing the outcomes. Some reviewers organize their findings around commonly used outcomes, while others do the opposite, and count or describe the number of programs dealing with outcomes of special interest.

Computer programs are available for preparing and updating reviews. They will allow you to enter protocols (and even a complete review) including text, characteristics of studies, and comparison tables.

Making the Grade:
How to Identify Evidence That Matters

Research consumers in their role as literature reviewer can adopt or adapt an existing study grading system such as the USPSTF's, or they can create their own unique system. The choice is dependent upon the reviewers' resources, the pertinence of the existing literature to decision makers' needs, and the quality of the literature.

Example 7.5   Sample Excerpts From a Literature Review Abstraction
Form

The Study Participants

Describe the eligible sample by placing the number and percentage in each
of the appropriate spots.

	65 Years of Age to 74 Years (n =)	75 Years of Age and Older (n =)
Men		
Women		

Describe the participating sample.

	65 Years of Age to 74 Years (n =)	75 Years of Age and Older (n =)
Men		
Women		

Are reasons given for incomplete or no data on eligible participants?

(Circle all that apply)

No   1 (Go to next question)
Yes   2

IF YES, what are they?

Incorrect address   1
Medical problems, specify:_____ 2
Failure to show for an appointment   3
Other, specify:_____ 4

Study Setting

From which settings are the study's participants drawn? (Circle all that
apply)

Retirement communities   1
General community   2
Community health centers   3
Senior centers   4
Medical clinics   5
Veterans Administration   6
Other, specify:_____ 7

Data Collection

Which of the following variables are explored in the study? (Circle all that
apply)

(Continued)

Example 7.5 (Continued)

Use of medicine (Check all that apply)

antihypertensives	1
antipsychotics	2
antidepressants	3
nonsteroidal anti-inflammatory (NSAIDs)	4
aspirin	5
barbiturates	6
Other, specify:_____	7
Quantity and frequency of alcohol consumption	8
Medical conditions or problems	9
Social functioning	10
Mental/psychological functioning	11
Physical functioning	12
Other, specify:_____	13

Outcomes

How large was the effect? (Write in results.)

Risk (need for services) before program participation (Baseline risk): X	
Risk with therapy: Y	
Absolute Risk Reduction (Risk Difference): X − Y	
Relative Risk: Y/X	
Relative Risk Reduction (RRR): [1 − Y/X] x 100 or [(X − Y) / X] x 100	
95% Confidence Interval (CI) for the RRR	

Funding

Who funded this study? (Circle all that apply)

Federal government	1
State government	2
Local government	3
National foundation	4
State or local foundation	5
University	6
Health care agency. If yes,	7
Public	8
Private	9
Other, specify:_____	10

Example 7.6 Sample Literature Review Data Table Format

Data Table 1. Alcohol and the Elderly: A Review of Counseling Programs

Study ID	Sample[1]				Reasons Data Are Incomplete	Settings	Medication Variables	Other Variables
	Men 65 to 74 years	Men 75+	Women 65 to 74 years	Women 75+				
001								
002								
003								
004								
Etc.								

1. Record numbers and (%)

Data Table 2. Interventions for Fathers With Infants or Toddlers

Study	Outcomes	Measures	Time Since Intervention	Finding (statistically significant unless indicated otherwise)	Quality Rating	Comments
Randomized control studies (n = 7)						
Belsky, 1985	Mother–child interaction	O; unnamed	1, 3, and 9 months	NS change in either maternal involvement or infant behavior	Moderate	

SOURCE: Magill-Evans, Harrison, Rempel, and Slater (2006).

(Continued)

Example 7.6 (Continued)

Data Table 3.   Describing the Phenomenon of "Palliative Sedation at the End of Life" From a Nursing Perspective

Authors, Publication Year, Country	Aim of Study	Design	Data Collection Method, Analysis Method	Participants (dropout rate)	Results	Quality (type of study)
Chater et al., 1998, Canada	To propose a definition for "terminal sedation," to estimate the frequency of this practice and the reasons for its use, to identify the drugs and dosages used, to determine the outcome, and to explore the decision-making process.	Quantitative	Questionnaires, descriptive statistics	61 (0)	89% agree that terminal sedation is sometimes necessary. The reasons for using it were both physical and psychological. The use of palliative sedation was regarded as successful in 90% of the cases.	II (P)

SOURCE: Engström, Bruno, Holm, and Hellzén (2006).

NOTE: Tables 2 and 3 are much longer in actuality. Some literature review data tables are 50 pages long (printed). Table length depends upon the amount of information abstracted and the number of articles that are reviewed.

Resources

Literature reviews are extremely costly and time consuming. Among the costs are those associated with training the reviewers, doing the review, and monitoring the quality of the review. It takes time and expertise to identify an entire body of literature. A search strategy must be developed and tested. Sometimes, search strategies are revised several times, and multiple databases and other sources need to be checked with each search strategy. Once articles are identified, their methods may need additional verification. For instance, it is not uncommon for reviewers to check the original sources of a measure used in an evaluation to make certain it has been tested within a population that is pertinent to decision makers and that the results are convincing. Reviewers can find themselves spending hours completing literature review questionnaires that call for detailed explanations of statistical methods, effect sizes, results, and conclusions.

Decision-Making Needs

The choice of which parameters to include in a review depends on their pertinence to the decision makers and clients who are to use the results. Some decision makers, for instance, may be concerned with explicit details on the program's objectives and implementation while others may focus on the research design and whether differences in baseline characteristics were identified and how these were handled. Because of conflicting values and expectations among clients, research consumers should consider involving clients in the selection of factors for the review by using focus groups, Delphi techniques, and other participatory methods. (See Chapter 8.)

Quality of the Literature

The literature varies in quality from discipline to discipline. Evidence on ultimate outcomes is unavailable in some fields, so consumers will have little choice but to expect studies that focus on proximal outcomes. The Promising Practices Network (PPN), for example, aims to improve outcomes for children. The organization will recommend a program as "promising" (as opposed to "proven") if it has an effect on proximal outcomes and if evidence suggests that it is associated with one of the PPN outcome indicators (e.g., youths not using alcohol, tobacco, or illegal drugs).

The research consumer should be aware of the possibility that, in actual practice, the link between proximal and ultimate outcomes may not pan out. Remember the diabetic education study (Sanchez, Newby, McGuire, et al., 2005) that aimed to improve blood sugar control, cholesterol levels, weight management, or mortality rates? In that study, the researchers found that, for diabetics, improved disease knowledge (proximal outcome) did not translate into improvements (ultimate outcomes). A focus on proximal outcomes may limit the study's overall ability to produce evidence that matters.

Research Limitations

Almost every study contains flaws that may limit its findings' validity. The flaws are due to methodological weaknesses and to deliberate selection or exclusion of types of study participants, settings, or outcomes. Researchers are ethically obligated to discuss their study's limitations, even though consumers are ultimately responsible for uncovering all limitations and evaluating how critical the limitations are. Critical limitations can turn valid evidence into evidence that does not matter. For instance, suppose the study excludes people whose characteristics (e.g., age, ethnicity, or language ability) mimic those of your target group. Then, the study's conclusions are unlikely to matter even if it is methodologically sound and deals with a relevant topic.

Discussions of study limitations are typically found at the conclusion of a report or article as illustrated in Example 7.7.

 CAUTION: Expect researchers to describe their study's limitations in detail. Study limitations can be due to methodological flaws, or they can be intentionally imposed by including or excluding populations or focusing on specific outcomes. After research consumers identify the limitations, they must next decide on the strength and importance of these limitations.

Reliable and Valid Reviews

A reliable review is one that consistently provides the same information about methods and content for every study reviewed, whether the review is conducted by one person (reliable "within") or by several reviewers (reliable "across"). A valid review is an accurate one.

Large literature reviews nearly always have more than one reviewer, and small ones should aim for at least two. The idea is that each reviewer examines each evaluation, and the results of the

Example 7.7 A Mental Health Intervention for Schoolchildren Exposed to Violence: Limits on Findings as Described in the Evaluation Report

The CBITS intervention was not compared with a control condition such as general supportive therapy, but rather with a wait-list delayed intervention. As a consequence, none of the informants (students, parents, or teachers) were blinded to the treatment condition. It is possible that the lack of blinding may have contaminated either the intervention or assessments. School staff and parents may have provided more attention and support to students who were eligible for the program while they were on a waiting list; alternatively, respondents may have been more likely to report improvement in symptoms for those students whom they knew had received the intervention. Using blinded evaluators is an important step for the future, to provide an objective rating of outcomes.

Future research comparing CBITS with an alternative intervention, such as generic support and attention, also would be an important next step, in part to reduce biases among respondents and also to control for the attention that children receive by being part of the program. However, such designs are often difficult to implement in school settings, where there is a push to provide the same program to all students and randomization to a placebo can be seen as insensitive to the needs of students and families. Further research is also needed to determine if our findings would be replicated in nonurban and non-Latino populations and to examine the intervention's effectiveness in alternative settings treating large numbers of children, such as pediatric clinics, adolescent medicine clinics, and community mental health centers.

Comment:
The authors discuss at least three limitations resulting from their study.

1. Failure to blind any of the participants
   "The CBITS intervention was not compared with a control condition such as general supportive therapy, but rather with a wait-list delayed intervention. As a consequence, none of the informants (students, parents, or teachers) were blinded to the treatment condition. It is possible that the lack of blinding may have contaminated either the intervention or assessments."

2. Need to compare the intervention with a suitable alternative
   "Future research comparing CBITS with an alternative intervention, such as generic support and attention, also would be an important next step, in part to reduce biases among respondents."

3. Limits on generalizability because the study population was restricted to an urban Latino population
   "Further research is also needed to determine if our findings would be replicated in nonurban and non-Latino populations and to examine the intervention's effectiveness in alternative settings treating large numbers of children, such as pediatric clinics, adolescent medicine clinics, and community mental health centers."

SOURCE: Stein, Jaycox, Kataoka, et al. (2003).

examinations are compared. Perfect agreement between (or among) reviewers means perfect inter-rater reliability. You came across this concept when we discussed measurement reliability (Chapter 6).

Sometimes, to promote objectivity, one or more of the reviewers are not told the names of the authors of the study, the name of the publication, or when or where the study took place; they are "blinded." In relatively smaller reviews (reviews with scant resources and just one reviewer), objectivity can be improved by having the single reviewer re-review a randomly selected sample of studies. Perfect agreement from the first to the second review is considered perfect intra-rater reliability.

Measuring Review Reliability: The Kappa Statistic

Suppose two reviewers are asked to evaluate independently the quality of 100 studies on the effectiveness of prenatal care programs in preventing low weight births. Each reviewer is asked, "Do the study's authors include low-risk as well as high-risk women in their analysis?" Here are the reviewers' answers to this question.

	Reviewer 2		
Reviewer 1	*No*	*Yes*	
No	20[C]	15	35[B]
Yes	10	55[D]	65
	30[A]	70	

Reviewer 2 says that 30 ([A]) of the studies fail to collect prospective data, while Reviewer 1 says that 35 ([B]) fail to do so. The two reviewers agree that 20 ([C]) studies (out of the 30 and 35 each picked) do not collect prospective data.

What is the best way to describe the extent of agreement between the reviewers? A 20% ([C]) agreement is probably too low; the reviewers also agree that 55% ([D]) of studies include low-risk women. The total agreement arrived at through this calculation—55% + 20%—is an overestimate because, with only two categories (yes and no), some agreement may occur by chance.

The measuring of agreement between two reviewers is called *kappa*, defined as the agreement beyond chance divided by the amount of agreement possible beyond chance. This is shown in the following formula in which O is the observed agreement and C is the chance agreement.

$$\kappa = \frac{O - C}{1 - C} \quad \begin{array}{l}\text{(Agreement beyond chance)}\\\text{(Agreement possible beyond chance)}\end{array}$$

Here is how the formula works with the above example.

1. Calculate how many studies the reviewers may agree by chance DO NOT collect prospective data. This is done by multiplying the number of no answers and dividing by 100 because there are 100 studies: 30 x 35/100 = 10.5

2. Calculate how many studies they may agree by chance DO collect prospective data by multiplying the number of studies each found collected prospective data. This is done by multiplying the number of yes answers and dividing by 100: 70 x 65/100 = 40.5.

3. Add the two numbers obtained in Question 1 and 2 and divide by 100 to get a proportion for **chance agreement**: (10.5 + 45.5)/100 = 0.56.

The **observed agreement** is 20% + 55% = 75% or 0.75. Therefore, the **agreement beyond chance** is 0.75 – 0.56 = 0.19: the numerator.

The **agreement possible beyond chance** is 100% minus the chance agreement of 56% or 1 – 0.56 = 0.44: the denominator.

$$\kappa = \frac{0.19}{0.44}$$

$$\kappa = 0.43$$

As with other measurements of reliability, a kappa of 0.0–0.2 = slight; 0.2–0.4 = fair; 0.4–0.6 = moderate; 0.6–0.8 = substantial, and 0.8–0.10 = almost perfect. In a literature review, you should aim for a kappa of 0.6 to 1.0.

How do you achieve substantial or almost perfect agreement—reliability—among reviewers? You do this by making certain that all reviewers collect and record data on exactly the same topics and that they agree in advance on what each important variable means. The "fair" kappa of 0.43 obtained by the reviewers above can be due to differences between the reviewers' definitions of high- and low-risk women or between the reviewers' and researchers' definitions.

Reviewing Other Reviews:
Narrative Reviews and Systematic Reviews

Until now, we have been discussing how to find relevant articles and evaluate their quality and appropriateness. As a research consumer, however, you may find that others have beaten you to it—have already produced a literature review on the topic of interest. These good people appear to have done all the work for you by searching the literature, identifying several pertinent articles, and summarizing the results. However, research consumers who find an existing review must evaluate the quality and timeliness of these reviews before accepting that their findings constitute evidence that matters. To evaluate the quality means first determining the type of review you are dealing with.

Reviews of the literature are either systematic or narrative. A systematic review follows a detailed set of procedures or a **protocol** that includes a focused study question (remember PICO in Chapter 2?); a specific search strategy (that defines the search terms and databases that are used as well as the criteria for including and excluding studies); and specific instructions on the types of data to be abstracted on study objectives, methods, findings, and quality.

Narrative reviews often do not have a specific protocol. For example, they rarely describe their search strategy or inclusion and exclusion criteria. Such reviews may be subject to selection bias because the reviewer may include or exclude studies at will. Narrative reviews do not apply quality standards, so they may contain studies of unknown or varying reliability and validity. The credibility of a narrative review is almost entirely dependent upon the reviewer's credibility.

Systematic literature reviews take two forms (Figure 7.4). The first produces **qualitative summaries** of the literature based on trends the review finds across the initially reviewed studies. In some fields (e.g., nursing) this review is called meta-synthesis. The second form of literature review uses statistical methods to produce a quantitative summary of the program effects that were presented in the initial reviews. It is called **meta-analysis**.

Example 7.8 contains descriptions of systematic literature reviews whose results are qualitative: No attempt is made to combine the studies statistically. Note in the "Methods" section, the investigators record that they searched more than one database and reviewed multiple articles. In the review of studies about children who have been exposed to intimate partner violence, for example, the researchers searched four databases and reviewed 94 articles. The review of research on mothers who murder also used four databases and summarized 39 articles.

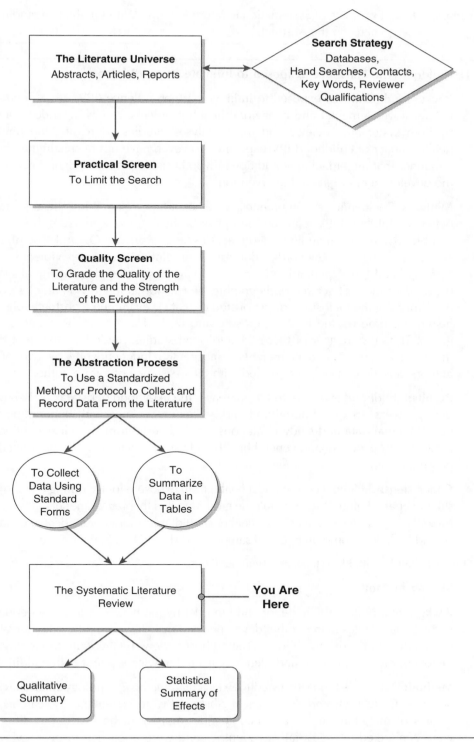

Figure 7.4   Systematic Reviews With Qualitative Summaries

Example 7.8 Examples of Systematic Literature Reviews With Qualitative Findings: Focus on the Abstracts

---

1. Children Who Have Been Exposed to Intimate Partner Violence

Background: Children exposed to intimate partner violence (IPV) are at increased risk for adverse mental and behavioral health problems, as has been documented by both systematic reviews and meta-analyses. Studies addressing the physical health impact of childhood IPV exposure, however, have not been summarized in a manner that might facilitate additional hypothesis-driven research and accelerate the development of targeted interventions.

Methods: To identify a comprehensive set of articles examining the association between childhood IPV exposure and physical health, we searched online bibliographic databases including Medline, CINAHL, PsychINFO, and Sociological Abstracts using the keywords "domestic" or "intimate partner violence" and "infant," "child," or "pediatric." From >2,000 articles retrieved in the initial search, we used online abstract and bibliographic information to identify 94 articles potentially meeting the inclusion criteria of studies that (1) examined a postnatal physical health outcome related to IPV exposure and (2) had a contemporaneous control group. Thorough review of these 94 published studies yielded 22 that met these inclusion criteria. The data then were abstracted independently by two of the authors, and differences were settled with the assistance of a third author.

Results: Childhood exposure to IPV increases the likelihood of risk-taking behaviors during adolescence and adulthood and is likely associated with underimmunization. Minimal data and study limitations preclude establishing a clear connection between IPV exposure and general health and use of health services, breastfeeding, or weight gain.

Conclusions: The impact on physical health from exposure to IPV during childhood is still uncertain. Future studies should be grounded in a theoretical model that specifies how IPV exposure can affect child health, should adjust for confounders adequately, should include a community-based sample, and should be of larger scale.

SOURCE: Bair-Merritt, Blackstone, and Feudtner (2006).

2. Murder by Mothers

Background: Maternal filicide, or child murder by mothers, occurs more frequently in the United States than in other developed nations. However, little is known about factors that confer risk to children. The authors review the literature to identify predictors of maternal filicide and identify gaps in knowledge about maternal filicide.

Method: Databases [PubMed (Medline), PsychINFO, the Psychology and Behavioral Sciences Collection, and Sociological Abstracts] were systematically searched for studies of maternal filicide and neonaticide (murder in the first day of life) that were conducted in industrialized countries and were published in peer-reviewed,

English-language publications after 1980. Search terms included "filicide," "infanticide," "neonaticide," and "fatal child maltreatment." The database search yielded more than 250 references in the extant literature. The majority consisted of case reports, reports on a series of filicide cases, and conceptual theoretical papers, and these publications were excluded. Eighty-three studies of child homicide were identified. Forty-two of these 83 studies reported on child homicide but did not distinguish maternal filicide from paternal filicide or murder by a stepparent or a nonparent. Those studies were not included in our analysis because they did not yield specific information about maternal perpetrators. Two studies of maternal filicide were excluded because they presented data that were primarily historical (dating to 1850 or the early 1900s) and did not separately consider more recent data. After exclusions, there remained 39 studies that were appropriate for use in our analysis.

Results: Women who committed filicide varied greatly by the type of sample studied. Neonaticide was often committed by young, poor, unmarried women with little or no prenatal care.

Conclusions: The results of the review suggest that little is known about the predictors of maternal filicide and that a systematic, focused program of research on reliable markers for maternal filicide is needed to better prevent these events.

SOURCE: Friedman, Horwitz, and Resnick (2005).

 CAUTION: A good systematic literature review that is out of date will still result in faulty findings. Consumers should check the literature for new or contradictory information when they are using reviews that are one year old or more.

Systematic Reviews: Meta-Analysis

A meta-analysis is a systematic review of the literature that uses formal statistical techniques to sum up the results of separate studies on the same topic. The idea is that the larger numbers obtained by combining study findings provide greater statistical power than any of the individual studies do.

Effect Size

The concept of effect size is central to meta-analysis. An effect is the extent to which an outcome is present in the population, and it is a crucial component of sample size selection. Learning about effect and sample size means taking a lesson in statistical terminology and understanding two ideas taken from statistics:

1. To find an effect, you need the appropriate sample size.

2. If the outcome of a study is continuous (e.g., a score from 1 to 100; blood pressure measurements) then the effect size is defined as the difference in means or average scores between the intervention and control groups divided by the standard deviation of the control or of both groups.

Effect sizes can be based on proportions, if the outcome is nominal, or on correlations, if the outcome is an association. Effect sizes can also be expressed as differences between **odds ratios** or **relative risks.**

Although research consumers do not have to actually select samples or determine effect sizes, to be an informed practitioner, you will want to stay tuned to the following discussion.

How Many People and What Effect?

The likelihood that an evaluation will be able to uncover an association between program participation and a good outcome—an **effect**—depends on the actual magnitude of that association in the target population.

Effect Size and Sample Size

Remember target populations? These are the people who are supposed to benefit from a program, even though only a sample of them actually participates in it. For example, suppose a program aims to prevent child neglect (the outcome or desired effect) on the part of young parents who have a history of neglect (the target) by providing them with parental coping skills (the program). Suppose also that the evaluators cannot enlist all young parents with histories of neglect in their study because there are too many and some live far from the research site. Moreover, good statistical practice says that not every member of a population needs to participate anyway if a representative subgroup is carefully selected. In response, the evaluators set specific eligibility criteria for participation. In their case, the evaluation sample consists of parents 21 years of age and under who have a previous history of child neglect and who attend any one of the city's prenatal care clinics.

Ideally, the evaluators of the parental coping program would like to see an effect (prevention of child neglect) that is clearly linked to participation in the program (which aims to provide parental coping skills). Previous research shows that, if the effect in the target population is large, it is easier to uncover in a smaller sample than a smaller effect. In fact, the smaller the effect, the larger the sample needs to be in order to detect it. Unfortunately, the evaluator has no way of knowing the size of the association in the target population. In fact, one of the jobs of the study is to find that out. Without that advance knowledge, the evaluator is forced to figure out how large an association he or she would *like* to find or that *is meaningful* (or both). That quantity—the size of the association—is known as the **effect size**.

Expert evaluators do not just come up with uninformed effect sizes. They find data from prior studies in related areas to make estimates. Sometimes, these are confirmed with experts who can help decide the clinical relevance of hoped-for effect sizes. When programs are designed to influence large numbers of people, small differences (e.g., 5 points on a standardized test of reading) might be important, especially if they are relatively easy to achieve. The choice of effect size is always somewhat arbitrary, however, with feasibility always uppermost in the researcher's mind. Sometimes, when the number of available participants is limited, evaluators will work backward and ask this question: If I have this many participants, what is the effect size I can hope to see?

The evaluator uses statistical techniques to determine how large a sample is needed to uncover the hoped-for effect. If the sample for the evaluation is too small, a true difference in effect may be missed. This is a serious error. Unfortunately, it is not an uncommon one. You will find many evaluations in which neither the sample nor effect size is justified.

The determination of sample size is also referred to as **power analysis** because the number of persons in the study determines (to some degree) the power the evaluator has to detect an effect or a true difference in experimental and control groups.

Experts in research design and sampling encourage researchers to choose one primary outcome on which to base sample size calculations. They are also enjoined to anticipate attrition by planning to recruit a larger number than needed to obtain a full sample. Sample size calculators can be found on the Web.

Effect Size, Odds and Risks

Risks and **odds** are alternative methods for describing the likelihood that a particular effect will or will not take place, but they do so in different ways. For example, suppose that, for every 100 persons who have headaches, 20 people have headaches that can be described as severe. The *risk* of a severe headache is 20/100 or 0.20. The *odds* of having severe headaches is calculated by comparing the number of persons with severe headaches (20) against the number without (100 − 20 or 80) or 20 / 80 = 0.25. The difference between risks and odds is shown in the table below.

Odds and Risks: Compare and Contrast

Number of Persons With Outcome	Risk	Odds
20 of 100	20/100 = 0.20	20:80 = 0.25
40 of 100	40/100 = 0.40	40:60 = 0.66
50 of 100	50/100 = 0.50	50:50 = 1.00
90 of 100	90/100 = 0.90	90:10 = 9.00

Because risks and odds are really just different ways of talking about the same relationship, one can be derived from the other. Risk converts to odds by dividing it by 1 minus the risk, and odds can be converted to risk by dividing odds by odds plus 1.

$$Odds = (Risk)/(1 - Risk)$$

$$Risk = (Odds)/(1 + Odds)$$

When an outcome is infrequent, little difference exists in numerical values between odds and risks. When the outcome is frequent, however, differences emerge. If, for instance, 20 of 100 persons have headaches, the risks and odds are similar: 0.20 and 0.25, respectively. If 90 of 100 persons have headaches, then the risks are 0.90 and the odds are 9.00.

Both risks and odds are used to describe the likelihood that a particular outcome will occur within a group (e.g., the group with or the group without headaches). But risks and odds can also be used in comparing groups (e.g., the experimental and control groups). When they are, you are comparing the *relative* likelihood that an outcome will take place. The **relative risk** expresses the risk of a particular outcome in the experimental group relative to the risk of the outcome in the control group. The odds ratio is a description of the comparison of the odds of the outcome in the experimental group with the odds in the control group.

The relative risk and the odds ratio will be less than 1 when an outcome occurs less frequently in the experimental than in the control group. Similarly, both will be greater than 1 if the outcome occurs more frequently in the experimental than in the control group. The direction of the relative risk and odds ratio (less than or greater than 1) is always the same. The extent to which the odds ratio and relative risk deviate from one another can be quite different.

But what significance do measurements of risk or odds have for meta-analysis? These measurements are crucial in any systematic, quantitative review because it is the effect sizes that are combined statistically in meta-analysis, and these are sometimes expressed as relative risk or an odds ratio. Suppose you do a literature review to find out the effect of a low-fat diet on your blood pressure. Typically, an effect size that expresses the magnitude and direction of the results would be calculated for each study in the review. For example, a positive effect of fish oil might be expressed as the difference in mean blood pressure levels between a group given a low-fat diet and a group not on a low-fat diet (possibly divided by a within-group standard deviation). A positive sign can be given if the low-fat diet group has lower post intervention blood pressure and a negative sign given when the opposite is true. As a second example, think of a group of studies examining whether attitude toward reading is associated with age. The effect size can be the correlation between age and satisfaction (as a component of the concept of "attitude"), with positive correlations indicating that older students are more satisfied than younger. In this example, the effect size is an expression of the degree of relationship between two variables.

There are many ways to define the average or typical effect size. Among the most commonly reported is the weighted mean, where weighting is by the size of the study. The idea is that effect sizes based on larger studies have more stability and should be weighted more heavily than the more variable effect sizes based on smaller studies. But this may be misleading. Suppose, for example, interventions in larger studies were intrinsically weaker and had less of an impact than the more intensive interventions that might be possible in smaller studies; the average effect size weighted by study size would be systematically biased toward the weaker interventions and could lead to a pessimistic conclusion. Because of this, many meta-analytic practitioners urge the reporting of both weighted and unweighted average effect sizes.

A Checklist of Seven Questions to Guide in Evaluating the Quality of a Meta-Analysis

A meta-analysis is an observational study in which the "participants" are research articles and not people. As a research consumer, you need to be able to evaluate the quality of a synthesis of research just as you must when you review a single study. The following are seven questions to use in the evaluation.

Checklist of Seven Questions for Evaluating the Quality of a Meta-Analysis

✓ **Question 1:** Are the objectives of the meta-analysis unambiguous?

The objectives are the purposes for doing the analysis. Meta-analyses have been done about subjects as diverse as school-based smoking prevention programs, adolescent gambling disorders, consumer choice and subliminal advertising, cesarean childbirth and psychosocial outcomes, and the effectiveness of intravenous streptokinase during acute myocardial infarction and of the use of electroshock in the treatment of depression. But just listing a topic is not the same as describing how the literature will be used to learn more about the topic.

Example 7.9 illustrates the statement of unambiguous meta-analysis objectives.

✓ **Question 2:** Are the inclusion and exclusion criteria explicit?

Very conservative meta-analysis practitioners assert that only true experiments or randomized trials are eligible to be included in a systematic review. More liberal practitioners will accept all "high" quality studies. They often group them by study design characteristics, such as random or nonrandom assignment, in order to estimate if differences exist between the findings of higher and lower quality studies. The technique used to conduct separate analyses of studies of different quality is called **sensitivity analysis**. As a consumer, you should check that the meta-analyst specifies and justifies quality criteria and that high quality studies are not analyzed together with studies of lower quality.

Example 7.9   Unambiguous Meta-Analysis Objectives

Objective 1: To examine the association between birth spacing and relative risk of adverse perinatal outcomes, we performed a systematic review, including meta-analysis, of the relationship between birth spacing and the risk of adverse perinatal outcomes that provided an overall summary of the effect measure and determined both the riskiest and the optimal interpregnancy intervals. In addition, we determined whether estimates of the effect size depend on dimensions of study quality of the primary studies.

Comment: This statement is unambiguous because it tells the research consumer exactly what to expect from the analysis. For instance, the consumer can expect to obtain information on

> Birth spacing and relative risk of adverse perinatal outcomes
>
> An overall summary of the effect
>
> The riskiest and optimal intervals between pregnancies
>
> Estimates of whether the effect size depends on study quality

Objective 2: A key prevention strategy is improved screening of depressed patients by primary care physicians and better treatment of major depression. This review considers what is known about this and other prevention strategies to permit integration into a comprehensive prevention strategy.

Comment: This analysis will provide information on what is known about improved screening for depression and other prevention strategies.

Objective 3: The purpose of this article is to conduct a meta-analysis on the facilitative effects of offering young children the opportunity to draw as part of an interview process and to determine if sufficient evidence exists to include drawings in research and clinical protocols and practice as a method of facilitating communication with children.

Comment: This analysis will provide information on what is known about offering children the opportunity to draw when interviewing them and if the strength of the evidence is sufficient to include drawing as part of clinical protocol and practice.

✓ **Question 3:** Are the search strategies described in detail?

Electronic and manual literature searches that are supplemented by consultation with experts in the field are the order of the day for all literature reviews. In meta-analyses, it may be important to make certain that data are included from ongoing studies that have not yet been published. If they are not, the analysis may fall victim to **publication bias,** a term used to mean that a review unfairly favors the results of published studies. Published studies may differ from unpublished in that they tend to have positive findings; negative findings or findings of no difference between groups do not get published as frequently (in the English-language literature). The general rule in estimating the extent of the bias is to consider that, if the available data uncovered by the review are from high quality studies and are reasonably consistent in direction, then the number of opposite findings will have to be extremely large to overturn the results.

A number of statistical techniques are available to help deal with publication bias. Formulas are available that you can use to estimate the number of published studies showing no differences between programs that are needed to convert a statistically significant pooled difference into an insignificant difference. If the number of unpublished studies needed to overturn your findings is small relative to the number of published studies pooled in the meta-analysis, then you should be concerned about potential publication bias.

Other methods include estimating the size of the population from which each study group is drawn. Using this information and the study's sample size, potential publication bias can be calculated for individual studies. Software is available for investigating publication bias by graphically displaying sample size plotted against effect size. Some researchers suggest that this graphic display (which is called a funnel plot) should always be examined as part of a meta-analysis, if a sufficient number of studies are available.

✓ **Question 4:** Is a standardized protocol used to screen the literature?

Usually, two or more reviewers determine the quality of each study in the total number of potential studies to be included in the review. To ensure a consistent review, researchers should prepare a screening protocol. This means that each study is reviewed in a uniform manner.

✓ **Question 5:** Is a standardized protocol or abstraction form used to collect data?

Once studies are selected, they are reviewed and information is abstracted. The best meta-analyses describe the coding of information. Information may, for example, be coded by type of intervention, sample size, setting, age of participants, or any number of factors.

As with the screening process, valid data collection often requires at least two reviewers using a standard protocol.

Check to see who conducted the review, if they were trained, and how disputes were handled.

✓ **Question 6:** Do the authors fully explain their method of combining or "pooling" results?

An underlying assumption of one of the most commonly used meta-analytic approaches is that the reason you can **pool** (merge) individual study results to produce a summary measure is that all study results are homogeneous in that they reflect the same "true" effect. Differences, if you find any, are due to chance alone (sampling error). If the assumption is correct, then when the results are combined, any random errors will be canceled out and one meta-study will be produced. A meta-study—a merging of many studies—is presumed to be better than just one.

In large meta-analyses, you can expect disagreement in results among studies. Sometimes the differences may be due just to chance. But not always. Other factors, such as variations in study settings or the age or socioeconomic status of the participants, may be the culprits. Rather than being **homogenous** (with any observed variations due to chance) studies may be **heterogeneous** (with observed variations due to initial differences in design, setting, or sample).

In reviewing the results of a meta-analysis that assumes that study results are homogeneous, check to see if the authors systematically examine their assumption of homogeneity or compatibility of the study results. Investigations of homogeneity may be done graphically or statistically or both ways. It is generally considered good practice for a meta-analysis to examine sources of variation based on theoretical or other empirical considerations regardless of the outcomes of the homogeneity tests. These tests alert the investigator to the likelihood that differences in effect size may be due to influences on the intervention that vary from study to study. Thus, a significant test result for homogeneity obligates the meta-analyst to search for variations in study settings or participants' characteristics; a nonsignificant test does not preclude the search.

✓ *Meta-Analysis Illustrated*

One method of describing the results of a meta-analysis is by plotting the results on a graph, as shown below in Figure 7.5. The objective of the meta-analysis in Figure 7.5 was to estimate the effects of international adoption on behavioral problems and mental health referrals. The investigators used a statistical technique called Cohen's criteria represented by *d* to describe the difference between international adoptees and nonadopted controls.

Finally, international adoptees were overrepresented in mental health referrals (*d*, 0.37; Figure 7.5) and this effect size was medium. According to Cohen's criteria, *d*s of <0.20 are considered small effects; *d*s of about 0.50, moderate effects; and *d*s of about 0.80, large effects.

Fixed Versus Random Effects. In reviewing meta-analyses, critics often focus on the reviewers' choice of one or two models called **fixed effects** versus **random effects**. The fixed effects model assumes that all experiments are similar in that they share the same underlying treatment effect. Thus, the observed differences in their results are considered to be due to chance alone (sampling error within each study).

The random effects model incorporates the potential heterogeneity of the treatment effect among different studies by assuming that each study estimates a unique treatment effect that, even given a large amount of data, might still differ from the effect in another study. Compared with the fixed effects model, the random effects model weights smaller studies more heavily in its pooled estimate of treatment effect. The fixed effects and random effects models are equivalent when there is no heterogeneity of the treatment effect among different studies.

Cumulative Meta-Analysis. A **cumulative meta-analysis** is a technique that permits the identification of the year when the combined results of many studies (almost always randomized controlled trials or true experiments) first achieve a given level of statistical significance. The technique also reveals whether the temporal trend seems to be toward superiority of one intervention or another or whether little difference in treatment effect can be expected, which allows investigators to

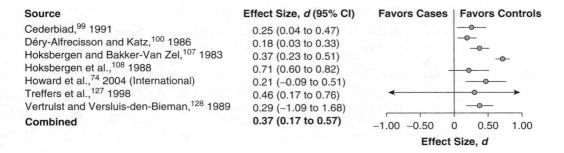

Source	Effect Size, d (95% CI)	Favors Cases	Favors Controls
Cederbiad,[99] 1991	0.25 (0.04 to 0.47)		
Déry-Alfrecisson and Katz,[100] 1986	0.18 (0.03 to 0.33)		
Hoksbergen and Bakker-Van Zel,[107] 1983	0.37 (0.23 to 0.51)		
Hoksbergen et al.,[108] 1988	0.71 (0.60 to 0.82)		
Howard et al.,[74] 2004 (International)	0.21 (−0.09 to 0.51)		
Treffers et al.,[127] 1998	0.46 (0.17 to 0.76)		
Vertrulst and Versluis-den-Bieman,[128] 1989	0.29 (−1.09 to 1.68)		
Combined	**0.37 (0.17 to 0.57)**		

Figure 7.5   Meta-Analysis of Mental Health Referrals in International Adoptees

SOURCE: Juffer F, van IJzendoorn MH. Behavior Problems and Mental Health Referrals of International Adoptees: A Meta-analysis. *JAMA.* May 25, 2005;293(20):2501–2515. Reprinted by permission of the American Medical Association.

assess the impact of each new study on the pooled estimate of the treatment effect.

✓ **Question 7:** Does the report summarize the flow of studies, provide descriptive data for each study, and summarize key findings?

A report of a meta-analysis should describe how the reviewers arrived at the final number of articles that were included. For instance, the reviewers should report on how many potentially relevant studies were identified for retrieval, screened (with the practical screen), and excluded. The reasons should be stated: e.g., closer review revealed that the setting was inappropriate. The reviewers should then discuss how many articles were excluded from the final number because they did not meet methodological or nonmethodological criteria.

The meta-analysis report should also present descriptive data for each study, including the study's objectives outcomes, sample size, intervention, settings, data collection methods and the reliability and validity of data collection, effect sizes, results, and conclusions. Key findings should also be summarized, and clinical and policy implications should be given. The meta-analysis' limitations should also be discussed. These may include concerns about the comprehensiveness of the review (e.g., only articles and reports in English) and its quality (e.g., only a few high quality randomized controlled trials).

> **CAUTION:** A good meta-analysis of badly designed studies will still result in faulty findings.
>
> **CAUTION:** A good meta-analysis that is out of date will still result in faulty findings. Consumers should check the literature for new or contradictory information when using any review that is one year old or older.

Funding and Support: The Role of Sponsor

It is axiomatic among many researchers that the study's funding sources should always be acknowledged. Perhaps you have noticed that the AHRQ includes *funding* as one in its critical domains in evaluating the quality of RCTs as well as observational studies. An increasing number of journals, in fact, will not publish research without full disclosure of all financial and material support for the research. Some even require that the specific role of the funding organization or sponsor be specified for each of the following: design and conduct of the study; collection, management, analysis, and interpretation of the data; and preparation, review, or approval of the manuscript. The reasoning is that full disclosure is the ethical way to enable research consumers to consider if biases may have been introduced either directly or indirectly because of a sponsor's potential interest in a study's findings.

Summary of Chapter 7: Getting Closer

Words to Remember

> abstraction, CONSORT, cumulative meta-analysis, effect, effect size, fixed effects, heterogeneous studies, homogenous studies, meta-analysis, methodological quality, narrative reviews, nonmethodological quality, odds, odds ratio, pool, power analysis, protocol, publication bias, qualitative summaries, random effects, relative risks, risks, sensitivity analysis, systematic literature review, TREND

Research consumers conduct literature reviews to learn about effective programs and practices and to evaluate the quality and strength of their supporting evidence. Doing a review means applying highly systematic, explicit, and reproducible methods for identifying, evaluating, and reporting on one or more studies, articles, or reports.

Researchers have identified domains considered absolutely critical for grading the methodological quality of RCTS and observational or nonrandomized research studies. The critical domains for RCTs are the study population, randomization, blinding, interventions, outcomes, statistical analysis, and funding. The critical domains for nonrandomized studies are the comparability of participants, the program or intervention, outcome measures, statistical analysis, and funding.

To help the research consumer evaluate the quality of research *reports*—that is, to begin to grade the extent to which they adequately cover each domain—proponents of evidence-based medicine have developed the Consolidated Standards of Reporting Trials (**CONSORT**), consisting of standards for *reporting* on randomized controlled trials in health and medicine. In addition, the American Public Health Association has issued the **TREND** (**T**ransparent **R**eporting of **E**valuations with **N**onrandomized **D**esigns) statement. Another important grading system is the one used by the U.S. Preventive Services Task Force (USPSTF), an independent panel of experts in primary care and prevention that systematically reviews the evidence of effectiveness and develops recommendations for clinical preventive services.

Most reviewers rely on a form that tells them what to look for when assessing reported research (e.g., "Describe the program's objectives") and provides them with a place to record the data. The process of reading and recording studies is called **abstracting** the literature. Once the information is abstracted onto the forms, it is typically summarized in tables or on spreadsheets.

Reviews of the literature are either **systematic** or **narrative**. A systematic review follows a detailed set of procedures or a **protocol** that defines a focused study question, a specific search strategy (that defines the search terms and databases that are used as well as the criteria for including and excluding studies), the types of data on study quality and findings to be abstracted, and how the data will be synthesized (either qualitatively, as text, or in a quantitative summary accompanied by text).

Systematic literature reviews take two forms. The first produces qualitative summaries of the literature based on trends the reviewer finds across studies. The second type of review uses statistical methods to produce a quantitative summary of program effects. It is called **meta-analysis**.

A meta-analysis uses formal statistical techniques to sum up the results of individual studies on the same topic. The idea is that the larger numbers that are obtained by combining study findings provide greater statistical power than any of the individual studies alone.

The concept of **effect size** is central to meta-analysis. The effect size describes the magnitude of the relationship between two variables. In meta-analytic studies, the effect sizes are used as a common measure and combined statistically.

The Next Chapter

The next chapter discusses how to assess your clients' needs, come to consensus when there is uncertainty, and evaluate your own performance in order to find out if it needs improvement.

Exercises

1. Find these three articles. Tell if they are systematic or narrative reviews. Explain why.
   A. Bair-Merritt, M. H., Blackstone, M., & Feudtner, C. (2006). Physical health outcomes of childhood exposure to intimate partner violence: A systematic review. *Pediatrics, 117*(2), e278–290.
   B. Crook, J., Milner, R., Schultz, I. Z., & Stringer, B. (2002). Determinants of occupational disability following a low back injury: A critical review of the literature. *Journal of Occupational Rehabilitation, 12*(4), 277–295.
   C. Weyandt, L. L., & Dupaul, G. (2006). ADHD in college students. *Journal of Attention Disorders, 10*, 9–19.

2. You are interested in programs to enhance the health and development of children under four years of age and of their families, who live in poor communities. Your search of the literature has led you to the article below. You have been asked to create an abstraction form that can be used to evaluate the article's methodological quality.

   Belsky, J., Melhuish, E., Barnes, J., Leyland, A. H., Romaniuk, H., & the National Evaluation of Sure Start Research Team. (2006). Effects of Sure Start local programmes on children and families: Early findings from a quasi-experimental, cross sectional study. *British Medical Journal, 332*(7556), 1476–1479.

   a. Which methodological domains should you include in the abstraction form?
   b. Write at least three questions for abstracting nonmethodological information.

3. Read the following two meta-analyses. Compare and contrast each with respect to whether or not they adhered to following recommendations for reporting meta-analytic results.

   Mitchell, T. L., Haw, R. M., Pfeifer, J. E., & Meissner, C. A. (2005). Racial bias in mock juror decision-making: A meta-analytic review of defendant treatment. *Law and Human Behavior, 29*, 621–637.

   Horowitz, J. L., & Garber, J. (2006). The prevention of depressive symptoms in children and adolescents: A meta-analytic review. *Journal of Consulting Clinical Psychology, 74*, 401–415.

Recommendations	Mitchell, Haw, et al.		Horowitz and Garber	
1. Describes eligibility for inclusion and exclusion	Yes	No	Yes	No
2. Discusses databases that were searched	Yes	No	Yes	No
3. Gives specific search terms	Yes	No	Yes	No
4. Discusses effect size and why chosen	Yes	No	Yes	No
5. Provides results of tests of study homogeneity	Yes	No	Yes	No
6. Discusses effects of publication bias	Yes	No	Yes	No
7. Depicts the flow of literature from potentially useful through those that passed through all screens (e.g., practical, methodological)	Yes	No	Yes	No

4. Two reviewers evaluate 110 studies on the impact of home-safety education in preventing accidents. The reviewers are asked to tell if the study investigators adequately describe the education intervention by defining its objectives, activities, participants, and settings. Reviewer 1 says that, in total, 30 of the studies do not adequately describe the intervention, but Reviewer 2 says that 45 do not give an adequate description. The two reviewers agree that 20 specific studies do not adequately describe the intervention. Use the kappa statistic to describe the extent of agreement between the reviewers. Is the kappa slight, fair, moderate, or nearly perfect?

5. Locate the following article: Hovell, M. F., Seid, A. G., & Liles, S. (2006). Evaluation of a police and social services domestic violence program: Empirical evidence needed to inform public health policies. *Violence Against Women, 12*(2), 137–159. List the study's limitations as described by the researchers.

8

The Ethical Research Consumer Assesses Needs and Evaluates Improvement

This chapter discusses the context in which the process of discovering evidence that matters takes place and focuses on three topics: identifying clients' needs, determining if programs have met those needs, and applying ethical standards when practicing research.

Discovering evidence that matters depends upon integrating the best research with clients' values and needs to make decisions about the effectiveness and appropriateness of programs and practices. This chapter discusses techniques that can be used to **assess the needs** and priorities of institutions, communities, and society. The techniques include using key informant methods, public or community forums, focus groups, the nominal group process, the Delphi technique, the RAND/UCLA Appropriateness Method, surveys, and consensus development conferences.

An important step in evidence-based practice is to evaluate one's own effectiveness and efficiency and seek ways to improve both. The chapter therefore discusses improvement evaluation, which is designed to study and enhance the effectiveness of already established evidence-based programs and practices. Did the evidence-based process meet the needs and conform to the values of clients? Is improvement needed in the process?

This chapter also focuses on the **ethical concerns** associated with assessing needs, conducting research with human participants, and practicing research.

After reading this chapter, you will be able to

- Distinguish among social, behavioral, administrative, environmental, communal, physical, and educational needs that affect the choice of evidence-based programs and standards for selecting evidence that matters
- Identify the features of techniques for assessing needs and priorities, such as key informant techniques, public or community forums, focus groups, the nominal group process, the Delphi technique, the RAND/UCLA Appropriateness Method, surveys, and consensus development conferences
- Compare the characteristics of improvement and effectiveness evaluations or evaluation research
- Identify the characteristics of research ethics and research misconduct in doing all types of evaluation research
- Identify the limitations of evidence-based practice and their ethical implications
- Distinguish among the ethical concerns that may occur when conducting research
- Distinguish among the ethical concerns that may occur when deciding if evidence matters

Figure 8.1 shows your location on the way to discovering evidence that matters.

Identifying Needs, Preferences, and Values

Evidence-based practitioners count on the experimental method to provide evidence that matters and agree on the need to incorporate users' needs, preferences, and values and expectations into treatments, practices, and programs. A systematic effort to identify user needs and provide a context for them is called a **needs assessment.**

Needs occur when gaps in services and programs lead to unsolved problems affecting health, education, and social well-being. Needs are intertwined with values and preferences, which together affect priorities. For example, a community may need better social services for its elderly but may prefer to spend most of its resources on preventing violence in teens.

Needs can be arranged into six categories: social, communal or epidemiological, behavioral, environmental, educational, and administrative.

Social needs usually refer to the community's perceptions of its problems. For example, one community may see gang warfare or teen

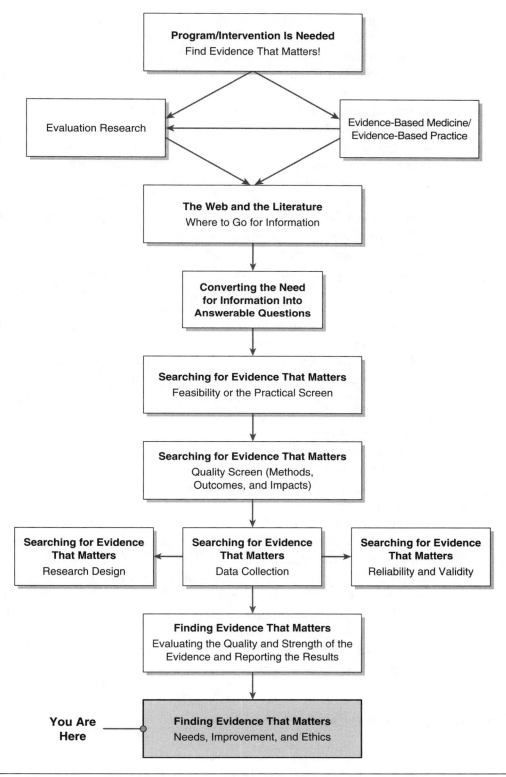

Figure 8.1   Location on the Way to Discovering Evidence That Matters

violence as its major problem, while another may regard the unemployment of its youth as the most pressing need.

Communal or epidemiological needs refer to problems that can be documented to affect a large number of people in the community. For example, school records may reveal inadequacies in meeting the needs of special education students in a school district, and a review of the state's statistics on low-weight births may reveal higher than state averages for three counties. Data on communal or epidemiological needs usually come from school or medical records, administrative documents, and other databases like vital statistics and local and national surveys of the public's health, educational status, and welfare.

Behavioral needs refer to individual and communal lifestyles and beliefs that affect a community's well-being. Abundant evidence exists, for example, that some communities rely on diets that are high in fat and that this contributes to high rates of obesity and to concomitant illnesses in those communities. As another example, prenatal care may be viewed by some in Community A as a necessity, while in Community B it may be seen as an attempt to make a medical problem out of a natural process.

Physical needs refer to social or physical factors that are external to an individual or a community. If access to nutritious food is limited in a community, for instance, then it will be difficult to implement a program to instill good eating practices.

Educational needs refer to individual and community knowledge, attitudes, skills, and self-efficacy beliefs. Some communities are interested in the social and political process and have knowledge about how the "system" works. Others are less interested in or knowledgeable about these things.

Administrative needs refer to policies and resources that exist in the organizations and institutions (e.g., schools, hospitals, businesses, nongovernmental organizations) that might facilitate or hinder the adoption of a new program. Evaluation of these needs helps to answer questions like these: What are the barriers to implementation (e.g., lack of staff commitment, lack of space)? What policies should be changed to remove the barriers?

Table 8.1 summarizes each of the six needs that can be explored through a needs assessment.

Techniques for Assessing Needs

At least seven methods are commonly used in assessing individual and public needs. Each has its advantages and limitations.

Table 8.1   Exploring Six Needs

Need	Explanation	Question/Comment
Social	People's perception of their own needs	What are the community's needs and preferences? Does the community have the resources to solve problems? How readily can the community implement programs?
Communal/ Epidemiological	Determination by researchers or practitioners of which problems are important for specific groups in a community	Information comes from analyses of school records, national databases, and administrative databases
Behavioral	Determination of individual and community lifestyles or behaviors that contribute to existing needs	For instance, these may include dietary preferences that lead to obesity and diabetes; customs regarding receipt of prenatal care
Environmental	External social and physical factors	For instance, how healthy are the foods served to children in school cafeterias? How accessible is prenatal care? Fresh fruits and vegetables?
Educational	Individual and community knowledge, attitudes, skills, and self-efficacy beliefs	A major question is how these factors interact to assure the implementation of new programs and practices
Administrative	Refers to policies and resources prevailing in the organizational context that might facilitate or hinder program implementation	What are the barriers to implementation (e.g., staff commitment, lack of space)?

Key Informant

The purpose of the **key informant method** is to collect information about a community's needs by interviewing community leaders who are likely to be in a position to know what the needs are. Key informants in most communities include religious leaders, physicians, teachers, selected members of public service organizations, the mayor, public safety administrators, business owners, and so on.

The key informant technique is relatively inexpensive to implement because the interviews are almost always conducted locally, and no travel costs are incurred. Because only a relatively few people are interviewed (say, 25), analyzing the results is relatively simple. Further, the technique is useful for getting a variety of perspectives on any single set of problems and an "insider's" view of events.

The main disadvantage of the key informant technique is that you cannot be sure that you have interviewed all relevant people, and, if you did not, the results may not be representative or correct. Also, the leaders who are willing and able to participate may not always be the "voice" of the people. If you want input from the community itself, a technique like the public forum may be a better choice.

Public or Community Forum

A community forum consists of a group of people who meet together to discuss a common problem. The meeting is open to all members of the community.

The purpose of convening one or more public forums is to obtain information from a relatively large number of people in the community at one time. The community may share a geographic area (e.g., a school district) or a special interest (e.g., parents whose children are threatened by school gangs). Usually, a single agency—a community college, a homeowners' association, the local Parent Teacher Association—sponsors the forum and drafts the initial questions for participants. The questions focus on the needs that should have highest priorities in the community, what is being done currently to meet the needs, what should be done in the future, and where resources might come from.

Public or community forums are useful in enabling a large number of interested participants with diverse perspectives to have their say. If done well, a forum can provide a relatively quick look at the community's present needs. Good leadership and advance preparation are crucial if only to make sure that good community debate does not turn into pointless argument.

Focus Groups

A focus group is designed to collect information from "insiders" or "people in the know." The group usually consists of about 10 carefully selected participants and a trained moderator. The session lasts about two hours and is centered on getting answers to four or five carefully constructed questions. Focus group participants almost always receive financial rewards for participation.

The advantage of a well-conducted focus group is that it can produce answers to difficult questions in a short period of time. **Focus groups** are, however, among the most costly needs assessment methods. The questions asked of the group must be skillfully assembled, and an experienced moderator is needed to conduct the discussion. Often, many focus groups are deemed necessary to get a full complement of community views, so, if you add in the incentives, the costs can become pretty steep.

Nominal Group Process

In the nominal group technique, participants are brought together for a discussion session led by a moderator. After the topic of concern has been presented to session participants and they have had an opportunity to ask questions or briefly discuss the scope of the topic, they are asked to take a few minutes to think about and write down their responses. The session moderator will then ask each participant to read, and elaborate on, one of his or her responses. These are noted on a flipchart. Once everyone has given a response, participants will be asked for a second or third response, until all of their answers have been noted on flipchart sheets posted around the room.

Once duplications are eliminated, each response is assigned a letter or number. Session participants are then asked to choose up to 10 responses that they feel are the most important and rank them according to their relative importance. These rankings are collected from all participants and aggregated. Here is an example:

Response	Participant 1	Participant 2	Participant 3	Columns Inserted Here for Participants 4–12	Relative Importance of Each Response
A	ranked 1st	ranked 2nd	ranked 2nd		5 participants ranked A 1st
B	ranked 3rd	ranked 1st	ranked 3rd		7 participants ranked B 3rd
C	ranked 2nd	ranked 3rd	ranked 1st		6 participants ranked C 2nd
D	ranked 4th	ranked 4th	ranked 4th		12 participants ranked D 4th

Sometimes, the results are given back to the participants in order to stimulate further discussion, and perhaps a readjustment in the overall rankings will be assigned to the various responses. This is done only when group consensus regarding priorities is important.

The **nominal group process** can be used in a wide variety of settings. For example, a nominal group process was used to collate information for the development of a mental health program for victims of drought in rural Australia (Sartore). Twenty-three participants were recruited in consultation with rural mental health organizations. They were asked questions about the best mental health service strategies to minimize and respond to the mental health impact of drought. Three general strategies emerged: community-building and education about the physical, financial, and mental health effects of drought; cooperation between and coordination among agencies in delivering mental health and other drought support; and continuity and planning of improved mental health services.

Delphi Technique

The **Delphi technique** is a structured method of determining the degree of agreement on a topic, selecting alternatives, or setting priorities. Delphi techniques use questionnaires that are completed by participants on their own, in groups, or both. The questionnaires are structured to ask people to rate or rank the importance or validity of certain ideas. For example, Delphi participants might be asked to rate the importance of a particular program objective (1 = *definitely important* to 5 = *definitely not important*) as well as the likelihood that it might be achieved in a particular institution (1 = *definitely likely* to 5 = *definitely not likely*). The results of the ratings (round 1) are sent back to the respondents who are asked to review them and re-rate the items (round 2).

In "mailed" Delphi's (regular mail, e-mail, or on the Web), the participants are usually not known to one another. "Anonymity" is thought to encourage people to focus on the issues rather than on each other. In a Delphi variation in which round 1 is mailed but round 2 is a face-to-face meeting, the participants are known to each other, but their individual ratings are not. The idea behind a face-to-face discussion of the first round's results is that the dialogue increases attention to the subtleties of the issues and introduces new views into the rating process.

The following example (Example 8.1) describes an actual use of the Delphi method to identify the essential characteristics of cognitive behavioral treatment manuals.

Example 8.1   Using Delphi by E-Mail: What Do Experts Agree Should Be in a Cognitive Behavioral Treatment Manual?

Who Were the Delphi Participants?

All participants were experts who were defined as individuals who have published treatment manuals or have used them in published research. Potential participants' names were gathered primarily through an electronic search of the online literature.

How Was Anonymity Guaranteed?

Twenty-nine prospective participants were e-mailed a pre-notification letter inviting them to participate in the study. A positive response was viewed as informed consent. The e-mail process enabled the mass mailing of all correspondence without individuals' knowledge of each other.

What Was the Study Plan?

Round 1. An e-mail, with attachment, was sent to the consenting sample. In the attachment, participants were asked to list their preferences for the contents of a good cognitive behavioral therapy treatment manual.

Round 2. Items generated from round 1 were thematically analyzed by the investigators and a colleague experienced in using treatment manuals. When initial disagreement regarding the categorization of items occurred, discussion took place until the investigator and his colleague reached agreement. Following analysis, a questionnaire was designed for the subsequent rounds. In order to facilitate completion, a 3-point rating scale was generated for each item:

E = Essential. Each manual must contain this item

D = Desirable. Inclusion of this item enhances the manual

I = Inappropriate. Not applicable to the manual

Round 3. The results of round 2 were collated, and the percentage agreement for each category was placed next to each item. The returned questionnaire included the participants' original responses, and participants were given the opportunity to amend their selections (if desired) in response to viewing the overall feedback.

How Was Consensus Defined?

As there is no agreement concerning the required degree of consensus in a Delphi study, the investigators set consensus levels at two-thirds of the responses.

What Did the Delphi Find to Be Essential?

Only 11 (13%) of the generated items were rated as essential:

(Continued)

Example 8.1 (Continued)

General characteristics of treatment manuals

Appropriate for the problem addressed

Coherent and focused

Based on a clear theoretical model

General information that should be found in treatment manuals

A clear specification of what the intervention aims to do

A statement of the aims and objectives of each session

A detailed description of the problem for which the manual has been designed

Intervention strategies/chapters

Rationale of therapy should be linked to intervention

Treatment procedures should be detailed

Treatment procedures should be illustrated with realistic clinical case examples

Specific content of patient led treatment manuals

User friendly

Give hope that therapy will work

A unique feature of the Delphi technique is the anonymity of participants or responses. If participants are not known to one another, the method can be used to obtain agreement among groups and individuals that are normally hostile to one other. But Delphi participants may not be representative of the very group whose needs are being assessed, and this is a limitation. Participation requires the completion of written questionnaires through at least two rounds. Not everyone is survey savvy and can spend the required time. If the results are seen as nonrepresentative, then they might not be taken seriously. Further, no established definition of agreement or consensus exists, and this alone can make Delphi findings appear arbitrary for those who would use a different definition. Finally, the method tends to encourage a middle-of-the-road view, especially if average ratings or majority ratings are used.

The RAND/UCLA Appropriateness Method

The **RAND/UCLA Appropriateness Method (RUAM)** is a method for determining the extent of agreement on controversial topics and those for which the research base is poor or ambiguous (a mixture of positive and negative findings).

The RUAM was originally created to determine the appropriateness of certain medical procedures and surgical operations, such as gallbladder removals or coronary artery bypass surgery. Because the method has proven to be flexible, reliable, and valid (Shekelle, 2004), it has been adapted for use in a variety of other health and mental health contexts, including the creation of indicators of quality of care for children with ADHD, conduct disorder, and major depression (Zima et al., 2005) and the identification of indicators of quality care for elderly patients undergoing surgery (McGory, Shekelle, Rubenstein, Fink, & Ko, 2005).

The RUAM incorporates elements of the NIH consensus development process, the Delphi, and the nominal group techniques. It has the following characteristics:

- Six to fourteen panelists are assembled. The panelists are well known in their fields and differ in their expertise.
- The study team compiles a state of the art review of the literature for the panelists.
- The panelists participate in a two-round rating process using a 9-point scale.
- Round 1 is usually done by each panelist independently, before a group meeting.
- A highly skilled moderator conducts a meeting to discuss the ratings and clarify individual concerns. After discussion, the panelists do their ratings a second time; this constitutes the second round.
- The second and final ratings are used for the statistical analysis. Do the panelists agree? Disagree?

How is the RUAM used in identifying needs? Example 8.2 shows how the RUAM was used in developing a manual to address the intermediate and long-term mental health needs of students and staff after incidents of school-related violence. In this RUAM, 10 panelists were given a literature review and asked to rate scenarios in a two-round process. The first round of ratings was conducted by each panelist in his or her office while the second was done in a telephone group session.

Surveys

Surveys are usually used to gather information from large numbers of people. Several types are possible. A face-to-face interview may

Example 8.2   Using the RAND-UCLA Appropriateness Method (RUAM): School-
Related Violence and Intermediate and Long-Term Mental Health Needs

---

Problem: Many American communities have suffered and continue to suffer from school-related violence. School administrators and teachers have found that the mental health recovery needs of students and staff often span months or even years beyond the initial date of the tragic event. What are the needs of administrators and teachers in dealing with this problem?

Method:

Panel Composition

Ten teachers, administrators, school police, and school mental health personnel who represented urban, suburban, and rural school districts from geographic regions across the United States agreed to participate.

Round 1

The panelists were mailed a review of the literature on immediate, intermediate, and long-term mental health services after school-related violence. At the same time, they were asked to review five scenarios, based on actual events. They were also asked to respond to 34 questions about each scenario. The questions focused on which mental health services would be appropriate after each event in four different time frames: in the first week after a violent event, between one week and one month after the event, between one and six months after the event, and more than six months after the event.

One of the five scenarios was as follows:

Sample Scenario Used for a RUAM: School-Related Violence

At 10 a.m. on Thursday morning, students and teachers in several classrooms at South Suburban High School heard a loud noise. No one was sure what it was, but, a few seconds later, there was another, similar noise, this time followed by screams. Teachers followed school crisis procedures by locking classroom doors and making the students get down on the floor, away from the windows. Cellular phones from throughout the school peppered the 911 operators with calls.

Police, firefighters, and paramedics were at the scene within minutes, and they cautiously began evacuating the school. Gradually they discovered the classroom from which the gun had been fired. Its door was locked, the teacher lying bleeding, but still alive, in the hallway. Most of the students had escaped, but there were still seven inside, being held hostage by Tom Georgian, their fifteen-year-old classmate, who was armed with a semi-automatic pistol.

Hostage negotiators tried without success to engage Georgian in conversation. Yelling and crying could be heard from the classroom, and then screaming, and more shots. A window opened, and a sobbing girl started trying to climb out, despite the fact that the classroom was on the second floor. Emergency personnel yelled to her to stop, and she began screaming, "He's blocking the door! I can't get out! There's blood everywhere, and I can't get out!"

Firefighters brought a ladder up to the window, and helped the screaming girl and three other terrified but unharmed students down to the ground. Inside the classroom, one of the hostages was dead and two others were wounded. Tom Georgian had shot himself in the head, and his body was blocking the classroom door.

Mr. and Mrs. Georgian had seen no signs of trouble in their son. He had left no clues to his intentions. The surviving hostages said he had been incoherent but that he seemed to be saying something about the school play, which had been scheduled to begin rehearsals the next day.

School administrators closed the school temporarily and met to determine how to proceed.

One of the 34 questions about the scenario was this:

Question Asked in Connection With the Scenario

For the **first week** following this event:

Teachers should provide trauma-specific mental health services to students in the classroom.

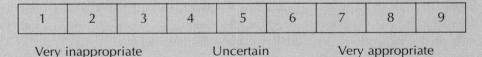

| 1 | 2 | 3 | 4 | 5 | 6 | 7 | 8 | 9 |

Very inappropriate   Uncertain   Very appropriate

Panelists were asked to rate the appropriateness of services on a scale of 1 to 9, with 1 being the least appropriate and 9 being the most appropriate. A rating of 7, 8, or 9 indicated that the panelist thought that a service was "definitely appropriate" and that the benefits of the service exceeded the costs or risks by a sufficient margin, that is, that the service was definitely worth providing. A service was deemed "definitely inappropriate" if the costs or risks exceed the benefits (ratings 1, 2, or 3). If the benefits and costs were determined to be about equal, or if there was not enough information to make a definite decision, then panelists were asked to assign a rating of 4, 5, or 6.

The results were compiled and summarized into a re-rating form. This form was very similar to the original questionnaire, but it indicated how many panelists had selected each answer, identified the panelist's original answer, and provided a graphic median and inter-quartile range for each question. This is an example of the summary of the ratings.

(Continued)

Example 8.2 (Continued)

Example of the Ratings for Round 1 Summarized

1	2	2				2	1	2
1	2	3	4	5	6	7	8*	9

   Very inappropriate   Uncertain   Very appropriate

In this example, one (1) panelist rated the appropriateness as 1, two (2) rated it at 2, two (2) at 3, one (1) at 6, two (2) at 7, and two (2) at 9. This particular panelist rated the appropriateness as 8 because the 8 has an asterisk (*).

Disagreement/Agreement

Did the panelists agree with one another? A standard definition for disagreement is that it occurs if 3 or more panelists rate a statement in the high range (7–9) AND 3 or more rate it in the low range (1–3). Any other combination of ratings is considered agreement. In the example above, the panelists disagreed.

Round 2

Panelists were given the summary of the round 1 ratings. They then participated in a two-hour telephone conference to discuss the ratings, with particular emphasis on disagreement. After discussion, the panelists re-rated the scenarios. Needs for services were recommended if, after the second round of ratings, a service received a rating of 7 or higher (very appropriate) *and* there was no disagreement.

---

result in in-depth information but requires a skilled interviewer. Telephone surveys also require skilled interviewers, but it has become increasingly difficult to get people to agree to participate. People hanging up, the need to call back, and messages left on voice mail are costly.

E-mail, Web-based, or electronically distributed surveys can reach large numbers of people. However, technical expertise is needed to design the survey, and you have to make certain that the people who are selected to participate can access the survey, and complete it.

Mail surveys are in some ways the simplest because they do not require staff training (as do interviews) or technical expertise. The number of people who return questionnaires that are mailed to them, however, is often extremely low unless they are given an

Example 8.3   A Survey of the Needs of Women With Diabetes

Purpose: The purpose of this survey was to explore food purchasing, preparation, and consumption among black women with type 2 diabetes mellitus in an urban setting to assess barriers to medical nutrition therapy recommendations.

Methods: A telephone survey asked about shopping habits, the use of community resources for food supplementation, use of restaurant/fast-food establishments, dining habits, food purchasing and consumption, and food preparation methods. The survey contained 38 items.

Results: The respondents identified ways in which their participation in a culturally competent intervention of diabetes care and education helped them to change their dietary behaviors. The most common areas of change included purchasing, preparation, and portion size. The most commonly cited barriers to medical nutrition therapy included low income, time constraints, competing demands, and knowledge deficits.

Conclusions: Culturally sensitive diabetes interventions are an effective way to overcome some of the barriers to medical nutrition therapy. The results of the survey suggest that identification of more affordable healthy food resources in the community is needed. In addition, transportation to grocery stores should be on the public policy agenda. Finally, alternate sites for nutrition education, such as a supermarket forum, warrant further investigation.

SOURCE: From Galasso P, Amend A, Melkus GD, Nelson GT. Barriers to medical nutrition therapy in black women with type 2 diabetes mellitus. *Diabetes Educ.* Sep-Oct 2005;31(5):719-725. Used with permission of Sage Publications, Inc.

incentive to do so. The use of incentives in surveys may be costly and may boost the number of responses only slightly. Writing survey questionnaires requires a great deal of skill. Poorly designed questionnaires result in low response rates. Low response rates mean invalid survey results.

An illustrative use of a survey to identify needs is given in Example 8.3 (Galasso, Amend, Melkus, & Nelson, 2005) . The purpose of the survey was to assess the nutritional needs of black women with type 2 diabetes as well as the barriers they encounter in meeting these needs.

Table 8.2 summarizes the objectives, characteristics, advantages, and limitations of some of the main needs assessment methods. They should be considered as part of the research consumer's store of techniques for finding out about individual and community needs and about the place of new programs and practices in meeting those needs.

Table 8.2   Needs Assessment Methods

Name	Objectives	Implementation	Advantages	Limitations
Key Informant	Gather views from members of community who know the community from the "inside" because of their training or affiliations	Identify key informants (e.g., elected officials, religious and public services leaders, professionals, teachers, lawyers) Interview or survey them	Relatively inexpensive Provides perspectives from different viewpoints Can get "insider's" view	Limit on how many people can be included and so results may not be representative Cannot be sure that all "key" people are included
Public or Community Forum	Get views from a wide range of community residents in public meetings	A sponsoring agency puts on public forums A list of discussion questions is generated by the sponsors	A large number of views can be heard Enables people to participate in generating ideas about their community Relatively easy to implement Provides a quick view of community needs and preferences	Requires good leadership and advance organization Only some people might attend and so the views expressed may not be representative May generate more questions than answers
Focus Group	A small group technique with up to 10 people The purpose is to answer no more than about 5 important questions in two hours	A trained moderator leads a discussion of each question in a "permissive" atmosphere (that is, "anything goes")	Provides answers to important questions in a relatively short period of time	Need a trained and experienced moderator Questions must be formulated so they are important and answerable by the group within the time allotted May be costly because you need several groups and each person must be compensated financially

Name	Objectives	Implementation	Advantages	Limitations
Nominal Group Process	A small group process in which all members' views are heard The purpose is to make decisions on competing alternatives	A moderator and a group of people are assembled Ideas are put on paper Discussion leads to listing ideas on a board Ideas are voted on	Leads to definite conclusions Gives all participants an equal opportunity to express their views	Need an experienced moderator who makes sure everyone is heard Results may not be representative because group size is relatively small
Delphi	A method for generating ideas and also coming to consensus	Respondents complete a questionnaire The results are summarized and sent to participants Participants review the summary and complete the questionnaire a second time Process is repeated until general agreement is reached	Participants are unknown to one another, which encourages frankness Conducive to independent thinking Can be used to get agreement among groups that are hostile to each other because of the anonymity of participation	Participants may not be representative Tends to encourage a middle-of-the-road view Can be time consuming because method requires several "rounds" Definition of agreement may be considered arbitrary
RAND/UCLA Appropriateness Method (RUAM)	A panel method to identify areas of agreement, disagreement, and uncertainty (not enough evidence to make a decision)	Panelists are given a review of the literature and sent a set of items to rate On their own, they rate the appropriateness of each item using a standardized scale, where 1 = definitely not appropriate and 9 = definitely appropriate	Provides an opportunity to combine existing research with expert opinion Statistics on reliability and validity of the process are known and acceptable	An expert leader is essential The process is expensive because it is relatively lengthy Potential bias in choosing panelists whose views are likely to be accepted

(Continued)

Table 8.2 (Continued)

Name	Objectives	Implementation	Advantages	Limitations
		The ratings are summarized and given to the panelists The panelists meet face-to-face in a one to two day session to clarify ratings and discuss them Panelists rate each of the items once again Extent of agreement, disagreement, and uncertainty is identified	Process is flexible and can be used in a variety of settings and for a variety of topics	Does not force consensus and allows for uncertainty as well as providing a reliable portrait of current knowledge
Surveys	To obtain information from a large number of participants	A survey questionnaire (interview, mail, online) is developed The sample is selected The survey is conducted	Can reach a relatively large number of people with diverse perspectives	Requires expertise in survey research including questionnaire development, sample selection, and data analysis (including statistical analysis) Can be costly to reach some people who do not like written surveys (mail or Web)

_____ Facing Uncertainty and Coming to Consensus

Research consumers may find themselves confronted with the need to make decisions on topics for which data are inconsistent, of poor quality, or even missing. The need to "do something" in situations of uncertainty is certainly characteristic of the health professions. In response, the U.S. National Institutes has supported a program since 1977 whose aim is to produce "state-of-the-science" reports (www.consensus.nih.gov). Although not yet widely implemented in the other helping professions, **consensus development conferences** are an integral part of evidence-based health care, and their methods can be usefully adapted to other fields. In fact, as can be seen from the sample topics in Table 8.3, many of the NIH reports are applicable to a wide variety of disciplines other than health care.

NIH Consensus and State-of-the-Science statements are prepared by independent panels of health professionals and public representatives on the basis of (1) the results of a systematic literature review, (2) presentations by investigators working in areas relevant to the conference questions during a two-day public session, (3) questions and statements from conference attendees during open discussion periods that are part of the public session, and (4) closed deliberations and a production of a report by the panel during the remainder of the second day and morning of the third. Consensus statements are independent reports of the panel; they are not policy statements of the NIH or of the federal government of the United States. Each statement reflects the panel's assessment of knowledge available at the

Table 8.3   National Institutes of Health Consensus Development
              Conferences: A Small Sample

Manifestations and Management of Chronic Insomnia in Adults

Preventing Violence and Related Health-Risking Social Behaviors in Adolescents

Symptom Management in Cancer: Pain, Depression, and Fatigue

Diagnosis and Treatment of Attention Deficit Hyperactivity Disorder

Interventions to Prevent HIV Risk Behaviors

Effective Medical Treatment of Opiate Addiction

Sunlight, Ultraviolet Radiation, and the Skin

Treatment of Destructive Behaviors in Persons With Developmental Disabilities

The Health Benefits of Pets

Pain, Discomfort, and Humanitarian Care

time the statement was written. Thus, it provides a "snapshot in time" of the state of knowledge on the conference topic.

One consensus development conference, Preventing Violence and Related Health-Risking Social Behaviors in Adolescents, was a two-and-a-half-day conference at the U.S. National Institutes of Health. The conference participants examined and assessed the current state of knowledge regarding adolescent violence and related health-risking social behavior and identified directions for future research.

Twenty-one experts presented the latest research findings on risk and protective factors involved in the development of adolescent violence and related behaviors and on interventions to reduce those behaviors. The presenters had expertise in public policy, social learning and development, pediatrics, psychiatry, community development, psychology, social medicine, violence prevention, sociology, and nursing.

After a day and a half of presentations and public discussion, an independent panel of 13 people weighed the available evidence and drafted a statement addressing the following questions:

1. What are the factors that contribute to violence and associated adverse health outcomes in childhood and adolescence?

2. What are the patterns of co-occurrence of these factors?

3. What evidence exists on the safety and effectiveness of interventions for violence?

4. Where evidence of safety and effectiveness exists, are there other outcomes beyond reducing violence? If so, what is known about effectiveness by age, sex, and race/ethnicity?

5. What are the commonalities among interventions that are effective and those that are ineffective?

6. What are the priorities for future research?

The panelists had expertise in pediatrics, psychiatry, law, sociology, nursing, research methods, adolescent health, and social work. In their statement, they gave specific examples of programs that effectively reduced arrests or precursors to violence. They also discussed the characteristics shared by these programs, such as being derived from sound theoretical rationales, addressing strong risk factors, involving long-term treatments (lasting a year and sometimes much longer), working intensively with those targeted for treatment and often using a clinical approach, following a cognitive/behavioral strategy, being multimodal and multicontextual, focusing on improving social competency and other skill development strategies for targeted youth and their families, being developmentally appropriate, not being delivered in coercive institutional settings, and having the capacity to be delivered with fidelity.

The panelists also named specific programs that are not effective even though they are in use (and in some cases widely) and cited reasons for the lack of success of these programs. These reasons included implementation protocols that are not clearly articulated, staff that are not well supervised or held accountable for outcomes, programs limited to scare tactics, programs limited to toughness strategies, and programs that consist largely of adults lecturing at youth.

The panelists concluded (among other things) that some interventions have been shown by rigorous research to reduce violence precursors, violence, and arrest. However, many interventions aimed at reducing violence have not been sufficiently evaluated or proven effective, and a few widely implemented programs have been shown to be ineffective and perhaps harmful. The panelists also recommended funding sufficient to promote the dissemination of violence prevention programs that have been shown to be effective through rigorous RCT (randomized controlled trial) research. Funding, they said, must include support for research, and monitoring must continue as these programs are more widely implemented.

NIH Consensus Development Conferences are the gold standard for developing agreement. And the NIH literature reviews that form the research base for these panel reviews are world class. Also, the speakers and panelists participating in NIH consensus development are internationally renowned. Of course, these characteristics encourage acceptance of the conference statements.

Improvement Evaluations: How Are We Doing? Can We Do Better?

The fifth step of evidence-based medicine or evidence-based practice calls for practitioners to evaluate their own effectiveness and efficiency and seek ways to improve both next time (Chapter 1). Evaluation may be as specific as analyzing performance with respect to asking questions or searching for evidence, or it may pertain to the extent to which evidence-based methods made a difference in the processes or outcomes of care.

Evaluation has a long history as a mechanism for improvement. The American Evaluation Association states that purposes of evaluation include bettering practices, personnel, programs, organizations, governments, consumers, and the public interest; contributing to informed decision making and more enlightened change; precipitating needed change; and empowering all stakeholders by collecting data from them and engaging them in the evaluation process.

The search for evidence that matters is almost completed when the evidence about needed programs has been compiled. If a program is to be adopted or a campaign to change practices is to be implemented, an evaluation of the effectiveness of the entire process and its outcomes is in order. The purposes of the evaluation would be to (1) examine the extent to which the newly adopted programs met clients' needs and (2) identify where improvements should be made to improve future efforts to find evidence that matters. The type of evaluation that is used to accomplish these purposes is called an **improvement evaluation**.

The ideal improvement evaluation takes place as follows:

1. The evaluators identify the services, programs, or outcomes that should be improved based on a needs assessment. This can be done by reviewing existing records (e.g., school or case records); observing behavior (e.g., in a classroom, a village); or surveying members of the community (e.g., politicians, leaders) and practitioners (e.g., nurses, social workers). Requests or demands for change can also come from political pressure or legislation.

2. The evaluators set performance standards. These are the benchmarks against which improvement is measured, and, to the extent possible, they should come from evidence-based sources. In other words, they should be selected because evidence exists that, if the standards are met, beneficial results are more likely to occur than otherwise.

In the health field, performance standards are derived from research findings and the consensus of experts. The American Diabetes Society, for example, has issued clinical practice recommendations for the diagnosis and treatment of diabetes, while the Joint National Committee on the Prevention, Detection, Evaluation, and Treatment of High Blood Pressure has released recommendations for the prevention and treatment of high blood pressure. Proponents of evidence-based health care often use published recommendations or guidelines as the basis for setting performance standards in improvement evaluations. For instance, here in Example 8.4 is a very small portion of the practice recommendations issued by the American Diabetes Association:

Example 8.4   Psychosocial Assessment and Care Recommendations

- Preliminary assessment of psychological and social status should be included as part of the medical management of diabetes.
- Psychosocial screening should include but is not limited to attitudes about the illness, expectations for medical management and outcomes, affect/mood, general and diabetes-related quality of life, resources (financial, social, and emotional), and psychiatric history.
- Screening for psychosocial problems such as depression, eating disorders, and cognitive impairment is needed when adherence to the medical regimen is poor.
- It is preferable to incorporate psychological treatment into routine care rather than wait for identification of a specific problem or deterioration in psychological status.

SOURCE: Derived from the American Diabetes Association (2006).

3. An evidence-based program is selected and adapted for implementation. Implementing programs is an extremely complex activity. Effective strategies for translating solutions from one setting to another are not readily available. Also, introducing a new "solution" may pose new problems if the organization is not prepared or is resistant to it.

4. The program is implemented. The program's implementation should be monitored to make certain all of its components are being put in place as planned. If any component is difficult to implement or proves to be unsatisfactory to participants, revision may be necessary.

5. The evaluators assess performance using the agreed upon standards and measures.

6. The evaluators provide data on the results to all participants so that they can review their progress toward meeting the identified need.

7. If the need has been met, participants decide if they want to continue with the program. If the need has not been met, participants decide if they want to continue or revise their activities until the standards are achieved.

Implementing and evaluating programs to improve the quality of services and care is an emerging discipline. EBM researchers have urged caution in adopting programs without a solid evidence base and careful evaluation (Auerbach, Landefeld, & Shojania, 2007).

Improvement and Effectiveness Evaluations: Two Purposes for One Discipline

What are the differences between evaluations that are conducted primarily to improve provision of services to meet specific needs and evaluation research that is designed to provide evidence of effectiveness? Listen in on a conversation between an improvement and an effectiveness evaluator (Table 8.4).

Table 8.4   A Conversation Between an Improvement and an Effectiveness Evaluator

Improvement evaluator: We are planning to find out if an improvement evaluation will improve the quality of care we give to patients with diabetes or high blood pressure.

Effectiveness evaluator: Where are the patients located?

Improvement evaluator: In a rural health clinic. We have three physicians in the clinic and two full-time registered nurses.

Effectiveness evaluator: Why did you decide to focus on diabetes and high blood pressure?

Improvement evaluator: These are the two most common medical problems treated in the clinic. We looked at a sample of medical records and found that many patients did not receive recommended care.

Effectiveness evaluator: What do you mean by recommended care?

Improvement evaluator: Recommended care are the standards—processes and practices—that are likely to result in optimal outcomes based on the conclusions of experts like the American Diabetes Association and the Joint National Committee on the Prevention, Detection, Evaluation, and Treatment of High Blood Pressure. The practices are based on clinical expertise and research-based evidence.

Effectiveness evaluator: You say the evaluation aims to improve the quality of care. Are you interested only in the process of care, that is, what is done to and for the patient, or are you also interested in the outcomes?

Improvement evaluator: We are interested in both.

Effectiveness evaluator: So what will the clinic do to improve care?

Improvement evaluator: The physicians and nursing staff have created a program that they are fairly sure will work for them. It includes providing quarterly feedback to physicians, empowering nurses to remind patients of the essentials of their diabetes and high blood pressure care, and flagging medical records to remind physicians of the care due for each patient. The program was chosen because a recent analysis of 25 studies showed that physician reminders improved the quality of care for diabetic patients. Patients will be given educational materials so that they can see the standards we were aiming for. Two recent studies have shown that patients who are informed of the standards of care are more likely to be compliant with treatment than those who are not.

Effectiveness evaluator: How will you decide which patients are eligible to be in the evaluation?

Improvement evaluator: We have decided that they must be 18 years of age or older and have diabetes and/or high blood pressure. We have about 5,000 patients in the clinic, and we anticipate that, by the end of the study's first 12-month period, we will have about 250 diabetics and 650 patients with high blood pressure enrolled in the evaluation.

Effectiveness evaluator: Do you have a comparison group?

Improvement evaluator: Not one that is created especially for this evaluation. The clinic is interested in improving its performance to meet established standards. In essence, the standards are what an ideal control group who is receiving "perfect" care would receive. Education experts might call this a **criterion-referenced** design.

Effectiveness evaluator: How will you evaluate whether or not improvement takes place?

Improvement evaluator: The standards we plan to use are evidence based and state that all diabetic patients should have an eye exam, be vaccinated for pneumococcal pneumonia, and have a cholesterol screening test. The standards also state that patients with high blood pressure should achieve a measure of less that 140/90mm hg and should be taking a "baby" aspirin (81mg) daily. We have done extensive needs assessments and have found out the proportion of patients who currently receive the recommended care. To find out if the standards are met, we will compare the proportions achieving the criterion before we begin the intervention and in two months. Our aim is not just to increase the proportion, but to ensure that every patient receives recommended care to meet his or her particular, individual needs.

Effectiveness evaluator: How will you keep track of the patients and the changes in care?

Improvement evaluator: We have an electronic medical record system and plan to hire a programmer and statistician to help us. However, before we do the hiring, I am going to check out some ordinary data management programs to determine if they can handle the data management and the statistics.

Effectiveness evaluator: We are both evaluators, but my perspective is different from yours. I do evaluation research, which means that I rely upon experiments to test the comparative outcomes, impact, and costs of programs. You, on the other hand, evaluate whether programs designed to meet specific needs live up to evidence-based standards.

Table 8.5 compares effectiveness and improvement evaluations.

The effectiveness and improvement evaluators' perspectives are compared in Table 8.6. Effectiveness evaluators aim to determine if a program is successful when compared to an alternative. Improvement evaluators want to find out if a successful program is specifically beneficial in their setting.

Table 8.5 Effectiveness and Improvement Evaluations: Compare and Contrast

	Effectiveness Evaluation	Improvement Evaluation
Study Objective	Hypotheses or research questions are derived from reviews of previous research. Purpose is to find out if a program "works": Did it accomplish its objectives? What were its outcomes, impact, and costs?	The aim is to determine if evidence-based programs and practices have progressed to satisfying a public need. If not, can the newly adopted program be improved? Was the process of choosing the project meticulous?
Main Outcomes	A program is effective if its outcomes compare favorably to comparable alternative programs or to any new program and are clinically or practically meaningful.	Improvement is manifest if evidence-based standards are achieved; comparisons to alternative programs are sometimes made to determine the extent to which the new and the alternative meet justifiable standards. Is the new program more effective? Cost-effective?
Programs/ Interventions	The choice of programs to evaluate depends upon which ones have a sound theoretical base and promising evidence of effectiveness based on previous research. The implementation of the program is carefully monitored to make certain it is implemented as planned.	Recommended programs should have sound research evidence suggesting a high likelihood of success. Consultation with clients or the public can ease the new program's transition into the existing culture of the community, organization, etc. The implementation of the program is carefully monitored to make certain it is implemented as planned.

	Effectiveness Evaluation	*Improvement Evaluation*
Research Design	Research designs are rigorous (e.g., randomized controlled trial).	Research designs are not always a critical concern; however, unless rigorous designs are used, the evaluation results may only apply to a particular setting. If control groups are used, the comparability of the groups at baseline must be established and the control program must be a justifiable alternative to the experimental one.
Sampling	Sampling methods may be complex; inclusion and exclusion criteria are very specific and relatively restrictive; sample size is a concern: It must be large enough to detect a true difference.	Sampling may not be a major concern because everyone who is eligible is invited to participate in the improvement evaluation. Inclusiveness is often a goal.
Data Collection	Data collection relies on demonstrably reliable and valid measures.	Data collection is focused on measuring progress toward meeting needs; measures are often adapted for the local setting and must be tested to ensure that they "fit in" and still produce valid data.
Data Analysis and Data Management	Data management and analysis are often multi-faceted; expert statistical knowledge is essential.	Although expert statistical assistance is recommended, it may not always be necessary. Ability to maintain a database and use inferential statistics is almost always required.

Table 8.6   The Effectiveness and Improvement Evaluators' Perspectives

The Effectiveness Evaluator's Perspective: "Here is a program that is grounded in theory and is likely to be effective, based on findings from previous research in a similar population and setting. I plan to do a randomized controlled trial to find out if the program achieves its objectives in this population and setting and if it is associated with beneficial outcomes when compared to an appropriate alternative program."

The Improvement Evaluator's Perspective: "Here is a program with evidence that matters. It has been selected after an extensive review of the literature and consultation with experts and other decision makers. We held public meetings to discuss the program and received positive reactions. We have pilot tested the program in our organization, with favorable results. Now, I am interested in finding out if the program increases the number of people being served and improves the quality and outcomes of their services. I plan to use a comparison group to help us decide if any observed differences in numbers and quality are truly due to the program."

Research and Ethics: An Indomitable Connection _____

Research with human participants raises ethical concerns because people accept risks and inconvenience in order to contribute new knowledge and provide benefits to others. Research consumers are not responsible for ensuring that research has been conducted in an ethical manner, but they can benefit greatly if they understand the characteristics of ethical research. Consumers are responsible for the use of research results, so it is important for them to learn about the ethical consequences of applying evidence-based practices. In recognition of the strong link between research and ethics, many medical journals require that authors state that their study protocol was reviewed and approved by an **ethics committee** or **institutional review board (IRB)**.

Research and the Institutional Review Board _____

An **institutional review board (IRB)** or ethics committee is an administrative body whose purpose is to protect the rights and welfare of **human research subjects** who are recruited to participate in research activities. Research is defined by the U.S. Department of Health and Human Services (DHHS) as systematic investigation (including research development, testing, and evaluation) designed to develop or contribute to *generalizable knowledge*. The key point here is that knowledge resulting from research must be presumed in advance to apply to other people in other settings. Thus, using the DHHS definitions, **effectiveness evaluations** are research whereas **improvement evaluations** are usually not. (The exception, which we discuss below, occurs when the results of improvement evaluations are considered generalizable and made public through publication.)

According to the DHHS a **human subject** is a living individual about whom an investigator (whether a professional or a student) conducting research obtains (1) data through intervention or interaction with the individual (e.g., in a counseling session or a classroom) or (2) identifiable private information (e.g., birth date or school record number). (For more information about this and other definitions, see the U.S. Department of Health and Human Services, 2005.) The IRB is in charge of determining if the research is structured to guarantee that each participant's privacy and rights are protected. If it is, the research can proceed. If it is not, the IRB will not allow any data collection. All major and reputable social, health, and welfare agencies (school districts, departments of mental health and social services, health departments, and so on) have ethics committees and protection requirements for **human subjects**. Research that receives any U.S. government support (e.g., from the National Institutes of Health, the National Science Foundation, the U.S. Department of Education) must be formally approved by an IRB or ethics committee that itself has been approved by the U.S. Office for Human Research Protections (OHRP: http://www.hhs.gov/ohrp/). Many other countries are equally rigorous as the United States in applying human subject protection, and most of the principles are similar if not identical.

Three Guiding Principles

According to the U.S. government, all IRB activities related to human subjects research should be guided by the ethical principles in *The Belmont Report: Ethical Principles and Guidelines for the Protection of Human Subjects of Research* (www.ohrp.osophs .dhhs.gov). *The Belmont Report* was prepared by the National Commission for the Protection of Human Subjects of Biomedical and Behavioral Research in 1979 and is still the foundation for ethical research. Three major principles come from the Belmont Report:

Respect for Persons. Respect for persons requires investigators to obtain **informed consent** from research participants, to protect participants with impaired decision-making capabilities, and to maintain confidentiality.

Beneficence. This principle requires that research design be scientifically sound and that the risks of the research be acceptable in relation to the likely benefits. The principle of beneficence also means that persons are treated in an ethical manner not only by respecting their decisions and protecting them from harm, but also by actively making efforts to secure their well-being.

Justice. Justice refers to the balance between receiving the benefits of research and bearing its burdens. For example, to ensure justice, the selection of research participants needs to be scrutinized in order to determine whether some classes (e.g., welfare recipients, persons in institutions) are being systematically selected simply because of their easy availability rather than for reasons directly related to the problems being studied.

U.S. government policy also mandates that an IRB must have at least five members, with varying backgrounds. When selecting members, the IRB must take into account racial and cultural heritage and be sensitive to community attitudes. In addition to possessing the professional competence necessary to review specific research activities, the IRB members must also be able to ascertain the acceptability of proposed research in terms of institutional commitments and regulations, applicable law, and standards of professional conduct and practice.

U.S. government policy requires that, if an IRB regularly reviews research that involves a vulnerable category of participants (such as children, prisoners, pregnant women, or handicapped or mentally disabled persons), it must consider the inclusion of one or more individuals who are knowledgeable about and experienced in working with these participants. Also, the IRB must make every nondiscriminatory effort to ensure that it does not consist entirely of men or entirely of women.

Table 8.7 lists the major criteria used by IRBs and ethics committees in approving research protocols.

Obtaining Informed Consent

The informed consent process requires researchers to disclose information that will be relevant to the potential participant's decision about whether to participate in the research. Disclosure means answering questions such as these: Why is the research being done? What will participants do? What are the risks and benefits of participating?

Informed consent is usually obtained in writing. If written consent cannot be obtained (participant is blind or cannot write), then the researchers must provide evidence that consent was administered (say, on the phone) and understood. The consent form is designed to

Table 8.7   Criteria Used by an Institutional Review Board (IRB) in Approving Research Protocols

- **Study Design:** Many experts agree that an IRB should approve only research that is both valid and of value. The thinking is that a poorly designed study will necessarily lead to misleading results. Study design includes subject recruitment, selection, and assignment to groups; measure or instrument reliability and validity; and data analysis.

- **Risks and Benefits:** IRBs evaluate whether the risks to participants are reasonable in relation to the anticipated benefits, if any, to the participants, and they asses the importance of the knowledge reasonably expected to result from the research.

- **Equipoise:** The ethical basis for assigning treatment by randomization is the judgment that current evidence does not favor the superiority of the experimental over the control program.

- **Equitable Selection of Participants:** The IRB usually considers the purpose of the research and the setting of the research and closely examines studies involving vulnerable populations, such as children, prisoners, participants with cognitive disorders, or economically or educationally disadvantaged people.

- **Identification of Participants and Confidentiality:** The IRB is required to review the method for prospective identification of research participants. IRB members examine the researchers' means of identifying and contacting potential participants and the methods for ensuring the participants' privacy and confidentiality.

- **Participant Payment:** Many medical and health-related studies provide financial and other incentives to study participants to compensate them for their time. Ethical concerns arise if the payment is high or too low. If the payment is high, some participants may be induced to take risks against their better judgment. If the payment is too low, some participants may not believe the study is worth their time.

- **Qualifications:** The IRB examines the qualifications of the evaluator and the evaluation team. In addition, the IRB considers the facilities and equipment used to conduct the research and maintain the rights and welfare of the participants.

- **The Informed Consent Process: Informed consent** means that participants who agree to participate in the research are knowledgeable about the risks and benefits of participation and the activities that comprise participation. They also agree to the terms of participation and are knowledgeable about their rights as research subjects.

protect all parties: the participant, the researcher, and the institution. Therefore, it is important that consent forms present information in an organized and easily understood format.

In some studies, researchers design separate informed consent forms for parents and assent (verbal) forms for children.

Table 8.8 contains the contents of an informed consent form that should be discussed with research participants.

Table 8.8   The Contents of Informed Consent

1. **The Characteristics of the Research.** The participant should be told directly that research is being conducted, what the research's purpose is, and how participants were chosen.

2. **The Study Procedures.** Participants should be told what they are going to be doing in the project, how much time will be needed, and when participation will begin and end. Alternative procedures should be discussed as should blinding or randomization.

3. **Potential Risks and Benefits.** Although some research may pose significant risks (a new drug therapy, for example) other research may not. Almost all research results in some discomfort (e.g., feeling embarrassed by questions about drug or alcohol use).

    Also, participation in research is sometimes mistakenly assumed to mean benefit, especially for people who know they are in the experimental group (not blinded). Researchers should state clearly that they do not know if the experimental treatment is better than the control or an alternative.

4. **Assurance That Participation Is Voluntary.** Participants should be told that they are free not to enroll or to enroll and drop out.

5. **Procedures to Maintain Confidentiality.** These include coding research data, storing it in locked computers and file cabinets, and limiting the number of people who have access to it. These measures should be discussed with research participants.

The Special Case of Evaluations That Are Exempt From IRB Approval

A program evaluation is considered to be research by many IRBs when the evaluator intends to create generalizable knowledge that will be shared outside of the program being evaluated in professional presentations, reports, or published articles. In all likelihood, process and implementation and improvement evaluations will not be considered research. Process and implementation evaluation data are used, typically, to assess progress and better understand operations within a program, while improvement evaluations are designed to assess quality within an institution. The results of these evaluations are almost always not designed for publication. If the evaluators do not intend to generalize or publicize the results, their studies may be exempt from IRB scrutiny. Consider Example 8.5.

Limits to Confidentiality

Depending on the research's aims, there may be limits to the investigator's promise of confidentiality to the subject. An example would be if a participant reveals information about child or elder abuse, and you were required by law to report this information.

Example 8.5   An Evaluation That Is Exempt From IRB Approval

The Health Center wants to improve its influenza vaccination rate. An automatic e-mail system is set up to remind physicians of their patients who are due for the vaccination. An evaluation is conducted of the effectiveness of the e-mail reminder system, and data are collected each year for two years. Information from the evaluation will not be shared with anyone outside the Health Center.

Comment: This evaluation is probably exempt from being reviewed by the ethics committee because the findings are going to be used only by the Health Center. It does not conform to the definition of human subjects' research, which results in generalizable information and may be published.

Research Misconduct

Research misconduct includes such factors as fabrication, falsification, and plagiarism. Fabrication means making up results and recording or reporting them. Falsification includes changing or omitting data or results. Plagiarism means taking another person's ideas, results, or work without giving due credit.

Research misconduct is becoming an increasingly important concern throughout the world. The following (Table 8.9) are problematic behaviors and definitions of misconduct that may apply to many situations in which evaluations are conducted.

Faking the data is a clear example of research misconduct. More subtle examples include

- Exaggerating findings to support the researcher's point of view
- Changing the research protocol or method of implementing the program without informing the IRB before doing so
- Failing to maintain adequate documentation of the research methods (such as preparing a code book or operations manual)
- Releasing participant information without permission to do so
- Having insufficient resources to complete the research as promised
- Having financial or other interests in the funders or supporters of the evaluation (conflict of interest)

Many agencies and professional organizations provide guidelines for ethical research. Table 8.10 lists some of these organizations and their Web sites.

Table 8.9   Problematic Behaviors in Research Leading to Charges of Misconduct

Problematic Behavior	Definition
Misconduct	Fabrication, falsification, or plagiarism
Questionable research practices	Actions that violate values of research and may be detrimental to the research process but do not directly threaten the integrity of the research record Examples include failing to retain research records for a reasonable period or using inappropriate statistics to enhance findings
Other misconduct, not pertaining to scientific integrity	Unacceptable behaviors subject to generally applicable legal and social penalties but that are not unique to research Examples include sexual harassment, misuse of funds, or violations of federal regulations
Other misconduct, pertaining to scientific integrity	Unacceptable behavior that does not directly affect the integrity of the research process but is nevertheless directly associated with misconduct in science Examples include cover-ups of scientific misconduct or reprisals against whistleblowers
Sloppiness	Negligent or irregular research practices that risk distortion of the research record but that lack the intent to do so

Table 8.10   Agencies That Have Policies and Guidelines for Conducting Ethical Research

American Psychological Association (APA)

- Ethical Principles of Psychologists and Code of Conduct
  http://www.apa.org/ethics/code2002.html
      The current version of this document was adopted by the American Psychological Association Council of Representatives on June 1, 2003. It includes information about issues pertaining to privacy and confidentiality, therapy, publishing, and more.

- Ethical Principles of Psychologists and Code of Conduct (1992)
  http://www.apa.org/ethics/code1992.html
      Between 1992 and 2003, the APA was guided by this ethics code.

- Guidelines for Ethical Conduct in the Care and Use of Animals
  http://www.apa.org/science/anguide.html
      This is a set of guidelines developed by APA to be used by psychologists working with animals. The document covers areas such as housing of animals, experimental procedures, and educational use of animals.

American Public Health Association (APHA): Public Health Code of Ethics

http://www.apha.org/programs/education/progeduethicalguidelines.htm

The ethical guidelines can be accessed from this Web site highlight issues that are unique to the public health field.

American Statistical Association (ASA): Ethical Guidelines for Statistical Practice

http://www.amstat.org/profession/index.cfm?fuseaction=ethicalstatistics

ASA's Committee on Professional Ethics prepared these guidelines, and they were approved by their Board of Directors on August 7, 1999. This document contains two sections: the preamble and ethical guidelines.

Applied Research Ethics National Association (ARENA)

http://www.primr.org/membership/overview.html

ARENA is a national membership organization that deals with biomedical and behavioral research issues such as scientific misconduct, ethical decision making in health care, and the protection of human and animal subjects. The group was organized in 1986.

Association for Practical and Professional Ethics

http://www.indiana.edu/~appe/

The Association for Practical and Professional Ethics was founded in 1991 with the support of Indiana University and a Lilly Endowment. Its mission is to "encourage interdisciplinary scholarship and teaching of high quality in practical and professional ethics by educators and practitioners." This site includes association information, association activities, association publications, and electronic networking opportunities.

Association of University Professors (AAUP): Statement on Professional Ethics

http://www.aaup.org/AAUP/pubsres/policydocs/statementonprofessionalethics.htm

The statement that appears at this site is a revised version of one that originally appeared in 1966. In 1987, the AAUP adopted this current document that was endorsed at its seventy-third annual meeting.

Center for Academic Integrity (CAI)

http://www.academicintegrity.org

The Center for Academic Integrity is affiliated with the Rutland Institute for Ethics at Clemson University. CAI's mission is "to identify and affirm the values of academic integrity and to promote their achievement in practice."

Council on Undergraduate Research (CUR)

http://www.cur.org/conferences/responsibility/ResRespons.html

The mission of CUR is to "support and promote high-quality undergraduate student-faculty collaborative research and scholarship." In June 2002, CUR held a major symposium titled *Research Responsibility and Undergraduates*. Manuscripts, post-conference workshop summaries, and news on guidelines related to responsible research are merely a few of the resources posted at this site.

Creating a Code of Ethics for Your Organization

http://www.ethicsweb.ca/codes/

Chris MacDonald, PhD, Philosophy Department, St. Mary's University (Halifax, Canada) has put together this site with links to resources to assist individuals and groups

(Continued)

Table 8.10 (Continued)

in writing a code of ethics. He discusses why organizations and institutions should even have a code and provides guidance in writing one. He also provides links to essays on ethics, sample codes, and contacts for ethics consultants.

Federal Policy on Research Misconduct

http://www.ostp.gov/html/001207_3.html

The Office of Science and Technology Policy has posted this site, which includes information on issues such as requirements for findings of scientific misconduct, responsibilities of federal agencies and research institutions, and guidelines for fair and timely procedures and agency administrative actions.

Framework for Policies and Procedures to Deal With Research Fraud

http://www.aau.edu/reports/FrwkRschFraud.html

This Association of American Universities document grew out of the belief that universities should be held responsible for the actions of their faculty and staff, not research sponsors. As a result of this belief, an interagency group got together to develop this "framework" in 1988. Areas such as "Definition of Research Fraud" and "Process for Handling Allegations of Research Fraud" are covered in this document.

Illinois Institute of Technology Codes of Ethics Online

http://ethics.iit.edu/codes/coe.html

Illinois Institute of Technology's Center for the Study of Ethics in the Professions (CSEP) developed this online collection of over 850 codes of ethics. CSEP received a grant from NSF in 1996 to put its collection of codes on the Web, a collection that grew out of CSEP's paper archive of codes. In addition to the codes, resources for authoring a code, case studies, and other information can be found at this site.

Office of Human Research Protections (OHRP)

http://www.hhs.gov/ohrp/

This OHRP site, part of the U.S. Department of Health and Human Services, provides links to IRB registration and filing information, policy guidelines, compliance oversights, educational materials, and upcoming workshop events.

Office of Research Integrity (ORI)

http://ori.dhhs.gov

The goal of the ORI is to "promote integrity in biomedical and behavioral research supported by the Public Health Service (PHS)." This site has links to resources like breaking news stories, tips for handling misconduct, publications, and policies, regulations, and statutes.

Scientific Freedom, Responsibility & Law

http://www.aaas.org/spp/sfrl/

This program is part of the AAAS Directorate for Science & Policy, and it focuses on the ethical, legal, and social issues associated with the conduct of research and with the advances in science and technology. Information and links to projects and activities, publications, and access to the PER newsletter (http://www.aaas.org/spp/sfrl/per/per.htm) can be found at this site.

University of California, San Diego: Office of Graduate Studies and Research

http://ogs.ucsd.edu/

The Office of Graduate Studies and Research at the University of California, San Diego (UCSD) has posted policies that are applicable to those doing research.

Training in research ethics and the proper conduct of research can be done online. Many institutions require that researchers complete such training before doing research with human subjects. (See, for example, the OHRP site *Human Subject Assurance Training*: http://ohrp-ed.od.nih.gov/CBTs/Assurance/login.asp.)

Practicing Research and Ethics

From an ethical perspective, the strongest arguments in support of evidence-based practice are that it allows the best evaluated programs (and useless or harmful ones) to be identified and that it facilitates informed decisions. But all may not be well because the body of research is often incomplete, methodologically flawed, or unresponsive to important social and cultural needs. Further, although evidence is emerging in health care that research-based interventions produce better outcomes, little evidence is available for other fields (although those studies are being done). Therefore, consumers who adopt evidence-based methods should do so cautiously, keeping in mind the ethical implications of the emerging field of evidence-based practice.

Table 8.11 lists some of the major ethical concerns associated with the use of evidence-based practices.

Table 8.11   Ethics and Evidence-Based Practices

Ethical Concern	Explanation
Many important outcomes cannot be measured.	Evidence-based practice aims to provide a simple, logical process for reasoning and decision making. But to make balanced decisions, all the relevant consequences of an action must be considered. Current measures of some outcomes (such as pain) are inadequate, while others (such as justice) may not be measurable. Further, other complex outcomes (such as quality of life) may not even be adequately definable (across cultures, generations, and over time). Often, researchers "settle" for imprecise measures or proximate outcomes.
Stakeholders' needs may differ markedly from those of researchers and policy makers.	The community—recipients of evidence-based practices—has relatively little influence over the priorities and funding of research.

(Continued)

Table 8.11 (Continued)

Ethical Concern	Explanation
Because the large quantities of data required to meet the standards of evidence-based practice are available for relatively few interventions, a systematic bias may be inevitable toward those interventions.	The bias may ultimately result in the allocation of resources to those interventions for which there is rigorous evidence of effectiveness or toward those for which there are funds available to show effectiveness. This may be at the expense of other areas where rigorous evidence does not currently exist or is not attainable (such as palliative care services). Allocating resources on the basis of evidence may therefore involve implicit value judgments, which is at odds with evidence-based practices that emphasize explicit "objective" criteria.
The application of cost-effectiveness measures to decisions about who does or does not receive services may adversely affect the position of the weaker groups in our society.	People who are expected to benefit only slightly from particular programs, such as the elderly and the disabled, may be excluded from access to such programs particularly when they are expensive. Many vulnerable people have been excluded from large-scale research because of the perceived (or real) difficulty of retaining and caring for them.
Use of the term "evidence-based" may be misleading (Steinberg & Luce, 2005). Research consumers, policy makers, and others acting on the basis of recommendations labeled as being "evidence-based" should not blindly assume that the label truly applies.	EBP methods are often not applied consistently or interpreted properly. The potential exists for great variation in the validity of decisions and recommendations that claim to be "evidence-based." In addition, evidence may be available for some but not all issues related to a decision or recommendation that has to be made, or the evidence that is available may not be directly relevant to the situation to which it is being applied.

Acknowledging the limitations of evidence-based practice and its associated ethical problems should not deter research consumers from searching for the best evidence when making decisions about the selection of programs and interventions to improve the public's health and welfare. Research consumers who understand the complexity of the issues have more data to work with when making decisions than those who unthinkingly accept or reject the methods and findings of evidence-based practice. Informed consumers may even decide to use their knowledge to demand that researchers devise more publicly responsive methods of collecting evidence—so that it truly matters.

Summary of Chapter 8:
The Ethical Research Consumer
Assesses Needs and Evaluates Improvement

Words to Remember

administrative needs; behavioral needs; beneficence; communal or epidemiological needs; consensus development conferences; Delphi technique; educational needs; effectiveness evaluation; equipoise; ethics committee; evidence that matters; focus groups; human subject; improvement evaluation; informed consent; institutional review board; justice; key informant; needs assessment; nominal group process; physical needs; public or community forum; the RAND/UCLA Appropriateness Method; research misconduct; respect for persons; social needs; surveys

Evidence-based practitioners count on the experimental method to provide evidence that matters, and they agree on the need to incorporate users' needs, preferences and values, and expectations into treatments, practices, and programs. A systematic effort to identify user needs and provide a context for them is called a **needs assessment.**

Needs can be arranged into six categories: social, communal or epidemiological, behavioral, environmental, educational, and administrative.

At least seven methods are commonly used to determine individual and public needs:

1. The purpose of **the key informant method** is to collect information about a community's needs by interviewing community leaders who are likely to be in a position to know what the needs are.

2. A **community forum** consists of a group of people who meet together to discuss a common problem. The meeting is open to all members of the community.

3. A **focus group** is designed to collect information from "insiders" or "people in the know." The group usually consists of about 10 carefully selected participants and a trained moderator. The session lasts about two hours and is centered on getting answers to four or five carefully constructed questions.

4. In **the nominal group technique**, participants are brought together for a discussion session led by a moderator. After the topic of concern has been presented to session participants and they have had an opportunity to ask questions or briefly discuss the scope of the topic, they are asked to take a few minutes to think about and write down their responses. The session moderator will then ask each participant to read, and elaborate on, one of his or her responses. These are noted on a flipchart. Once everyone has given a response, participants will be asked for a second or third response, until all of their answers have been noted on flipchart sheets posted around the room.

5. **The Delphi technique** is a structured method of determining the degree of agreement on a topic, selecting alternatives, or setting priorities. Delphi techniques use questionnaires that are completed by participants on their own, in groups, or both. The questionnaires are structured to ask people to rate or rank the importance or validity of certain ideas.

6. **The RAND/UCLA Appropriateness Method** (RUAM) is a method for determining the extent of agreement on controversial topics and on subjects for which the research base is poor or ambiguous (a mixture of positive and negative findings).

7. **Surveys** are usually used to gather information from large numbers of people. Several types are possible. A face-to-face interview may result in in-depth information but requires a skilled interviewer. Telephone surveys also require skilled interviewers, and it has become increasingly difficult to get people to agree to participate. People hanging up, the need to call back, and messages left on voice mail are costly. E-mail, online, and mailed surveys can reach large numbers of people.

Although not yet widely implemented in the other helping professions, **consensus development conferences** are an integral part of evidence-based health care, and their methods can be usefully adapted to other fields. NIH Consensus and State-of-the-Science statements are prepared by independent panels of health professionals and public representatives on the basis of (1) the results of a systematic literature review, (2) presentations by investigators working in areas relevant to the conference questions during a two-day public session, (3) questions and statements from conference attendees during open discussion periods that are part of the public session, and (4) closed deliberations and the production of a report by the panel during the remainder of the second day and the morning of the third.

Some evaluations are designed to examine the extent to which the newly adopted programs met clients' needs and identify where improvements should be made to improve future efforts to find evidence that matters. The type of evaluation that is used to accomplish these purposes is called an **improvement evaluation**.

Effectiveness and improvement evaluators have differing goals. Effectiveness evaluators aim to determine if a program is successful when compared to an alternative. Improvement evaluators want to find out if a successful program is specifically beneficial in their setting.

Research with human participants raises **ethical** concerns because people accept risks and inconvenience in order to contribute new knowledge and provide benefits to others. Research consumers are not responsible for ensuring that research has been conducted in an ethical manner, but they can benefit greatly if they understand the characteristics of ethical research. Consumers are responsible for the use of research results, so it is important for them to learn about the limitations of research methods and evidence-based practices and how some of these limitations have ethical implications.

An **institutional review board (IRB)** or **ethics committee** is an administrative body whose purpose is to protect the rights and welfare of human research subjects who are recruited to participate in research activities. The IRB is in charge of determining if the research is structured to guarantee that each participant's privacy and rights are protected. If it is, the research can proceed. If it is not, the IRB will not allow any data collection.

Three major principles guide much of health research.

Respect for Persons. Respect for persons requires investigators to obtain **informed consent** from research participants, to protect participants with impaired decision-making capabilities, and to maintain confidentiality.

Beneficence. This principle requires that research design be scientifically sound and that the risks of the research be acceptable in relation to the likely benefits. The principle of **beneficence** also means that researchers treat people in an ethical manner, not only by respecting their decisions and protecting them from harm but also by actively making efforts to secure their well-being.

Justice. Justice refers to the balance between receiving the benefits of research and bearing its burdens. For example, to ensure justice, the selection of research participants needs to be scrutinized in order to determine whether some classes (e.g., welfare recipients, persons in institutions) are being systematically selected simply because of their easy availability rather than for reasons directly related to the problems being studied.

The informed consent process requires researchers to disclose information that will be relevant to the potential participant's decision about whether to participate in the research. Disclosure means answering questions such as these: Why is the research being done? What will participants do? What are the risks and benefits of participating?

Research misconduct includes such factors as fabrication, falsification, and plagiarism. Fabrication means making up results and recording or reporting them. Falsification includes changing or omitting data or results. Plagiarism means taking another person's ideas, results, or work without giving due credit.

Research consumers should be aware of at least four ethical concerns in the application of evidence-based practices to their own settings. First, many important outcomes of treatment cannot be measured. Second, it may be impossible to decide between the competing claims of different stakeholders. Third, because the large quantities of data required to meet the standards of evidence-based practice are available for relatively few interventions, a systematic bias may be inevitable toward adapting those interventions. Finally, the application of cost-effectiveness measures to decisions about who does and who does not receive services may adversely affect the position of the weaker groups in our society.

Exercises

1. Name the assessment technique used in each of the following studies.

   a. Home Injury Hazard Risks and Prevention Methods for Young Children

   The Board requested a list of 5–7 injury hazards and 5–7 potential prevention behaviors and/or devices for children aged 1–5 years in each of the following areas of the home: bedroom/play area, kitchen/dining area, bathroom, living room, basement/garage (including other outdoor areas such as the driveway), pool, stairs/hallway, and multiple rooms/general safety. We asked participants to develop their lists of hazards by considering the *frequency, severity,* and *preventability* of the potential injury from each hazard, as well as the *efficacy* and *feasibility* of each prevention method. Efficacy was defined as the ability of the behavior or the device, if implemented, to eliminate the hazard and/or to prevent the injury. Feasibility was defined as the likelihood of implementation of the behavior or the device (depending on acquisition, installation, utilization, and maintenance).

   Round 2 asked participants to *rate* each hazard and behavior/device listed in the responses submitted to survey 1 using a scale of 1 to 3 (with 3 being highest priority). Participants could also assign a score of zero (0) if they believed that an item should not remain on the list. In rating each item, the participants were instructed to consider the same factors used in the first round (for example, children aged 1–5 years; frequency, severity, and preventability for the hazards; and efficacy and feasibility for the behaviors/devices). We calculated a mean score for each item by summing all ratings reported for a single item. Items were subsequently listed in descending order of priority.

   The 47 hazards and 52 prevention methods with the highest mean scores were selected for inclusion in survey 3 based upon natural clusters, rather than just choosing the top 50 of each.

   For the 99 selected items, the third round asked participants to *rate* each hazard using a Likert scale of 1 to 5 (with 5 being the most important) considering overall importance in an injury prevention program for preschool aged children, 3–5 years of age. This age group request differed from previous rounds as we sought to use the panel's findings for a future injury prevention program targeted at children aged 3–5 years.

SOURCE: Katcher, Meister, Sorkness, et al. (2006).

b. Impact of Smoke-Free Residence Hall Policies: The Views of Administrators at Three State Universities

Interviews with XXX aimed to (1) explore staff interpretation of trends and data, (2) assess observed changes in campus constituent with attitudes and behaviors resulting from the policy change, and (3) determine the impact of the policy change on personnel workload. We designed questions tailored to each department to elicit information and to enrich understanding of the policy's impact. As appropriate, the interviewer requested additional existing documentation during interviews.

In total, we contacted 47 personnel for interviews. Thirty campus personnel contributed to the study through telephone interviews, e-mail correspondences, providing data, or a combination thereof. We conducted 27 telephone interviews: 10 at URI, 7 at MSU, and 10 at OSU. Three additional xxx answered questions by e-mail correspondence. At MSU and URI, personnel from all identified departments, except admissions, participated in the interviews. At OSU, personnel from all 7 departments participated. In some cases, we interviewed multiple personnel from a single department. The interviewer took copious notes during the interviews and then compiled them along with e-mail correspondence into an interview report.

SOURCE: Gerson, Allard, and Towvim (2005).

2. Match each need with its appropriate definition.

Need	Definition
A. Social	1. Individual and communal lifestyles and beliefs that affect a community's well-being
B. Behavioral	2. Community's perceptions of its problems
C. Administrative	3. Problems that can be documented to affect a large number of people in the community
D. Communal/ Epidemiological	4. Social or physical factors that are external to an individual or a community
E. Physical	5. Policies and resources that exist in the organizations and institutions (e.g., school, hospital, business, nongovernmental organization) that might facilitate or hinder the adoption of a new program
F. Educational	6. Individual and community knowledge, attitudes, skills, and self-efficacy beliefs

3. Which of these should be applied to improvement evaluation? Check all that apply.
   ☐ Evidence-based programs
   ☐ Randomized controlled trials with blinded observers
   ☐ Evidence-based performance standards
   ☐ Very detailed study inclusion criteria

4. Which of these should be applied to effectiveness evaluations? Check all that apply.
   ☐ Reliable and valid measures
   ☐ Inclusive study eligibility criteria
   ☐ Assessment of evidence-based programs
   ☐ Flexible evaluation designs

5. Match the following statement with the concept that supports or defines it.

1. In our RCT, we went to great trouble to ensure that the alternative program has not been proven superior to the experimental.	a. Informed consent
2. Participants in the research are knowledgeable about the risks and benefits of participation and the activities that comprise participation. They also agree to the terms of participation and are knowledgeable about their rights as research subjects.	b. The ethics committee or institutional review board (IRB)
3. U.S. government policy also mandates that it must have at least five members, with varying backgrounds. When selecting members, the committee must take into account racial and cultural heritage and be sensitive to community attitudes.	c. Equipoise
4. The selection of research participants needs to be scrutinized in order to determine whether some classes (e.g., welfare recipients, persons in institutions) are being systematically selected simply because of their easy availability rather than for reasons directly related to the problems being studied.	d. Justice

6. Which of these is characteristic of research misconduct? Circle all that apply.

Plagiarism	a
Falsification	b
Conflict of interest	c
Fabrication	d

7. Which of these is a potential ethical concern when considering the adaptation of evidence-based practices? Circle all that apply.

The application of cost-effectiveness measures to decisions about who does or does not receive services may adversely affect the position of the weaker groups in our society.	a
Many important outcomes cannot be measured.	b
Because the large quantities of data required to meet the standards of evidence-based practice are available for relatively few interventions, a systematic bias may be inevitable toward those interventions.	c
It may be impossible to decide between competing claims of different stakeholders.	d

8. What is the primary reason that research with human participants raises ethical concerns? Circle one.

Participants are not always told why they are being asked to join a study.	a
Participants accept risks they might not otherwise agree to.	b
Participants frequently get paid for their participation.	c
Participants are rarely part of the ethics committee to approve the study protocol.	d

9. Which of these is a defining characteristic of the ethical principal of beneficence? Circle one.

Scientifically sound research design	a
A balance between benefits and risks	b
Informed consent	c

Appendix _____

Answers to Exercises

Chapter 1. The Evaluation Research and _____ Evidence-Based Practice Partnership

1.
   a. Yes. This is an evaluation study. The program is an intervention to prevent high HIV risk sexual behaviors for Latina women in urban areas.
   b. Yes. This is an evaluation study. The intervention is a spit tobacco intervention.
   c. No. This is not an evaluation study. The researchers are not analyzing the process, outcomes, impact, or costs of a program or intervention.

2.
   a. The intervention is the Hawaii Healthy Start Program (HSP), which is operated at three sites by community-based agencies. This program provides home visiting services to families identified as at-risk of child abuse; it hopes to prevent child abuse and neglect in the first three years of life.
   b. The main outcomes studied were (1) to prevent child abuse or (2) promote the use of nonviolent discipline and (3) to prevent neglect.
   c. There were three hypotheses:
      • No difference exists between HSP and the control in preventing child abuse
      • No difference exists between HSP and the control in promoting the use of nonviolent discipline
      • A difference exists between HSP and the control in preventing neglect

3.

Evaluation research
1. Is a systematic investigation
2. Uses scientific method
3. Uses experimental methods
4. Focuses on process, outcomes, impact, and costs of a program
5. Provides new knowledge about social behavior
6. Results are accurate
7. Results are helpful to users

4.

EBM/EBP
1. Relies on best research evidence
2. Incorporates patient values into options for decisions about treatment
3. Uses clinical expertise to integrate best evidence and patient values

5.

Evaluation research and EBM are similar in that they both are concerned with evidence that matters about programs and interventions. Evidence that matters is valid because it is derived from scientific evaluations. To be useful, research results must be based on studies that address the needs, values, and expectations of patients and other clients. Both evaluation research and EBM are concerned with the ethical implications of research with human participants. EBM, however, is usually characterized by its emphasis on using research results to work with individual patients to choose their best treatment options.

6.

Evaluation research is always concerned with the process, impact, outcomes, and costs of programs and interventions. Evaluation research almost always takes place in an institutional and organizational context, whereas other types of research often do not. Evaluators need management and group skills as well as research savvy.

7.

The best evaluation and social research adhere to the scientific method.

8.

Evaluation consumers rely upon evaluation research to provide information about a program's process, outcomes, impact, and costs. Many evaluations include sponsors and other users in some or all phases of the research process and have developed techniques for ascertaining their values and preferences. These same participatory techniques can be used by evaluation consumers in working with their clients in selecting high quality programs that are also appropriate. EBM practitioners have developed explicit systems for locating and analyzing research findings and for grading their quality and strength. The evaluation consumer needs these to identify the best research evidence and the highest quality programs.

9.

Definitions 1, 3, and 4 emphasize research or empirically driven data as a contribution of evaluation. Definitions 2 and 3 state that evaluation's purpose is to determine if a program has achieved its objectives. Definition 4 emphasizes evaluation's goals of influencing decision making through empirically driven feedback. Definition 1 is the broadest definition because (like definition 2) it states that evaluation also includes attention to process (formative) information. Like Definition 4, Definition 1 describes research evidence that matters in terms of the aptness of the "fit" between the evidence and the stakeholders' values and expectations.

Chapter 2. The Research Consumer as Detective: Investigative Program and Bibliographic Databases

1.

First look through the lists of resources provided in Table 2.1. If you cannot find what you are looking for, consider contacting government agencies, research institutes, school districts, and universities for information. Program databases may not be available in all fields.

2.

The consumer should contact the program site and ask the site or project coordinator to send copies of the relevant articles. If the project is unwilling to do so, the consumer should be extremely cautious about adopting the programs that the site recommends.

3.

a and d

4.

Note: These answers are purely illustrative. Other articles databases may also be useful.

a. PsycINFO; MEDLINE/PubMed; Social Sciences Citation Index
b. ERIC; Social Sciences Citation Index

    c. MEDLINE/PubMed; PsycINFO

    d. MEDLINE/PubMed

5.

    a. How does an online educational program compare to printed materials in reducing the number of home-based falls in older adults?

    b. How do home visits and small group sessions compare in fostering parenting skills in first-time parents?

    c. Do ads on local television stations and e-mailed newsletters to community leaders increase parental involvement in the Parent-School Organization (PSO)?

    d. How do pharmacists and health educators compare in their ability to teach adults 75 years of age and older the names, dosages, and purposes of their medications?

6.

    a. How does an online educational program compare to printed materials in reducing the number of home-based falls in older adults?
       Key words: online, Web, Internet; aged 65+; printed materials; education; falls; program; evaluation; evaluation research; English

    b. How do home visits and small group sessions compare in fostering parenting skills in first-time parents?
       Key words: home visits; small groups; parenting; program evaluation; evaluation research; English

    c. Do ads on local television stations and emailed newsletters to community leaders increase parental involvement in the Parent-School Organization (PSO)?
       Key words: advertisement; television; e-mail, electronic newsletter, e-news; community leaders; parents; program evaluation; evaluation research; English

    d. How do pharmacists and health educators compare in their ability to teach adults 75 years of age and older the names, dosages, and purposes of their medications?
       Key words: pharmacists; health educators; older adults, adults 75+; medications, medication use; health literacy; program evaluation; evaluation research: English

7.

    a. Example Boolean operators: Aged 65+ AND education AND falls AND English (as of August 2006, this search yielded 431 entries from PubMed)

b. Example Boolean operators: parenting AND education AND program OR evaluation AND English (as of August 2007, this search yielded 468 publications from PubMed)

8.

You can limit your search by author's name, journal name, article title, date of publication, language, age group, gender, publication type, human or animal studies, and many more parameters; the limitations available depend on the database you are using.

9.

Other sources of information about programs and practices include
1. Reference lists in high quality studies
2. Colleagues and other experts (including authors of articles that interest you)
3. Government, university, and foundation Web sites

_____ Chapter 3. The Practical Research Consumer

1.

(1) Disagree; (2) Agree (data on how program participants' outcomes compare to nonparticipants'); (3) Disagree; (4) Cannot tell; (5) Disagree

2.

Practical criteria can include publication language, journal or origin of publication, program characteristics, program's theoretical foundation, research design, setting, data collection dates, duration of data collection, publication date, participants, content, and outcomes. Not all these criteria were discussed by the authors of the study on whether a fetus feels pain. The practical criteria that were used to select articles for this study were

Publication language: English

Publication dates: No restrictions on start date; last article reviewed was June 6, 2005

Participants: Human studies of fetuses of less than 30 weeks' gestational age

Content: Fetal pain, anesthesia, and analgesia; fetal pain perception or nociception

3.

Official name of the program: Cognitive-Behavioral Program for Veterans with Trauma (CBV)

Characteristics of target population: Veterans who have symptoms of posttraumatic stress syndrome, commonly called PTSD

Characteristics of comparison group: Not described

Data on the outcomes that are being compared: Trauma scores

How the program is implemented: The CBV program incorporates cognitive behavioral therapy (CBT) skills in a group format (five–eight veterans per group) to address symptoms of posttraumatic stress disorder (PTSD). Generally, in each session, a new set of techniques is introduced by a mixture of didactic presentation, and individuals work on worksheets during and between sessions. Homework assignments are developed collaboratively between the veteran and the clinician in each session and are reviewed at the beginning of the next session.

Duration of each activity: Not described

Duration of the program: The CBV program was implemented on a continuous basis from the late autumn through the spring of 200X-200Y by one part-time and two full-time psychiatric social workers from the Veterans Affairs Mental Health Services Unit. The groups most often met once a week at a time mutually agreed upon at the end of each session. Most groups met during the late afternoon.

Resources needed to perform each major activity: One part-time and two full-time psychiatric social workers; two hours of training for each; a meeting place that holds from eight to eleven people.

Information on costs, cost-effectiveness, or cost-benefit: Not described

As you can see, the report does not provide information on three potentially important factors:

- The group
- The duration of each activity
- Costs

How important are these three factors? The answer depends upon you, your needs, and the availability of information on all the important factors from reports on practices of similar quality.

4.

The researchers conducted a cost-effectiveness analysis in which they found that one model of care (hospital-based home care) had both improved outcomes and lower costs when compared to another model of care (conventional outpatient services).

5.

Outcomes: Self-reported incidence of abuse and possibly changes in disease morbidity or mortality

Comparison groups: No intervention control, a usual care control, or a group receiving an alternate intervention for study purposes

_____ Chapter 4. The Designing Research Consumer

1.

Article 1: Impact of School-Based Health Centers on Children With Asthma

Objective: To assess the impact of school-based health centers (SBHCs) on hospitalization and emergency department (ED) visits for children with asthma.

Assessment for Eligibility: Children with asthma with at least two years of continuous enrollment who had medical claims for asthma diagnosis and anti-asthmatic medications were selected. Two comparison (non-SBHC) school districts (six schools) were selected to reflect students with similar characteristics to those in SBHC schools based on Ohio census data from local education departments, including information on rural/urban setting, percentage of student body that was nonwhite, and percentage of students eligible for free or reduced lunch.

Evaluation Research Design: The study was conducted at four SBHC intervention school districts and two comparable non-SBHC school districts in Greater Cincinnati, Ohio. A longitudinal, quasi-experimental, time-series repeated measures design was used.

Findings: Asthma was one of the major diseases for SBHC encounters. After the opening of the SBHC, relative risks of hospitalization and ED visits in the SBHC group decreased. The cost of hospitalization per child decreased significantly over time for children in SBHC schools. Costs of ED visits for children in SBHC schools were significantly lower than for children in non-SBHC schools.

Article 2. Acupuncture for Patients With Migraine: A Randomized Controlled Trial

Objective: To investigate the effectiveness of acupuncture compared with sham acupuncture and with no acupuncture in patients with migraine.

Assessment for Eligibility: Patients with migraine headaches (based on International Headache Society criteria) who were treated at 18 outpatients centers in Germany over a nine-month period.

Evaluation Research Design: Three-group, randomized controlled trial with patients participating in one of three programs: acupuncture, sham acupuncture, or waiting list control.

Results: Between baseline and weeks 9 to 12, the mean number of days with headache of moderate or severe intensity decreased by 2.2 days from a baseline of 5.2 days in the acupuncture group compared with a decrease to 2.2 days from a baseline of 5.0 days in the sham acupuncture group, and by 0.8 days from a baseline of 5.4 days in the waiting list group. No difference was detected between the acupuncture and the sham acupuncture groups, while there was a difference between the acupuncture group compared with the waiting list group. Acupuncture was no more effective than sham acupuncture in reducing migraine headaches although both interventions were more effective than a waiting list control.

2.

ST users tended to be upperclassmen (sophomores, juniors, and seniors); only 11% were freshmen. Eleven percent said they currently smoked. Thirty-eight percent reported having little or no confidence that they could quit ST use, whereas 43% were very confident. Forty-three percent were daily ST users, 23% used ST within 30 minutes of waking, and 93% used dip or dip and chew ST. There were slightly more control than intervention subjects at upper levels of all three of these addiction-related variables; otherwise, the groups were similar.

3.

Answers are highlighted and in parentheses except for commentary on this author's note concerning the second study.

1. The Role of Alcohol in Boating Deaths

Although many potentially confounding variables were taken into account, we were unable to adjust for other variables that might affect risk, such as the boater's swimming ability, the operator's boating skills and experience, use of personal floatation devices, water and weather conditions, and the condition and seaworthiness of the boat. Use of personal floatation devices was low among control subjects (about 6.7% of adults in control boats), but because such use was assessed only at the boat level and not for individuals, it was impossible to include it in our analyses (*Selection resulting in potentially nonequivalent groups*). . . . Finally, although we controlled for boating exposure with the random selection of control subjects, some groups may have been underrepresented (*Selection*).

2.

Violence Prevention in the Emergency Department

The study design would not facilitate a blinding process (*Expectancy*) that may provide more reliable results. . . . The study was limited by those youth who were excluded, lost to follow-up, or had incomplete documents (*Selection; Attrition*). Unfortunately, the study population has significant mobility and was commonly unavailable when the case managers attempted to interview them (*Attrition*). The study was limited by the turnover of case managers (*Attrition; Instrumentation*).

Note: The first statement regarding the length of time needed for the program's effects to be observed is not a limitation in the study's research design but in the evaluators' rush to try out a program with insufficient evidence. Limitations like this can be avoided in practice by relying only on programs that are known to work and that define the circumstances in which they work best.

Regarding the second limitation concerning the evaluation tool, the problem here is that the evaluators used a measure of unknown validity. This is a serious (and not uncommon) problem. Invalid measures do harm to any study no matter how carefully it is designed. That is, a brilliantly designed RCT with an invalid test or other measure will produce inaccurate results. Measurement validity is discussed in Chapter 6.

4.

RCTs and wait-list controls guard against most biases. They produce the most internally and externally valid results. In their "purest" forms, they may be somewhat complex to implement. It is often difficult, if not impossible, to "blind" evaluation participants, for example.

Quasi-experimental designs are often more realistic designs for clinical and other real-world settings. However, preexisting differences in groups may interfere with the results so that you cannot be certain if group differences or programs are responsible for outcomes.

Time-series designs can provide (or refute) evidence of impact. However, their implementation requires a justifiable and often relatively long period of time for outcomes to be visible.

Observational designs are convenient because the researcher does not have to develop and implement a research protocol—complicated activities, to say the least. At the same time, the researcher may have little "control" over data collection or the assignment of participants.

5.

The covariates are the baseline scores on the primary outcome measures: (1) child problem behavior and (2) positive and negative parenting skill, confidence, and depression.

6.

The variables used in the propensity score analysis were as follows: age, gender, marital status, level of education, household income, race/ethnicity, immigrant status, language spoken, borough of residence, exposure to WTCD events, history of mental health treatment, history of depression, and having experienced a peri-event panic (PEP) attack during the WTCD.

Chapter 5. The Research Consumer Reviews the Measures

1.

a. Self-administered questionnaires

The Suicidal Ideation Questionnaire—Junior (SIQ-JR; Reynolds, 1988) is a 15-item self-report questionnaire used to assess the frequency of a wide range of suicidal thoughts.

The Spectrum of Suicide Behavior Scale (Pfeffer, 1986) is a 5-point rating of the history of suicidality (none, ideation, intent/threat, mild attempt, serious attempt).

Measures of internalizing symptoms include the Youth Self-Report (YSR; Achenbach, 1991) internalizing scale and the Reynolds Adolescent Depression Scale (RADS; Reynolds, 1987). The YSR consists of 119 problem behavior items that form internalizing and externalizing scales. The RADS is a 30-item self-report questionnaire that assesses frequency of depressive symptoms on a 4-point scale with endpoints of *almost never* and *most of the time.*

The CAFAS (Hodges & Wong, 1996) assesses functional impairment in multiple areas, including moods/self-harm. On the basis of parent responses to a structured interview, a trained clinician rates level of functioning on a 4-point scale (0, 10, 20, 30) ranging from 0 (*minimal or no impairment*) to 30 (*severe impairment*).

b. Large database

The 2002 National Health Interview Survey (NHIS), a national household survey sponsored by the National Center for Health Statistics, was used to collect data on whether participants had a diagnosis of diabetes or other illness, the use of complementary and alternative medicine, demographic and socioeconomic characteristics, preventive health care practices, and the use of conventional medical services.

c. *Audio records*
A computer-implemented acoustic voice measure was used to track slight as well as profound cognitive impairment.

2.

a. Categorical (nominal)
b. Continuous
c. Continuous
d. Categorical (nominal, dichotomous)
e. Discrete
f. Ordinal
g. Categorical
h. Continuous

3.

	True	*False*
Most evaluations only report the results of measures with preset choices. Some social scientists refer to data collected from these as quantitative because the measures produce results that can be quantified or enumerated.	T	
Qualitative data are rarely collected from open-ended questions, observations, and reviews.		F
A most important use of qualitative measures is in determining the fidelity with which a program is implemented.	T	
A content analysis relies on trained personnel to search the data for themes that commonly occur in the data.	T	

Chapter 6. The Research Consumer Evaluates Measurement Reliability and Validity

1.
Underlined text should be replaced with the answer.
A measure has <u>internal consistency</u> (**Answer:** test-retest) reliability if the correlation or reliability coefficient between scores recorded at

different times is high. A commonly used method for determining the agreement between observations and observers results in a statistic called _alpha_ (**Answer:** _kappa_), defined as the agreement beyond chance divided by the amount of agreement possible beyond chance.

Content validity refers to the extent to which a measure thoroughly and appropriately assesses the skills or characteristics it is intended to measure. (**Answer:** No change)

Predictive (**Answer:** concurrent) validity is demonstrated when a new measure compares favorably with one that is already considered valid.

A sensitive measure will correctly detect disease (such as alcohol-related risk) among people who have the disease. (**Answer:** No change.)

Specificity refers to the proportion of people without disease who have a negative test result. (**Answer:** No change.)

Some researchers refer to the use of multiple measures as triangulation. (**Answer:** No change.)

A Type II (**Answer:** Type I) error is analogous to a false positive in that the evaluator concludes that a difference exists when one does not.

The null hypothesis postulates that no difference exists between experimental and control program participants. (**Answer:** No change.)

With intention to treat analysis, outcomes between study groups are compared with every participant analyzed according to his or her randomized group assignment regardless of whether she received the assigned intervention or produced any data, under most circumstances. (**Answer:** No change.)

In practice, it is not uncommon for program developers and researchers to find that programs accomplish one or a few proximate outcomes rather than the hoped-for ultimate outcomes. Proximate outcomes are intermediate outcomes. (**Answer:** No change.)

2.

Answer A: Content validity
Answer B: Inter-rater reliability
Answer C: Test-retest reliability

3.

a. Diagnostic Interview Schedule for Children; Child Behavior Checklist; Divorce Adjustment Project Externalizing Scale; Child Depression Inventory; Children's Manifest Anxiety Scale; Monitoring the Future Scale; 7-point scale to measure number of times used alcohol and marijuana; use of other drugs and polydrug use also counted; self-administered questionnaire on number of different sexual partners.

b. In the following text, outcome measures are indicated in bold italics, and information about reliability and validity is in italics.

Mental disorder and drug abuse or dependence were assessed at six-year follow-up using the computer-assisted parent and adolescent versions of the *Diagnostic Interview Schedule for Children* (scoring algorithm version J). Diagnoses were derived separately for mental disorder and drug abuse or dependence and were based on meeting two conditions: (1) according to either self or parent report, adolescents met symptom criteria for diagnosis of one or more disorders in the past year and (2) two or more of the impairment items for the disorder(s) were rated as intermediate or severe according to adolescent or parent report.

Parents completed the *Child Behavior Checklist*, which includes a 33-item *externalizing problems subscale*. The researchers state that the subscale has *adequate test-retest and internal consistency reliability and construct and predictive validity*. Adolescents completed a 27-item *self-report scale of externalizing problems*. *Aggression and hostility* were assessed by items from the *Divorce Adjustment Project Externalizing Scale*; items were added by the researchers to assess delinquent behavior. The researchers indicate that the full 27-item scale has been found to be *sensitive to detecting intervention-induced change and has acceptable internal consistency*.

Parents completed the *Child Behavior Checklist*, which includes a 31-item *internalizing subscale*. Adolescents completed the 27-item *Child Depression Inventory* and the 28-item revised *Children's Manifest Anxiety Scale*. These measures, according to the researchers, have *adequate test-retest and internal consistency reliability and construct and predictive validity*.

Items from the *Monitoring the Future Scale* were used at the six-year follow-up. The researcher states that *this scale has adequate reliability and construct validity*. To *maximize validity of responses*, adolescents responded on a *self-administered questionnaire*. *Alcohol and marijuana use* were measured by a 7-point scale of times used (1 = 0 to 7 = 40) in the past year. *Other drug use* was computed as the sum of ratings on this scale for 13 other drugs (e.g., heroin). *Polydrug use* was assessed by counting the number of different drugs, including alcohol, used in the past year.

Adolescents responded to a *self-administered question on the number of different sexual partners* they had had since completion of the New Beginnings Program.

4.

The first article by MacMillan and colleagues describes in detail how they defined missing data and tells how they handled these data statistically. The researchers found that, although proportions of missing data differed by instrument, statistical analysis revealed the differences were not significant. MacMillan and colleagues also provide a detailed flow chart that shows how many participants were assessed for inclusion into the study and how many remained for the analysis—even if they had missing data (intention to treat analysis).

In the second article, Riggs and colleagues do not provide a flow diagram. They do discuss in the text that they started with 1,267 parents, 584 completed a time 1 survey and 351 completed a survey at time 2. No information (e.g., demographics) is provided on parents who did not complete either of the surveys or on those who completed only one. No information is provided on whether the 351 participants completed all survey questions or just a proportion.

Riggs et al. found no differences between experimental and control group parents who completed the second survey, so they concluded that "although the current sample is 28% of all parents reached at baseline, the lack of group differences at baseline coupled with a lack of program group differences in survey completion rates at follow-up allows us to reasonably expect that the current sample is representative of the overall study sample."

Chapter 7. Getting Closer: Grading the Literature and Evaluating the Strength of the Evidence _____

1.
A and B are systematic reviews. They describe their objectives, search terms, databases, and reviewing process. C is a narrative review because it only explains key words and databases. The authors of review C accepted all studies regardless of quality, and no description of the review process is given.

2.
   a. The evaluation uses a quasi-experimental research design. Therefore, you should use the critical methodological domains: comparability of participants, program/intervention, outcome measures, statistical analysis, and funding.
   b.

Question 1. Which of the following child health and development outcomes are measured in this study? (Check all that apply.)

Outcomes	Page Number	Comment
Birth weight	☐	
Duration of breast feeding	☐	
Frequency of accidents	☐	
Hospital admissions	☐	
Social competence	☐	
Behavioral problems	☐	
Verbal ability	☐	
Nonverbal ability	☐	

Question 2. Describe the background of families in experimental and control groups by indicating the number (N) and percentage (%) in each category.

	Experimental Group		Control Group	
	N	%	N	%
Child's age*				
1 year and younger				
2–3 years				
4 years				
Child's gender				
Male				
Female				
Mother's age				
19 years or younger				
20–25 years				
25–30 years				
Etc.				
Primary language spoken at home				
English				
Spanish				
Etc.				

*Note that the categories that you are interested in may not correspond directly to the ones used in each of the studies that you review.

Question 3. Record the study's main conclusions: _____

_____

_____

_____

_____

_____

Question 4. Do the authors report that the study received approval from an ethics or institutional review board?

Yes ☐

No ☐

3.

Recommendations	Mitchell, Haw et al.		Horowitz and Garber	
1. Describes eligibility for inclusion and exclusion	Yes X	No	Yes X	No
2. Discusses databases that were searched	Yes X	No	Yes X	No
3. Gives specific search terms	Yes X	No	Yes X	No
4. Discusses effect size and why chosen	Yes X	No	Yes X	No
5. Provides results of study and of homogeneity among studies	Yes	No X	Yes	No X
6. Discusses effects of publication bias	Yes	No X	Yes X	No
7. Depicts the flow of literature from potentially useful through those that passed through all screens (e.g., practical, methodological)	Yes	No X	Yes	No X

4.

The following describes the way in which the two reviewers' responses look.

	Reviewer 2		
Reviewer 1	*No*	*Yes*	
No	20	25	45
Yes	10	55	65
	30	80	

This is the formula for deriving the kappa statistic:

$$k = \frac{O - C \text{ (Agreement beyond chance)}}{1 - C \text{ (Agreement possible beyond chance)}}$$

Here is how the formula works with the above example.

1. Calculate how many studies the reviewers may agree by chance DO NOT adequately describe the intervention. This is done by multiplying the number of no answers and dividing by 110 because there are 110 studies: 30 x 45 / 110 = 12.3.

2. Calculate how many studies they may agree by chance DO describe the intervention by multiplying the number of studies each found included an adequate description and dividing by the total number of studies. This is done by multiplying the number of yes answers and dividing by 110: 80 x 65/110 = 47.3.

3. Add the two numbers obtained in Question 1 and 2, and divide by 110 to get a proportion for **chance agreement:** (12.3 + 47.3) / 110 = 0.54.

The **observed agreement** is 20 / 110 or 18% + 55 / 110 or 50% = 68% or 0.68. Therefore the agreement beyond chance is 0.68 − 0.54 = 0.14: the numerator.

The **agreement possible beyond chance** is 100% minus the chance agreement of 54% or 1 − 0.54 = 0.46: the denominator

$$k = \frac{0.14}{0.46}$$

$$k = 0.30$$

A kappa of 0.30 is considered fair.

5.

a. Unknown uncontrolled variables (confounders) permit alternative explanations for the results.

b. The intervention was not standardized (e.g., variation among case managers).

c. Intervention (combined police and social services) may have sensitized family members to domestic violence and to calling for help or for increasing domestic violence.

d. Rates of recidivism in the control group were artificially low. They were lower than would have been found if individuals could have been followed instead of addresses.

e. Time frames for the intervention and control samples were not concurrent.

f. In 1997, Child Protective Services (CPS) California began recognizing the witnessing of domestic violence as a form of child abuse. This change in CPS policy could have resulted in decreased rates among intervention participants in notifying law enforcement of domestic violence.

Chapter 8. The Ethical Research Consumer Assesses Needs and Evaluates Improvement _____

1.
   a. Delphi
   b. Key informant

2.
   A-2
   B-1
   C-5
   D-3
   E-4
   F-6

3.
   Evidence-based programs; evidence-based performance standards

4.
   Reliable and valid measures; assessment of evidence-based programs

5.
   1c; 2a; 3b; 4d

6.
   All (a–d) are characteristic of research misconduct.

7.
   All are potential ethical concerns.

8.
   b

9.
   a

Glossary _____

A

An **abstract** is an abbreviated version of the objectives, methods, findings, and conclusions of a much larger report.

Abstracting the literature is the process of reading and recording data from research articles and reports.

Administrative needs refer to policies and resources that exist in the organizations and institutions (e.g., schools, hospitals, businesses, nongovernmental organizations) that might facilitate or hinder the adoption of a new program.

Alternate-form reliability refers to the extent to which two instruments measure the same concepts at the same level of difficulty.

Analysis of covariance (ANCOVA) is a statistical procedure that results in estimates of intervention or program effects "adjusted" for participants' background and for potentially confounding characteristics or **covariates** (such as age, gender, educational background, severity of illness, type of illness, motivation, and so on).

Article databases consist of citations and abstracts of articles that have been published either in print or online pertaining to a particular subject, such as psychology (e.g., PsycINFO) or medicine (e.g., MEDLINE). You find article databases online.

Attrition is the loss of participants during the course of an evaluation (also called **loss to follow up**). Participants that are lost during the study are often called dropouts. Attrition can be a threat to an evaluation's internal validity if participants drop out from one or more study groups on a nonrandom basis.

B

Baseline information refers to information collected about study participants and staff before the program begins, and it is sometimes referred to as **pretest** data.

Behavioral needs refer to individual and communal lifestyles and beliefs that affect a community's well-being.

Beneficence is an ethical principle. It requires that research design be scientifically sound and that the risks of the research be acceptable in relation to the likely benefits. The principle of beneficence also means that persons are treated in an ethical manner. Researchers must not only respect people's decisions and protect research participants from harm but also make efforts to secure their well-being.

Bibliographic databases: see **article databases**.

Blinding is the process of preventing those in an experiment from knowing to which comparison group a particular participant belongs. The risk of bias is minimized when as few people as possible know who is receiving the experimental program and who the control program. All participants, including members of the research team, are candidates for being blinded.

Blocked randomization is a method of randomization ensuring that, at any point in an evaluation study, roughly equal numbers of participants have been allocated to all the comparison groups.

Boolean operators are words such as AND, OR, and NOT. They are used to combine search terms to either broaden or narrow the retrieval results of a research literature search.

C

Case-control designs are generally retrospective. They are used to explain why a phenomenon currently exists by comparing the histories of two different groups, one of which is involved in the phenomenon. For example, a case-control design might be used to help understand the social, demographic, and attitudinal variables that distinguish people who, at the present time, have been identified with frequent headaches from those who do not, at the present time, have frequent headaches.

Categorical response choices force respondents to put answers into categories. The responses are sometimes called **nominal** because they ask people to "name" the groups to which they belong. Are you male or female? This is an example of a question requiring a response that places people into one of two named categories. Other ways of "categorizing" respondents include asking about religious affiliation, school last attended, or last job held. These categories have no natural order.

Clinical expertise, according to evidence-based medical practitioners, means the ability to use clinical skills and past experience to identify rapidly each patient's unique health state and diagnosis, his or her individual risks and benefits of potential interventions, and his or her personal values and expectations.

Clinical trials are evaluations of medical and surgical treatments, drugs, and other interventions that are conducted in health care settings such as clinics and hospitals. The outcomes investigated in clinical trials may be medical (e.g., reductions in blood pressure), psychosocial (improvements in health-related quality of life), and economic (which of two equally effective programs costs less).

Closed questions, sometimes called **forced-choice questions,** are ones in which participants choose their answers from a set of response choices.

Clusters are naturally occurring groups (e.g., classrooms, hospitals, social work agencies) that are used as single sampling units.

A **cohort** is a group of people who have something in common and who remain part of a study group over an extended period of time. In public health research, **cohort studies** are used to describe and predict the risk factors for a disease and the disease's cause, incidence, natural history, and prognosis.

Communal or epidemiological needs refer to problems that can be documented to affect a large number of people in the community.

A **community forum** consists of a group of people who meet together to discuss a common problem. The meeting is open to all members of the community.

Concurrent validity is demonstrated when two measures agree with one another or when a new measure compares favorably with one that is already considered valid.

A **confidence interval (CI)** is a measure of the uncertainty around the main finding of a statistical analysis.

A **conflict of interest** is a situation in which someone in a position of trust, such as a researcher, practitioner, or policy maker, has competing professional or personal interests.

A **confounding** variable is an extraneous variable that affects the dependent variables but has either not been considered or has not been controlled for. The confounding variable can lead to a false conclusion that the dependent variables are in a causal relationship with the independent variable. Such a relation between two observed variables is termed a spurious relationship. An experiment that fails to take a confounding variable into account is said to have poor internal validity.

Consensus development conferences aim to produce "state-of-the-science" reports using best evidence and expertise (www.consensus .nih.gov).

The **Consolidated Standards of Reporting Trials (CONSORT)** consists of standards for *reporting* on randomized controlled trials in health and medicine.

Construct validity is established experimentally to demonstrate that a measure distinguishes between people who do and do not have certain characteristics.

Content analysis is the process of systematically reviewing, analyzing, and interpreting data from open-ended questions, observations, and records—from all types of human communication. A content analysis relies on trained personnel to search the data for "**themes**" that consistently occur.

Content validity refers to the extent to which a measure thoroughly and appropriately assesses the skills or characteristics it is intended to measure. A depression scale may lack content validity if it only assesses the affective dimension of depression but fails to take into account the behavioral dimension.

Continuous measures use response options that result in numerical data. They can have an infinite number of values (e.g., weight) or be discrete (e.g., number of drinks per day).

A **control group** is a group assigned to an experiment, but not for the purpose of being exposed to the program under investigation. The performance of the control group usually serves as a standard against which to measure the effect of the program on the experimental group. The control program may be typical practice ("usual care"), an alternative practice, or a placebo (a treatment or program believed to be inert or innocuous).

A **controlled experiment** generally compares the outcomes obtained from an experimental group against a control group, which is practically identical to the experimental group except for the one aspect (the experimental program) whose effect is being tested.

Convergent validity means that performance on the new measure correlates with one or more measures of a similar characteristic.

A **correlation** is a numerical index that reflects the linear relationship (described by a straight line) between two numerical measurements made on the same group of people. A correlation coefficient—r—ranges from -1 to $+1$, with 0 indicating no relationship. The absolute value of the coefficient reflects the strength of the correlation so that a correlation of $-.60$ is stronger than a correlation of $+.50$.

Cost is the value of money that has been used to produce something, so it is not available for use anymore. In deciding on the costs of programs, the evaluator might consider the amount of money expended to train personnel, to administer the program, and to design the intervention.

Having a **cost benefit** means that a program has value because its benefits (expressed in monetary terms) are equal to or exceed its costs. To determine whether this is the case, a researcher might perform a **cost-benefit analysis**.

Cost minimization refers to attempts to determine which of two equally effective programs has lower costs.

Cost utility means that the outcomes of hypothetical programs A and B are weighted by their value or quality and measured by a common metric such as "quality of life" years.

Cost-effective programs save costs and offer equal or better outcomes than the alternative. A program is also cost-effective when no other program is as effective at lower cost.

In statistics, a **covariate** is a variable that is possibly predictive of the outcome under study. A covariate may be of direct interest or be a confounding variable.

Criterion validity is a general term for predictive and concurrent validity because both involve comparing a measure to something else (the criterion).

Cronbach's α (alpha) is a measure of internal consistency that reflects the extent to which a set of test items can be treated as measuring a single latent variable. Latent variables, as opposed to observable variables, are those variables that cannot be directly observed but are rather inferred from other variables that can be observed and directly measured. Cronbach's alpha can range between 0 and 1. A measure with an alpha .61 and above is usually considered to be internally consistent.

Cross-sectional study is a study measuring the distribution of some characteristics in a population at a particular point in time. (It is also called a **survey** study.)

Cumulative meta-analysis is a technique that permits the identification of the year when the combined results of many studies (almost always randomized controlled trials or true experiments) first achieve a given level of statistical significance.

D

A **data set** consists of a subset of information that was extracted from a database for a specific analytic purpose. A researcher who extracts the information on all persons 85 years of age and older from a database consisting of statistics on all people in the nation who are 65 years of age and older has created a data set.

A **database** contains all the information collected on a population of people.

Decision makers are users of evaluation information.

The **Delphi technique** is a structured method of determining the degree of agreement on a topic, of selecting alternatives, or of setting priorities. Delphi techniques use questionnaires that are completed by participants on their own, in groups, or both. The questionnaires are structured to ask people to rate or rank the importance or validity of certain ideas.

A **dependent variable** is a variable (improved health) that may be predicted by or caused by one or more other variables called independent variables (e.g., a health education intervention). In evaluation research, outcomes are dependent variables.

Descriptors are terms used by some article databases to describe the articles listed (e.g., their content or subject or language); they are similar to key words except that, like **identifiers**, they are taken from a controlled language prepared and monitored by the librarians or indexers who categorize, sort, and store information in the database.

A **dichotomous** result occurs when a question has only two possible response choices (e.g., male and female).

Discriminant validity means that performance on the new measure does not correlate with measures of dissimilar characteristics.

E

Educational needs refer to individual and community knowledge, attitudes, skills, self-efficacy, and beliefs.

An **effect** is an association between program participation and an outcome.

Effect size is a generic term for an estimate of the effect of being in a study. It is viewed as a dimensionless measure of effect that is typically used for continuous data and is usually defined as the difference in means (average scores) between the intervention and control groups (on the primary outcome of interest) divided by the standard deviation (a measure of variation from the average scores) of the control or both groups.

An **effectiveness evaluation** is a form of research whose purpose is to find out if program works in "real life" situations. A program is effective if its outcomes compare favorably to comparable alternative or currently available programs.

Effectiveness studies examine the outcomes and impact of programs that evaluators observe in "real life" settings.

Efficacy studies consider the outcomes and impact of programs that evaluators observe in laboratory-like or ideal settings.

Equipoise means that current evidence does not favor the superiority of the experimental over the control program. Equipoise is associated with randomized controlled trials.

Ethics, also called moral philosophy, involves systematizing, defending, and recommending concepts of right and wrong behavior.

An **ethics committee,** sometimes called an **institutional review board** or **IRB,** is an administrative body whose purpose is to protect the rights and welfare of human research subjects who are recruited to participate in research activities.

Evaluation researchers use scientific methods to assess the process, outcomes, impact, or costs of programs and to provide new knowledge about social behavior.

Evidence that matters is meaningful to its users as well as scientifically valid.

Evidence-based health is the application of the principles of EBM to all professions associated with health care, including purchasing and management.

Evidence-based medicine (EBM) is the conscientious, explicit, and judicious use of current best evidence in making decisions about the care of individual patients.

Evidence-based practice (EBP) is the conscientious, explicit, and judicious use of current best evidence in making decisions about the care of individual clients.

Expectancy is a threat to an evaluation's internal validity that is caused by the expectations of the evaluator or the participants or both.

The **experimental group** is the group in an experiment that receives the program that is being studied.

Experimental research designs involve the collection of information to compare two or more groups, one of which participates in a new program while the other does not. An example of an experimental design is the randomized controlled trial in which the groups are constituted at random, which means that chance dictates which participants receive the experimental program.

Experimental studies are tests that are conducted under controlled conditions to examine the validity of a hypothesis or determine the effectiveness or efficacy of something (e.g., a program or intervention) previously untried.

External validity refers to the extent to which the design produces results that are applicable to other programs, populations, and settings. Another term for external validity is **generalizability**.

F

Face validity refers to how a measure appears on the surface: Does it seem to cover all the important domains? Ask all the needed questions?

False negatives occur as a result of measures with poor specificity. They incorrectly classify people as not having a disease (such as an alcohol-related risk) when in fact they actually do.

False positives occur when people without a disease get a positive test anyway, one that says they do have the disease. Insensitive, invalid measures lead to false positives.

Fidelity of program implementation, also called **integrity of implementation**, refers to the extent to which a program's protocol was followed.

The **fixed effects model** assumes that all experiments are similar in that they share the same underlying treatment effect. (Compare **random effects**.)

A **focus group** is designed to collect information from "insiders" or "people in the know." The group usually consists of about 10 carefully selected participants and a trained moderator.

Forced-choice questions, also called **closed questions,** are those in which respondents provide answers from a list of response options.

Formative evaluations are evaluations that focus on the program's activities and organization rather than on the outcomes of participation. These evaluations are sometimes called implementation or process evaluations.

G

Generalizability refers to the extent to which the design produces results that are applicable to other programs, populations, and settings. Another term for generalizability is **external validity.**

H

The **Hawthorne Effect** is a threat to an evaluation's external validity that occurs when participants know that they are participating in an experiment. These sorts of threats are also described as the **reactive effects of experimental arrangements.**

Heterogeneous studies are those with observed variations due to initial differences in their design, setting, or sample. (Compare **homogenous studies.**)

Using **historical controls** means comparing the outcomes for participants who receive a new program with the outcomes for a previous group of participants who received the standard intervention. Selection bias often arises because subjects who receive the new intervention are typically not comparable to subjects who received the standard intervention.

History is a threat to internal validity that is caused by unanticipated events that occur while the evaluation is in progress.

Homogenous studies are those in which any observed variations are due to chance. (Compare **heterogeneous studies.**)

A **human subject** is a living individual about whom an investigator (whether professional or student) conducting research obtains (1) data through intervention or interaction with the individual (e.g., in a counseling session or a classroom) or (2) identifiable private information (e.g., birth date or school record number).

A **hypothesis** is an unproven theory that can be tested through research. To properly test a hypothesis, it should be prespecified and clearly articulated, and the study to test it should be designed appropriately.

I

Identifiers: see **descriptors**.

Impact refers to the magnitude and duration of program effects.

Implementation evaluations focus on the program's activities and organization rather than on the outcomes of participation. They are sometimes called **formative** or **process** evaluations.

Improvement evaluations aim to (1) examine the extent to which a newly adopted program met clients' needs and (2) identify where improvements should be made to improve future efforts.

Independent variables are the factors such as gender and age that are not expected to change because of the program. The program itself is an independent variable. Independent variables are also known as **predictor variables.**

Informed consent means that subjects who agree to participate in the research are knowledgeable about the risks and benefits of participation and about the activities that comprise participation. They also agree to the terms of participation and are knowledgeable about their rights as research subjects.

In-person observations are made by one or more trained observers who are actually present at the events of interest. Observations may be summarized by using checklists, notes, cameras, and audiotapes.

An **institutional review board (IRB)**, also called an **ethics committee,** is an administrative body whose purpose is to protect the rights and welfare of human research subjects who are recruited to participate in research activities.

An **instrument** (often called a measure) is a formalized data collection method (e.g., the XYZ Checklist or the ABC Behavioral Survey).

Instrumentation is a threat to an evaluation's internal validity that is due to changes in a measuring instrument or changes in observers or scorers.

Integrity of program implementation (also called **fidelity of program implementation**) refers to the extent to which a program's protocol was followed.

Intention to treat analysis (ITT) is a technique for analyzing data from a randomized controlled trial. All participants are included in the study group to which they were allocated, whether or not they received (or completed) the intervention given to that group. Intention to treat analysis prevents bias caused by the loss of participants, which may disrupt the baseline equivalence established by randomization and which may reflect non-adherence to the program's activities and protocol.

Interaction effects of selection biases and the experimental treatment is a threat to an evaluation's external validity that occurs when an intervention or program and the participants are a unique mixture, one that may not be found elsewhere. This threat is most apparent when groups are not randomly constituted.

Internal consistency is an indicator of the cohesion of the items in a single measure. That is, all the items in an internally consistent measure actually assess the same idea or concept.

Internal validity refers to the extent to which a study's design permits the evaluator to make valid inferences about a program's outcomes, impact, and costs (e.g., Program A caused Outcome A).

Inter-rater reliability refers to the extent to which two or more observers or measurements agree with one another.

The **interrupted or single time-series** design without a control group (hence, the "single") involves repeated measurement of a variable (e.g., reported crime) over time, encompassing periods both before and after implementation of a program. The goal is to evaluate whether the program has "interrupted" or changed a pattern established before the program's implementation.

Intra-rater reliability refers to the extent to which an individual's observations are consistent over time.

Item is a term often used interchangeably with "question" when referring to a survey questionnaire, test, or other evaluation measure.

J

Justice is an ethical principle that refers to the balance between receiving the benefits of research and bearing its burdens. For example, to ensure justice, the selection of research subjects needs to be scrutinized in order to determine whether some classes (e.g., welfare recipients or persons in institutions) are being systematically selected simply because of their easy availability rather than for reasons directly related to the problems being studied. The concern is that participation in research always involves burdens including the time participants spend in activities and the risk of being exposed to untested interventions. Ethicists believe that these burdens must be equitably distributed. A sample drawn from a captive audience (e.g., people in an institution) may be unjust because it unfairly distributes risk. The captive audience has a better, rather than random, chance of being selected from all potentially eligible participants. Of course, some researchers study these groups specifically to learn more about them. Special ethics safeguards exist for research about "vulnerable populations."

K

Kappa is a statistic that results from a commonly used method for determining the agreement between observations and observers. It is defined as the agreement beyond chance divided by the amount of agreement possible beyond chance.

A **key informant** is an individual in a given position who is able to give researchers important or expert information. The purpose of the key informant method is to collect information about a community's needs by interviewing community leaders who are likely to be in a position to know what the needs are.

Key words are informative words chosen to indicate the content of a document; these words can be used to search indexes and databases.

Kuder-Richardson refers to a statistical technique for estimating internal consistency in measures with dichotomous response choice (e.g., yes or no; true or false).

L

Levels of measurement refers to measures (e.g., online or paper and pencil surveys, achievement tests, interviews, record reviews) that result in either categorical, ordinal, or numerical data.

The **Likert scale** is a type of response format that shows responses on a continuum and has response categories such as "strongly agree," "agree," "disagree," and "strongly disagree."

A **linear** relationship between two numerical measurements is described by a straight line.

Longitudinal studies provide information on changes over time (from one time to the next). See **time-series designs**.

Loss to follow-up: see **attrition**.

M

Matching is the process of ensuring that participants in a study's experimental and control groups are as alike as possible in age, gender, problem severity, motivation, etc. at baseline.

Maturation is a threat to internal validity that is the result of processes occurring inevitably within participants as a function of time (e.g., physical and emotional growth).

Measurement error is a term used to describe the discrepancy between responses to a measure and the true value of the concept.

Measurement scales or response choices are variously referred to as rating or measurement scales and levels of measurement.

Measures refer to data collection devices or instruments such as self-administered surveys or achievement tests.

A **meta-analysis** is the use of statistical techniques in a systematic literature review to integrate the results of included studies.

Methodological quality is the extent to which all aspects of a study's design and implementation combine to protect its findings against biases. A focus on methodological quality means intensively examining factors such as the scientific soundness of the research design and sampling strategy, measurement, and data analysis.

Multiple program interference is a threat to an evaluation's external validity that results when participants are in other complementary activities or programs that interact with the one being tested.

N

Narrative literature reviews are interpretations of the research literature that do not describe their research question or search strategy. (Compare **systematic literature review**.)

A **needs assessment** is a systematic effort to identify user needs.

The **negative predictive value** is the probability that the patient will not have the disease when restricted to all patients who test negative.

In the **nominal group technique**, participants are brought together for a discussion session led by a moderator. After the topic of concern has been presented to session participants and they have had an opportunity to ask questions or briefly discuss the scope of the topic, they are asked to take a few minutes to think about and write down their responses.

Nominal response choice: see **categorical response choices**.

Nonmethodological quality means analyzing the clarity and relevance of the program's objectives, theoretical basis, and content; the trustworthiness of the research's funding source; and the adequacy of the resources, setting, and ethical considerations.

Nonrandomized controlled design is the same as **quasi-experimental design**.

The **null hypothesis** is the statistical hypothesis that one variable (e.g., the program a study participant was allocated to receive) has no association with another variable or set of variables (e.g., whether or not a study participant acquired a skill), or that two or more population distributions do not differ from one another. In simplest terms, the null hypothesis states that the factor of interest (e.g., the program) has no impact on outcome (e.g., acquiring a skill).

The **number needed to treat** (**NNT**) is an estimate of how many people need to receive the program before one person would experience a beneficial outcome. For example, if you need to give violence prevention therapy to 20 people before one violent act is prevented, then the number needed to treat to benefit for that violence prevention program is 20.

Numerical is a type of response choice. It may be continuous (e.g., weight) or discrete (number of witnesses).

O

Observational research designs are those in which the evaluators do not seek to intervene; they simply observe the course of events. Changes or differences in one characteristic (e.g., whether or not people received the program of interest) are studied in relation to changes or differences in other characteristics (e.g., whether or not they reduced their harmful drinking), without action by the evaluator.

The **odds** are a way of expressing the chance of an event, calculated by dividing the number of individuals in a sample who experienced the event by the number for whom it did not occur. For example, if, in a sample of 100, 20 people did not improve and 80 people improved, the odds of improving are 20/80 = ¼, 0.25 or 1:4.

An **odds ratio** (**OR**) is the ratio of the odds of an event in one group to the odds of this event in another group. In studies of treatment effect, the odds in the treatment group are usually divided by the odds in the control group. An odds ratio of one (OR = 1.0) indicates no difference between comparison groups. For undesirable outcomes, an OR that is less than one (OR<1) indicates that the intervention was effective in reducing the risk of that outcome. When the risk is small, odds ratios are very similar to risk ratios.

Online bibliographic or article databases contain bibliographic citations, abstracts, and, sometimes, the full text of documents and articles; these databases can be searched online.

Online or electronic journals can be found directly online or through online databases.

An **open-ended question** is one in which respondents provide answers in their own words. (Compare **closed** and **forced-choice questions**.)

Ordinal response choices have a built-in order to them such as highest level of education attained. The order may be imposed: e.g., poor, fair, good, very good, excellent.

Outcomes are the results of program participation. Beneficial outcomes include improvements in health, education, social well-being, and economic prospects.

P

P **value** is the probability (ranging from zero to one) that the results observed in a study (or results more extreme) could have occurred by chance if, in reality, the null hypothesis was true.

Participant observation requires the researcher actually to live within or somehow join in the community being observed.

Participatory evaluations include stakeholders as partners in setting the evaluation agenda and in doing all phases of the research including analyzing or reporting on the results.

Patient values, according to evidence-based medical practitioners, are the unique preferences, concerns, and expectations that each patient brings to a clinical encounter and that must be integrated into clinical decisions if they are to serve the patient.

The **Pearson product-moment correlation coefficient** is a statistical technique for estimating test-retest reliability.

Physical needs refer to social or physical factors that are external to an individual or a community.

PICO is a framework for asking research questions. It consists of four components: the population or problem of concern; the intervention, practice, or program; a comparison program; and the hoped-for outcomes.

An underlying assumption of one of the most commonly used meta-analytic approaches is that the reason you can **pool** (merge) individual study results to produce a summary measure is that all study results are homogenous in that they reflect the same "true" effect.

The **positive predictive value** of a test is the probability that a person has the disease when restricted to those patients *who test positive.*

Power (also called **statistical power**) is the probability of rejecting the null hypothesis when a specific alternative hypothesis is true. The power of a hypothesis test is one minus the probability of Type II error. In clinical trials, power is the probability that a trial will detect, as statistically significant, an intervention effect of a specified size. If an evaluation study had a power of 0.80 (or 80%), and assuming that the prespecified treatment effect truly existed, then, if the trial was repeated 100 times, it would find a statistically significant treatment effect in 80 of those repetitions. Ideally, we want a test to have high power, close to the maximum, which is one (or 100%). For a given size of effect, studies with more participants have greater power. Studies with a given number of participants have more power to detect large effects than a small effect.

The determination of sample size is also referred to as **power analysis** because the number of persons in the study determines (to some degree) the power the evaluator has to detect an effect or a true difference in experimental and control groups.

Practical clinical trials (also called **pragmatic clinical trials**) are studies in which the hypothesis and study design are developed specifically to answer questions faced by decision makers.

The **practical screen** consists of criteria that an article or report absolutely must achieve if it is to be included in the literature review. The criteria include attention to the language of the article or report, the study design, the nature of the program and its participants, the date of publication, and the study's funding source.

Practical significance is an outcome or result (e.g., a program effect) that is large enough to be of practical importance to participants and all others (e.g., teachers, prison officials) concerned with program outcomes. This is not the same thing as **statistical significance**. Assessing practical significance takes into account factors such as the size of the program's effect, the severity of the need being addressed, and the cost.

Pragmatic clinical trial: see **practical clinical trial**.

Predictive validity refers to the extent to which a measure forecasts future performance.

Predictor variable: see **independent variable**.

Pretest information refers to information collected about study participants and staff before the program begins. This information is sometimes referred to as **baseline** data.

Pretest-posttest designs (also called **self-controlled designs**) are designs in which each participant is measured on some important program variable and serves as his or her own control. Participants are usually measured twice (at baseline and after program participation), but they many be measured multiple times afterward as well.

Process evaluations focus on program activities and organization. (They are sometimes called **formative** or **implementation evaluations**.)

A **program** consists of activities and resources that have been specifically selected to achieve beneficial outcomes.

Program processes refer to the staff, activities, materials, and methods that are used to accomplish the outcomes.

Propensity score analysis is a technique for dealing with confounding variables; it is used in analyzing data from quasi experiments. The goal of a propensity score analysis is to create subgroups of study participants who are similar across a broad range of confounding variables or covariates and then to test the program effect within those groups. That is, within homogenous subgroups (such as all older participants or all at risk for dropping out), the evaluator compares the outcomes of those who did and did not receive the program.

With a **prospective design**, the direction of inquiry is forward in time. (Compare **retrospective design**.)

A **protocol** is a planned set of procedures to follow in a research study or systematic literature review. In literature reviews, the protocol includes a focused study question, a specific search strategy (that defines the search terms and databases that are used as well as the criteria for including and excluding studies); detailed instructions on which data are to be abstracted on study objectives, methods, findings, and quality; and a plan for how the data will be synthesized (either qualitatively, as text, or in a quantitative summary accompanied by text).

Proximate outcomes are intermediate outcomes. They are chosen because they are meaningful in themselves and because previous research and clinical insight suggest that they are associated with the hoped-four outcome.

Psychometrics is a discipline concerned with the theory and technique of psychological measurement, which includes the measurement of knowledge, abilities, attitudes, and personality traits.

Public forum: see **community forum**.

Publication bias means unfairly favoring the results of published studies.

Q

Qualitative methods involve investigating participants' opinions, behaviors, and experiences from their point of view and using logical deduction.

Qualitative summaries of the literature describe and analyze trends across studies. In some fields (e.g., nursing) doing this is called meta-synthesis.

Quality of evidence depends on factors such as the characteristics of a study's research design, the adequacy of the sample size, the composition of the participants, and the validity of the outcomes.

Quantitative evaluation methods rely on mathematical and statistical models.

A **quasi-experimental design** is one in which the control group is predetermined (without random assignment) to be comparable to the program group in critical ways, such as being in the same school or eligible for the same services.

R

The **RAND/UCLA Appropriateness Method (RUAM)** is a method for determining the extent of agreement on controversial topics and on those for which the research base is poor or ambiguous (a mixture of positive and negative findings).

Random allocation (also called **random assignment**) is a method that uses the play of chance to assign participants to comparison groups in a trial, e.g., by using a random numbers table or a computer-generated random sequence. Random allocation implies that each individual or unit being entered into a study has the same chance of receiving each of the possible interventions.

Random assignment is the same as **random allocation**.

The **random effects model** incorporates the potential heterogeneity of the treatment effect among different studies by assuming that each study estimates a unique treatment effect that, even given a large amount of data, might still differ from the effect in another study. (Compare **fixed effects model**.)

Random error occurs when the concept underlying a measure is subject to debate and, thus, imprecise (e.g., quality of life, economic well-being). Random error comes from three sources: variability in the measure itself, variability in the respondents, and variability in the observer.

Randomization is the process of randomly allocating participants into one of the groups that make up a controlled trial. There are two components to randomization: the generation of a random sequence and its implementation, ideally in a way so that those entering participants into a study are not aware of the sequence (**concealment of allocation**).

A **randomized controlled trial** (**RCT**) is an experimental study in which eligible individuals or groups of individuals (e.g., schools, communities) are assigned at random to receive one of several programs or interventions. The group in an experiment that receives the specified program is called the **experimental group**. The term **control group** refers to another group assigned to the experiment, but not for the purpose of being exposed to the program. The performance of the control group usually serves as a standard against which to measure the effect of the program on the experimental group. The control program may be typical practice ("usual care"), an alternative practice, or a placebo (a treatment or program believed to be inert or innocuous).

Rating scales are measurements based on descriptive words or phrases that indicate performance levels. Qualities of a performance are described (e.g., advanced, intermediate, novice) in order to designate a level of achievement.

RCT is the same as a randomized controlled trial.

Reactive effects of experimental arrangements or the **Hawthorne Effect** is a threat to an evaluation's external validity that occurs when participants know that they are participating in an experiment.

Reactive effects of testing pose a threat to an evaluation's external validity that occurs when a baseline measure interacts with the program resulting in an effect that will not generalize.

Record reviews are analyses of an evaluation participant's documented behavior such as their school or medical records. The documentation may be in print, online, on or audio or video.

The **relative risk** expresses the risk of a particular outcome in the experimental group relative to the risk of the outcome in the control group.

Reliability coefficient: see **correlation.**

Reliable means consistency over time and within an instrument.

Research is a diligent and systematic process of inquiry aimed at discovering, interpreting, and revising information about programs and interventions. Research is also a term that is used to describe a collection of information about a particular subject and is associated with the scientific method.

Research-based is a synonym for **evidence-based.**

Research consumers use research as the basis for making decisions about programs, practices, and policy. Consumers practice research and are concerned with the practical applications of research findings.

Research design is the structure of research. At its most stingy, the structure consists of the intervention or program that is to be compared to an alternative, participants who are assigned to be part of the new program *or* of the alternative, and a schedule of measurements (e.g., before program participation and immediately after).

Research ethics concern the rights and wrongs associated with research. Evaluations always include "human subjects," and so, research ethics are of great concern. The evaluator must demonstrate that the study design respects participants' privacy, ensure that the benefits of participation are maximized, and provide all participants with equal access to the benefits. Research that is not sound is unethical in itself because it results in misleading or false conclusions, which when applied may result in harm.

The best **research evidence,** according to evidence-based medical practitioners, is clinically relevant research, often from the basic sciences of medicine but especially from patient-centered clinical research. Patient-centered clinical research is analogous to evaluation research, particularly in its advocacy and use of experimental methods to test effectiveness, impact, and cost.

Research literature review is a highly systematic, explicit, and reproducible method for identifying, evaluating and synthesizing one or more studies or reports that comprise the existing body of completed and recorded work produced by researchers, scholars, and practitioners about programs.

Research misconduct includes such offenses as fabrication, falsification, and plagiarism. Fabrication means making up results and recording or reporting them. Falsification includes changing or omitting data or results. Plagiarism means taking another person's ideas, results, or work without giving due credit.

A **research question** is the objective of the evaluation, the uncertainty that the evaluator wants to diminish.

Respect for persons is an ethical principle that requires investigators to obtain **informed consent** from research participants, to protect participants who have impaired decision-making capabilities, and to maintain confidentiality.

Respondent refers to the person who completes a survey.

Response choices are also known as **rating** or **measurement scales** and **levels of measurement**. There are three basic measurement types: **categorical**, **ordinal**, and **numerical**.

With a **retrospective design**, the direction of the inquiry is backward in time. (Compare **prospective design**.)

Risks and odds are alternative methods for describing the likelihood that a particular effect will or will not take place.

S

The **scientific method** is a set of techniques for investigating phenomena and acquiring new knowledge of the natural and social worlds; this knowledge, scientific knowledge, is based on observable, measurable evidence.

Selection of participants is a threat to internal validity that results from the selection or creation of groups that are not equivalent. Selection can interact with history, maturation, and instrumentation.

Self-administered survey questionnaires ask participants to answer questions by writing ("paper-and-pencil" surveys) or online. Some paper-and-pencil surveys are mailed to participants, and others are completed on site, at a clinic or school, for example.

Self-controlled research designs (also called **pretest-posttest designs**) are designs in which each participant is measured on some important program variable and serves as his or her own control. Participants are usually measured twice (at baseline and after program participation), but they may be measured multiple times afterward as well.

Sensitivity refers to the proportion of people with disease who have a positive test result. Said another way, a sensitive measure will correctly detect disease (such as alcohol-related risk) among people who have the disease. A sensitive measure is a valid measure.

Sensitivity analysis is a technique that is used to conduct separate analyses of different quality studies.

The **single time-series design** (also called **interrupted time-series design**) is a research design without a control group (hence, the "single"). It involves repeated measurement of a variable (e.g., reported crime) over time, encompassing periods both before and after implementation of a program. The goal is to evaluate whether the program has "interrupted" or changed a pattern established before the program's implementation.

Social needs usually refer to the community's perceptions of its problems.

Spearman-Brown prediction formula is a statistical technique for estimating split-half reliability.

Specificity refers to the proportion of people without disease who have a negative test result. Measures without good specificity lead to **false negatives.** They invalidly classify people as not having a disease (such as alcohol-related risk) when in fact they actually do.

Split-half reliability requires the researcher to divide a measure into two equal halves (say by choosing all odd numbered questions to be in the first half and all even numbered questions to be in the second half). Then, using, a technique called the **Spearman-Brown prediction formula,** the researcher calculates the correlation between the two halves.

Stakeholders are users or consumers of evaluation information.

Statistical regression is a threat to an evaluation's internal validity when participants are selected on the basis of extreme scores and regress or go back toward the mean (e.g., average score) of that variable.

Stratified blocked randomization is a method used to ensure that equal numbers of participants with a characteristic thought to affect response to the intervention will be allocated to each comparison group. Stratification variables often include age, gender, marital status, and socioeconomic status.

Strength of evidence refers to the number of high-quality studies that consistently support the effectiveness of a program or intervention.

Study quality refers to the validity of the research design, the adequacy of the sample size, the composition of the participants, and the pertinence of the outcomes.

Summative evaluations examine outcomes and impact after most (if not all) of a program's activities are completed. (Compare **formative** and **process evaluations.**)

A **systematic literature review** is the same as a research review. It follows a protocol that includes a focused study question; a specific search strategy (that defines the search terms and databases that are used as well as the criteria for including and excluding studies); and specific instructions on the types of data to be abstracted on study objective, methods, findings, and quality. (Compare **narrative literature reviews.**)

T

Testing is a threat to internal validity; it refers to the effect of previous testing upon the scores of subsequent tests.

Test-retest reliability refers to the extent to which a measure produces consistent results over time.

Themes are fundamental and common ideas, perceptions, values, and attitudes expressed by respondents or participants in a study.

Threats to an evaluation's validity arise because of factors such as imperfect randomization and attrition. Both internal and external validity may be affected.

Time-series designs are longitudinal studies that enable the evaluator to monitor change from one time to the next.

The **TREND** (Transparent Reporting of Evaluations with Nonrandomized Designs) statement is a checklist developed to guide reporting on studies having a nonrandomized controlled design or a quasi-experimental design.

Triangulation is the use of multiple measures to collect data on a single outcome, with the expectation that, if the findings converge, then confidence in the results is enhanced.

A **true experiment** is the same as a **randomized controlled trial** (RCT).

A **Type I error** (also called a **false positive**) is a conclusion that a program works, when it actually does not work. The risk of a Type I error is often called alpha. In a statistical test, the term describes the chance of rejecting the null hypothesis when it is in fact true.

A **Type II error** (also called a **false negative**) is a conclusion that there is no evidence that a program works, when it actually does work. The risk of a Type II error is often called beta. In a statistical test, the term describes the chance of *not* rejecting the null hypothesis when it is in fact false. The risk of a Type II error decreases as the number of participants in a study increases.

U

Unobtrusive measures obtain data about evaluation participants by relying on existing documentation (e.g., from medical and school records).

The U.S. Preventive Services Task Force (USPSTF) is an independent panel of experts in primary care and prevention that systematically reviews the evidence of effectiveness and develops recommendations for clinical preventive services. The USPSTF is now under the auspices of the Agency for Health Care Quality and Research.

V

Valid is the accuracy of a measure, or the extent to which the measure represents the concept of interest.

Validity refers to the degree to which a measure assesses what it is supposed to measure. For example, a test that asks students to *recall* information is an invalid measure of their ability to *apply* information.

Variables are quantities or factors that may assume any one of a set of values such as age (e.g., 13 through 19 years), educational level (e.g., elementary or high school), reading ability (e.g., reads at the 3rd grade level or reads below it).

A **vignette** is a short scenario that is used in collecting data in "what if" situations.

W

A **wait-list control** refers to a research study design in which one group receives the program first and others are put on a waiting list. If the program appears to be effective, participants on the waiting list receive it. Participants are randomly assigned to the experimental and wait-list groups.

References _____

Alkin, M. C. (Ed.). (2004). *Evaluation roots: Tracing theorists' influences.* Thousand Oaks, CA: Sage.

Allen, S., Resnik, L., & Roy, J. (2006). Promoting independence for wheelchair users: The role of home accommodations. *Gerontologist, 46*(1), 115–123.

American Diabetes Association. (2006). Standards of medical care in diabetes—2006. *Diabetes Care, 29,* s4–s42. Retrieved August 15, 2007, from http://care.diabetesjournals.org/cgi/content/full/29/suppl_1/s4#SEC9

Auerbach, A. D., Landefeld, C. S., & Shojania, K. G. (2007). The tension between needing to improve care and knowing how to do it. *North England Journal of Medicine, 357*(6), 608–613.

Bair-Merritt, M. H., Blackstone, M., & Feudtner, C. (2006). Physical health outcomes of childhood exposure to intimate partner violence: A systematic review. *Pediatrics, 117*(2), e278–290.

Bandell-Hoekstra, I., Abu-Saad, H. H., Passchier, J., & Knipschild, P. (2000). Recurrent headache, coping, and quality of life in children: A review. *Headache: The Journal of Head and Face Pain, 40*(5), 357–370.

Belsky, J., Melhuish, E., Barnes, J., Leyland, A. H., Romaniuk, H., & the National Evaluation of Sure Start Research Team. (2006). Effects of Sure Start local programmes on children and families: Early findings from a quasi-experimental, cross sectional study. *British Medical Journal, 332*(7556), 1476–1479.

Bifulco, A., Bernazzani, O., Moran, P. M., & Jacobs, C. (2005). The childhood experience of care and abuse questionnaire (CECA.Q): Validation in a community series. *British Journal of Clinical Psychology, 44,* 563–581.

Booth, B. M., Kirchner, J. E., Fortney, S. M., Han, X., Thrush, C. R., & French, M. T. (2006). Measuring use of health services for at-risk drinkers: How brief can you get? *Journal of Behavioral Health Services and Research, 33*(2), 254–264.

Boscarino, J. A., Adams, R. E., Foa, E. B., & Landrigan, P. J. (2006). A propensity score analysis of brief worksite crisis interventions after the World Trade Center disaster: Implications for intervention and research. *Medical Care, 44*(5), 454–462.

Brockington, I. F., Fraser, C., & Wilson, D. (2006). The Postpartum Bonding Questionnaire: A validation. *Archives of Women's Mental Health, 9*(5), 233–242.

Bruinsma, F. J., Venn, A. J., Patton, G. C., Rayner, J., Pyett, P., Werther, G., et al. (2006). Concern about tall stature during adolescence and depression in later life. *Journal of Affective Disorders, 91*(2–3), 145–152.

Buchanan, D., Doblin, B., Sai, T., & Garcia, P. (2006). The effects of respite care for homeless patients: A cohort study. *American Journal of Public Health, 96*(7), 1278–1281.

Campbell, D. T., & Stanley, J. C. (1963). *Experimental and quasi-experimental designs for research.* Chicago: Rand McNally.

Campbell, M. K., Elbourne, D. R., & Altman, D. G. (2004). CONSORT statement: Extension to cluster randomised trials. *British Medical Journal, 328*(7441), 702–708.

Centre for Health Evidence. (2007). *Users' guides to evidence-based practice.* Retrieved August 21, 2007, from http://www.cche.net/usersguides/main.asp

Chen, P.-H., Rovi, S., Vega, M., Jacobs, A., & Johnson, M. S. (2005). Screening for domestic violence in a predominantly Hispanic clinical setting. *Family Practice, 22*(6), 617–623.

Cook, D. C., & Campbell, D. T. (1979). *Quasi experimentation: Design and analysis issues for field settings.* Boston: Houghton Mifflin.

Crook, J., Milner, R., Schultz, I. Z., & Stringer, B. (2002). Determinants of occupational disability following a low back injury: A critical review of the literature. *Journal of Occupational Rehabilitation, 12*(4), 277–295.

Des Jarlais, D. C., Lyles, C., & Crepaz, N. (2004). Improving the reporting quality of nonrandomized evaluations of behavioral and public health interventions: The TREND statement. *American Journal of Public Health, 94*(3), 361–366.

DeSena, A. D., Murphy, R. A., Douglas-Palumberi, H., Blau, G., Kelly, B., Horwitz, S. M., et al. (2005). SAFE Homes: Is it worth the cost? An evaluation of a group home permanency planning program for children who first enter out-of-home care. *Child Abuse and Neglect, 29*(6), 627–643.

Dolan, K. A., Shearer, J., MacDonald, M., Mattick, R. P., Hall, W., & Wodak, A. D. (2003). A randomised controlled trial of methadone maintenance treatment versus wait list control in an Australian prison system. *Drug and Alcohol Dependence, 72*(1), 59–65.

Drummond, M. F., Richardson, W. S., O'Brien, B. J., Levine, M., & Heyland, D. (1997). Users' guides to the medical literature. XIII. How to use an article on economic analysis of clinical practice. A. Are the results of the study valid? Evidence-Based Medicine Working Group. *JAMA, 277*(19), 1552–1557.

Duggan, A., McFarlane, E., Fuddy, L., Burrell, L., Higman, S. M., Windham, A., et al. (2004). Randomized trial of a statewide home visiting program: Impact in preventing child abuse and neglect. *Child Abuse and Neglect, 28*(6), 597–622.

Ebell, M. H., Barry, H. C., Slawson, D. C., & Shaughnessy, A. F. (1999). Finding POEMs in the medical literature. *Journal of Family Practice, 48*(5), 350–355.

Eccleston, C., Yorke, L., Morley, S., Williams, A. C., & Mastroyannopoulou, K. (2003). Psychological therapies for the management of chronic and recurrent pain in children and adolescents. *Cochrane Database of Systematic Reviews 1*, CD003968.

Engström, J., Bruno, E., Holm, B., & Hellzén, O. (2006). Palliative sedation at end of life—A systematic literature review. *European Journal of Oncology Nursing, 11*(1), 26–35.

Feuerstein, M., & Nicholas, R. A. (2006). Development of a short form of the Workstyle measure. *Occupational Medicine, 56*(2), 94–99.

Fink, A. (2004). *Evaluation fundamentals: Insights into the outcomes, effectiveness, and quality of health programs* (2nd ed.). Thousand Oaks, CA: Sage.

Fink, A., Elliott, M. N., Tsai, M., & Beck, J. C. (2005). An evaluation of an intervention to assist primary care physicians in screening and educating older patients who use alcohol. *Journal of the American Geriatrics Society, 53*(11), 1937–1943.

Fix, G. A., & Schaefer, C. (2005). Note on psychometric properties of playfulness scales with adolescents. *Psychological Reports, 96*(3, Pt. 2), 993–994.

Foa, E. B., Johnson, K. M., Feeny, N. C., & Treadwell, K. R. H. (2001). The Child PTSD Symptom Scale: A preliminary examination of its psychometric properties. *Journal of Clinical Child Psychology, 30*(3), 376–384.

Friedman, S. H., Horwitz, S. M., & Resnick, P. J. (2005). Child murder by mothers: A critical analysis of the current state of knowledge and a research agenda. *American Journal of Psychiatry, 162*(9), 1578–1587.

Friedmann, P. D., Hendrickson, J. C., Gerstein, D. R., & Zhang, Z. W. (2004). Designated case managers as facilitators of medical and psychosocial service delivery in addiction treatment programs. *Journal of Behavioral Health Services & Research, 31*(1), 86–97.

Gache, P., Michaud, P., Landry, U., Accietto, C., Arfaoui, S., Wenger, O., et al. (2005). The Alcohol Use Disorders Identification Test (AUDIT) as a screening tool for excessive drinking in primary care: Reliability and validity of a French version. *Alcoholism: Clinical and Experimental Research, 11*, 2001–2007.

Galasso, P., Amend, A., Melkus, G. D., & Nelson, G. T. (2005). Barriers to medical nutrition therapy in black women with Type 2 diabetes mellitus. *Diabetes Education, 31*(5), 719–725.

Gardner, F., Burton, J., & Klimes, I. (2006). Randomised controlled trial of a parenting intervention in the voluntary sector for reducing child conduct problems: Outcomes and mechanisms of change. *Journal of Child Psychology and Psychiatry, 47*(11), 1123–1132.

Garrow, D., & Egede, L. E. (2006). Association between complementary and alternative medicine use, preventive care practices, and use of conventional medical services among adults with diabetes. *Diabetes Care, 29*(1), 15–19.

Gerson, M., Allard, J. L., & Towvim, L. G. (2005). Impact of smoke-free residence hall policies: The views of administrators at 3 state universities. *Journal of American College Health, 54,* 157–165.

Gibbs, L. E. (2003). *Evidence-based practice for the helping professions: A practical guide with integrated multimedia.* Pacific Grove, CA: Brooks/Cole-Thomson Learning.

Glasgow, R. E., Magid, D. J., Beck, A., Ritzwoller, D., & Estabrooks, P. A. (2005). Practical clinical trials for translating research to practice: Design and measurement recommendations. *Medical Care, 43*(6), 551–557.

Grembowski, D. (2001). *The practice of health program evaluation.* Thousand Oaks, CA: Sage.

Guo, J. J., Jang, R., Keller, K. N., McCracken, A. L., Pan, W., & Cluxton, R. J. (2005). Impact of school-based health centers on children with asthma. *Journal of Adolescent Health, 37*(4), 266–274.

Gustafson, D. H., McTavish, F. M., Stengle, W., Ballard, D., Hawkins, R., Shaw, B., et al. (2005). Use and impact of eHealth System by low-income women with breast cancer. *Journal of Health Communication, 10* (Suppl. 1), 195–218.

Guyatt, G. H., Cairns, J., Churchill, D., & Group, E.-B. M. W. (1992). Evidence-based medicine: A new approach to teaching the practice of medicine. *JAMA, 268,* 2420–2425.

Ha, B. T. T., Jayasuriya, R., & Owen, N. (2005). Increasing male involvement in family planning decision making: Trial of a social-cognitive intervention in rural Vietnam. *Health Education Research, 20*(5), 548–556.

Hartman, C., Luteijn, E., Serra, M., & Minderaa, R. (2006). Refinement of the Children's Social Behavior Questionnaire (CSBQt): An instrument that describes the diverse problems seen in milder forms of PDD. *Journal of Autism and Developmental Disorders, 36*(3), 1–18.

Horowitz, J. L., & Garber, J. (2006). The prevention of depressive symptoms in children and adolescents: A meta-analytic review. *Journal of Consulting and Clinical Psychology, 74,* 401–415.

Hulley, S. B., Cummings, S. R., Browner, W. S., Grady, D., Hearst, N., & Newman, T. B. (Eds.). (2001). *Designing clinical research* (2nd ed.). Philadelphia: Lippincott Williams and Wilkins.

Juffer, F., & van IJzendoorn, M. H. (2005). Behavior problems and mental health referrals of international adoptees: A meta-analysis. *JAMA, 293*(20), 2501–2515.

Katcher, M. L., Meister, A. N., Sorkness, C. A., Staresinic, A. G., Pierce, S. E., Goodman, B. M., et al. (2006). Use of the modified Delphi technique to identify and rate home injury hazard risks and prevention methods for young children. *Injury Prevention, 12*(3), 189–194.

King, C. A., Kramer, A., Preuss, L., Kerr, D. C. R., Weisse, L., & Venkataraman, S. (2006). Youth-Nominated Support Team for Suicidal Adolescents (Version 1): A randomized controlled trial. *Journal of Consulting and Clinical Psychology, 74*, 199–206.

Landis, J. R., & Koch, G. G. (1977). The measurement of observer agreement for categorical data. *Biometrics, 33*, 159–174.

Lieberman, P. M. A., Hochstadt, J., Larson, M., & Mather, S. (2005). Mount Everest: A space analogue for speech monitoring of cognitive deficits and stress. *Aviation, Space, and Environmental Medicine, 76*, 1093–1101.

Linde, K., Streng, A., Jurgens, S., Hoppe, A., Brinkhaus, B., Witt, C., et al. (2005). Acupuncture for patients with migraine: A randomized controlled trial. *JAMA, 293*(17), 2118–2125.

Lindqvist, J. K., Daderman, A. M., & Hellstrom, A. (2005). Internal reliability and construct validity of the Novaco Anger Scale-1998-S in a sample of violent prison inmates in Sweden. *Psychology Crime & Law, 11*(2), 223–237.

Lohr, K. N. (2004). Rating the strength of scientific evidence: Relevance for quality improvement programs. *International Journal of Quality Health Care, 16*(1), 9–18.

Love, J. M., Kisker, E. E., Ross, C., Constantine, J., Boller, K., Banks Tarullo, L., et al. (2005). The effectiveness of early Head Start for 3-year-old children and their parents: Lessons for policy and programs. *Developmental Psychology, 41*, 885–901.

MacMillan, H. L., Thomas, B. H., Jamieson, E., Walsh, C. A., Boyle, M. H., Shannon, H. S., et al. (2005). Effectiveness of home visitation by public-health nurses in prevention of the recurrence of child physical abuse and neglect: A randomised controlled trial. *The Lancet, 365*(9473), 1786–1793.

MacMillan, H. L., Wathen, C. N., Jamieson, E., Boyle, M., McNutt, L. A., Worster, A., et al. (2006). Approaches to screening for intimate partner violence in health care settings: A randomized trial. *JAMA, 296*(5), 530–536.

Magill-Evans, J., Harrison, M. J., Rempel, G., & Slater, L. (2006). Interventions with fathers of young children: Systematic literature review. *Journal of Advanced Nursing, 55*(2), 248–264.

Marshall, B. J., & Warren, J. R. (1984). Unidentified curved bacilli in the stomach patients with gastritis and peptic ulceration. *The Lancet, 1*(8390), 1311–1315.

McFarlane, J. M., Groff, J. Y., O'Brien, J. A., & Watson, K. (2006). Secondary prevention of intimate partner violence: A randomized controlled trial. *Nursing Research, 55*, 52–61.

McGory, M. L., Shekelle, P. G., Rubenstein, L. Z., Fink, A., & Ko, C. Y. (2005). Developing quality indicators for elderly patients undergoing abdominal operations. *Journal of the American College of Surgeons, 201*(6), 870–883.

McQuay, H. J., & Moore, R. A. (1997). Using numerical results from systematic reviews in clinical practice. *Annals of Internal Medicine, 126*(9), 712–720.

Mitchell, T. L., Haw, R. M., Pfeifer, J. E., & Meissner, C. A. (2005). Racial bias in mock juror decision-making: A meta-analytic review of defendant treatment. *Law and Human Behavior, 29,* 621–637.

Montgomery, P., Stores, G., & Wiggs, L. (2004). The relative efficacy of two brief treatments for sleep problems in young learning disabled (mentally retarded) children: A randomised controlled trial. *Archives of Disease in Childhood, 89*(2), 125–130.

Nemet, D., Barkan, S., Epstein, Y., Friedland, O., Kowen, G., & Eliakim, A. (2005). Short- and long-term beneficial effects of a combined dietary-behavioral-physical activity intervention for the treatment of childhood obesity. *Pediatrics, 115,* e443–449.

Nickel, M. K., Nickel, C., Lahmann, C., Mitterlehner, F., Tritt, K., Leiberich, P., et al. (2005). Recovering the ability to function socially in elderly depressed patients: A prospective, controlled trial. *Archives of Gerontology and Geriatrics, 41*(1), 41–49.

Patel, A., Knapp, M., Perez, I., Evans, A., & Kalra, L. (2004). Alternative strategies for stroke care: Cost-effectiveness and cost-utility analyses from a prospective randomized controlled trial. *Stroke, 35*(1), 196–203.

Patrick, K., Calfas, K. J., Norman, G. J., Zabinski, M.F., Sallis, J.F., Rupp, J., et al. (2006). Randomized controlled trial of a primary care and home-based intervention for physical activity and nutrition behaviors: PACE+ for adolescents. *Archives of Pediatrics and Adolescent Medicine, 160*(2), 128–136.

Patton, M. Q. (2001). *Qualitative research and evaluation methods.* Thousand Oaks, CA: Sage.

Pelissier, B. M. M., Camp, S. D., Gaes, G. G., Saylor, W. G., & Rhodes, W. (2003). Gender differences in outcomes from prison-based residential treatment. *Journal of Substance Abuse Treatment, 24*(2), 149–160.

Peluso, M. A. M., Hatch, J. P., Glahn, D. C., Monkul, E. S., Sanches, M., Najt, P., et al. (2007). Trait impulsivity in patients with mood disorders. *Journal of Affective Disorders, 100*(1–3), 227–231.

Peragallo, N., Deforge, B., O'Campo, P., Lee, S. M., Kim, Y. J., Cianelli, R., et al. (2005). A randomized clinical trial of an HIV-risk-reduction intervention among low-income Latina women. *Nursing Research, 54*(2), 108–118.

Reed, D. B., & Kidd, P. S. (2004). Collaboration between nurses and agricultural teachers to prevent adolescent agricultural injuries: The Agricultural Disability Awareness and Risk Education model. *Public Health Nursing, 21*(4), 323–330.

Riggs, N. R., Elfenbaum, P., & Pentz, M. A. (2006). Parent program component analysis in a drug abuse prevention trial. *Journal of Adolescent Health, 39*(1), 66–72.

Rossi, P. H., Freeman, H. E., & Lipsey, M. W. (2003). *Evaluation: A systematic approach*. Thousand Oaks, CA: Sage.

Sackett, D. L., Straus, S. E., Richardson, W. S., Rosenberg, W., & Haynes, R. B. (2000). *Evidence-based medicine: How to practice and teach EBM* (2nd ed.). New York: Churchill and Livingstone.

Sanchez, C. D., Newby, L. K., McGuire, D., K., Hasselblad, V., Feinglos, M. N., & Ohman, E. M. (2005). Diabetes-related knowledge, atherosclerotic risk factor control, and outcomes in acute coronary syndromes. *The American Journal of Cardiology, 95*(11), 1290–1294.

Santa Mina, E. E., Gallop, R., Links, P., Heslegrave, R., Pringle, D., Wekerle, C., et al. (2006). The Self-Injury Questionnaire: Evaluation of the psychometric properties in a clinical population. *Journal of Psychiatric and Mental Health Nursing, 13*(2), 221–227.

Shah, R., & Ogden, J. (2006). "What's in a face?" The role of doctor ethnicity, age, and gender in the formation of patients' judgments: An experimental study. *Patient Education and Counseling, 60*(2), 136–141.

Shekelle, P. (2004). The appropriateness method. *Medical Decision Making, 24*(2), 228–231.

Sinclair, V. G., & Scroggie, J. (2005). Effects of a cognitive-behavioral program for women with multiple sclerosis. *Journal of Neuroscience Nursing, 37*(5), 249–257, 276.

Smith, G. C. S., & Pell, J. P. (2003). Parachute use to prevent death and major trauma related to gravitational challenge: Systematic review of randomised controlled trials. *British Medical Journal, 327*(7429), 1459–1461.

Smith, G. S., Keyl, P. M., Hadley, J. A., Bartley, M. A., Foss, R. D., Tolbert, W., et al. (2001). Drinking and recreational boating fatalities: A population-based case-control study. *JAMA, 286*(23), 2974–2980.

Stein, B. D., Jaycox, L. H., Kataoka, S. H., Wong, M., Tu, W., Elliott, M. N., et al. (2003). A mental health intervention for schoolchildren exposed to violence: A randomized controlled trial. *JAMA, 290*(5), 603–611.

Steinberg, E. P., & Luce, B. R. (2005). Evidence based? Caveat emptor! *Health Affairs, 24*(1), 80–92.

Stutts, J., Feaganes, J., Reinfurt, D., Rodgman, E., Hamlett, C., Gish, K., et al. (2005). Driver's exposure to distractions in their natural driving environment. *Accident Analysis & Prevention, 37*(6), 1093–1101.

Svendsen, K., Kuller, L. H., Martin, M. J., & Ockene, J. K. (1987). Effects of passive smoking in the Multiple Risk Factor Intervention Trial. *American Journal of Epidemiology, 126*, 783–795.

Ter Meulen, R. (2007). *Ethical issues of evidence based medicine*. Retrieved August 21, 2007, from http://www.ccels.cf.ac.uk/archives/other/launch/meulenpaper.html

Trochim, W. M. K. (2006). Evaluation research. *Research methods knowledge base*. Retrieved August 21, 2007, from http://socialresearchmethods.net/kb/evaluation.htm

Tsai, S. L., Chen, M. B., & Yin, T. J. (2005). A comparison of the cost-effectiveness of hospital-based home care with that of a conventional

About the Author _____

Arlene Fink, PhD, is Professor of Medicine and Public Health at the University of California Los Angeles and President of the Langley Research Institute. Her main interests include evaluation and survey research and the conduct of research literature reviews as well as the evaluation of their quality. Dr. Fink has conducted many research studies in medicine, public health, and education and has trained hundreds of practicing researchers. She is on the faculty of UCLA's Robert Wood Johnson Clinical Scholars Program and its Health Services Research Center and is on the Advisory Board of the University of Southern California's Minority Health Services Research Center. Dr. Fink is also a consultant to the American Society for Bioethics and Humanities, the International Society for Clinical Bioethics, and L'Institut de Promotion de la Prévention Secondaire en Addictologie (IPPSA), Paris, France. Professor Fink has lectured extensively in the United States and internationally and is the author of 100 peer-reviewed papers and 15 textbooks.